ENTHUSIASTIC MATHEMATICS

REVIVING MYSTICAL EMANATIONISM

in

MODERN SCIENCE

Bernie Lewin

The Platonic Academy of Melbourne

Also by Bernie Lewin:

Searching for the Catastrophe Signal

Copyright © 2018 Bernie Lewin
All rights reserved

Published by:
The Platonic Academy of Melbourne
Australia

Formatted by the Author
Printed by Createspace

ISBN: 9781982930523

Cover design by Ben Tiefholz

CONTENTS

	Letter to the Reader	vii
	Introduction	1
Part I	**Incredible & Triumphant Logical Empiricism**	
	1. The Lost Object of Empiricism	9
	2. The Failure of Logical Method	30
	3. The New Scepticism	53
Part II	**Towards a Mathematical Epistemology**	
	4. Rediscovering Pre-Communicative Knowing	69
	5. The Knowing Being is a Self-Referencing System	80
	6. Distinction: the Mathematical Element	94
	7. A Calculus of Distinction	106
	8. The Dynamics of Form	120
Part III	**Enthusiastic Mathematics**	
	Introduction to Part III	151
	9. The Mathematici	153
	10. Foundations of Arithmetic	170
	11. Logos and Analogia	207
	12. Alternating Analogia	230
	13. Dyadic Emanation	248
	14. The Dyadics of Leibniz	267
	15. Dyadics Discovered in Ancient China	304
	16. The End of the Road	328
	Acknowledgements	336
	Notes	337
	Greek Glossary	344
	Index	345

道可道非常道
名可名非常名

In Memory

of

George Spencer Brown

1923-2016

Dear Reader,

Have you ever wondered what it is to know something: not so much that you have an idea, but to have ideas <u>about</u> something? You know it. And yet how? Everything you know is ideas in your mind. So, how do you know something that is not in your mind? You see it and feel it, right? But what you see and feel are your sensations—there is no part of <u>your</u> feeling that is <u>it</u>, the thing. So again: <u>How do you know it</u>?

Thus so, we arrive quickly and effortlessly at the unsolved problem that is the contradiction of all the modern Western theories of knowledge that you are ever likely to encounter in a university or school. 'Epistemology', as it is called, is supposed to teach what it is to know something, and yet the essential connection between <u>the knowledge</u> and <u>the thing</u> is never satisfactorily explained. In all these theories the object remains unknown and essentially unknowable. All modern accounts of science are founded in a leap-of-faith establishing the existence—the 'ontology'—of the known object. We have all just got to agree that it's out there <u>external</u> to our knowledge of it, <u>providing</u> our knowledge of it, and <u>corresponding</u> to our knowledge of it…and so, <u>just get on with it</u>!

To do otherwise is only to ponder the absurd. The existence of the external objects of knowing must be accepted on faith, or otherwise, as Immanuel Kant would say, 'we should be landed in the absurd conclusion that there can be appearance without anything that appears'. Any alternative is in the realm of delusion. Madness. As John Locke had said before Kant: without such faith in the unknown object of our knowing, our common beliefs by which we live, and our science, would only be 'castles in the air'.

How strange, dear Reader, that it has come to this. Our experts and fathers of reason are telling us that our theory of knowledge must be founded in faithful ignorance. <u>Why</u>? For the negative reason that the only alternative is absurd. We must accept such an unsatisfactory doctrine only to avoid worse. And in order to do so we must force ourselves to believe that the things we all know and feel as <u>real</u> and as <u>present</u> are <u>absent</u>; and that what we do know and feel, is in urgent need of tethering to some phantom unknowable essence. Surely, upon arriving at such a failed explanation, if we were good scientists about it, we would go back to the elements, to the foundations, to the initial assumptions, and look for another way. And yet we don't. <u>Why</u> <u>not</u>? Now that is very strange.

It hasn't always been like this. During the 16th and 17th centuries there was a broad controversy over the epistemological question before this way of thinking was instituted at the beginning of the 18th century. The new dogma came to be promoted as 'Empiricism' but at the time it was known by its opponents as 'Materialism' *because the unknown external ontology of the known object was its essential materiality. And for some obscure reason, your teacher of philosophy will invariably associate the advent of this unbridgeable divide between <u>matter</u> and <u>ideas</u> with the 17th century mathematical intuitionist René Descartes. Whereas, in fact, this duality is ever so clearly traceable down through Christian theology to the Greeks, and the overwhelming influence here is Aristotle. In as much as Aristotelianism still dominates Western philosophy, this dualism remains, and so too the contradiction it entails.*

The contradiction of materialist epistemology is traceable to Aristotle's modification of Plato's ontology of <u>Forms</u>. Aristotle was taught by Plato that things are only ever at essence the expressions of mathematical forms. Aristotle would not abide the grounding of the sensible world entirely in the insensible, and so to avoid a complete mysticism he introduced <u>matter</u> as the content of the <u>Forms</u>. <u>Form-and-content</u> dualism always seems to work so well on the surface, but sure enough a contradiction soon emerges that is so fundamental and so intractable that most modern philosophers choose to stay quiet about it. Descartes never fully escaped the Aristotelian paradigm, and he did indeed get stuck on this problem, but he was not afraid to say so. To blame Descartes, and many now do blame him, looks much like shooting the messenger; or worse, it is to load up as a scapegoat one hero of the vanquished opposition.

What I propose here, dear Reader, is that we can come to an account of <u>knowing</u> that does not fall victim to the contradiction of this modern Empiricism. But we can only do this after retreating into consideration of our knowing practices at their most elementary level. Here we find a basic habit as the source of the problem. And we let go of it. And we start again. You see, we seem to have confused the form of language (the subject-refers-to-the-predicate) with the essential form of knowledge. Many also consider that knowledge is in the form of signification (the-sign-refers-to-what-it-signifies). The habit of taking the <u>form-of-knowledge</u> as nothing more elementary than the <u>form-of-its-communication</u> has become so entrenched that we cannot imagine it otherwise. Once we find that it can be otherwise (actually, that we knew this all along), it becomes apparent that this mistake of conflating <u>knowing</u> with <u>communicating</u> has been forcing the contradiction all along.

You see, the problem with the Aristotelian way is not limited to this particular problem of epistemology. Rather, it gives but one expression to a contradiction implicit in his methodological tool. And this has been the main motive perpetuating this bad habit down though our tradition. This tool that he calls 'analysis' is what we call 'logic', more precisely 'predicate logic'. Now logic, as a reduction and formalisation of linguistic reasoning, is a fine disciple, and all very useful. But Aristotle makes logic the elementary 'tool' of his philosophy, thereby replacing the mathematical *tools used in the Greek mathematical philosophy called 'Pythagorean'. Aristotle objected to the Pythagorean approach not only because of its mystical grounding but also because of its self-referencing character. For the Pythagorean, <u>being</u> is always acting upon itself, or returning to itself. In fact, their philosophy (epistemology and ontology) is founded in a primary and mystical unity that generates all difference through action upon itself. It is a 'monistic' philosophy, in that there is only one source, or 'monotheistic' if you follow the Platonists and call this creator-origin 'God'. Otherwise, the names for this origin can be translated as 'the one', the 'one-alone' or 'the singularity', and we might best describe this philosophy of self-generation as 'Emanationism'. I call it 'Mystical Emanationism'.*

What Aristotle especially liked about logic is that it is <u>other-referring</u>; the subject refers not to itself but to the predicate, just as <u>the-idea-of-a-thing</u> refers not to itself but to <u>the-thing-itself</u>. And it is not as though I am the first to point to its failure as a philosophical tool. It might surprise the reader (as it once did me) that the failure of this logical method is most explicitly identified throughout the Aristotelian tradition, from Aristotle down to our time. That is to say, it is common among methodological Aristotelians to explicitly state just how they cannot escape its contradiction: the tradition is littered with confessions like those little tastes I have just given from Locke and Kant. But still they persist with it. <u>Why</u>?

External reference must be retained in order to avoid the absurdity of self-reference and the airy castles of mysticism.

So they say.

Just how truly pathetic is this condition of modern epistemology I ask you to consider in the first part of this book; but only so that I can motivate you to consider something that seems a little weird at first. This is that knowledge, including modern scientific knowledge, is found to be fully self-referencing and fully mystical in both its elementary form and in its over-all structure. The reward for your persistence is that once you get used to it, you find not only a way out of the contradiction we started with, but a marvellously powerful vision of what it is to know.

Plato developed the Pythagorean methodology in particular ways so as to meet the challenges Pythagorean doctrine was experiencing at the time. This revolutionised the mathematical tradition, and as 'Platonism' it waxed and waned down through the millennia, competing or blending with Aristotelianism, until the 18th century and the period we now call 'The Enlightenment'. This is when a 15th century renaissance of Platonic mathematical mysticism fell dramatically from favour, and Empiricism emerged triumphant. The Enlightenment was many things, but one thing it most definitely delivered was a triumph of Logical Empiricism over Mathematical Mysticism.

In this view of the history of philosophy, it is just at the time when scientific knowledge was advancing so wonderfully well that promising work towards a better epistemology was abandoned for an approach that is so apparently and perfectly contradictory. In this view, we now live not only in a contradiction of knowledge, but also in a contradiction of history. <u>How can this be explained</u>?

The answer awaits us in the theo-political controversies of Restoration England. The Enlightenment emerged in England after its political establishment had endured long decades of turmoil, where it was battered by, even torn apart by, and continued to be threatened by, waves upon waves of religious 'enthusiasm'. Sporadic, uncontrollable and sometimes utterly devastating, this threat to society came from within society, where apocalyptic fanaticism could develop unpredictably, seemingly anywhere, and at any time, to unleash its formidable power with terrible impact. The threat was perceived to be so serious—and Protestant England so feeble in its defence—that the urgency to contain and control enthusiasm became one of the chief concerns of British political theory and strategy in the late 17th and early 18th centuries. It was in this political context that astute English apologists for natural science found an opportunity for its promotion as a sobering antidote to enthusiasm.

The Royal Society of London received its royal charter almost directly upon the restoration of the monarchy —returned after the decades of political uncertainty that followed the previous King's murder in a parliamentary rebellion fuelled by millenarian fanaticism. Not long into the still precarious Restoration came the Plague, and then the Fire of London in the apocalyptic year of 1666. Meanwhile, the Royal Society had been preparing an apology for science, which it published in 1667. This <u>History of the Royal Society</u> presents a political strategy most explicit. It positions experimental science in the context of these 'enthusiastic times', as a 'sensible prescription' to 'allay the violence of spiritual madness'. Science is just the 'remedy' required for 'the late extravagant excesses of Enthusiasm'.

Now, as this <u>History</u> points out, the epistemological source of enthusiastic prophesy is 'a pretence to inspiration', or an 'immediate communication with God'. If science is to be an antidote to such pretensions then it could not promote itself as also inwardly inspired—and so any suggestion of a mystical foundation to science must be obscured or denied. The Greek term 'enthuse' means 'god-within' and it was used by Plato to explain his belief that all wisdom comes from a source within us that is more primary than reason. But in its derogatory use during the 17th century British political debate, the term 'enthusiast' invoked someone who ranted apocalyptic prophesy in the belief that the voice inside their head is the very *commanding voice of God, in other words, someone who today would be assessed as mad, would be sedated and perhaps locked away.*

The trouble for mystical science was that the mystic and such prophets were confused. The controversy exaggerated a link that was already there in fact. Plato did say that the truly insightful can appear mad, comparing his mysticism to the 'divine madness' of the oracle. Then Platonic mystics, some Jews and some Christian also indulged fantastic forebodings. Startling allegorical 'revelations' even made it into the Christian canon. When these were revived and interpreted for the British political context, the social order was turned upon its head. Clearly, the restoration of order under the crowned head of church and state required the quiescence of enthusiasm. When the Royal Society then offered science to that effect, the fate of mystical epistemology was sealed; for, not only in London, but across Europe, this strategy was so marvellously successful in the marketing of natural science that it ended up delivering its long sought breakthrough. Thus, we cannot account for the church-tolerated and state-sponsored science that we have today without acknowledging this extraordinary marketing success.

A big part of this success was the Empiricism of John Locke. Poorly defended, well refuted and incongruous with the science with which it was packaged to promote, the success of Locke's epistemology had much to do with the stand he took against 'innate ideas', i.e., *against any <u>internally</u> grounded knowledge. His insistence that all knowledge has an <u>external</u> grounding via the senses was just the thing for a new secular science positioned to avoid threatening the spiritual authority of the church and the political authority of the state. The only trouble for us now is that this means to the much heralded success of the Enlightenment exacted a price when this marketing spin ossified into dogma. Today, while the political exigency has fallen away, we yet still live and breathe this ancient apology. We still eschew a mystical ground for an external ground, however absurd we know it to be, and only to dismiss as absurder any return to the site of its error in search of another way.*

In a nutshell, that is how it happened. But this is another story beyond the scope of this book. My task is much more important and primary. It is to identify the contradiction in its various manifestations across modern philosophy of science, before then offering an alternative approach to knowledge. This then prepares the way for a re-awakening to the long history of this alternative understanding of science prior to its extinction in the Enlightenment.

My final advice is to the reader not fully initiated into academic philosophy. To you I say, if when first perusing these pages you are alarmed by the incomprehensible jargon and strange symbols, do not despair. It is true that those uninitiated into this philosophical tradition may find the going hard at *times. Your consolation is that the rest of us must unlearn the habits instilled by 300 years of tradition. Indeed, it is because you escape this disadvantage that I am so eager for your unjaded attention. Do trust that I have made every effort to remove any unnecessary labours as I guide you into this understanding. New terminology will only emerge as it is naturally required in the narrative. And you may rest assured, at least as a base rule that when a term is not adequately explained in the <u>Oxford Concise Dictionary of English</u>, then I do so. As for the mathematics, it is so ridiculously basic that nothing is assumed. My primary concern is with the nature of the arithmetic series 1, 2, 3, ..., and with various notational systems used to express this series, which are all carefully introduced. This care for the reader not withstanding, I do concede that there will be those who may wish to avoid some of the developments in the interpretation of Pythagorean science by skipping over some sections of Part III. Whatever you make of this book, I do believe that your efforts to connect with the underlying vision of science will be amply rewarded.*

Bernie Lewin
1 June, 2009

This book originated as a doctoral dissertation abandoned in the early 1990s. The project was expanded and reconfigured in the early 2000s as 'A Remedy for Enthusiasm'. That manuscript was reworked with a reduced scope during 2008-9 and circulated under the title 'Enthusiastic Mathematics'. During preparations for publication new sections were added at the ends of Chapters 10 and 14, but otherwise the content and structure are little changed.

B. L., Nov, 2018

xvii

INTRODUCTION

The New 'Natural' Philosophy

Out of the Renaissance and through to the 17th century there was a growing push to create a socio-political space for a new type of knowledge. This new knowledge was being generated by networks of *virtuosi* across Europe all with interests in the direct observation of nature. This movement began within disparate communities, protestant and catholic, clerical and secular, working in a variety of ways towards sometimes opposing goals, yet developments did occur which had universal impact. Early in the Renaissance Leonardo da Vinci's records of his natural observations inspired others to follow. Later, Tycho Brahe (1546-1601) spent a fortune and a lifetime building astronomical records of an unprecedented volume and accuracy to which Johannes Kepler (1571-1630) was then able to apply mathematical models and so advance the understanding of the dynamic geometry of the wandering stars. The telescope, promoted by Galileo (1654-1642), and the microscope that was to follow, were early examples of observational tools that continued to develop and further catalyse interest in the examination of nature. The founders of the Royal Society of London (Chartered in 1662) were also interested in observational tools. In particular, they promoted their use in more interactive methods of observation, much like those developed in alchemy, where physical transformation was performed and observed. Boyle's air pump and Newton's glass prism became icons of this 'experimental' method, and the Society often referred to itself as the 'Royal Society for the Advancement of *Experimental* Philosophy'.

Advocates of natural science exhorted others to question accepted dogma and to end futile controversies about competing authorities and competing interpretations. As well as inquiring into the book of Scriptures, they encouraged the examination of God's other dispensation, the 'book' of creatures. Why rely upon what is written about nature by 'the philosopher', Aristotle, when we can experience nature for ourselves? Rather than blindly following what Aristotle *said*, natural philosophers should do as Aristotle *did* and observe nature directly—only then comparing their account with his. Trust nothing in words was the Royal Society's motto.

The new natural science was, in sum, firstly about an interest in nature, secondly about direct methods, both active and passive, for studying nature, and finally it was about building systems of natural explanation. The latter aspect concerned not the method of obtaining knowledge but the new natural knowledge, itself. This natural knowledge was often referred to by the Greek derivation 'physics', but we get 'nature' from the Latin translation of *physios* and we get 'science' from the Latin *scientia*, meaning knowledge. This aspect of the movement, this development of natural systems of knowledge by the 'naturalists' of the 17th century, is perhaps best referred to by the derogatory 18th century currency, 'naturalism'.

Naturalism eschews supernatural explanations of events—involving the intervention of gods, angels, demons and so forth—so as to discover natural causal mechanisms. Taking the lead from Aristotle, and then from the revival of Epicureanism, Naturalism advanced to build new theoretical systems which called for little or no supernatural intervention. When in Book III of *The Mathematical Principles of Natural Philosophy* (1687) Isaac Newton applies his mathematical principles to 'The Systems of the World', only God's steadying hand was required in a solar system of perfect dynamic equilibrium. In the 18th century, Newton's *Principles* was upheld and proclaimed exemplar of the triumph of Naturalism.

A New Theory of Knowledge

But what is this new philosophy doing exactly? How is it generating knowledge, and how do we know its claims are true? Successive attempts were made to give an account of this new method, and of how the truths established in this way related to truths established in other ways, especially religious truths. Across Europe during the 17th century there were a remarkable variety of such accounts, proffered by practitioners, apologists and adversaries alike. What we now call 'philosophy of science' was a domain of intense debate within—and difficult to separate from—a wider controversy over the status of knowledge derived variously from *revealed* (scriptural), *mystical*, as well as *natural* sources. In fact, the sources of knowledge, and its nature and variety—what is now studied as '*epistemology*'—had been a hot topic for the European *literati* since Martin Luther's appearance at the Diet of Worms in 1521. But in the 17th century this debate broadened and deepened with social and political implications beyond elegances in the protestant wars. While French epistemology was still recovering from the devastation of counter-Renaissance scepticism, the English scene was commanded by extraordinary local events beginning with the rebellion of British parliament against its King during the summer of 1642. The ensuing war and 'interregnum' opened a vacuum of authority, unprecedented in Christendom, which sucked this controversy unrestrained into the broader public sphere.

The eruption of competing systems of belief onto the streets and into the presses during the kingless years was not yet exhausted nor extinguished with the return of a Stuart to the British throne. However, during the 'Restoration' (1660-) we witness a growing movement within the elites for an end to ideological conflict—achievable if not through a 'comprehension' into a single church authority, then by settling for a truce and a 'toleration' of non-conformity. It was in this mood of debate that the push to give natural science a legitimate socio-political space gathered momentum and eventually achieved formidable political success. But who would have guessed how it was to happen? I doubt that any pundit could have guessed before the 1660s—not the sceptic, Michel de Montaigne (1533-92), nor the advocates John Dee (1527-1608) or Francis Bacon (1561-1626)—that the apologetic for science most tolerable to a state and its church attempting to re-establish its spiritual authority would be the epistemology synonymous with Atheism. And yet that is exactly what happened. By the beginning of the 18th century one account of natural science had emerged a clear leader. This was a revived and renewed Empiricism, and its popularity in England spread into the French Enlightenment and across Western Europe. It is, in essence, this Empiricism which continues to dominate philosophy of science to this day.

Now, from the historian's perspective, in order to come to an understanding of the present condition of epistemology, it would seem natural to ask why Empiricism triumphed at this time and why it remains triumphant. The tacit answer found in our histories is that it was inevitable that Empiricism would triumph, either then or later, as it is the *true*, or, at least, the *best*, account we have of natural science. The question then is not *Why Empiricism?*, but rather, *Why science?* The story we are told presumes that modern Empiricism *is* science, and that any retreat from Empiricism is a retreat to fantasy and superstition, fairies and demonic intervention. If there were earlier and competing accounts of the new philosophy, they were at best *transitional*—incompletely detached from the old religious ways out of which modern Naturalism emerged.

If we view Empiricism in this way then it is *not* remarkable, let alone incredible, that Empiricism's reign is undisputed in philosophy of science today. But could this complacency suggest that we are trapped in the victor's view of history? What if this account of science contains a contradiction that is as fatal as it is fundamental? What if this contradiction had been identified again and again—by advocates and adversaries alike—every time Empiricism emerged in the Western tradition, and yet it has never been successfully answered? In fact, as we shall see, any fair survey of the history of Empiricism reveals a flawed system under continual attack. Moreover, any fair survey of the history of Western epistemology also reveals that there have always been other approaches to the problem of knowledge that avoid its pitfalls, thereby offering a better account of knowledge.

This book aims to persuade the reader to this view by making three broad moves, the first critical, the second constructive and the third historical. The criticism in the first part is necessary in order for us moderns to see the great failure of modern epistemology behind its overwhelming academic triumph. In Part II we build an alternative account of knowledge using recently developed symbols, metaphors and tools. Empowered by this new understanding, we return in Part III to the history of science. Here we find, beneath the Enlightenment gloss, at the heart of our long tradition, the powerful beat of mathematical mysticism. This is where, in our final move, we reconnect with a broad tradition that we might best call 'Mysticism Emanationism'.

If at any point in the reading, this book manages to persuade the reader towards this view, then the historical question of the current dogma is left largely unanswered, and so it might start burning in the readers mind:

> *If modern Empiricism has always been known to be so fundamentally flawed, then why did it emerge and remain triumphant?*

A full answer to this question is a project beyond the scope of this book. However, to avoid premature rejection of the already ambitious aim of present work—namely, to revive an alternative to this prevailing dogma —a quick summary here might help dampen the flames.

Introduction

A Remedy for Enthusiasm

Empiricism triumphed as the dominant philosophy of science at end of the 17th century not because it was the best account of science (it was not) but, instead, its rise was largely an outcome of socio-political forces. The account of science offered by the modern empiricists, from Locke to Kant and beyond, would have science occupying an epistemological corral where its impact on the spiritual—and therefore *political*—authority of the state church could be contained and controlled. Other accounts of science, sometimes better accounts, could not be so contained and their very existence threatened political authority and social stability. This was not only because they challenged dogmatic theology but also because of their associations (real and imaginary) with the rampant millenarian fanaticism known as 'enthusiasm'.

This is the overwhelming reason why, contrary to first appearances, and despite its associations with Atheism, the state church was relatively tolerant of the new Empiricism. And it explains why other theories of knowledge that did constitute a theology were roundly condemned as, if not atheistic, then 'enthusiastic'. Successful Restoration advocates of science, if they were not genuine believers in modern Empiricism, then they were those quick to recognise that *politically* they had no other option, and so they proceeded to obscure or suppress any association that they, or their fellows, had with the various competing systems of thought that were threatening the spiritual authority of the newly reconstituted state church. Science was promoted not only as intolerant to enthusiasm but even as a social panacea for it. The title, *Enthusiastic Mathematics*, identifies this present work as an attempt to revive Mystical Emanationism in direct challenge to what is now a habitually perpetuated suppression.

PART I

Incredible & Triumphant
LOGICAL EMPIRICISM

Chapter 1
THE LOST OBJECT OF EMPIRICISM

It was a large room
Full of people,
All kinds,
And they had all arrived at the same building at more or less
the same time,
And they were all free,
And they were all asking themselves the same question:
What is behind that curtain?
Laurie Anderson

What is Modern Empiricism?

The term 'Empiricism' comes from the Greek word '*empeiria*', meaning '*experience*', and so the association of Empiricism with the natural sciences is in the first place not surprising, as the claim that all knowledge comes from experience—exclusively or primarily *sensual* experience—privileges the study of natural phenomena. From the information gained by sensual experience we develop ideas about the world. If we call these ideas 'knowledge', then, for the empiricist who claims *there is nothing in our ideas that was not first in our senses*,* the flow of information is entirely from the senses, and our complex systems of knowledge are built from primary ideas about sensation. For extreme empiricists like John Locke (1632-1704), there are no 'innate ideas', there is no knowledge *a priori*, nothing

---

* The Latin expression is *Nihil est in intellectu quad non prius fuerit in sensu*. For its use in the positive epistemology of the Enlightenment prior to John Locke, see the Port Royal *Logic*, where *Omnis idea orsum ducit a sensibus* is also discussed by implicit reference to the *Institutio Logica* of Pierre Gassendi (1592-1655) [1], p. 28. For this doctrine as the basis of sceptical epistemology of the 16th century, see for example Montaigne's 'Apology for Raymond Sebond' [2], p. 663–4. For an ancient discussion, see Plato's *Theaetetus*, p. 151e.

that the mind contributes of itself. For Locke, the mind is as though a *tabla rasa*, a white paper void of all characters, upon which sensual knowledge is written.*

Not all Empiricists claim sensations as the *only* source of knowledge. Today most would agree that this extreme proposal is difficult to defend and that it was not even upheld by Locke in his very defence of it.# More typical is an Empiricism moderated by concessions to the formal sciences. That is, in order for us to develop ideas and theories *about things* we use formal principles—like those of logic or mathematics—which we, perhaps, become aware of, or learn, *by way of* our experience of things, but which are not themselves *derived* from experience. In this way we build knowledge of the things we experience from our various perceptions of them. This was Kant's critique of Locke but it was also St Thomas Aquinas' view, which itself has ancient origins.

The term 'Empiricism' covers so much, but for modern Empiricism we can take our definition a step further and introduce the term 'Representationalism'. Not all Empiricism is Representationalist, but Representationalism is a tendency of Empiricism and, at least since the beginning of the 18th century, it is synonymous with it. The leap to Representationalism is in the claim that the information in the senses, upon which our knowledge is built, is itself derived from *external* objects which this sensual information *represents*. The 'experimental method' of philosophising about nature, advocated by Isaac Newton (1643-1727), and famously promoted in his name and in the name of the Royal Society, is not intrinsically bound to a Representationalist epistemology. The formulation of a Representational account of science was made by Newton's Society fellow and friend, John Locke. It is with Locke that the known object is positioned explicitly and absolutely external, and this doctrine quickly became the account of knowledge promoted within and around the empirical science movement.+

---

* The foundation of the epistemology in Locke's *An Essay Concerning Human Understanding* is that all ideas come from sense and 'reflection', reflection being internal sense of the minds own operations. See [3] Bk II, Ch 1, Section 2-5. See also Aristotle's *On the Soul*, p. 430a, for the first appearance of the idea of the mind (*'nous'*) as a blank page/tablet.
\# The main problem is with Locke's deferral to the role of reason in the development of knowledge. We don't get a clear picture of the nature of reason and its powers. The actor/operator 'reason' is collecting, analysing reflecting on and developing the sensible ideas. If Locke had elaborated he might have found that there are some ideas used to analyse experience that are innate, including, for example the idea of logical non-contradiction and number. Historically, this critique is that of Kant, and yet Locke already anticipates it in his own inconsistencies. See for example where he discusses archetypes which are ideas of the mind's own making not intended to be the copies of anything nor referred to the existence of anything, as to their originals ([3], Bk IV, Ch 4, Part 5). In 1883 long after Kant, John Stuart Mill's *A System of Logic* [4] would return to the strict empiricism of Locke, arguing even that mathematics and logic are from experience.
+ For an account of the popularity and influence of Locke's brand of Empiricism, see Porter [5], p. 60–71.

Unhindered by the lack of a proper defence, Representationalism rapidly rose to become an Enlightenment dogma. Not that it came entirely out of the blue, with Locke drawing upon recent continental developments. Back further, Representationalism had been long upheld in the Western tradition to account for that type of knowledge gained from the senses, and especially since the institution of Aristotelian philosophy by St Thomas Aquinas.

St Thomas (1225-74) worked on the Aristotelian principle that things are *matter* with *form* impressed on them. For him, mind can only contain the form of things, so minds take in likenesses of things' forms abstracted from matter.* This way of thinking has evolved somewhat through the centuries and the notion of a primary formless matter became increasingly difficult beyond the close of the 19th century with the advances in the study of the (sub-atomic) *form* of matter itself. However, this way of thinking does persist in the belief that the difference between our ideas and sensations *of things* and the *things-in-themselves* is that the *things-in-themselves* have some essential and non-sensual 'material' reality, which our thought and sense of them do not have. This is the difference between the ice cream in the mind and the ice cream in the mouth. Even if we don't grant this as a *material* distinction, we might at least say that the ice cream in the mind is a *representation* of ice cream itself, which is not in the mind. Whether the Empiricism is absolute or moderated by the *a priori*, and whether or not it is an overt *Materialism*, there are two things we can safely say about modern Empiricism:

1. The idea we have of a thing *corresponds*, through our sensual experience of it, to the *thing-in-itself*; and, in this way, the idea *represents* the thing.

2. The *thing-in-itself* is *external to* our experience and our knowledge of it.

The Contradiction of Representationalism

Representationalism works something like this: if knowledge is ideas (in minds) about the way things are, then natural knowledge is about the *being* of natural things, like the *being* of rocks, plants, animals, the sun and the

---

* *Summa Theologiae*, Vol 12, 84, 2. Plato does not describe his forms as abstractions drawn from things, rather the forms themselves (auta ta eide) are the underlying reality expressed in things. See *Parmenides*, p. 129. Equating Platonic *forms-in-themselves* with 'abstracted ideas' or abstract entities (*aphaireseôs*) is an Aristotelian distortion that pervaded Medieval scholasticism.

stars. These things *exist* not in our minds but *external* to them. That is to say they have an *external* 'ontology'. They exist not in our science but in nature itself. Now, the way we come to know an externally existing object is *through* our senses: *knowledge-of-the-thing* is derived from the *thing-itself* through the medium of our senses. To the extent that we can rely on the fidelity of the mediation performed by our senses—and we might apply *internal* faculties, *a priori* knowledge, memory and the like to assist in assessing this fidelity—we can say that our *idea-of-the-thing corresponds to* the *thing-in-itself*, which it *represents*. For example, the idea of a horse *corresponds to* and *represents* the horse itself and, likewise, the idea of a molecule represents, in our minds, and in our science, the molecule in itself.

This epistemology that gives our ideas of things as *corresponding to* the things they *represent* in the *external* world was labelled approvingly by Bertrand Russell the 'Correspondence Theory of Truth' and later disapprovingly by Richard Rorty as 'Representationalism'.* This is not Empiricism as such. We cannot always presume that the assignment of experiences as the *source* of knowledge necessarily implies correspondence to an external ontology. But almost without exception, and as we shall see, when this term is used, correspondence with an external ontology is implied or else it is found implicit. Nor is Representationalism restricted to Materialism, although Materialism—with a *material* external object—was its first manifestation. In fact, while 'Materialism', and more broadly 'Empiricism', are common labels for versions of what we are calling 'Representationalism', the use of these terms in the modern context could be misleading because there is a consensus in this representational model across many theories of knowledge that would resist association with either of these labels. This is why Rorty's term 'Representationalism' is so useful, as it allows me to state my negative case most precisely, for it is precisely this type of epistemology (as it remains triumphant since the beginning of the 18th century) that is the first concern of this book.

---

* In 1910 Russell contrasted 'correspondence' with the 'coherence' theory of Idealists in Chapter 6 and 7 of his *Philosophical Essays* [6], p. 156–185. For Rorty's presentation of correspondence theory as 'representationalism', see the introduction to his 1991 essay collection: *Objectivity Relativism and Truth* [7], p. 1–8. The critique of representational epistemology is earlier elaborated in his *Philosophy and the Mirror of Nature* [8]. Earlier critiques can be traced anecdotally to Wittgenstein's abandonment of his 'picture theory' [9] p. 260–1, to his posthumously published rule-following investigations [10], and to Quine's 'Two Dogmas of Empiricism' [11]. In the 1970s, and altogether outside the school of Philosophical Analysis, came Maturana and Varela's '*Autopoiesis*', a non-representationalist theory of perception [12]. Their resolution of the problem of 'representation(al)ism' (which we come to below) is clearly presented in their *Tree of Knowledge* [13] p. 129–135 & 252–4.

Chapter I: The Lost Object of Empiricism

It was not until Immanuel Kant (1724-1804) two generations after Locke that a thorough, overt and self-conscious Representationalism was defended.* However, the need for such a defence first arose as a consequence of the intervention of a young contemporary of Locke. His critique of Locke's epistemology was so powerful that it has smouldered in the background of every attempt to reform Representationalism from Kant to the present. It was George Berkeley (1685–1753), while still a young fellow at Trinity College Dublin, who launched a long career as a vigilant critic of the new natural sciences by pointing to a fundamental flaw in the argument of Locke and the 'new materialists'.

Berkeley's case can be restated as follows: If everything I know about things are ideas in my mind, then how do I know that the things represented in my mind exist in reality? Sensation is supposed to be the medium between things and knowledge, and yet all sensation, all experience, is internal; it is *my* experience, and it does nothing to establish the existence of the things from which the sensations are supposed to have arrived. [16] What we need is some way of establishing the existence of *the-thing-in-itself*. Locke tells us that the real essence of the object has insensible and unknown...primary qualities from which are derived the sensual secondary qualities. And he tells us that there is a conformity between our ideas and the reality of things because our *ideas-of-things* must necessarily be the product of things operating on the mind. But he does not tell us how he knows that these objects exist, let alone how he knows that the way they operate upon our minds guarantees conformity with their reality.# Not only does Locke neglect to tell us, but he cannot, and Berkeley shows that this contradiction places in doubt the very *being* of the material object upon which this epistemology is grounded.

How do we know that an object is producing these sensations of itself when the real essence of the object is unknown? This is as though to say we know there is a dragon hidden in the Alps because we have seen the smoke and heard it roar. Surely there is no credibility in a theory of knowledge that begins with the assumed existence of an unknown and unknowable field of objects from which our experience and knowledge—our apparent reality—is derived? The irony is that the impulse to Empiricism

---
* The closest Locke came to a defence of Representationalism was in answer to Stillingfleet's concern that Locke was almost discarding substance out of the reasonable part of the world. See Locke's 'Letter to the Bishop of Worcester' [14], p. 344–346. See also Cranston [15], p. 276.
# Paraphrase from Locke's *An Essay Concerning Human Understanding*, see: Bk II, Ch 8.9; Bk III Ch 6.2; Bk IV, Ch 3.12 & Ch 12.9. Perhaps the clearest outline of Locke's Representationalism is in Bk IV, Ch 4, where his external known object presents strong resonances with Descartes' external material reality as reduced to extension and confirmed by the goodness of God.

is so often a keenness to build knowledge from the real and present objects in our experience, but what we end up with is a claim that the object itself —its 'reality', 'substance' or 'essence'—is hidden, unknown and unknowable. Berkeley shows how in Representationalism the real object of common experience is removed and replaced by a sensual representation of it. In this account of our empirical knowledge of things, *the-thing-in-itself* has become an absence in our very experience of it.

Berkeley, the Whipping-Boy of the New Empiricism

Berkeley's critique was acute, but his attempt to escape Representationalism and to re-establish the object of knowledge within experience failed. His strategy is to abolish the external material realm and claim that just as everything we know is ideas-in-minds, so *all-known-things* exist only as *ideas-in-minds*. The *being* of objects is always and only *in perception*. But then how does he establish the apparent independent and continuing existence of things? Surely a tree deep in the forest exists even when no one observes it? His answer is that all things exist as *ideas-in-God's-mind*. But in abolishing the mind/body divide Berkeley has not solved the problem of Representationalism. By establishing the independence of objects in this way he has re-established their externality. There is no way out but that my *ideas-of-things* in my mind are representations of the divine originals. Berkeley has done little more than re-invent the external material world as the *mind-of-God*. Aristotle's primary matter, then Locke's primary qualities and now Berkeley's *mind-of-God* all play the role of the external ontology in a Representationalist epistemology. The problem Berkeley found in Materialism has re-emerged in his own Empiricism, where the objects of knowledge are, once again, absent in our experience of them.

It is fair to say that Berkeley's solution to the problem of Representationalism never really caught on. Berkeley's epistemology was novel, unpopular and revealed a failure in its own time.* One would therefore expect it to have gone the way of the vast majority of 18th century controversial literature—forgotten but for a British Museum catalogue entry. But remember it we do. What Berkeley himself called 'the immaterialist

---

* One astute critic was Samuel Johnson (1696-1772), an American educator and admirer of Berkeley's work who should not be confused with Boswell's friend of the same name. In a letter of 10 September 1729, Johnson politely shows how Berkeley's 'immaterial' epistemology (i.e., that our sensations are imperfect copies of divine archetypes) has not escaped the correspondence form. The clear implication is that the contradiction of Locke's Representational epistemology remains. Alas, Berkeley's reply does not directly address the problem. For extracts from Johnson's critique and a commentary see [17] p. 223–32.

Chapter 1: The Lost Object of Empiricism

hypothesis' acquired the label 'Idealism' on account of its 'ideal' ontology, and it was later opposed to a new 'Realism' which (in contrast to Medieval Realism) defended the real existence of material objects in an external realm. The Enlightenment man, if not entirely sceptical of the whole science thing, is a Realist. Yet, again and again, the ghost of Berkeley reappears, often implicitly but sometimes explicitly. To this day Berkeley's epistemology remains a classic of philosophy, always in print. Why so?

Certainly the criticism was acutely felt by all those attempting to make a go of epistemology in the 18th century Enlightenment, the golden age of Representationalism. It was on this account that Berkeley's Idealism became a foil, a scapegoat and even a whipping boy for the new Empiricism. It served to remind the faithful that giving way to your doubts about the reality of the external object could only be a descent into the realm of Berkeley's wacky Idealism. And even if you yield to the *mind-of-God* ontology that doesn't solve the problem anyway. It is primarily in this role as a safe foil for Materialism that Berkeley remains on undergraduate philosophy reading lists. In this role Berkeley became much more than a man of his times. In the enlightened new age of science he came to stand for the last hurrah of the old, theological way of doing epistemology.

Berkeley published the more popular account of his 'immaterialism' in London in 1713. [18] This was 26 years after Newton's *Mathematical Principles of Natural Philosophy*, nine years after his more empirical *Opticks*, and 23 years after Locke first published his *Essay Concerning Human Understanding*, by then after the author's death, in its profusely inflated fifth and final edition. This was at the English dawn of the movement that has come to be known as 'The Enlightenment', and soon the Enlightenment proper was to emerge in France, captivated by intellectual developments across the channel. After Voltaire's *Lettres anglaises* (1733) Locke's Empiricism quickly gained acceptance amongst these French radicals; and, as incredible as it may seem, Newton's *Mathematical Principles of Natural Philosophy*, as celebrated as it was unread, was soon given to exemplify the power of Locke's (most unmathematical) approach to science.* It is in this view of the English scene that Berkeley's failed attempt to overcome the contradictions of Locke's Representationalism acquired a status above and beyond its initial controversial context. Voltaire actually

---

* Locke's continental début came in 1700 with the French translation of the 4th edition. In 1713, with the 2nd edition of *Principia Mathematica*, Lockean epistemology was impressed upon the already-famous text in reaction to concerns over the 'occult' nature (i.e., action-at-a-distance) of gravitational planetary motion. Firstly, a new preface by Roger Cotes defends Newton's method as empirical. All true philosophy, he says, is founded on the appearance of things as manifest to us by God, and so he asks that fair judgement be given to the most excellent method of philosophy founded on experiments and observations. Secondly, the

met Berkeley during his exile in England, and thirty years later he had this to say about him in his entry on 'body' in *The Philosophical Dictionary* of 1764:

> Berkeley, bishop of Cloyne, is the last who claims to have proved, by a hundred captious sophisms, that bodies do not exist. They have, he says, neither colours, nor odours, nor heat. These modalities are in your sensations, and not in the object. He could have saved himself the trouble of proving this truth: it is well enough known. But from this he goes on to extension and solidity, which are essences of a body, and he thinks he has proved that a piece of green cloth has no extension because this cloth is not really green. The sensation of green is only in oneself: therefore the sensation of extension is also in oneself alone. And he concludes, having thus destroyed extension, that the solidity which is attached to it falls automatically, and that there is thus nothing in the world but our ideas. So that, according to this theologian, 10,000 cannon shots are at bottom nothing but 10,000 apprehensions of our understanding; and when a man begets a child on his wife, it is only an idea that lodges itself in another idea, from which a third idea is born.*

For Voltaire, Berkeley's ridiculous excess can be avoided if we admit that we know nothing about the inner meaning of the material object, and yet at the same time he claims that this object exists none the less since it has essential properties of which it cannot be deprived. [19, p. 158] Voltaire is following Locke in asserting—without defending—the being of the external object of sensation in its non-sensual essence. After falsely situating Berkeley as the last of the old school, after ridiculing his solution to the problem of the external object, Voltaire then agrees with Berkeley that we know nothing about its non-sensual inner meaning…only then to say, in effect, *but of course we know it is there!* #

---

text itself changes. With help from Cotes, Newton fashioned a new 'General Scholium' added to Bk III where its mathematical account of gravitational motion is famously defended in the Latin, '*Hypotheses non fingo*':

> I feign no hypotheses; for whatever is not deduced from the phenomena is to be called a hypothesis, and hypotheses, whether of occult qualities or mechanical, have no place in experimental philosophy.

This all stands against the presentation of the text itself where mathematical principles (hypotheses?) are first developed in two books before their application to the systems of the world (phenomena?). For Voltaire's portrayal of Newtonian physics as a product of Lockean method, see especially his writings on Newton in *Lettres philosophiques* (1734) and *Elements de la philosophie de Newton* (1738).
* [19] p. 157. By the time of Voltaire's *Dictionary*, Lockean epistemology had been taken up in the French Enlightenment, promoted by such works as Étienne de Condillac's *Essay on the Origin of Human Knowledge* (1746).
# This confused Representationalist *rationale* became popular, typically serving injunctions to a strict empirical methodology. Denouncements of 'speculation' and the framing of 'hypotheses' would often preface brilliant works that nevertheless continued to indulge these proscribed practices. Consider Lavoisier's preface to his *Elements of Chemistry* (1789). In introducing this classic elaboration of material atomism, Lavoisier confesses that we know nothing at all about those simple and indivisible atoms of which matter is composed. This presents no epistemological crisis even though Lavoisier also proclaims one rigorous law from which I have never deviated, of forming no conclusions which are not fully warranted by experiment.

Rescuing the Object of Science

Voltaire was not the last to have this sort of response to Berkeley. It became a pattern for those unwilling or unable to address the contradiction of Representationalism: the alternative is old fashioned, anachronistic, self-destructive, absurd and devoid of common sense. It is as though to say: *Let's not fall into the absurdity of denying the reality of things...of course we know they exist!* With no alternative in view, any Berkeleian critique of an *external* ontology would invariably be taken as denial of existence altogether—as denying epistemology its rightful and plainly obvious ontology. This led to a standard non-verbal refutation, which we might call *Kick-the-Stone* Realism. James Boswell gives us this 18th century scene:

> After we came out of Church, we stood talking for some time together of Bishop Berkeley's ingenious sophistry to prove the non-existence of matter, and that everything in the universe is merely ideal. I observed, that though we are satisfied his doctrine is not true, it is impossible to refute. I never shall forget the alacrity with which Johnson answered, striking his foot with mighty force against a large stone till he rebounded from it, 'I refute it thus.'

Boswell's own feelings on the matter were less forceful, and although it was inconceivable to him how Berkeley can be answered by pure reason, he did hold out hope that an admirable display of subtlety united with brilliance might resolve the problem. [21, p. 248] Of course, it was not Berkeley but Locke who had removed the stone from experience. Thus, if a *Kick-the-Stone* demonstration is doing anything, then it should be reminding us of the real *presence* of the object in our experience of it—the very *presence* which is denied in Locke. Rarely is it seen that way. On the contrary, the critique of Locke's new ontology is invariably taken as a challenge denying the very *being* of such ordinary objects. And for three centuries this has so often been the supposed axis of the debate: *Well, do things exist or don't they?*

One might suppose that this scorn and ridicule directed at Berkeley and other opponents of the new epistemology was motivated by a confidence that modern Empiricism had finally got it right. However, close inspection suggests otherwise. The excited reactions to critics appear more the projections of insecurities about the integrity of the theory. Indeed, grave concerns are explicitly addressed by its chief advocates in our very canon of modern Empiricism.

[20, p. 16] It was only when the rhetoric of a strict Empiricism was taken seriously by German physicists in the late 19th century that it stifled innovation by inhibiting the development of (hypothetical/-metaphysical) models to explain the nature of things (see below on p. 25-8).

Consider first Locke's *Essay*. In Book IV, Chapter 4, Locke is mulling over his striking admittance that despite our ability to discern from disparate sensual experiences what is true of reality, there remains no discernible connection between any one of these experiences and the external qualities of the reality upon which it depends. Locke then reflects upon this problem by invoking a protest by his imagined reader:

> I doubt not but my reader, by this time, may be apt to think that I have been all this while only building a castle in the air and be ready to say to me: *To what purpose all this stir? Knowledge, say you, is only the perception of the agreement or disagreement of our own ideas; but who knows what those ideas may be? Is there anything so extravagant as the imaginations of men's brains?...* [If knowledge is only this then] *the visions of an enthusiast and the reasonings of a sober man will be equally certain. It is no matter how things are...it is all truth, all certainty. Such castles in the air will be as strongholds of truth as the demonstrations of Euclid...But of what use is all this fine knowledge of men's own imaginations to a man that inquires after the reality of things?* *

In other words, the alternative epistemology (using the coherence or 'agreement' of ideas) provides no discernment of sober reasoning from enthusiastic madness. Locke's answers is firstly that truth must come through grounding in reality: Our knowledge, therefore, is *real* only so far as there is a conformity between our *ideas* and the reality of things. But again: what shall be the criterion? How shall the mind when it perceives nothing but its own ideas, know that they agree with things themselves? The answer is that the conformity of our simple perceptions (what Locke calls 'ideas') is guaranteed by the wisdom and will of our Maker. [Bk IV, Ch 4.3] And so here is the link: by the wisdom and (good) will of God we know that our world of appearances conforms to—is a projection of—this unknowable unknown world of real things. Thus, Berkeley is only following Locke in pulling in God to uphold his reality. Moreover, in Locke's own divine faith we find the hint of a line back to that great bastion of 'innate ideas', the school of Descartes. It was René Descartes (1596-1650) who had grounded the certainty that *external-material-objects* correspond to our *sensation-of-them* by way of his proof of the existence of God, and then by the proof of God's goodness—for *such a good God would not deceive us in such a matter.* #

---

* Bk IV, Ch 4.1. Note that Locke's 'ideas' is better understood as 'sensations'.
# '6th Meditation' [22] p. 158. The convenient dogmatic context is more evident in his 'Principles of Philosophy'. Just before final submission to the authority of the Church in his ultimate principle (N° 206), the certainty of the unknown external material existence of the known object is founded in that God is supreme, good and in no way a deceiver. [23, p. 211–2] No one could argue with that.

Chapter 1: The Lost Object of Empiricism

Whatever we might feel about deferring to faith or to a religious dogma, it is worth examining what is happening here. What this is really saying is that *if* we are *thus so* alienated from reality, *then* God would not deceive us and deny the fidelity of our experience with it. Consider, by substituting this problem in this theory with some other theoretical *non sequitur*, then we may well enlist God's invisible hand to bridge that gap as well. Indeed, it is hard to see how this appeal to the divine is any less absurd than Berkeley's immaterialist hypothesis. There is no faith here, no retreat to any principle of Christian belief, only a fudge. Not for the first time, nor the last, but across the entire history of Representational epistemology and into our secular age, if this question is not ridiculed, buried or shouted down, then there is some sort of fudge.

But, oh, how one can sympathise! For those trapped in this model of knowledge, and yet really trying to make it work, the inability to establish the very *beingness* of things would be maddening. Voltaire and Johnson might have got excited in their responses but they probably did not worry their days away. It was not so easy for those who faced up squarely to the challenge of bringing sense to Representationalism. They would dwell on the problem for too long unresolved, and some found it hard to keep their cool.

George E Moore (1873-1958) was a leader of the great reinvigoration of Representationalism at Cambridge around the beginning of the 20th century, but he was far from resolute, and he anguished his life away over proof of the external world. One account gives a scene at a philosophy conference with Moore 'tearing his hair in despair' before exclaiming,

Look here!

All looked while Moore tapped the table with ferocious fingers.

This table does not exist. IT DOES NOT EXIST. *

Even Kant: while he was not one to lose his cool, all the same he saw no way out but to follow Berkeley in degrading bodies to mere illusion.[#] And if bodies are found to be illusions, then, for the iconoclast who dares, scepticism is just around the corner. Indeed, when David Hume (1711-76) lit that path it had awoken Kant to action. Kant's *Critique of Pure Reason* was an

---
* [24] p. 138. See also [25] p. 248–9. Similar scenes were played out in 20th century French controversy, see Descombes' *Le Même et L'Autre* in translation [26], p. 20–1.
\# *Critique of Pure Reason*, B, p. 71.

heroic attempt to avert the course to mere illusion and the descent into scepticism. It tries to establish the reality of the (represented) object despite the contradiction. In the second edition, Kant makes this project most explicit: though we cannot *know* these objects as *things-in-themselves*, Kant confesses, we must yet be in a position at least to *think* them as *things-in-themselves*... Why? Because ...otherwise we should be landed in the absurd conclusion that there can be appearance without anything that appears. [B, xxvii]

Kant's new Metaphysics was designed to save philosophy from the scandal that the existence of things outside us...must be accepted merely on faith. [B, xl] With its dependence on faith in a non-deceiving God now a scandal, Enlightenment science had come a long way from Descartes, Locke and Berkeley. Kant's ambition for demonstrative reason was not only to rise above the tutelage of the Medieval schools, but also above the faith of Descartes and Locke, and yet still escape the self-destructive impulses that this faith was design to avert. Kant is rescuing the object of science for the sake of science—a science fully independent from religious dogma and yet not destroyed by scepticism. Ever since, Representationalism has seen itself not just as a philosophy of science but also the great defender of the autonomous republic of science. When this heroic mission was taken up by a group of young philosophers at Cambridge, it gave rise to a powerful new movement in Western philosophy.

At the close of the 19th century, after Bertrand Russell (1872-1970) turned with Moore to re-establish Logical Empiricism, physical reality was again threatened by resurgent Idealism. The purpose of Russell's new (physical) 'Realism' was to rescue the physical world from the idealists.* Particularly threatening was the tide of mathematical 'Intuitionism' washing over from the continent (more on that below). Russell's protégé, the precocious Frank Ramsey (1903-30), saw this movement threatening the demonstrative method of the mathematical logicians: after it saved mathematics from sceptics, it now had to contend with Intuitionism, which he depicted as the Bolshevik menace. At the time he was drawing this analogy, shocking news from Russia was spreading fear through the English upper classes that the breakdown of civil order might spread Westward across the continent, and so Ramsey's message was clear: the outbreak of Idealism on the continent threatened a breakdown of philosophical order and a descent into the chaos of scepticism.#

---

* Quoted in [27] p. 535.
# In a highly technical defence of Russell's complete theory of classes, Ramsey proclaims his purpose: I am following the great school of mathematical logicians who in virtue of a series of startling definitions have saved mathematics from sceptics, and provided a rigid demonstration of its propositions. Only so can we preserve it from the Bolshevik menace of Brouwer and Weyl. [28, p. 56] Ramsey refers to the Mathematical Intuitionists Luitzen

Chapter 1: The Lost Object of Empiricism

For Russell and Ramsey, the defence of Realism may have been the defence of natural science, but watching this epistemological controversy from the sidelines provides a very different perspective. The heroic rescuers of science appear to have built Representationalism as a prison for themselves where the prisoner is presented with two clear options: either you find a way to live with yourself in defending the bastion of Realism; or you abandon science, deny the reality of nature, and throw yourself over to the delusion of Idealism or the disarray of scepticism. For so many influential philosophers and teachers who chose the new Realism, the practice of epistemology descends into a preoccupation with shoring up epistemological orderliness to allay this madness. For Bertrand Russell, perhaps the most influential Representationalist in 20th century academic philosophy, this struggle seems to have had deep personal resonances.

Russell's youth was filled with the 19th century revival of Idealism in continental philosophy, but he was soon repulsed by its lack of scientific credibility. Nineteenth century Idealism, with its strong romantic and aesthetic associations, was never popular in the sciences. And whenever it did attempt a science, as Georg Hegel (1770-1881) did, it was not a good look.* Russell decided (as Kant had before him) that he wanted to establish a philosophy to support (his view of) science. He would be the first to admit that he never succeeded, with every attempt spiralling into an abyss of self-contradiction. Sure, he built some props to avert disaster, but he never expressed full confidence in them. Yet this is not to say that his philosophical perspective collapsed. The school of Analytic Philosophy, of which he is a patriarch, still dominates Anglophone academic philosophy schools. And so with Analytical Philosophy triumphant, academic philosophy has become a prisoner to the contradiction of Representationalism. Although there is episodic rattling of the chains, it has never been able to escape its bounds.#

Russell's booklet, *The Problems of Philosophy*, is a delightfully short and well-crafted introduction to epistemology. It is by far the most read of Russell's philosophical texts, and the most familiar book on epistemology in English. To the uninitiated, it also serves well in displaying the formative attitude—although not the later complexities and subtleties-—of the epistemology of the philosophy that continues to dominate the

---

Brouwer and Hermann Weyl. This combative attitude angered Wittgenstein. For more on the controversy see Monk [9] p. 245–6.
* Russell said later that he had found Hegel's mathematics to be both ignorant and stupid. [29, p. 106]
# Despite powerful critiques by Wittgenstein [10], Quine [11], Davidson [30] and Rorty [7, p. 1–18], there is no epistemology in the Philosophical Analysis school that has escaped the representation form. This is not surprising considering that Representationalism is fundamental to the Analytic understanding of science.

universities. Its first chapter starts with the problem of the 'appearance' and the 'reality' of Russell's writing table, which leads into a discussion of Berkeley. The chapter winds up with this rhetorical observation:

> It has appeared that, if we take any common object of the sort that is supposed to be known by the senses, what the senses *immediately* tell us is not the truth about the object as it is apart from us, but only the truth about certain sense-data which, so far as we can see, depend upon the relations between us and the object. Thus what we directly see and feel is merely 'appearance', which we believe to be a sign of some 'reality' behind. But if the reality is not what appears, have we any means of knowing whether there is any reality at all? And if so, have we any means of finding out what it is like? *

Such questions are bewildering, says Russell, but in suggesting the possible paths beyond this point it is clear that we do not have the complete liberty of conjecture, as he claims, for we are in fact prisoners of Representationalism. Beyond Representationalism there is only ontological despair—perhaps there is no table at all.

> If we cannot be sure of the independent existence of objects, we shall be left alone in a desert—it may be that the whole outer world is nothing but a dream, and that we alone exist. This is an uncomfortable possibility.
> [31, p. 7]

The problem, the possibility, the fear of solipsism, of being alone in the world with no connection to things or people, is often expressed by Russell, and perhaps his struggle with philosophical solipsism is symptomatic of his own psychopathology.# But Russell's fears, and his fight against them, can also be seen as symptomatic of a general malaise in philosophy of science. If it is not suffering the abyss, as Russell so candidly did, then it is otherwise trying to obscure or avoid it. Indeed, at the end of Chapter 2 Russell has resolved the issue. Matter *does* exist after all and we know it by our instinctive beliefs:

---

* [31] p. 6. Note that pagination varies in the many editions of this book.
\# Russell's psychological disturbances are sometimes used to understand his peculiar approach to philosophy, and they can also be related to the peculiar nature of his thinking. In the first volume of his biography, called *The Spirit of Solitude*, Ray Monk shows how solipsism was, for Russell, much more than an intellectual curiosity. Russell's strong feelings of alienation from the world (of people and things) might be related to a deficiency of his pictorial memory. Russell noted that he could not imagine familiar objects such as his own breakfast table. Moreover, extraordinary results from a psychological test suggest that he could not directly remember geometric patterns. He could only remember them if he had a name for them and then remembered the name. It seems that Russell's contact with the world was mediated by words. See Monk [27] p. 87 & Crawshay-Williams [32] p. 31–2.

Chapter I: The Lost Object of Empiricism

> Of course it is not by argument that we originally come by our belief in an independent external world. We find this belief ready in ourselves as soon as we begin to reflect: it is what may be called an *instinctive* belief. We should never have been led to question this belief but for the fact that, at any rate in the case of sight, it seems as if the sense-datum itself were instinctively believed to be the independent object, whereas argument shows that the object cannot be identical with the sense-datum. This discovery, however...leaves undiminished our instinctive belief that there are objects corresponding to our sense-data. Since this belief does not lead to any difficulties, but on the contrary tends to simplify and systematise our account of our experience, there seems no good reason for rejecting it. We may therefore admit...that the external world does really exist, and is not wholly dependent for its existence upon our continuing to perceive it.
> [31, p. 11]

The context of this resolution of the problem of external material ontology (published in 1912) is Russell's mounting offensive against 'Mysticism' and 'Intuitionism' in speeches and in print. Here we are not talking about old German romanticism. The new 'Idealists' from whom Russell is attempting to rescue science and the physical world are much more pretenders to science in the garb of mathematical philosophy and evolutionary theory. Most especially prominent at this very time was Henri Bergson's *L'Evolution créatrice* (1907), the enormous fame of which crossed the channel in 1911 with a translation into English and two visits by the author.

The critical response from Cambridge was an heroic defence of science against its adversaries. Russell saw Bergson's 'Creative Evolution' not as science but an attack on science. [33, p. 176] It moves against both logic and sense. Such mystics as Bergson read the book of Nature in the conviction that it is all illusion. [33, p. 26] For Russell, what is at stake is the internal grounding of science—whether by insight, intuition or instinct. Bergson, under the name of 'intuition', has raised instinct to the position of sole arbiter of metaphysical truth.*

Thus, if we turn back again to *The Problems of Philosophy*, we can now see how Russell is sailing close to the wind when, after failing to

---

* [33] p. 19. Russell first attempted to read *Creative Evolution* while in Paris, Easter 1911, just before meeting Bergson for the first time. [27, p. 202–3 & p. 233]. Here we have paraphrased Russell's critical essay 'Mysticism and Logic' [33, p. 18–19], first published in 1914. For Russell, a truly scientific philosophy comes nearer to objectivity than any other human pursuit, and gives us, therefore, the closest constant and the most intimate relation with the outer world that it is possible to achieve.' [33, p. 36–37] This essay makes most evident that Russell found utterly inconceivable the mystical claim that *knowing* finds intimacy with *being* internally, through *in*sight into the knower's own *being*. [33, p. 18–37]. For an earlier critique of Bergson, see especially the essay 'On the Notion of Cause', which was the presidential address to the Aristotelian Society in November 1912, first published in 1913. More on Russell's views of Intuitionism can be found, along with these essays, in the collection we reference here, which is also called *Mysticism and Logic*, first published in 1918. For the social context see Monk [27], p. 232–247.

establish the external ontological ground *externally*, he then resorts to instinct. The difference he makes is subtle. In the Intuitionist controversy, Russell concedes that instinct, intuition, or insight is what first leads to foundational true beliefs, yet such insight, untested and unsupported is an insufficient guarantee of truth. It is *reason* that confirms or confutes these basic instincts. [33, p. 18–19] Thus, in the quoted passage above, to establishing external reality in correspondence with its appearance, we can see how Russell uses, not just 'instinctive belief', but argument and good reason to confirm this belief. Logic remains the saviour of the object of science.

Russell had saved the object of empirical science, but Russell remained uncomfortable about his means of rescue. We know this in a number of ways: firstly, in the next paragraph, where he confesses that this conclusion is doubtless less strong than we could wish; secondly, by his conclusion to the chapter where he gives a brief and surprisingly conciliatory statement of the very foundation of philosophy—that philosophy should be founded on a hierarchy of instinctive beliefs; and thirdly, by his continuing obsession with the problem.

Indeed, Russell should not be comfortable because his atheistic deferral to *reasonably-confirmed-instincts* has no more philosophical credibility than the theological deferral of his 18th century predecessors. If the reader considers Russell's case again, she will find that the appeal to instinct is not to establish *externality*. Rather it is an appeal to the common,

---

An interpretation of Russell's reasonable confirmation that the external world really exists:

1. *Instinct* gives us the existence of the independent world.
2. *Instinct* gives that this independent world is present in our experience.
3. However, *argument* shows that this world is not identical to our experience of it. So, in fact,
4. The world cannot be immediate in our experience.
5. As there must be an independent world,
   but it cannot be in our experience,
   then it must be...
   external to our experience of it, in correspondence with it.

This is how we reasonably interpret our original instinct of the immediate independent world as in fact external to, but in correspondence with, our experience of it.

untutored belief in the real presence of the independent object in our experience—*of course the table is there!* Russell then steps out of instinct to reasons ('argument shows...') that the object is *not* present in our experience, while then coming back to the original appeal to instinct to confirm this absence. Only in this way is the corresponding external reality confirmed. In other words, it is a fudge. In fact, when reason has shown that we experience not *things*, but *appearances-of-things* (i.e., only sense data), it does not confirm the original instinct but confutes it.

The reader could ask herself at this point: *Does my instinct tell me that my table is real and present, or rather that it is a simulacra of itself built of sense data?* Even if you feel that the objects around you are (re)present as Russell reasons, then it is hard to see how this refutation of their immediate presence serves to simplify and systematise our account of experience. Russell's only other defence is entirely negative: that the alternatives to this account are absurd, unworkable and uncomfortable. Anyway, with the inserted argument for the *absence* of the *real* from our experience, we only return, unresolved, to the precise contradiction of Empiricism given by Berkeley and by all the fathers of modern Empiricism. What Russell and the other patriarchs of Representationalism seem to find inconceivable is that the world could be causally *independent* from our experience but yet remain *internal* to it. This is just what we propose in Part II. But that is jumping ahead of ourselves, for meanwhile, over in German, another movement of Empiricism was developing in response to 19th century Idealism. In an effort to reform scientific methodology, these Germans took to the contradiction of Representationalism with brave resolve to conquer it. External ontology would be abolished with the empirical object returned fully to immediate sensual experience.

Returning the Empirical Object to Experience

On continental Europe in the 19th and 20th centuries (and at times in England and America as well) the system and the language of Kant's *Critique of Pure Reason* was difficult to avoid, and, inevitably, it was in Kantian terms that these attempts to retrieve the empirical object were formulated. Kant had two object-fields in correspondence: the *phenomenal*, presented in our sensations, and the *noumenal*, the independent, external and insensible source. Discomfort with this new metaphysics was expressed from the beginning, but the first great rebellion came from within German ıcism. Hegel's *Phenomenology of the Mind* (1807) shows how the ₂an come around to unmediated experience in a direct experience of . Later in the 19th century we find other attempts to establish *being* in *experience*, which were more or less influenced by Hegelian Idealism, but which were much more orientated to, and expressed within, the context of the contemporary empirical sciences. These projects discredited the metaphysical superstructure designed to keep the noumenal in place and re--established Empiricism in a new simplicity, where the object of science remains in the phenomenal. With the noumenal abandoned and the *being-of-things* now in the phenomenal, this approach came to be known, at least with Edmund Husserl (1859-38), as 'Phenomenology'.*

The close affinity of these post-Kantian movements with Berkeley's response to Locke is often lost in the changing conventions of terminology. To be precise about Berkeley, he insisted that *being* must remain in *perception*, that the object of knowledge must be in sensual experience (although he only achieved this by situating *being* in the independent domain of divine perception). A sensation, or sense datum, is not what is normally thought of as an 'idea', but this conforms to Locke's peculiar definition of an 'idea'. Thus, Berkeley's 'Immaterialism' is accurately described as an ontological *'Ideal*-ism' in this Lockean sense, but not in the sense we would normally associate with that term. This unusual usage suggests that Berkeley's Idealism has an affinity with what was often called Plato's 'Theory of Ideas' (now better described as the 'Theory of Forms') and with other *'form*-al' epistemologies, and not with modern Phenomenology, where the true affinity lies. With Berkeley's reputation as the enemy of modern physics in its early days, and with the anti-science associations of the term 'Idealism', the obscurity of this affinity was not unwelcome. Before we leave Representationalism, it will serve our purposes to visit but one of these attempts to overcome Kant in a new and rigorous Empiricism. This is the 'Sensationalism' of Ernst Mach.#

---

* This tradition has evolved and continues in France through the work of Maurice Merleau-Ponty and others. Its different branches have been assigned different, conflicting and overlapping classifications. Here I refer to Phenomenology broadly as the attempt to find *being* in *experience*, where experience is dealt with in terms of the Kantian idea of *phenomena* as *the-experienced-objects-of-knowing*. This simplified account of this post-Kantian project keeps the focus on our specific concern. The intention is not to suggest that in other respects Sensationalism, Positivism, Phenomenalism and Phenomenology can be reduced to each other, but only their similarity in that they have all failed to progress on the contradiction of epistemological Representationalism.

Identification with Berkeley's view was explicitly rejected by Mach. [34, p. 361–2]

Ernst Mach (1838-1916) is unusual among modern philosophers of science in that he was directly involved in the leading science of his time. Mach was a physicist at a time when physical theory was in a state of revolution, with all the old idols smashed and a continuing and broad debate about what was to replace them. Mach's philosophy influenced the course of this debate, if not the eventual outcomes.

By the end of the 19th century the scene was set in the physical sciences for a re-examination of the nature of empirical knowledge. Old-fashioned Materialism had become untenable in the advancing investigations of matter. The behaviour of matter at the most basic observable level appeared less and less like what would be expected of Aristotle's passive, impressionable, unformed *stuff-of-the-universe*. Locke had been sloppy in making claims about the unknown source of sensation without any justification for those claims. Kant answered the criticisms of Locke by establishing the unknown object through his metaphysics—we cannot *know* it but we can *think* it—and to the extent he did this, the external object was internalised as still absent, yet ideal. Ernst Mach was as critical of Kantian metaphysics as was Locke of 'innate ideas', and so his response to Kant can be seen as a return to Locke's sensual source without Locke's references to its insensible essence. In fact, Mach's strategy is to make inadmissible all claims not immediately sensible. Such claims can only be—like Kant's *thinking the noumenal*—metaphysical invention. For Mach, and the new 'Positivists' who followed, it is this 'metaphysics', which had been designed to establish reality and avoid illusion, that has itself become our modern illusion. In this renewed and rigorous Empiricism, to describe something as metaphysical is to discredit it. Instead, science should always and only concern objects present in our senses. For Mach, the world consists only of our sensations and the objects, or elements, of this world are the units of sensation—more or less what is later called 'sense data'. My sensation of *red*, when I see a red table, is what is *real* and *present*, and it is also something of which I am *certain*.* Science should always and only be *description* of this sensual world consisting of these sensational elements.

Where Mach's influence was most strongly felt in the debate over the fundamental nature of matter was in his rejection of theories, or models, that are not directly grounded in terms of sensations. For Mach, theory

---

*   [34] Mach's use of colour in an attempt to overcome Representationalist epistemology can be contrasted with Maturana and Varela's more recent use of colour to the same purpose. [13, p. 19–23] In the latter, it is the very difficulty of considering colour a primary object of experience that is exploited to make their case against Representationalism.

has at best a provisional role in leading to sensational description, but it can never constitute claims about what actually exists. If you do make existential claims of ungrounded theory, you are imposing ideal forms on to a world that does not evidently possess them. For example, if a theory about the atomic structure of matter were presented as something real *beyond* the experimental data, Mach would claim it to be metaphysics, not physics, an illusion inadmissible to science.

Mach's objections to speculative theory echoed the early 18th century advocates of 'experimental method' and their objections to theoretical speculation or 'hypothesis'.* As we have seen, the most famous and historically important advocates of experimental method were Locke, Newton and other members of the Royal Society. However, back then, this doctrine did not at all reflect practice. The great founders of modern science continued to speculate grandly despite this new propaganda. The mood was entirely different in German physics two centuries later. Mach's attempt to bring science into a strict and close adherence to its empirical foundation caused tension among Mach's contemporaries, who were at that very time groping around for increasingly complex mathematical models to explain the new experimental phenomena. In his *Analysis of Sensations* (1886), Mach used atomic modelling to exemplify inadmissible theorising, and as late as 1912 he was claiming that physical atoms must not be considered to really exist. This is one of those rare moments in modern science when the epistemological controversy enlivened at the frontier of experimental science. Mach's rejection of theoretical modelling featured in the heated debate between the 'energeticists' and the 'atomists', and it contributed to the neglect of Ludwig Boltzmann's kinetic theory of molecular motion, vindicated only after his suicide in 1906. Mach (and also Wilhelm Ostwald) held firm to the experiential ground of science, but it seemed to some at the time (and to many others, in hindsight) that their epistemological rigour inhibited the acceptance of some very sound theorising.#

---

* What Buchdahl says of early 18th century 'experimental Newtonianism' could, with appropriate substitutions, be said of this movement at the end of the 19th century:
> What has been called 'experimental Newtonianism' became an important 'image' for the 18th century thinker and writer. It emphasized observation and experiment, it officially denounced the employment of hypothesis, it stressed the aim of investigating nature at close range, and it ended up by operating *against* the very spirit of systematisation which we have seen to be such a central feature of that aspect of 18th century thought so far considered...[20, p. 12]

[35] Vol 2, p. 266-7. One of those who came to see it this way was Albert Einstein (1879-1955). Much influenced by Mach's physics in his early development, Einstein later came to view Mach's positivist epistemology as essentially untenable. Moreover, he felt that the hostility of Mach and Ostwald towards atomic theory can undoubtedly be traced back to their positivist philosophical attitude. Of this view of knowledge, Einstein observed: the belief that facts by themselves can and should yield scientific knowledge without free conceptual construction is a misconception only possible because one does not easily become aware of the free choice of such concepts, which, though success and long usage, appear to be immediately connected with the empirical material. [36] p. 21 & 47.

Chapter 1: The Lost Object of Empiricism

Mach had stripped Empiricism of its metaphysics and re-oriented science to its object in the sensual world, but had he escaped the contradiction of external representation? According to Mach, the objects of *my* knowledge are elements in *my* sensation, immediate, present and certain...to *me*. But how does he go beyond *my* experience and establish the world independent from my perceiving it? There is still a gap in his theory. Mach's attempt to make Empiricism work in physics exemplifies the difficulties—perhaps the impossibility—of Empiricism: how to avoid the leap to the external without slipping into the vortex of solipsism.* Where now? Surely not a new metaphysics?

Russell's discomfort in 1912 now has more context. From where Russell stood it was clear that knowledge of the world must come through the individual's experience of the world, otherwise it is an illusion, an Idealistic fantasy. Yet, either the world is *my* world and I retreat into solipsism, or otherwise some new metaphysics—some *non-experiential* presumption—is required to establish the very existence of this world. But if we were to take the latter path, then how could we say that a real world established by a new metaphysics is, itself, less than fantastic, and so avoid an outcome where, once again, the apologetic for science is revealed as its own enemy?

The predicament was dire, but it was about to get worse. Not only the foundation of knowledge *in things*, but the very logical form of knowledge itself was about to be consumed by a new scepticism. By the end of the 20th century scepticism would return with the all-consuming destructiveness that it had with the revival of ancient scepticism at the end of the 16th century. Indeed, Russell had already faced its chilling winds, ever since he stumbled upon 'the logical paradox' in 1901.

---

* The metaphor of the vortex is given after the Greek mythology of 'Scylla and Charybdis'. The former is a monster on the shoreline, while the latter is a whirlpool. One must navigate between these these perils through the Strait of Messina. Maturana and Varela's *Tree of Knowledge* [13, p. 134] presents this myth as an analogy of the choice between representation (Scylla) and the vortex of solipsism (Charybdis) that modern epistemologists fail to navigate.

Chapter 2
THE FAILURE OF LOGICAL METHOD

This contradiction comes like a thunderbolt from a clear sky.
How could we be prepared for anything like this in exact logic?...
The possibility of such a thing points to a mistake in the original design.

Gottlob Frege

Any proof of the syllogism would be absurd.
The syllogism is, to put it briefly, nothing but a rule of language to avoid contradiction:
At bottom the principle of non-contradiction is a principle of grammar.

Simone Weil

Contradiction: Why this one bogy?
This is surely very suspicious.

Ludwig Wittgenstein

Please accept my resignation.
I don't want to belong to any club
that will accept people like me as a member.

Groucho Marx

From Ontological Foundation to Methodological 'Element'

So far we have discussed the foundation of the new Empiricism in a Representational epistemology. We have seen how Berkeley identified the fundamental contradiction of Representationalism in Locke and how successive attempts to find a way out of the contradiction were unable to avoid the solipsistic vortex while establishing the independent object of science within experience. The problem is simple but monstrous and it has monstered many a modern philosopher brave enough to face it. But the problem is, in fact, even more monstrous than this. What we will do now is pull back from this problem, broaden the scope, and consider that the difficulty Representationalism has in establishing the ontology of its object may be but one inevitable outcome of the prevailing elementary method of modern philosophy. In order to show this we will put aside the problem of an epistemology finding its *foundation* in an ontology—which is to answer the question: *What is it that our knowledge is ultimately about?*—and turn our attention toward consideration of the formal '*element*' of a philosophical method. Let me explain what this means.

Instead of introducing this new term 'element', I might have said that we will now consider the *logic* of a philosophical method, but I didn't say 'logic' because it is precisely *logic* that is in contention. Throughout the history of Western philosophy there have been two competing elementary methodologies, the one logical and the other mathematical. The logical 'element' derives from a formalisation of linguistic reasoning. The mathematical 'element' is the unseen and ultimately inexpressible, or *mystical*, 'form' of mathematical reasoning. The first mathematical philosophers were the Pythagoreans, a religious cult reputedly founded by Pythagoras in the 6th century BC. Their elementary approach was eventually wholly embraced by Plato (428-347 BC) who collaborated with some brilliant mathematicians to revolutionise the Pythagorean teaching and thereby establish the foundations of the long tradition of Platonism. The lines of conflict between the two elementary approaches, the logical and the mathematical, were defined when a former student of Plato returned to Athens to set up his own school teaching a new and revolutionary method. The new school was the *Lyceum*, the method was predicate logic and the philosopher was Aristotle (382-322 BC).

LOGICAL EMPIRICISM

Both Platonism and Aristotelianism spread from Athens throughout the Hellenistic world*, sometimes as dynamic and evolving traditions, but often in dogmatic, degenerate or blended forms. The ongoing controversy over these two methodologies defines the historical dimensions of our story. Yet, this conflict is barely evident in most standard histories of science. As a consequence, a student of philosophy would find it difficult to appreciate just how the outcome of this controversy—i.e., the triumph of the logical—determines and legitimates most contemporary philosophical discourse. Thus, it is my first duty to prepare the reader by drawing out these two methods so they stand apparent and opposed in the reader's mind. Thus, for the rest of Part I, we will give our attention to the logical element, showing how inhibited, self-defeating and utterly unsuited to the task it truly is. It is only after this exposition of logical method that, in Part II, we launch into the likely less familiar but (I hope the reader will agree) liberating and truly marvellous domain of mathematical mysticism.

The exposition of the logical method in this chapter begins with an examination of predicate logic. Here I will demonstrate how the *'other-referring'* nature of this *element* tends to a philosophical system that is *foundationally* contradictory. My case is that logic is the elementary form of the approach to philosophy that is driven to found itself in an external, represented ontology; and that the contradiction of Representationalism, which we have been examining, is only a consequence of *the insufficiency of all logical systems*—that is, it is a consequence of their inability to contain themselves.

We will start by returning to Bertrand Russell but reaching beyond his defence of Representational epistemology to the crisis of logical method that he, as much as anyone else, lived and breathed. This crisis arose during the late 19th and early 20th centuries as part of what is sometimes called the 'Foundation of Mathematics Controversy'. This saw revived mathematical foundationalism pitched against the most concerted attempt we have ever witnessed to render mathematics finally and completely logical.# It is this logical reductionism that Ramsey was still defending

---

* 'Hellenistic' is an historical term referring to the spread across Europe, Asia and North Africa of Greek culture, and its infusion and transmission of host cultures after the conquests of Alexander the Great. The beginning is usually marked by the death of Alexander in 323 BC, but its decline is less well defined. Politically in the West, the Hellenistic period ends with the rise of the Romans. However, Hellenistic language, philosophy and religion thrived through the height of Roman domination and into the 6th century AD, only ending with the political disintegration and impoverishment of the Dark Ages. In the East, because there was no such disintegration, there was strong cultural continuity into Byzantine Christianity and right though to the fall of Constantinople in 1553.

\# Those positioned against the logicians included the leading 'mathematical Intuitionist', the Dutchman Luitzen Brouwer. Brouwer was also in a famous dispute over the 'Formalism' of the German, David Hilbert. Also involved was the French mathematician Henri Poincaré, who sided with the Intuitionists against the logicians, and we will come to him shortly.

against the Bolshevik menace of continental Intuitionism in the 1920s. Muc earlier, in the first decade of the 20th century, Ramsey's mentor had set about achieving this reduction. Very early in this project Russell discovered an elementary antinomy that became known as Russell's Logical Paradox.

Russell Discovers the Paradox

It all began well. In fact, Russell was doing so well in 1900 in reducing the whole of mathematics to a small set of logical statements, or primitive propositions, that he drafted a booklet with the none too humble title, *The Principles of Mathematics*. The difference with *The Principles of Mathematics* written by Russell's famous Cambridge predecessor, Isaac Newton, was that this book would have all mathematics wrapped up in a complete *logical* system. It was to be a complete Aristotelian revolution that would finally turn the tables on the supporters of mathematical foundationalism, who were by then making noises on the continent. There were still some problems to iron out, none of which seemed critical, when, in the spring of 1901, a new such problem emerged. It appeared a trifle at first, but over the next 10 years it developed into a giant cloud of doubt over the entire project, even in its apparent success.

The trouble began with Russell's attempts to assimilate to logic a remarkable but little known mathematics of infinite numbers. Whereas previously, infinity had been considered a concept of boundlessness or endlessness, Georg Cantor (1845-1918) identified a hierarchy of infinite numbers (transfinite cardinal numbers) as infinite 'sets', where the higher order set contains the lower order sets and more. Russell applied Cantor's theory of infinite sets to his logic of classes, which allowed him to invoke, say, *the class of all red things* as a class with potentially infinite members that yet remained definite and so containable within a higher class. Cantor had also developed a calculus for his infinite numbers and its application to Russell's logical system proved very powerful. While Russell championed Cantor for conquering infinity, he did have one outstanding objection.

Cantor had stipulated that there was no end to the hierarchy of infinite numbers, but Russell thought this could not possibly be. In principle, there must be a greatest number, which is the number of all things and all classes of things. Russell's idea was that, in principle, you could count every thing (and every *class-of-things*) in the world and so arrive at the

er.* As he reflected later, it was this innocent idea that ended
eymoon by leading him to the paradox that now bears his

> I applied [Cantor's] proof to this number to see what would happen. This process led me to the consideration of a very peculiar class. Thinking along the lines which had hitherto seemed inadequate, it seemed to me that a class sometimes is, and sometimes is not, a member of itself. The class of teaspoons, for example, is not another teaspoon, but the class of things that are not teaspoons, is one of the things that are not teaspoons. There seemed to be instances which are not negative: for example, the class of all classes is a class. The application of Cantor's argument led me to consider the classes that are not members of themselves; and these, it seemed, must form a class. I asked myself whether this class is a member of itself or not. If it is a member of itself, it must possess the defining property of the class, which is to be not a member of itself. If it is not a member of itself, it must not possess the defining property of the class, and therefore must be a member of itself. Thus each alternative leads to its opposite and there is a contradiction.

Russell first communicated his misfortune to Alfred Whitehead (1861-1947), with whom he intended to collaborate, but Whitehead failed to console him, quoting Browning: never glad confident mornings again. [38, p. 58]

How prophetic Whitehead's assessment was! Over the next 10 years the paradox would expand its effect on the logical approach, and over the next 14 years Russell would make his great contributions to modern philosophy. But this was not the Russell, glad and confident, of the first few years of his Logical Realism. Instead, this was a man expressly despondent and plagued by doubt. Indeed, as he put it, within two years of embracing logical reductionism, his logical honeymoon was over. Yet this did not mean the end of the marriage, as it did for others, including, famously, Gottlob Frege (more below). Eventually Whitehead also walked away, but not before Russell had develop a rule to disable the effect of the paradox, which then allowed the completion of their project in what became *Principia Mathematica* [1910-13]. The confidence suggested in appropriating again the title of Newton's great work, this time using the original Latin, was not reflected in a confidence that the problem of the paradox was finally and

---

* In an article published in 1901, and then republished in *Mysticism and Logic* with recanting footnote, Russell writes: There is a greatest of all infinite numbers, which is the number of things altogether, of every sort and kind. It is obvious that there cannot be a greater number than this, because if everything has been taken, there is nothing left to add. Cantor has a proof that there is no greatest number, and if this proof were valid, the contradiction of infinity would reappear in a sublimated form. But in this one point, the master has been guilty of a very subtle fallacy, which I hope to explain in some future work. [33, p. 87] Later, in *Principles*, at the beginning of Chapter X he says that he was led to the contradiction in an endeavour to reconcile Cantor's proof that there can be no greatest cardinal number with the very plausible supposition that the class of all terms (which we have seen to be essential to all formal propositions) has necessarily the greatest possible number of members. [37, p. 101]

completely resolved. Just as Russell did not shy from revealing his reservations about his *reasonably-confirmed-instinctive-belief* solution to the contradiction of Representationalism, here too he did not hide his doubts about his solution to the paradox.

How a proposition that contradicts itself could become so devastating to the logical approach is hard to see at this point. But by giving the Aristotelian background to this modern logical reductionism, I can demonstrate the profound impact of the paradox upon it, and this, in turn, will lead us to see the very contradiction of Representationalism as a particular expression of the paradox.

The Organon: Aristotle's New Method

When Aristotle returned to Athens, Plato's Academy after the death of Plato was engrossed in mathematical philosophy. Plato had moved more and more towards Pythagorean mathematical mysticism as he grew older, and now the Academy under Speusippus and then Xenocrates was thoroughly Pythagorean. Upon all accounts these first Academics followed the doctrine that the principles of mathematics are the principles of everything* due to the fact that the particular *being-of-things* is constituted as an expression of an emanation, a mathematical differentiation, of the mystical unity, the source of all things.# Aristotle found great difficulties with this mathematical emanationism, and in place of mathematical method, he introduced his own method, or 'organon' (meaning 'tool'), which is a reduction and formalisation of ordinary grammatical implication, what we now call 'predicate logic'.

In Aristotle's *Organon*, statements of fact are reduced to the form:

Subject	The verb *to be*	Predicate
e.g., Socrates	is	a man.

The predicate is seen both as an attribute of the subject and a qualification of the subject, and a subject can have any number of predicates attributed to it. The purpose of the logic is not so much to discover new truths but more to sort out what is already known, which is to say, it is a mechanism for the *analysis* of truths. Logical analysis does not solve the problem, for

---
* See for example Aristotle's account in *Metaphysics* p. 985b.
\# Mathematical emanationism is evident in Pythagoreanism from the earliest accounts. The emanation is from an original principle of unity (*arche hen*), which is often call the 'Monad' after the time of Plato. See the discussion below in Chapter 9.

35

LOGICAL EMPIRICISM

example, of propositions that are thought to be true (say, *All swans are white*) which are subsequently found to be false (because it is found that *Some swans are black*), but it can produce new conclusions from given premises as is shown in the form of the 'syllogism':

> *Socrates is a man.*
> *All men are mortal.*
> *Therefore, Socrates is mortal.*

If *predicates* are interpreted as sets of individuals or classes of attributes, then *subjects* as either classes or individual members of classes. In this interpretation we can take this example as invoking the class of all *men*, the class of *mortal* beings, and the individual *Socrates*. *Socrates*, on account of being in the class of *men*, which is contained in the class of *mortals*, is found to be, himself, *mortal*.* The power of the syllogism is in the implication of the premises, *if* they are true. So while the truth of a premise is something that is established externally (external to the logic), the *implication* is an internal issue and its effectiveness is maintained in a large part by the Law of Contradiction.

The Law of Contradiction

The Law of Contradiction will not allow a proposition that is, in any respect, both true and false.# Consider in our syllogism above what would happen if we also assert that there are God-men and so add the proposition: *Some men are immortal*. If this proposition is taken as *also* true, then *All men are mortal* is false. It has contradicted the original premises causing the original conclusion to collapse, for it is illogical to be conclusive about Socrates' mortality if the premise *Some men are immortal* is introduced. The Law of Contradiction is absolutely critical for this tool to be able to build systems of truth. For Aristotle's tool to work, all propositions must be found to be either true or false or otherwise meaningless and, therefore, able to be dismissed.

Just as two propositions that contradict each other are inadmissible, so too a single proposition that contradicts itself is either, by definition, false, or, otherwise, nonsense (e.g., *Bachelors are married* or *Paris is*

---
* In the *Organon*, see especially Aristotle's *Prior Analytics* Bk I, p. 24-9. It was the Stoics who used the term 'logic' for Aristotle's methodological 'tool'. Aristotle's term was 'analysis'—taking apart—and this term is accurately applied to the 20th century school called 'Analytic Philosophy'.
# In Aristotle, see *Metaphysics* Bk IV 3-6, especially p, 1008b, and also the discussion of contraries in Bk X, Ch 4-5, p. 1055ff.

London or *Pigs are birds* or *The unknowable is known*). What Russell discovered was a self-contradictory proposition which he could not easily dismiss as false or nonsense. It was not altogether trivial either. On the contrary, it presented necessary to define the class essential to all formal propositions, that is, the 'universal class'. [37, p. 101] As he recollects above, this paradoxical type of self-contradiction first appeared while he was trying to establish this *universal class* by experimenting with classes that were not members of themselves, and thereby the proposition about them: *The class-of-all-classes is a class*. Is this proposition true or false? As Russell said, if this class is a member of itself, it must possess the defining property of the class, which is to be not a member of itself and so the statement is true. Yet if it is not a member of itself, it must not possess the defining property of the class, and therefore must be a member of itself. And so it is false. Thus the predicate negates the subject, each alternative leads to is opposite and we have an alternating true/false vicious circle.

After Russell bravely offered his discovery to the arena of the mathematical foundations controversy, it was soon recognised that 'Russell's Paradox'—which plainly had a devastating impact on Russell's *particular* attempt to found mathematics in logic—was an instance of a broader class of self-contradictory propositions that had been used to attack logical method from the beginning. As Henri Poincaré (1854-1912) was to show, Russell's propositional vicious circle was similar to one of those used at the time of Plato and Aristotle for broad attacks on theory. [39, pp. 187–8] These attacks began with the 5th century Eleatic philosophers, Parmenides and Zeno, who found similar paradoxes in all attempts to account for difference, differentiation and the reference of words to things. Neither Plato nor Aristotle could, nor did they, ignore their apparent devastation of any pretension to elementary methodology.*

Poincaré found Russell's paradox to be of the same form as the famous ancient antinomy of 'The Liar'. The version Poincaré relates concerns the contradiction implicit in the Cretan poet, Epimenides, defending the immortality of Zeus by claiming *The Cretans* [are] *always liars*. While there is no suggestion that Epimenides' defence was considered self-contradictory

---

* There are no primary sources of the Eleatics nor of their followers, the early Megarians, who were contemporaries of Plato and Aristotle. Plato's dialogue on ontology, *Parmenides*—a supposed discussion between a (very young!) Socrates and Parmenides of Elea—is an attempt to deal with the critical impact of the Eleatics. Plato's dialogue on epistemology, *Theaetetus*, is introduced by Euclides of Megara. *Cratylus* and *Euthydemus* also address this form of scepticism. As for Aristotle, he discusses the challenges of Zeno and Parmenides in many places, see for example in *Metaphysics* p. 1001 & p. 1089a, and *Sophistical Refutations* p. 180. In addressing each of the major questions of philosophy, Aristotle tends to discuss and answer these sceptics, but he also often uses Eleatic arguments strategically to attack the views of the Pythagoreans and Plato. See also Russell's treatment of Parmenides in his *History of Western Philosophy* [40] Ch 5.

LOGICAL EMPIRICISM

in his time, the form of its contradiction is later discussed as 'the case of the Liar'. This is recorded as one of the paradoxes of Eubulides, who we know wrote a dialogue called *The Liar*. Eubulides was of the Megarian school, which continued the critical tradition of the Eleatics into the time of Aristotle. Indeed, Eubulides is said to have kept up a controversy with Aristotle and said much to discredit him. [41, Bk II, p.108-9] Various expressions of the self-contradiction paradox—including simply *I am lying*—were used to attack logical method from the beginning and right through the Hellenistic period. In the Medieval Aristotelians revival they were widely discussed, although with less gravity. Now, at the beginning of the 20th century, logical self-contradiction returned with full force to foment a crisis in a new attempt at logical reduction.*

So, what is the form of logical paradox? Russell found the answer. The common characteristic of all these troublesome propositions is self-reference or reflexiveness.#

Self-Reference: the Plague, the Antidote, the Victim

In a self-referencing proposition, instead of the predicate making some independent and new qualification of the subject, the predicate is referred to the proposition as a whole. The action of predication is an action of self-inclusion. In the *universe-as-classes*, the contradiction occurs when a class is a member of itself. The whole is one of its parts. Russell found that such propositions as *The class-of-all-classes is a class* presented themselves necessary at critical moments in the development of a complete logical system. But instead of completing or containing the system, they spin out into a vicious circle of self-contradiction. Not only Russell's project was threatened by the paradox, but it threatened the very power of logic to building systems of knowledge, and both Russell and Poincaré knew it. So what could Russell do to save logical reductionism?

Identifying the problem can be half the work in finding a solution. The paradox is self-referential. Now, while self-reference is the *condition* of the paradox, not all self-reference is paradoxical. For example, *This*

---

* [39] p. 187–8. Aristotle's response to the paradox [42, Bk XXV, p. 180a27-b7] is a source often cited in the Medieval discussion of what they called *insolubilia*. Cesare Burali-Forti found a similar paradox in Cantors set theory prior to Russell's discovery. [43]

[44] p. 61. Note that this statement and others on the analysis and treatment of self-reference that appear in *Principia* are more properly attributed to both the authors, Russell and Whitehead. However, it serves our narrative to attribute them to Russell as the driving force behind this aspect of the work about which Whitehead already held grave concerns.

Chapter 2: The Failure of Logical Method

sentence has five words is self-referential and plainly true. Whereas *This sentence has ten words* is self-referential and self-contradictory but false. There is also *This sentence is true*, which does not seem to be saying anything at all. These cases of logical self-reference, whether or not they are permissible, seem of little use to logic, and could be dispensed with. If they were outlawed nothing much would be lost, and yet the Law of Contradiction could be saved. And if the Law of Contradiction could be saved then logic, as elementary method, could be saved. And so it was. In his 'Hierarchy of Types', this is exactly what Russell did. He outlawed all self-reference.

In the history of logical philosophy the solutions to the Liar Paradox are often about finding a way to show that its self-reference is meaningless unless it is expanded into an *other-referencing* form. This expansion usually involves rectifying a confusion in the paradox between the plane of a discourse and the plane of *that-which-the-discourse-is-about*—i.e., the plane of its reference. This is not quite what Aristotle is doing when he comes to answer the challenge of the self-professed liars. In *Sophistical Refutations* Aristotle suggests that the logical self-contradiction, including the Liar Paradox, is due to a confusion between 'relative' and 'absolute' predications of a subject.* However, the strategy of realising the paradox out of a confusion in the orders of reference is found in many of the Medieval solutions—of which Paul of Venice (1368-1429) in his *Logica Magna* lists fourteen. [45, Vol 4, p. 534] In this way, the Christian Aristotelians anticipate Russell's Hierarchy of Types.

In Russell's *universe-as-classes* there are individuals that are members of classes and then there are classes of these classes. These classes-of-classes are 2nd order classes, and classes that contain 2nd order classes are 3rd order classes... and so forth. In this universe, just as a class cannot be one of its individual members, likewise, a *class-of-classes* cannot be one of its member classes. If this were allowed then self-referencing could occur and we open ourselves to the paradox. Paradoxical propositions are statements that confuse this hierarchical order of classes. Russell shows how the Liar Paradox entails such a confusion:

---

* [42, Bk XX,V 180a27-b7] In this passage Aristotle first deals with non-paradoxical (non-self-referencing) sets of two seemingly contradictory statements and says that the resolution of these contradictions is similar to the resolution of the Liar Paradox. A man who is not a keeper of oaths (absolute) can sometimes keep an oath (relative). The liar saying at the same time what is both true and false presents apparent difficulties, according to Aristotle, because it is not easy to see whether the qualification *absolutely* should be applied to *true* or *false*. However, there is no reason why the same man should not be absolutely a liar yet tell the truth in some respects, or that some of a man's words should be true but he himself not be truthful. For Aristotle, there is no self-reference if we consider that the liar is making a relative and true statement that he lies, but this statement, itself, is not affected by the absolute conclusion that he is a liar.

> If we regard the statement 'I am lying' as a compact way of simultaneously making all the following statements: 'I am asserting a false proposition of the first order', 'I am asserting a false proposition of the second order', and so on, we find the following curious state of things: As no proposition of the first order is being asserted, the statement 'I am asserting a false proposition of the first order' is false. This statement is of the second order, hence the statement 'I am making a false statement of the second order' is true. This is a statement of the third order, and is the only statement of the third order which is being made. Hence the statement 'I am making a false statement of the third order' is false. Thus we see that the statement 'I am making a false statement of order 2n +1' is false, while the statement 'I am making a false statement of order 2n' is true. But in this state of things there is no contradiction.
> [44, p. 62]

So, if such a hierarchy is instituted in a formal language, then the paradox can be avoided. But this still leaves Russell's original problem of closing or completing the system: What about the *class-of-all-classes*? Russell had said in *The Principles of Mathematics* that this class is essential to all formal propositions.* But by *Principia Mathematica* Russell has conceded to Cantor. The notion of a *class-of-all-classes-that-are-not-members-of-themselves* is meaningless and the hierarchy of classes goes on without limit. [44, p. 63] So, just as Cantor had avoided paradox by claiming no end to the hierarchy of infinite numbers—that there is an absolute infinity—likewise, for Russell: his Types theory requires no limit to the hierarchy of classes. By class, as by set, the universe is unbounded and (infinitely) infinite after all. From the first appearance of the paradox to its solution, Russell had come full circle.

Russell first hit on his Hierarchy of Types solution quite early, and an early version was put forward tentatively in an appendix to the final version of *The Principles* published in 1903. In the Preface he writes:

> For publishing a work containing so many difficulties, my apology is, that investigation revealed no near prospect of adequately resolving the contradiction discussed in Chapter X or of acquiring a better insight into the nature of classes. [37, p. xlvii]

And the book ends with this final sentence:

> What the complete solution to the difficulty may be, I have not succeeded in discovering; but as it affects the very foundations of reasoning, I earnestly commend the study of it to the attention of all students of logic.
> [37, p. 528]

---
* [37, p. 101] See also Chapter XLII and Chapter XLIII for discussions of the continuum and infinity.

Chapter 2: The Failure of Logical Method

It turned out that Russell was *never* entirely happy with his solution. Even when he was more confident that a Hierarchy of Types was a way out, it was never *the* way out. It was always a loophole, an exit or a stop gap. It was an interim adoption while he promoted the search for a better solution, and advertised, that if a better solution were found, he would happily accept it.*

Others not so wedded to logic responded differently. Many saw the emergence of the paradox as a sign that logic was not at the very foundation of reasoning. Poincaré and the mathematical Intuitionists naturally took the emergence of the paradox as a vindication of their opposition to the whole project from the beginning. But for the German mathematician, Gottlob Frege (1848-25), the paradox had perhaps the most profound effect.

After sending the manuscript of *The Principles* to the press, Russell's attention was drawn to Frege's own work on the foundations of mathematics. He found to his surprise that much of what he thought was original in *The Principles* had been pioneered by Frege. In fact, while Russell is always remembered as the popular advocate of the Analytic Philosophy, it is Frege who is regarded the principal founder of this school. Russell himself was first to recognise this and, in another appendix, he graciously drew the attention of Anglophone philosophers to Frege's little known work. Meanwhile, Russell was anxious to see how Frege had handled the paradox. He soon found that one of Frege's axioms (Law V) was critically exposed to it. In the summer of 1902 he pointed this out in a letter. Frege's response is now folklore:

> Your discovery of the contradiction has surprised me beyond words and, I should like to say, left me thunderstruck, because it has rocked the ground on which I meant to build arithmetic...It is all the more serious as the collapse of my Law V seems to undermine not only the foundations of my arithmetic but the only possible foundation of arithmetic as such.
> [48, p. 350]

Frege was devastated. His life work, his entire philosophic project, collapsed before his eyes. In 1893 Frege had published the first of the projected three volumes of his *Die Grundgetze der Arithmetick*, which was a re-work of his previous attempt to demonstrate the foundations of arithmetic in the propositional form. Frege received Russell's faithful letter when the second volume was at the press. Though he quickly modified his

---
* For 'loophole' and 'exit' see Russell's Introduction to the *Tractatus*, [46] p. 22; for 'stopgap' see George Spencer Brown's account of a 1967 conversation with Russell in the Preface to *Laws of Form* first American edition [47], p. xiv; for 'adoption' see *Principia* [44], p. vii.

Law V to head off the contradiction, this revelation now triggered a cascade of doubt. Volume III of *Die Grundgestze* was never written and Frege fell silent. Frege went on to become a hero of Anglophone Analytic philosophy for his earlier work, but already at his English *début* he was a fallen hero. We now know from Frege's later unpublished writings that by 1923 he had abandoned logical foundationalism. As Michael Dummett writes, in 1923 he became convinced that the whole project of founding arithmetic on logic was in error and that the theory of classes constituted the nub of the error.... By age 75, Frege had decided that his logical reductionism fails to understand the nature of number and that it is, instead, geometry that is elementary, and that number and analysis are derived from it. [49, p. 92]

Other-Reference as a Logical Imperative

I have used Russell to show the contradiction in the element of logical method. But it is not yet clear how this relates to the foundational contradiction of Representationalism. Remember, I proposed that the contradiction of Representational *epistemology* is but an expression of a contradiction inherent in the elementary *method*. While in modern Aristotelianism the elementary drive to find an external foundation is somewhat obscured, it was explicit in the works of its founder. So we can now use Aristotle himself as a guide. The key text for finding the logical character of Aristotelian foundationalism is a text that might be the most influential in the history of Western philosophy, the original *Metaphysics*.

Aristotle's style is to begin his major works with a lengthy survey of the vast array of philosophical opinions that was before him. One advantage for the modern reader in this style is that these accounts are sometimes the best source of information about earlier philosophers whose original works are long lost or were never written down. Another advantage is that we are able to witness Aristotle formulating his own position out of the critique of others, and thereby come to an understanding of the controversial context of his various doctrines. The early books of *Metaphysics* are invaluable on both counts.

In the *Organon* Aristotle had introduced his logic by making clear that it fits his requirement of an element that is linguistically demonstrative (not mystical).* Now, as he introduces his ontology in the *Metaphysics*, he

---

* Aristotle's word for logical demonstration is *apodeixis*. It means 'putting forth' or 'showing', and in philosophy it means 'putting forth logically', thus our 'proving'. By contrast, according to Aristotle, mathematics deals with the unseen, abstracted entities, *aphaireseôs*.

Chapter 2: The Failure of Logical Method

makes clear that he requires a foundation that is both logical and sensible (not mystical). His survey of the variety of ontologies before him finds two principle types: those that give fundamental *being* as some elementary matter (e.g., Heraclitus giving fire, Thales giving water, Anaximenes giving air); and the Pythagoreans and Plato who have an entirely formal ontology. [50, p. 996a]

Aristotle argues against the pure formalism of Plato and the Pythagoreans because their unseen source does not account for the generation of particular, sensible, material things. He also argues against a straight Materialism on the grounds that *being* cannot be reduced to the being of any *particular* material substance. Instead, he finds that the *being-of-things* has both formal and material origins. For Aristotle, there is form [*eidos*] and there is the underlying matter [*hupo-keimenon*], and, when form is applied to this substrate, something comes into being.* Aristotle's 'form', like the 'form' of the mathematicians, is insensible; that is, until it is applied to matter. Likewise, this underlying matter, or *primary matter*—matter that is not *in the form* of any particular material substance—is also insensible.

Insensible? After the critical survey in the early books of *Metaphysics* this at first appears a surprising result. Is Aristotle's dual foundation doubly mystical? This is, after all, the man who had spent his youth, and more, as a student of Plato (during the last 20 years of Plato's life) and who had only just reiterated his rejection of Platonic mysticism. Now, in bringing his own formalism to a sensible materialism, the result is not a logically demonstrable materialism, as we might expect, but a double mysticism.

This is not the way Aristotle saw it. Form alone and matter alone do not have *being* but only *potential-to-be* [*dynamis*]. They both have a potency that is only realised by application of one to the other. One analogy he uses is the generation of a statue. A block of wood has the *potential-to-be* any number of forms under the sculpture's chisel, but when the form of Hermes is applied, only then does it become a statue of Hermes.# And this analogy stuck as a new conception of the natural order and the order of its

---

* Transliteration of the Greek is in square brackets. For the original Greek, see the Greek Glossary at the end of this book. For Aristotle's reasoning for this view and the introduction of these term, see *Physics*, p. 191a15-22.

See *The Metaphysics* p. 1048a80]. The statue (of wood or bronze) is used in a number of places as an analogy to explain the four causes, including in *Physics* p. 191a & 194b-195b]. Elsewhere in *Metaphysics*, Aristotle uses the proverbial expression 'Hermes is not in the stone' in a refutation of Pythagorean ontology. [50, p. 1002a] An earlier proposal of such a primary stuff, or 'receptacle', is found in Plato's *Timaeus*, p. 50-51. This doctrine of generation had great currency in Platonism in sympathy with the Aristotelians but in conflict with the Platonic Forms and with Pythagorean doctrines of self-generation (see below p.160-1).

generation. The Greeks had no word for 'matter' and so for Aristotelians the stuff shaped by the sculpture became the stuff of the cosmos generally: all things are *form-applied-to-matter* and at the base is a formless insensible 'under-lay' [*hupo-keimenon*], the *underlying-stuff-of-the-universe* upon which layers of form have been applied. As this and various other doctrines of primary matter took hold, the Greek word for 'wood' [*hule*] came into use. Roman Aristotelians (and Epicureans) also found their language lacking and so they used their word for 'wood' as the material [*materia*] from which they made things. Thus, hidden in the term to which modern science was born is a hint to the profundity of the Aristotelian ontological innovation.

We must now consider how this ontology relates to Aristotle's epistemology. This is to ask: how do we come to know these in-*form*-ed material things? Was Aristotle an empiricist? Not at all. It is true that Aristotle is remembered for his interest in the empirical sciences, and he is even celebrated, for good reason, as their Western founder. However, with his very commitment to forms and with his elaborate *a priori* superstructure, he could never be construed as primarily committed to a sensual source. His was, after all, the first 'metaphysics'. Yet, this said, it in no way diminishes his importance for the development of modern Empiricism.

For Aristotle, the difference between *Hermes-in-the-sculptor's-mind* and the *Hermes* he creates—the statue that we can all see and touch—is its materiality. Form *applied to* matter gives things. Form *without* matter is *ideal. Thought*, as *ideas-in-minds*, is, at the very least, the paradigm of form for Aristotle. When we observe sensible things, our minds implicitly recognise their forms. We don't directly sense the forms—remembering that forms are insensible. As St Thomas would say much later, we know sensible things by abstracting the likenesses of things' forms...from matter (see above on page 11). While the process is different, this result is very much as per the Platonic 'recollection' of mathematical forms that we will be discussing later.* In this mode we might say that, in seeing Hermes' two round eyes, I am recalling/abstracting *twoness* and *roundness*, which are both, in themselves, insensible. Of course, it is important here to remember that Aristotle is re-inventing Platonic forms logically. This transformation has various implications which will become evident, but for now we only need think of these forms as *predicates*, and note that it is as *predicates*

---

* On Plato's doctrine of 'recollection' [*anamnesis*] see below, p. 76 & p. 233.

that mathematical forms are reduced to logical forms, and that forms in the material world *correspond to* our logical thoughts about them. The ontology expresses the method: while for the Pythagoreans, the *essence-of-things* is like the *essence-of-number*, for Aristotle the *form-of-things* is entirely logical.

If we know the *form-of-things* by abstracting, then how do we know the *matter-of-things*? How do we know the difference between forms *qua* thoughts and in-*form*-ed matter? How do we know that it is, and how do we know what it is? It turns out that we do not know it. Our senses give us the *form-of-things* but the *matter-of-things*, the primary matter, is only given negatively, as logically necessary: there must be some primary malleable stuff of things that gives them their sensible independent *thingness* making them more than mere *ideas-of-things*. It is in their primary matter that material things are independent existing objects of our observation. And it is the primary matter of Aristotle's empirical objects that finds an affinity with the external object of representation in modern Empiricism. I say 'affinity' because the key to understanding the Aristotelian influence on modern Empiricism is not in finding a direct continuity between this primary matter and Locke's primary qualities, the Kantian noumenal...and so forth. Rather, the key is the common *logical imperative* that keeps generating these strange monsters; monsters that will not go away and monsters that keep reappearing at the logical boundary in new garb every time we try to cross it. What we shall find is that it is this same logical imperative that produced that other monster, Russell's Paradox. Thus we arrive at the heart of the matter.

In Aristotle's ontology, a particular thing consists of layers of form applied to a primary matter that is an independent cause of its being. The forms are entirely logical, as in-*form*-ation is a predication. The matter is entirely logical as a logical necessity. It is necessary because all chains of predication require a foundation in an absolute subject, a subject prior to predication. In Aristotle's analysis, science must have this ultimate subject matter. That is to say, *the logical method commands the ontology*, it demands that, in the last analysis, science must be about *something-other-than-itself*. Science must have an external content, its subject; or, as we say in this context, its 'object'.* Aristotelian science is 'objective' in this sense. It is characteristically *other-referring* and it has this *other-referring* character due to its elementary form, predication.

---

* According to Aristotle, it is the terms predicated of individuals, rather than genera that are the first principle because they are the first inform of the primary matter. [50, p. 999a]

45

We should not be mistaken into thinking that this logic imperative is an obscured actor in Aristotle's writing, as it often is later in the tradition. Rather, he actually uses the language of predication every step of the way: to describe the in-*form*-ation of matter; to argue the logical necessity of primary matter; and to argue against competing ontologies as illogical and therefore absurd. It is worth re-visiting *Physics* and *Metaphysics* to be reminded of this, and I recommend the reader do so. It is no secret. This is explicitly how the tradition was founded. The outcome is a science that represents a world of things essentially external to it *by logical necessity.*

The Problem of Continence in Aristotelian Theory

This *other-referring* character of Aristotle's method is most distinctively Aristotelian. And its influence extends beyond the epistemology to inform all aspects of his physics and cosmology. In fact, I would go as far as to say that other-reference is the defining character of the Aristotelian influence on our tradition. And the contrast is plain with mathematical emanationism, which is fundamentally and elementarily self-referencing—it could not be any other way, given that it proposes the self-generation, from unity, of all particular *being*. This points us to perhaps the most elementary way in which the Renaissance *did* involve a successful and sustained transcendence of Christian Aristotelianism. Beginning in the Renaissance, and accelerating into the 20th century, the sciences, especially the mathematical sciences, have shown how they have abandoned the logical imperative to other-referencing formulations. Today, many standard scientific accounts of the world (e.g., the unbounded finite universe; feedback/dynamical/fractal processes in natural systems) and much of our technology (e.g., cybernetics) is built on self-referencing principles. By contrast, philosophy of science remains wholly committed to *other-reference*. We will consider later the elementary and foundational character of self-referencing mathematical emanationism, but for now it serves us well to consider some of the consequences of this logical imperative for Aristotelian natural philosophy.

As Russell was to discover, Aristotelian philosophy will not allow self-reference because it has no facility for it. Precisely because it has no facility for self-reference, it cannot contain itself and so it will always tend to exceed itself at its boundaries. Formally, in any predicative system, there will be two such boundaries. The first is at the level of the ultimate subject upon which the system is grounded. We will call this the *inner* boundary. The second is at the level of the ultimate predicate, which we will call the *outer* boundary. A simple example of these boundaries is found in Russell's universe-of-classes. The outer boundary is dealt with when we consider *the-class-of-all-classes*. The inner boundary is dealt with when we consider the individual members of the classes. In Analytic Philosophy these individuals are the objective facts derived from sensation (*this red table*). It is at this first order of predication (*this table is red*), in the 'object language', that the problem of the logical inner boundary becomes the problem of Representationalism given by George Berkeley.

This incontinence at the epistemological inner boundary is the one of most interest to us because in it we can see a formal reason why logical Empiricism cannot ground itself in an external reality. But this is not the only place where the inner boundary problem arises. Aristotle himself gives us an entire catalogue of examples of inner and outer boundary problems. He comes up against boundary difficulties not only with the essence of matter and the boundary of the universe, but also when he discusses the related topics of the origin of causation, the origin of motion, the material origin of the universe and the origin of mind. With each topic we find him considering the options, identifying and dismissing the illogical and then, finally, coming up with his own way out. In each case we get a system where the internal mechanics is logically *other-referring*, but where something drastic has been done at the boundaries. The outcomes vary, and sometimes they seem to contradict each other, but in Aristotle and in Aristotelianism generally, there are the following three familiar ways of dealing with the problem of continence in predicate systems:

1. **To impose an ultimate external referent:** This is the most common. It is where we simply and dogmatically impose a block that terminates the drive to exceed. At the *outer boundary* it is *a-predicate-that-is-not-itself-a-subject*. This non-predicable predicate is the 'universal set' or the outer sphere of the universe that contains all things, as per Aristotle's bounded universe and as per Russell's initial objection to Cantor where he supposed a cardinal limit. At the *inner boundary* it is *a-subject-that-is-not-itself-a-predicate*. In epistemology it is the insistence on an external, unknown object, of which we know some of its predicable qualities. But it is also, in causal theory, Aristotle's *Unmoved Mover*, the first cause in the universe, *a-cause-that-is-not-itself-caused*.*

---

* Aristotle's first cause of motion, his primary and unmoved mover, is defined by its logical requirement in *Physics*, Bk VIII, p. 266a-267b.

The infinite series: This is where the other-referencing is left unbounded and so goes on indefinitely. At the *outer boundary* this is not self-continence but endless containment, as where Russell concedes to Cantor and finds that *logically*—that is, in order to avoid the self-referencing paradox—the hierarchy of class types must ascend endlessly. At the *inner boundary* the outcome is usually sceptical, and it is avoided in all positive epistemology because it allows no ontological grounding—it denies science any definite object.

3. **To realise other-reference into self-reference:** This is where *reference-to-the-other*, seen as a self-negation, is found to be the perfect form of self-reference. That is, *self-negation* is *self-reference*. Here, *other-reference* folds back on itself and so the outer is contained in the inner. The container is part of its content. Russell discovered this to his horror and did not allow it. This is the purest form of sceptical Aristotelianism, and at the same time the principle of generation in self-referencing systems. We approach this outcome in Chapter 3, but a full account of its formal nature is given in Chapter 8.

Aristotle's Purge of Reflexive Science

Ten years after he re-discovered the logical paradox, an evidently weary Russell wrote in the preface to *Principia Mathematica*:

> A very large part of the labour involved in writing the present work has been expended on the contradiction and paradoxes which have infected logic and the theory of aggregates.

One feels that if Aristotle had written a preface to *Physics* or *Metaphysics* he might have said something similar. In both these texts the logical analogy to natural systems seems feasible and powerful until you come to the boundaries, and that is where the problems start. The struggle to find a solution comes to dominate over everything else. Then, as with Russell, the solution itself dominates the final outcome. The result is that logically dubious and obscured monsters—such as the 'primary mover' and 'primary matter'—loom large over the boundaries of the logical system; and so quickly become both the object of dogma and the object of ridicule.

Chapter 2: The Failure of Logical Method

Whether or not Aristotle, like Russell, had misgivings about these outcomes of his logical approach, we will never know. What is clear is that like Russell, and in the face of the Academic Pythagoreans, Aristotle could conceive no other way. In *Metaphysics*, when discussing the various ways that things can come into being, Aristotle says that everything that is generated, whether naturally or artificially, is generated by something, from something and becomes something. This 'by something' is given to mean the principle [*arche*] of the process of generation, whereas 'from something' should not be understood so much as a lacking but as matter.* Aristotle is insistent that, in order to generate *being*, the principle (that is, the *form*) must act upon *something else*. This ultimate *something-else*, this complete *lack of all form*, Aristotle came close to conceiving as *non-being*, as nothing. But it must be something (or potentially something). And it must be *something-other-than-form*, because form can never act upon itself, as the Pythagorean emanationists would have it.

There is nothing but nonsense in reflexive theory, and Aristotle has an acute eye for hunting it out. In his analysis of prior doctrines, where reflexivity is only implicit, he digs it out, reveals it and pronounces it illogical. We witness Aristotle ticking-off theory after theory, and we can only wonder what these theories were really all about, as they are mostly lost now, except as fragments seen dimly through Aristotle's logical glass. Repeatedly he pulls up on self-action and self-motion. That there must always be an *actor* and *that-which-is-acted-upon* is reiterated in every case.# Self-causing, self-acting, self-motion, all reflexive activities, are but *applied* cases of self-predication, and they are dismissed as such.

This routing of reflexivity is not limited to his natural philosophy. In *About the Psyche*,+ he is up against a broad agreement, both philosophical and cultural, that the *psyche* is both the origin of movement and that it moves itself.++ The Greek word '*psyche*' means, in the broad sense, the life/movement of animals, their very *animation*. Where the body is considered distinct from the mind, this self-movement could be found in the higher minds of humans, in their initiation of thought and of bodily action.

---

* See *Metaphysics* p. 1032a12-15 & p. 1033a24-1033b4.
\# In modern logic these are called the 'operator' and the 'operand'.
+ [51] The title *Peri Psyche* was translated into Latin as *De Anima* and often still goes by this title, or otherwise it is usually translated into English as 'On the Soul'. However, this translation of *psyche* carry significant Medieval Christian baggage. *Psyche* is closer to 'mind' as the object of the modern science of psychology. Because we are familiar with this root, and because '*Nous*' is sometimes translated as 'mind,' it seems best to leave *psyche* untranslated. As for translating '*peri*' meaning 'about', see my discussion below, Chapter 10, p. 176.
++ An early philosophical example is Heraclitus: the *psyche* has a *logos* which generates itself. [52, p. 66] For the self-moving *psyche* in Plato, see *Phaedrus* 245c-e.

In Platonism, it is not just that mind has self-movement but the whole universe, which is sometimes seen as commanded by a universal mind.* Aristotle objects to all this self-movement in every way. Mind may be subject to movement, but the movement always comes from the outside; as it does in perception, where the mind is first moved to think by the sensations of objects reaching it. He argues against the circularity in *thought-about-things* (practical thought) and *thought-about-thought* (that is, theory) by insisting on a reduction to the delimited linearity of the logical form.

> All practical processes of thinking have limits—they all go on for the sake of something outside the process, and all theoretical processes come to a close in the same way as the phrases in speech which express processes and results of thinking. Every such linguistic phrase is either definitory or demonstrative. Demonstration has both a starting-point and may be said to end in a conclusion or inferred result; even if the process never reaches final completion, at any rate it never returns upon itself again to its starting-point, it goes on assuming a fresh middle term or a fresh extreme, and moves straight forward.... Definitions, too, are all finite.#

Aristotle continues to throw, seemingly, every argument he can think of against the various accounts of a self-moving *psyche* before he finally comes to the most illogical of all the doctrines: that advanced by the then head of the Academy, Xenocrates.

> Of all the illogical theories about the *psyche* the most illogical is that which calls the *psyche* a self-moving number. In this theory there are inherent impossibilities, first those which are implied by the theory of the *psyche* being moved, and also special ones which follow from calling the *psyche* a number. For how can one conceive of a unity [*monad*] moving, by what is it moved, and in what way, being as it is without parts or differences? For if it can cause and suffer movement it must have differences.+

What Aristotle finds most absurd is a doctrine that finds the principle of the mind's activity to be a unity acting upon itself and so moving itself.++

---

* The Medieval notion of the self-moving *Anima Mundi*, or 'World Soul', derives in part from Plato's dialogues. See *Timaeus* p. 35-6 & *Laws* p. 892-896.

\# This is McKeon's translation, except where 'are closed groups of terms' is replaced with 'are all finite'. [53, pp. 407a 22–30] 'Extreme' and 'middle' terms are the names for the terms in syllogistic logic. In our example above, 'Man' is the middle term and 'Mortal' the extreme.

+ See [51], p. 408b30-409a4 for variance with Hett's translation. Xenocrates was the third head of Plato's academy, from 339 to 314 BC. Aristotle does not mention Xenocrates by name, but the reference is surmised from other sources and it was likely apparent to the contemporary readers. Some evidence suggests that Xenocrates and Aristotle were rival candidates for the head of the Academy after Plato's first successor Speusippus died in 339 BC. Four years later Aristotle founded his own school. [45, Vol 3, p. 383]

++ Aristotle protests that difference is required if something is to act upon itself. Indeed, as we shall

Chapter 2: The Failure of Logical Method

Russell built a formal language system which became 'infected' with self-reference. Aristotle found the sciences already plagued by reflexivity. Both had the same job to do: to rout out self-reference as best they could. While we find Aristotle swiping every which way he can, Russell had a cleaner job and a sharper razor, but both had more or less the same outcome: they routed self-reference, instituted their logical forms as the form of the world, and then invoked some obscured monsters at the boundaries to prop the whole thing up.

I will not discuss further Aristotle's routing of reflexivity, nor the logical pathways he took to his non-reflexive conclusions, but I do recommend in particular the various discussions of causation which lead to the supposition of a 'Prime Mover', particularly in *Physics* Book VIII, but also, in a more theological discussion, in *Metaphysics*, Book XII. In re-reading Aristotle with this understanding, one begins to see quite directly and explicitly how the very first application of logical method to philosophical problems presented with the antinomies of external reference as symptoms of the very method itself.

***

To conclude this chapter, we return to the epistemological problem of Representationalism and provide a concise statement on how Aristotle's primary matter is the very paradigm of the external object in modern Representationalism.

Primary matter is what distinguishes material things from *ideas-of-things*. Matter is *logical* in that it is the ultimate subject to which forms are predicated. When we perceive things we abstract their formal nature. We do not perceive the *matter-of-things*, yet logically it must be there, as the ultimate object of perception. It exceeds all our knowledge and sensation of things and yet it is that which is the ultimate subject matter of science. Aristotle attempts to avoid the problem of grounding his epistemology in a primary external ontology by claiming that matter is, in itself, only *potential-to-be*. But there is no getting around the fact that this imperceptible matter is ontologically primary in perceived things. Matter is what things *are* in that they *are not* what they are *in our perception of them*. Modern physics might look back on primary matter as one of those metaphysical

---

see in Part II, recognition of the mystical unity as a *principle difference* is the very key to understanding its self-referencing emanation.

imputations, like *aether*, shown to be wholly incompatible with the evidence. But we can now see that in philosophy of science the legacy of primary matter persists as the very model of what our science is supposed to be about.

Chapter 3

THE NEW SCEPTICISM

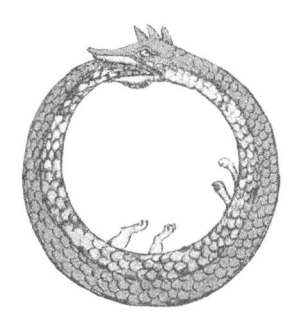

Chasing Linguistic Identity

At this stage I have only given crude expression to the form and behaviour of the logical element, now we will consider some more of its character before taking leave of it. We will do this by finding its similarity to other methodological elements, 'the sign' and 'the code', and thereby introduce the new scepticism. But firstly, as a prelude to the discussion of this scepticism, let us compare the mathematical and logical elements by considering how identity is established in both methods.

I have mentioned already how Mathematical Emanationism starts from unity and then self-differentiates to particulars. Logical Empiricism goes the other way, from the particulars to the general. In Aristotle's metaphysics the origin in the *generation-of-being* is in the first application of the form to the primary matter. In the ontological classification system professed in his *Categories*, it is these *primary beings* [*protai ousiai*] that are elementary. The analysis of *being* terminates at these individuals through classification by categories, genre and species.* Similarly, the

---

* See especially *Categories* p. 2a35-2b7. Aristotle is rightly credited a founder of modern biological taxonomy, but it is not often noted that Darwinianism represents a reversion to a taxonomy in accord with an emanationist notion of differentiation; for Darwin, all genetic difference evolves out of an undifferentiated origin.

analysis of knowledge in modern Empiricism gives the ontological ground of our knowledge via the particular units of sensual knowledge, or *sense data*. Even before any attempt to establish an ontological ground, the contrast between the two methods, mathematics and logic, is evident in the way they express identity. Arithmetic identity is found in mathematics by a retreat to the unit of value, *unity* or *one*, whereas logical identity is established by a retreat to the meaning of the particular terms. The difference between these processes of logic and mathematics are illustrated by comparing the proof of a simple equation with the analysis of a simple linguistic definition.

Consider first the proof:

To be proved:	$1/4 + 2/8$	$= 1/2$	
→	$2/8 + 2/8$	$= 1/2$	(multiply ¼ by ²/₂)
→		$4/8 = 1/2$	(add the two terms on the left)
→		$4/8 = 4/8$	(multiply ½ by ⁴/₄)
→		$1 = 1$	(multiplying both sides by 2)
		Q.E.D.	

The proof of the equation is that both sides have the same arithmetic value.

We can also define, without too much difficulty, the direct equivalence in different systems of two expressions of the same value, as for example when we say, 8 equals VIII. Indeed, an equation, or any piece of mathematical reasoning, will not alter if such a substitution is made. In Chapter 4 I will show why we have no difficulty in equating these numerical *expressions*. Now by contrast, consider the difficulties of equating linguistic terms with what they mean or represent.

Let's consider a simple linguistic definition. We could start with the word 'table', which means *the-table-in-itself*. This reference via the sensual facts to a table, as the external referent, is what we have been discussing for some time, but here we will consider a definition *qua* conceptual meaning. *Definition-of-meaning* is a very ordinary process in linguistic reasoning that is easily recognised as the elementary form of the dictionary. We could start or finish with the identity *table means table*, but such a tautology does not get us very far in logic. Nor would it sell many dictionaries. So we must remember, as the schoolteacher would say, the word defined cannot appear in the definition. Let's start by considering a simple likeness:

A stool is like a chair.

To get to a definition we need to arrive at the form A means B, which in predicate logic becomes:

A *is* B

Now, B is not, and is never, exactly A. Even if we could find a perfect synonym (where B = A) then we have only found another way of saying A *is* A. Here we are trying to move beyond this tautological loop. Thus, in any definition, there will be two aspects of B:

1. B-*that-is-the-same-as*-A, call this 'B$_A$'
   (where *chair* is meaningfully equivalent to *stool*)
2. B-*that-is-not*-A, call this 'B$_{not-A}$'
   (where *chair* differs in meaning from *stool*)

This gives the definition:

A *is* B$_A$ *and* B$_{not-A}$.

In our example we might give the definition:

A stool is a stool and a backrest.

This formalisation of the definition is only showing that while B is like A, it is not A because of the fact that it is B, which is not A. We have two *different* particulars in the language. We proceed in a search for the meaningful identity of our term (*stool*) by considering the meanings of the terms in the definition (e.g., *backrest*) and by qualifying them (*A stool is a-stool-and-a-back-rest without a backrest*). These terms themselves require definition (*What is a backrest?*), and in the definition will appear other terms requiring definition, and we can go on in the hope of finding some termination of this iterative process in an absolute meaning. But there is no such semantic ground because there will always be more words which themselves require more wordy definitions.

Let's now consider the form of this iteration, that is, the form of the *likeness* of the definition to the term defined. One part of this likeness is identity. Without the backrest we have *A stool is a stool*. To avoid this tautology we would need to remove this from the definition. With B_A removed we are left with:

A *is* $B_{\text{not-A}}$.

A is the negation of itself in another: *A stool is the backrest of a chair.* Any non-tautological definition retreats to this contradictory form. At first sight this appears a distortion or a trick. One objection could be that we get this result by conflating the domain of the *words-in-the-language* with the domain of their meanings: *Of course, we should not use the defined word in the definition, but it is precisely this word's <u>meaning</u> that is being defined in the definition, and so a word definition <u>should be</u> a tautological reference to that meaning.* Yet, even if we respect this hierarchy and grant that terms refer to the meaning field and each term does this in a unique way, then a tautological reference to meaning can only be the same as a return to A *is* A. It is as though to say: *Stool means…what stool means.* Furthermore, while the form A *is* $B_{\text{not-A}}$ looks extraordinary as a definition; it is, in fact, quite ordinary to modern epistemology. In order to make sense of this *definition-as-contradiction*, we can now consider the ontological definition that we avoided earlier, *viz.*, that the word 'table' means *the-table-in-itself*; that is to say, we skip semantics and give that the meaning of this word is the (external) object to which it refers. The definition of the known object in Representationalism can be found by the following steps:

> *My primary knowledge of the table itself is my perception it.*
> *But my perception of the table is not the table itself.*
> *So, what I know (i.e., the table) is, in my perception of it, exactly what I do not know.*

If *the-table-in-itself* is B and what I know of it is A, then A *is* $B_{\text{not-A}}$. This is only to say, as Locke and Berkeley both said, that there is nothing in my knowledge or sense of the table that is the table. As there is never any part of B that is A, this expression can be reduced to A *is* not-A. The elegant reflexivity of this terminal definition is of the 3rd outcome type given on page 48 above. It is the realisation of other-reference into self-reference through self-negation.

Now, to complete our comparison with number, we need to consider the equivalence, across different systems, of terms that serve to express the same value. The problem of identity across linguistic domains is the very problem of translation. And it is the humour of this old joke, which will suffice to make the point:

Q. What is French for 'London'?
A. Paris.

Every term in Aristotle's logic requires a definition: *Socrates*, *man* and *mortal* must mean something for the syllogism to make sense. As Whitehead wrote in 1927 after abandoning Logical Realism: whereas with mathematical algebra the manipulation of the algebraic symbols does your reasoning for you, in ordinary language you can never forget the meaning of language, and trust to mere syntax to help you out. [54, p. 2] If foundations are to be established linguistically then meaning must not collapse into self-reference or spin out in an endless pursuit of the meaning of the meaning of the meaning of the....

Formal language systems, like the Russell-Whitehead language of classification, are designed to avoid many of the problems of ordinary linguistic reasoning, and to some extent they do address semantic ambiguity. Yet the problem of identity persists in these systems because at some point terminal definitions are required...and if these definitions do not rest in ordinary language, then where else? Even if we accept that 'the table' and 'that chair' are grounded by external reference, no such grounding is available for abstract nouns such as 'class', 'one' or 'two'.

In *Principia Mathematica* self-evident mathematical intuitions were rejected for a linguistic ground enforced by 'dogmatic' affirmations. [44, p. v] This must have seemed an admission of defeat for both allies and opponents of logical reduction because dogmatism is anathema to the spirit of modern philosophers. Certainly it went no closer to answering Poincaré's earlier scathing criticism of their project.

In the essay of 1906 that identifies Russell's paradox with the ancient Liar Paradox (see above, page 37), Poincaré begins by arguing that logic can never get beyond tautology, and logic therefore remains barren unless it is fertilized by intuition. Poincaré then introduces the logical paradox so that the most famous mathematicians of the day could mock Russell's refusal of mathematical intuition by declaring that logic is not so barren after all as it engenders antinomies. [39, pp. 193-4] We will soon see how true this is.

LOGICAL EMPIRICISM

The Sign and its Scepticism

So far we have focused on the logical element and its expression in Logical Realism. But, in order to introduce what I see as a new sceptical Aristotelianism, we will now turn to continental philosophy and a related linguistic element, the *semion* or sign.

The rise of the sign to its defining role in modern French philosophy was assisted early by the immensely popular 'Port Royal Logic'. *La Logique ou l'art de penser* is a textbook on the art of thinking by two teachers at the Port Royal School, the famous Antoine Arnauld (1612-94) and his collaborator Pierre Nicole (1625-1695). First published anonymously in 1662, *The Logic* remained in print and influential throughout the 18th century Enlightenment. I will use it to introduce the semiotic element for us.

The first step is to move towards the view that knowing and communicating are formally the same:

> If reflecting on our thoughts never concerned anyone but ourselves, it would be enough to examine them in themselves, unclothed in words or other signs. But because we can make our thoughts known to others only by accompanying them with external signs, and since this habit is so strong that even when we think to ourselves, things are presented to the mind only in the words in which we usually clothe them in speaking to others, logic must examine how ideas are joined to words and words to ideas.
> [1, p. 23–4]

The next step is to define the communicative element, the sign, and recognise its important role in knowledge:

> When we consider an object in itself and in its own being, without carrying the view of the mind to what it can represent, our idea of it is an idea of a thing, such as the idea of the Earth or the Sun. But when we view a certain object merely as representing another, our idea of it is an idea of a sign, and the first object is called a sign.[*] This is how we ordinarily think of maps and paintings. Consequently *the sign includes two ideas, one of the thing which represents, the other of the thing represented. Its nature consists in prompting the second by the first....* Since the nature of (a particular type of) sign consists in prompting in the senses the idea of the thing symbolised by means of the idea of the symbol, we can conclude that the sign lasts as long as this effect lasts. That is, it lasts as long as this double idea is prompted, even if the thing in its own nature is destroyed.
> [1, pp. 35–6 (emphasis added)]

---
* This definition of the sign follows Saint Augustine (354-430 AD). Indeed, the semiotics of *The Logic* is generally so informed. See *On Christian Doctrine*, Bk II [55, p. 34] and also Confessions, Bk I, Ch 8 [56, p. 29].

The final step is the introduction of the problem of continence and the possibility of scepticism:

> Words are conventional signs of thoughts, and characters are conventional signs of words... It would be impossible to define every word. For in order to define a word it is necessary to use other words designating the idea we want to connect to the word being defined. And if we again wished to define the words used to explain that word, we would need still others, and so on to infinity. Consequently, we necessarily have to stop at primitive terms which are undefined.
> [1, pp. 37, 64]

As *The Logic* explains, the semiotic form consists of two parts, what we now call the *signifier* and the *signified*. So, just as *red* (the signifier) signifies *stop* (the signified) at the traffic signals, so the *letters* in written words signify the *sounds* of spoken words. We can go on and say that the *spoken word* in turn signifies its *meaning*, and that this is the basis of our communication as you read this. The spoken word is then, in this *chain*, first *signified* and then *signifier*.

The Logic professes to the importance of signs to knowledge and communication, but *does it give the sign as the very element of knowledge?* Not quite. Yes, it does say that there is a semiotic relationship between written and spoken words, and between spoken words and their meaning. But this is not to say that this relationship is epistemologically elementary. Yes, it does say that the sign is elementary to the *communication* of knowledge. But it also grants that thought can be unclothed in words or other signs and that we can consider an object in itself, that is, immediately and not merely as representing another.

Such quaint allowances for non-semiotic *knowing* have no place in the broad agreement today across various continental schools of philosophy. If they are true to the semiotic element then they are compelled to take our *chain-of-signifiers* further, so that the meaning of words signifies perceived things, and further still, that our *perceptions-of-things* signify *things-in-themselves*. This last step takes us to a semiotic version of epistemological Representationalism.

However much we may wish to avoid reducing this signification to predication, or *visa versa*, there is an unavoidable similarity between A *is* B and A *signifies* B found through interpreting A *means* B in both elementary forms. What is important for us at the moment is that both elements are *other-referring* and so they both present the problem of systemic continence. The scepticism of the semiotic element is a recognition of this.

The reader will recall that in order for a predication system to find a foundation, there must be an absolute subject, a *subject-that-is-not-itself-a-predicate*. In Logical Realism this 'inner boundary' is maintained by the external referent. The equivalent to the external referent in this semiotic foundationalism is the *signified-that-is-not-itself-a-sign*. In other words, the external referent is the *signified* that terminates the chain of signification. Sceptical semiotics recognises that it is self-contradictory to propose such an object. When the sceptics remove this block they find that the signification goes on endlessly without grounding itself. But this scepticism goes even further and attacks the very notion of the sign as an element of knowledge: it shows not only that no external foundation is possible, but it also shows the impossibility of internal foundation as one might hope for in a formalism or an Idealism. Let me explain.

If each unit of knowledge is a sign then each is presented in the system as a signifier. However, the signifier is only standing in for *what-it-signifies*. *What-it-signifies*, the signified, is absent or obscured in the sign. Yet when it is revealed, it is itself—it can only be—another sign. In this way, every word, every meaning and every idea is revealed to have indefinite signification. The implication is not only that no ontological foundation can be established but, also that the very notion of the *significance*, or the *meaning*, of a term is unstable and ultimately undefined. For example, when we reach for the meaning of a word we are presented with another set of signs, and, in defining these, we are presented with another set, and another and…as *The Logic* says…so on to infinity. A definition is indefinite unless it is terminated with a set of primitive terms. But on what basis are these established? Dogmatically? *The Logic* all but says so, but the rigour of the new scepticism will not allow it. When neither dogmatic nor intuitive terminations are allowed there is no stopping, and meaning dissipates like Chinese whispers in a crowd.

In the scepticism of semiotics, attention is drawn to these dissipating chains of signification, where the signifier/signified relationships have the following characteristics:

1. The signifier stands in the place of the signified, which is absent.
2. The signifier is non-identical to what it signifies (the relation is differential not tautological).
3. The signifier obscures the signified and yet leads to it.

Jacques Derrida (1930–2004) called this relationship deferred difference, which contracts to his neologism, différance. The process of signification is a movement of difference from signifier to signified. The difference is *deferred* in that it is not until the signified is revealed that it is, itself, presented as another sign. It is the *deferral* of the difference that affords the sign an apparent meaningful stability: while its signified is deferred/absent/hidden, the sign, as a unit of knowledge, appears definite and stable. The point is that this stable finitude is only apparent.

This, then, is the sceptical core of a movement in 20th century continental philosophy that rose to a peak of elegant clarity in a few short essays published in the late 1960s and early 1970s by Jacques Derrida.* It soon spread to Anglophone philosophy, mainly via literary and cultural studies, and it has become a powerful threat to all positive philosophical positions. This scepticism attacks Analytic Philosophy by way of a reduction of the logical element to the semiotic; but, as we have already seen, logic has always been susceptible to this form of scepticism on its own terms. What is historically interesting is how Analytic Philosophy has weathered its own sceptical tendencies so successfully for so long. Even as it continues to hold out in the academy, there is no exaggeration when comparing the sceptical threat it faces today with the threat of the Eleatics and Megarians on the Greek schools of the 5th and 4th centuries BC (see above on page 37), nor in a comparison with the outbreak of scepticism in 16th century France to which Descartes was responding.

The broad exposure to this scepticism is in the broad consensus within modern philosophy as to the elementary nature of knowledge. I have presented this consensus with the logical and semiotic elements, and I have shown that the exposure to this scepticism is in the *other-referring* nature of these methodological elements. Let me finish with a third and more contemporary take on this consensus, presenting it as *the consensus of the code*.

The Consensus of the Code

There is a consensus in modern philosophy that is in both positive Anglophone and sceptical continental schools, and in just about every position in between. This consensus is that the basic units of our knowledge, whether

---

* See especially the 1968 essay 'Différance' [57, p. 1–27] and also 'Signature Event Context' [57, p. 309–330].

LOGICAL EMPIRICISM

in our perception or in our thought, are codes, and that *to know* is *to decode*. We can take as the model for this form any simple code. We can take, for example, the codification of the books of *Metaphysics* in its modern translations, where in place of the Greek alphabetical names of each book, there are Roman numerals:

Book numeration in the translations	I	II	III	IV	V	VI	VII	VIII	IX
corresponds to	↕	↕	↕	↕	↕	↕	↕	↕	↕
the book names in the Greek.	A	Ά ΕΛΑΤΤΟΝ	B	Γ	Δ	E	Z	H	Θ

We use such codes all the time in communication, in knowledge, in thought. But in the consensus of the code, the form of the code is taken as the elementary form of knowledge. In all epistemology of the type that we are calling 'Representationalism', such a codification is found at the basic level of our knowledge where things known are codified. The code spans the border between *knowledge-of-things* and their *being*, where their being is entirely unknown. In Empiricism this is the correspondence in the Correspondence Theory of Truth, where the code (the Roman numeral) is presumed to align in correspondence with an unknown field of definite objects (the Greek letters). Similarly, in semantic foundationalism, words are given as encoding a fundamental set of definite meanings. In all such positive (non-sceptical) theories, at bottom, the objects that are encoded are not themselves codes. All the sceptics are doing is showing that there is no way to establish these final encoded object fields.

The consensus of the code reached its peak after what Richard Rorty labelled 'the linguistic turn' in Western philosophy. It came with Frege and Russell in their Logical Realism. But this 'turn' was not confined to the Analytic movement; it spanned Western philosophy. With the French, the semiotic element prevails. The evolutionary Intuitionism of Bergson and the various mathematical positions mentioned above—so promising in the early decades of the century—faded from view after World War II. In their place the consensus of the code strengthened despite failure to find a satisfactory solution to Russell's 'problems' of epistemology and his paradox of logic. And it strengthened again with the sceptical attacks by Derrida. Irrespective of any allegiances an observer may have, it remains a great question in the history of epistemology why this happened at this time. That is to say, why did we get this revival in Western epistemology of *other-referring elementism* synchronous with devastating and largely unanswered criticism of its very ability to frame an answer to the question: *What is knowledge?*

This book, I have to say, leaves this question largely unanswered. My case for the involvement of these doctrines in a resistance to mystical outcomes—from Aristotle to Russell, but especially within the 18th century Enlightenment—can only be part of the story. Even if the new Empiricism won as a remedy for the destabilising fanaticism of the 17th century, and even if the momentum was maintained through Lockean and Kantian motifs for 200 years and more, still, *Why?* Why this *revival*? Why the linguistic turn? Why this overwhelming consensus? I offer but one hint.

The consensus of the code is very often synchronous with a conflation of knowledge and communication. If there is no difference between knowledge and its communication, then, when we find the element of communication, we have found the element of knowledge. Thus, if we agree—and we mostly do—that communication is formally signs/representations/codes, then the form of knowledge is such. *Now, why would this conflation of knowledge with its communication become so strong in the 20th century?* That is hard to say, but it may have something to do with the privileging of the social domain in many academic schools of thought after World War II. This may have come about due to an increasing awareness of the social domain and its importance for social cohesion in increasingly secular societies. With the decline in the spiritual authority of the Christian churches, the situation became more fluid. At the same time efforts to introduce new ideological forms of social cohesion were facilitated by the increasing power of electronic communication. In this shift of emphasis to the social, Darwinism and Marxism, their theory and practice, their offshoots and perversions, undoubtedly played a role. By the 1960s and 1970s, the privileging of the social was so strong in the universities that there emerged various forms of sociological foundationalism. This is where reality is given as fundamentally a social construction.* An indication of the socialising trend that peak during the 1980s is ascendant schools of academic feminism deriding those who suggested, or implied, any biological foundations to sexuality ('gender') as 'essentialists'.

---

* The platform for this view is the sociological methodology introduced by Niccolò Machiavelli (1469-1527) and Thomas Hobbes (1588-1679), but it was only properly realised in 20th century sociology. See for example in Durkheim's *The Elementary Forms of Religious Life*: Since the universe does not exist except in so far as it is conceived in thought, and since it is not thought of as a whole except by society, it is comprised within the latter. [58, p. 265]. From the 1960s, and into the movement called 'post-Modernism', the 'social construction of reality' pervaded the humanities and social sciences. See for example Berger & Luckmann [59].

It is true that this socialising of knowledge was a rebellion against the prevailing flawed modes, yet it is often even more rigorously *other-referring*: *If all is social then there is nothing in knowledge beyond its communication*, which is to say, *the element of knowledge is the element of communication*, which is *the code*. Furthermore, the discovery of 'ideology', 'paradigm', 'episteme'* and other social constructors of reality provided a ripe new field of positive *other-referring* theory upon which scepticism could re-develop. The identification of this scepticism as 'post-' (i.e., post-structuralism, post-modernism) is apt, as it indicates the parasitic relationship of scepticism to positive theory. The current popularity of this scepticism might be due to its relative youth and the youth of its host.

This reduction of the elementary form of *that-which-is-communicated* to the elementary form of communication has a long pre-history, but we should be careful not to project it back to where it was yet fully formed. It is certainly suggested in Aristotle as where we quote him above (on page 50) saying that thought is limited in the same way as the phrases in speech which express processes and results of thinking. And we have seen it suggested in the Port Royal *Logic*. However, neither Aristotle, nor this pre-Enlightenment guide, go as far as to reduce knowledge to its communication. In *The Logic*, before the form of the sign is introduced (see above on page 58), recognition is given to a pre-semiotic knowledge, which is the knowledge we have in direct experience. As their chapter heading says, the difference is between 'Ideas of Things and Ideas of Signs'. Indeed, *The Logic* and other similar 17th century epistemological texts do contain the seeds of post-Lockean Representationalism and the seeds of the contemporary code consensus, but yet they all read so evidently of a bygone era.

If these cautious Frenchmen never took this final step to the complete hegemony of the sign then a bold Englishman would. The result was that a thorough Logial Empiricism could then be delivered back across the Channel clothed in terms familiar to the French (i.e., in terms of the signification) and wrapped up with the marvels of Newtonian mathematical physics.

In the final book of *An Essay Concerning Human Understanding* John Locke inserts a chapter 'On Truth in General' [Bk IV, Ch 5] where he says that truth seems to him in the proper import of the word, to signify nothing but the joining or separating of signs, as the things signified by them do agree or disagree one with another. Here he declares that this joining or separating of signs...is what

---

* For 'ideology', see: Marx and Engels, *The German Ideology* [60]; for 'paradigm', see Kuhn, *The Structure of Scientific Revolutions* [61]; for 'epistemes', see Foucault, *The Order of Things* [62].

by another name we call propositions. So, while truth has a relational dimension that is logical, its terms have a semantic dimension that is semiotic. And then in the very final chapter of the *Essay*, [Bk IV, Ch 21] Locke concludes his account of the understanding by giving the three most general and natural divisions of the sciences. Reverting to their original Greek script, he announces these as physics, ethics and semiotics.

Now, physics and ethics would have been familiar and expected by his readers, but then there is this new science in the place where one might expect to find the formal sciences of mathematics and logic. For Locke, the newly defined science of semiotics is counted as one of these three great provinces of the intellectual world but not for its role in the communication of ideas. Its primary importance is because it considers the nature of signs the mind makes use of for the understanding of things. Since the things the mind contemplates are not present to the understanding, it is necessary that something else, as a sign or representation of the thing it considers, should be present to it: and these are ideas. [3, pp. 634-5] In other words, ideas of things are signs. In prescribing the general science of semiotics at the closing his account of human understanding, Locke has the *code* spanning the border between the present idea and its absent object.

From Locke through to Kant, the Enlightenment established a new dogma that extinguished much of the debate witnessed in the 17th century. After Kant, any concession to the pre-communicative real presence of the object is marginalised as naïve, religious, mystical, unscientific. Today, the romantic opposition to the Kantians has all but disappeared from our schools, and the conflation of the medium of knowledge with knowledge itself now either goes without saying, or, when it is stated, it is stated dogmatically.

Not the least dogmatic is the great doubter of all doxy in our time, Jacques Derrida. Watching over the vast expanse of our tradition, his confidence in this dogma is blinding to any real regard for all pre-Enlightenment notions of the pre-communicative presence of the known object—notions that he finds curious and playful yet incredible and thus dismissible. The explicit mathematical elementism of Pythagoreans is never considered seriously on its own terms. If it is not ignored or avoided, then it is set up for misunderstanding by taking its linguistic aspects in isolation, as with Plato. [63, pp. 61-119] The closest Derrida comes to facing it head-on is when passing over pre-Enlightenment visions of a universal mathematical notation for science. He discusses among others, Descartes' vision of a *mathesis universalis*, but also, and more historically significant, the 'universal characteristics', the life-long project of the great mathematical philosopher Gottfried Wilhelm Leibniz (1646-1716). Regrettably, but predictably, these are both viewed by Derrida as no more than projects for a universal *language*; they are but instances of grammatology as a positive science propped up for demolition by Derrida's own negative grammatology, a sceptical semiotics otherwise known as 'deconstruction'.*

Derrida's obliquely expressed incredulous attraction to the mystical vision of the mathematical giants of 17th century is a sceptical echo of Russell's own positive interest; but it was Russell himself, at the other end of the century, who truly does personify the grand failure of what Derrida calls grammatology as a positive science.[#] A mark of the arrogance of our age is that when we try to engage our difference with *another* time, we only project an oppositional aspect of *our own* time: first we present Bishop Berkeley as though he is some messenger from the past, when, in both the success of his criticism and the failure of his theory, he is so quintessentially contemporary; and then we project upon the remote genius of the 17th century fathers of science—firstly for approval, now here for condemnation—an image of our own error in parting from them. In the strength of these delusions, and almost without a whimper of opposition, linguistic methodology—logical and semiotic, positive and sceptical—reigns over the entire domain of academic philosophical discourse. In this incredible triumph it is hard to find anyone in a philosophy school willing to bring into contention the consensus of the code. Most believe, or presume, that *to know is to decode*. What else could it be? That is what we will consider in Part II.

---

* For Derrida's linguistic treatment of these projects see *Of Grammatology* [64] p. 74–93. Descartes had his vision of a *mathesis universalis* in 1619 and incorporated it into his Rule N° 4 in 'Rules for the direction of our native intelligence', [23] p. 4–5. For Leibniz's 'universal characteristics', see Chapter 14 below.

\# Russell's interest in Leibniz and his interpretation of Leibniz's philosophical contribution are revealing. His interest is largely in Leibniz's logical successes and failures. His treatment of Leibniz as a logical reductionist is in stark contrast to how we present him in Ch 14 & 15 below. See [65] and [40], p. 563–76.

PART II

Towards MATHEMATICAL EPISTEMOLOGY

Chapter 4

Rediscovering
PRE-COMMUNICATIVE KNOWING

*Over and over
the thought, the picture
that what we see of the sign
is only the exterior of some inner thing
in which the real operation of meaning runs on.*
Wittgenstein, 1933

But we must go beyond words!
Leibniz, 1679

What is the form of knowledge that is more primitive than the form of its communication? We can begin to answer this question by contemplating very ordinary situations of knowing and learning. For example, imagine the following scenes:

> There is an introverted boy who likes taking apart machines to see how they work. It might be a mechanical clock, a wind-up toy or a bicycle. First he watches how it works. Then he takes it apart, puts it back together, and again watches it work. Once, after reassembly, a machine fails to work. He discovers that a component is missing. Finding the missing component on the floor, he reassembles the machine with this component in place and it works again. His friend arrives and he shows him what he has learnt about the machines and they tinker together.
>
> Later his father comes in with a broken machine that his son had been tinkering with. The boy discovers a bent cam and shows it

MATHEMATICAL EPISTEMOLOGY

to his father. They then talk about all the other mechanisms in that machine and the others. In the discussion the boy hears for the first time terms like 'cam', 'crank', 'lever', 'drive chain', 'torques', 'potential energy' and 'kinetic energy'. For the boy these words are like gifts from heaven. Later, when he uses these new names with his friend, it becomes much easier to talk about what they are doing. Better still, the father gives them the Reader's Digest Universal Repair Manual and they learn other ways to work with machines by following instructions that use many more technical terms to accompany labelled diagrams. Soon they start to sound like trained technicians.

The first question to consider about this story is: Did the boy have knowledge of the machines before he spoke about them with his father? If he did then the next question is: Was this knowledge in the form of codes, and was it acquired in a decoding? I suggest that the machines are real and present in the boy's experience and that he learnt about them directly in his experience. His knowledge at its basic level, consists of *distinguishing* the different components and functions of the things in his experience. He may have given some of the components his own names, but not necessarily. His ideas of the machine are not elementarily *codifications* of his experience. Rather, in making these distinctions in his experience, they *became* his experience. To take another thought experiment, imagine the boy at a much younger age learning with a toy that the square peg cannot go into the round hole. He distinguishes the difference between the shapes, and so his experience of the pegs changes, but he does not necessarily codify this difference, linguistically or otherwise.

The next question to consider about this story is: When the boy then starts communicating his knowledge with his friend using the new words 'cam' 'lever' etc., are these ideas now of the form of the code? It is true, codes are used to signify the components and the principles of the mechanics, and it is true that this signification is useful in his thought and communication about his ideas; but all the same, at the most basic level of knowledge, the components and the principles remain non-semiotic. The point is that one can *know* without signifying *that-which-one-knows*. In one's knowledge, *the distinction of something is prior to its naming.*

Participants in a beginner's wine tasting class can most likely already distinguish smells and tastes in wines before they take the class. For some of these tastes and smells they may know the conventional names. For others they may have their own names. But it is also likely that there are tastes and smells which they have already *distinguished* but not yet *named*. In the class they learn to align the right names to the right distinctions. Other names might be used to teach them new distinctions. But again, and in each case, the distinctions in themselves are not codes. Likewise, when feeling around in a pocket we can distinguish thousands of textures without naming them, and we can distinguish accents of people from different regions before we even attempt to define the patterns of difference. When we do attempt to linguistically define the differences, and we name them, and we refer to them, still they remain, at base, signified distinctions, which are not themselves signifiers.

Learning is all about coming to know how to do. Teaching is, in the first place, *showing* someone how to make the right distinctions. There are various ways *to show*, and one of these is by using codes. *Showing* by way of codes is useful, convenient, and often necessary, but in many cases, exclusive *code-mediated-learning* is inadequate. You could perhaps learn how to bake a cake by following a recipe, or learn how to play a tune by reading the score. But it would be with extreme difficulty that one could become a cook or a musician without being shown directly by example how to do it: *You do it like this, let me show you....* Imagine learning how to play cricket or tennis only from written instructions in a book.

Learning often involves various drills, imaginations and codified instructions. Once the learning is over, these can be dispensed with. Each time I ride a bicycle I don't need to think about the instructions I followed when first I learnt to ride. I dispensed with the following of rules, as I did my trainer wheels, once I got the knack. To put it another way: you can throw away the ladder once you have climbed up it. [1, p. 188] Some folk never need the ladder, like the greatest musicians who never learnt to read music, but who developed their ensemble by communicating directly in the sound patterns. Perhaps as a consequence, their innovation often could not be expressed in conventional notation. They discovered new ways that broke the old rules with beauty and elegance, leaving it for the literate music critics to explicate their genius.*

---

* Notional composition and transmission of music is a relatively recent convention that had little influence in most folkloric traditions until recently. In early Jazz, musical score was not generally used for either purpose. More recently, famous musical innovators could not read musical 'notes'. These include the gypsy Jazz guitarist Django Reinhardt, the electric Rock guitarists Jimi Hendricks and Eric Clapton, and the Pop singer Michael Jackson. Also, consider the imperative, attributed to Miles Davis, to play the silences between the notes: *Don't play what's there, play what's not there!* Notional determinism in music may be compared to the determinism of numerical notation considered below in Chapter 7.

MATHEMATICAL EPISTEMOLOGY

Showing and Saying

There are many different ways of *showing*, but now, if we consider only the sort of showing that uses codes, we should be careful not to confuse it with *'saying'*. For example, I could *say* the form of predication by defining it. Or I could *show* predication by examples. I did both in Chapter 2, but *showing-by-example* is the most powerful communicator. Definitions are secondary and interpretative even when they come first: *A Zebra is like a horse with stripes, but let me show you one and you will know what I mean.* Some things just cannot be said at all: I can define a table but I can only show you red. Language can be taught with great attention to defining meanings and structures, but often teachers find progress faster when teaching primarily by showing. This is a case, then, where saying, as in speaking, can be exemplary showing: *You don't say it like that, you say it like this....* Pre-school children learn language almost entirely by showing. Ultimately, all teaching (and communication generally) is showing. It can be a trap for the teacher/communicator to get bogged down in trying to say everything, but it is an error to try to say what can only be shown. This is because the *said* is always in the form of the code, it is *other-referring*, but that which is shown need not be.

Metaphor, analogy and allegory are the great prevailing showing techniques of the poetry, prose and painting in our religious tradition. Yet, while showing is often acceptable in philosophical explanation, what is particular about this *genre* of prose is that it tends to privilege saying: the impetus to completeness in Western philosophy is towards an *explicit* thesis, an argument fully said. Difficulty arises in trying to say what cannot be said. If a philosophical method is to transcend the form of its codified mediation, then the method of exposition must ultimately be a showing. The Austrian philosopher Ludwig Wittgenstein (1889-1951) never entirely abandoned linguistic method, yet he did recognise the limitations of linguistic explication very early in his career. In fact, here I am only following the distinction of *'sagen'* from *'zeigen'* in his *Tractatus Logico--Philosophicus*, which was eventually published after World War I in 1919. The right method of philosophy explains Wittgenstein, is to say nothing except what can be said. And what is it that *cannot* be said? All that which is 'philosophical' is unsayable. However, this is not to say that the philosophical is inexpressible: the unsayable shows itself; it is mystical.*

---

* For Wittgenstein's 'saying' and 'showing', see *Tractatus* from Prop 4.12. [1, p. 71ff] For his early and unambiguous logical reductionism, see Prop 6.2. [1, p. 168] His difficulties with Logicism, and

Chapter 4: Rediscovering Pre-Communicative ...

The road to publication for the *Tractatus* was not an easy one. Late in the war, the manuscript was secreted out of the Italian prison camp where Wittgenstein was been held, and forwarded to Russell in Cambridge. Russell had great difficulties with this first and strange offering of the son of a Viennese tycoon who had turned up one day at his Cambridge classes, and who continued to fascinate and bewitch him despite alarming philosophical differences. Now Russell, the renowned English philosopher, found himself in a situation similar to the time a few years earlier when he was asked to preface some translations of Poincaré—including the scornful attacks on his own work (see above, page 57). Then, Russell penned a polite but gently critical introduction, as he now did with the *Tractatus*, only this time it met with the fury of the author. The difference with Poincaré was not just that Poincaré was dead, but that he was already very famous, whereas Wittgenstein was entirely unknown, with no other advocate. Russell's 'Introduction' became the publisher's condition of publication.*

In this Introduction, Russell not only finds Wittgenstein's mystical philosophy inadequate, but he also finds a fundamental self-contradiction in its very affirmation: What causes hesitation about Wittgenstein's announcement that the philosophical is unsayable, is the fact that Mr Wittgenstein, after all, manages to say a good deal about what cannot be said. Russell advises that an escape from Wittgenstein's mysticism might be in a hierarchy of languages—an implicit reference to his Hierarchy of Types.

Wittgenstein's discomfort with the Introduction is entirely understandable. Russell seemed incapable of seeing what Wittgenstein was trying to show: that there is no need to look for an escape, that the way forward might be in *not forcing the saying*, in not trying to name everything, to hold back on linguistic referencing and let the unsayable show itself. In the words of the *Tractatus*' famous final injunction, *muss man schweigen*:

> Whereof one cannot speak, thereof *one must be silent*.

Representationalism generally, are raised but not entirely resolved in his *Philosophical Investigations*. [2] A shift towards mathematical foundationalism is evident in his notebooks from the late 1930s or early 1940s. [3] Wittgenstein's *sagen/zeigen* is picked up by Spencer Brown in *Laws of Form* [4], in his notes to Ch 2, p. 77–84. Spencer Brown's 'injunction' should also be compared with Wittgenstein's 'following a rule'. [2, Secs 201–2]

* Actually, Russell's 'Introduction' became a condition of publication as a monograph with a parallel English translation. The original German had already appeared in a 1921 issue of *Annalen der Naturphilosophie*.

...tion of mathematics is entirely 'silent' in this Wittgensteinian sense... metic value and geometric form can only ever be shown. Take for example the cardinal number two. The figure '2' can be used to *represent* twoness, but this twoness, itself, can also be directly expressed by examples, as two stones, two tables or two pencil marks. In the surviving Hellenistic Pythagorean textbooks of number theory, the preferred notation of number is to give a single mark—whether a circle, a dot or a letter—for every unit. Thus, the arithmetic sequence is expressed as, for example, •, ••, •••,.... Other similar 'topological' expressions of number are in finger counting, bead counting and 'bar' numerals. In a textbook that has survived complete from the 2nd century AD, Nicomachus of Gerasa explains that such expressions are the natural, unartificial, and therefore simplest indication of these numbers. This would have been all the more apparent to the ancient reader familiar with the counting board or abacus. Across the ancient world such computers were used for all large computations and they always expressed the unitary value by a unitary token. Number words or figures—'numerals'—were only used to name the computed results. Nicomachus explains that numerals only designate number by man's convention and agreement, not by nature. [5, Bk II, Ch 6] The Greek alphabetical numbers are like our modern Hindu-Arabic numerals in that they are graphic *representations* of number, a codified short hand. While numerals often contain a legacy of expressive notation, as do the numerals 1, 2, 3 and 4, they are no longer used to directly express the arithmetic form.

Expressed value: topological numerals					
Pythagorean	α	α α	α α α	α α α α	α α α α α
Universal	/	//	///	////	/////
Codified value: semi-topological numerals					
Roman	I	II	III	IV	V
Modern	1	2	3	4	5
Codified value: non-topological numerals					
Greek	A	B	Γ	Δ	E

Chapter 4: Rediscovering Pre-Communicative Knowing

It is important at this point in the discussion for the reader to develop a clear picture of the difference between the expression, or exemplification, of mathematical form, on the one hand, and the codified representation of things on the other. The graphic expression of two in '●●' does not *stand for* the formal concept of two in the same way that the letter 'T' codifies the sound 'tee', or the word 'table' represents the *table-in-itself*. One way to see the difference is in the arbitrary nature of the code. There is no formal reason why the graphic character 'T' is used to represent the phoneme 'tee'. Spelling is phonetic by convention and so any other shape could be used, as they are in other alphabets or in a cipher. In contrast, the mathematical expression of two as '●●' is non-arbitrary in its graphic form: its geometry or 'topology' of two distinct characters exemplifies two. The reference in this graphic pair is only a reference to a characteristic of itself, which is no reference at all. Twoness is present, not re-presented, on the page. The representation involved in the sound 'two' or the figure '2' occurs at another level. So, when wanting to explore the nature of number, and explore it religiously, as the Pythagoreans did, then clarity is retained when using notation that does not involve representation by remaining in primitive exemplification. Later, in Chapter 7, I will introduce yet another topological notation, more recently invented.

In the context of The Foundation of Mathematics Controversy (see above, page 32), we might say that we have just given an 'intuitive', or 'common sense,' account of the cardinal two. This is by contrast to the account found in *Principia Mathematica*. After hundreds of pages of symbolic deductions from non-intuitive ('dogmatic') principles, it arrives at a definition, which Russell later translated as follows:

> The cardinal number 2 consists of the class of all couples. These couples are defined as follows: there is some concept or other, which we will call p, such that, if A and B, which are not identical, are both members of p, and there are no other members, then p is a couple.*

Note that here two is defined through reference to particulars—to the class of all *couples*—and thus a mystical ground is apparently avoided. In contrast, the intuitive account of two gives *two-in-itself*, as entirely formal in the Platonic sense, which is to say, it is entirely *mystical*. Every instance of twoness is only an example, or expression, of the formal concept of two. The form of two has no particular name, expression or exemplar. It is invisible and nameless, yet knowable and immediate to the mind. It cannot

---

* Recalled in a memoir of Russell by Rupert Crawshay-Williams [6, p. 7]. Not until page 86 of Volume III is the occasionally useful equation, $1 + 1 = 2$, established as a logical proposition.

be *proven* but only perceived more or less clearly. I can show you twoness. I can define it only by showing you how it fits in with other aspects of the arithmetic system. But that is all. This then is one very ordinary way that mathematical reasoning is found to be mystical.

This mysticism of common mathematical reasoning extends into a Platonic dualism, and we should be careful to see how this dualism differs from Aristotelian form/matter dualism. In Platonism we would say that each example of two participates [*meteche*] in twoness.* That is, all instances of two present twoness, and so they all participate in the mystical concept of two. Likewise, all instances of a circle *present* and *participate* in mystical circularity. Circularity and twoness exist in the domain of form [*eidos*]. This is the domain explored by the formal sciences, arithmetic, geometry and music.# Entities in this domain exist independent of any actual expression, whether the expression is natural (two stones), notational (two marks), or technological (two cogs). Mathematicians like Leibniz and Poincaré are renowned for discovering and notating mathematical formulations for which applications (natural or technological) were not found for years, decades or centuries.+ And, of course, these formulations have an independence from their discovery; they are only 'inventions' in their actual notational presentation. The laws of trigonometry would still exist even if angular measurement were never invented. Plato called the expression of such formulations recollections [*anamnesis*]—mind remembering what in principle it already knew.++

Thus we have the two worlds of Platonism and the link between them. The first world is the world of form. We have immediate awareness of this world but it is only sensible and communicable in its expression. The second world is the world of its expression in our experience. In this dualism, the formal domain is privileged because Pythagorean mathematical elementism commands that this is the domain of *all* possible actualities. It is not just the abstract *form-of-things* in a form/matter dualism. Form is the essence of things. Remember, as Aristotle himself told us, for the

---
* For Platonic 'participation', see *Pheado* p. 100c-101c, where beautiful things participate in beauty, and any two things participate in twoness [*dyad*]. See *Parmenides* p. 129a-132c, where the theory of *participation-in-forms* is introduced in a non-mathematical context. See the discussion of forms in *Republic* p. 476, where things are images of reality, and later [p. 510] where this participation is discussed in relation to mathematics. In Platonism, down through the centuries, some terms evolve new meanings, including *metechei*, which come to mean the activity of generation. See, for example, Proclus *Elements of Theology*, Prop 1: Every multiple participates unity. [7] I will keep to Plato's usage.
\# Plato also includes 'Astronomy', but it is defined non-empirically as geometry of higher degree, see below, Chapter 13.
\+ For example, as Mandelbrot explains [8], both Leibniz and Poincaré were early explorers of topology, fractal geometry and chaos, for which powerful applications have only recently been discovered.
++ See especially *Meno* p. 81c-85d, where Socrates guides an uneducated slave to recall that the area of the square on the diagonal of any given square is double—a specific finding of Pythagoras' theorem, as discussed below on page 233. See also *Pheado* p. 72e-76d, and *Phaedrus* p. 249c-e.

Pythagoreans the principles of mathematics are the principles of everything. It is not just the shape of Hermes, but also the matter of the statue, the very wood, that is formal. Physical things are formal all the way down. Leibniz's division between necessary truths and contingent truths, between *law* and *fact,* follows this Platonic dualism. Necessary truths are truths of the formal sciences; whereas contingent truths are particular and relative to a region of experience. The domain of the necessary is the domain of the possibility of experience (what *could* happen) and it is infinite; whereas the regions of our experience (what *does* happen) are finite. It is only in this sense that something can be necessarily true (possible/hypothetical) but factually false (not expressly found in particular experience). For Pythagoreans that which is factually true must be necessarily true. The *phenomenal* must conform to the formal.*

This dualism expresses well the conventional relationship between mathematics and modern physics. Physical theory is about finding coherent formality in nature. Consider the search, since the time of Einstein, for a unified theory of force. This is only a search for a way to *formally* unite the quantum and the gravitational theories of force. Consider also the angst over the contradictions of quantum theory. The problem is that the *phenomenal* cannot be made to conform with the *formal* in any coherent way. And this formal nature of the *phenomenal* is wont to be *essential*, not *abstract*, because we have long since abandoned the notion of a primary matter beyond the reach of mathematical principles. In its implicit dualism, then, modern physics remains true to the Pythagorean empirical science introduced in the Renaissance by the likes of Leonardo, and advanced beyond its ancient origins by Kepler and Galileo. In reducing accounts of nature to mathematical expression, it remains true to Galileo's take on the familiar analogy of natural philosophy with biblical exegesis:

> Philosophy is written in this grand book—I mean the universe—which stands continually open to our gaze, but it cannot be understood unless one first learns to comprehend the language and interpret the characters in which it is written. It is written in the language of mathematics, and its characters are triangles, circles and other geometrical figures, without which it is humanly impossible to understand a single word of it; without these, one is wandering about in a dark labyrinth.#

---

* For Leibniz on *juris non facti*, see the extract from his 'Juris et aequi elementa' in Weiner [9] p. 1. Also in Weiner, 'Specimen calculi universalis' [p. 98] has a comparison of contingent truths with an infinite process. Leibniz explicitly relates his *truths-by-law* to Plato's doctrine of forms. In a different context, conformity can also be found with Plato's *Timaeus*. Before giving his account of the universe [at p. 27-29], Timaeus distinguishes eternal unchanging patterns (directly known by reason) from continually changing creation (known by the senses).
# From *Ill Saggiatore* ('The Assayer'), 1623, translated by Stillman Drake in [10], p. 237–8.

Summary

So far I have introduced the following ideas:

1. Knowledge (perception and thought) is not elementarily *codes* but is constituted of mere distinctions.

2. Experience is the experience of distinctions.
   When we make new distinctions in our experience they *become our experience*, our elementary empirical knowledge.

3. Distinctions are communicated socially by *showing*.

4. *Showing* using codes should not be confused with *saying*.
   Saying is an encoding technique and only codes can be decoded. The codification of distinctions is common and useful in our knowledge systems, but it is not elementary. At bottom we cannot *say* a *distinction*, we can only *show* it.

5. Mathematics expressed in notation may involve abbreviation and codification, but it is basically a *showing* of form, which itself is unsayable or 'mystical'.

6. In the tradition of mathematical elementism, which is more or less the Pythagorean tradition, things in our experience are regarded as essentially *formal*. The Platonic dualism of the *formal* and the *experiential* is more or less reflected in the modern relation of mathematics with physics.

This introduction has brought us some way towards transcending logical method, but still our two great questions remain unanswered and they are now likely pressing the reader's lips:

1. The ontological question: Even if we accept that *perceiving* is *distinguishing*, surely, in the story of the machine-tinkering boy, the machines must continue to have existence independent of his distinguishing them. If so, then doesn't the independent existence of these objects mean that they remain external to his knowing of them?

2. The methodological question: How does the mathematical element avoid the problems of *other-reference* that we found plaguing logical and semiotic modes?

These two questions shall be addressed in the next two chapters.

Chapter 5
THE KNOWING BEING
is a
SELF-REFERENCING SYSTEM

Whatever is thought of by us is either conceived through itself, or involves the concept of another. Whatever is involved in the concept of another is again either conceived through itself, or involves the concept of another; and so on. So one must either proceed to infinity, or all thoughts are resolved into those which are conceived through themselves. If nothing is conceived through itself, nothing could be conceived at all.
Leibniz, 1679

Know thyself
Inscription at the Delphic Oracle

The Analogy of the Living System

Consider for a moment this imaginary organism:

> There is an amoeba, a single cellular organism, living in an aqueous medium. Its only sensation is of pressure, that is, a primitive sense of touch. When another body presses upon it, it feel this pressure but it also feels a small area of least pressure, and, through tensing and relaxing segments of its cell wall, it moves into a new space away from the body that might well have crushed it.

This imaginary organism has only one sense, but we could say that through this sense of pressure it gains empirical knowledge. What is this

Chapter 5: The Knowing Being is a Self-Referencing System

knowledge of? It is knowledge of *perturbations*—pushes or pulls, knocks or tugs, on its cell wall. The knowledge it has is of what happens *to itself*. It is knowledge of its environment only in that it is knowledge *of itself* as affected by its environment. It is not knowledge *of things* in its environment. It does not know *the-things-that-go-bump*; rather, it only knows *the bump*—the effect upon itself. All it knows is what it feels within the limits of its sensation, and its sensation is always sensation of itself.

This primitive organism serves as a model for understanding the nature of knowledge in self-referencing Biological Systems Theory. We can develop our model of the organism to include *active sensation*; thus, while our amoeba could only passively *be touched*, we now have an organism that reaches out *to touch*. We can also add to our model the specialisation of sensation into taste, smell, hearing and sight. If we add a faculty for memory and learning, and these within a neural system, we are getting towards a model of higher organisms such as humans.

> *But surely we know the external world better and more directly than this blind amoeba?*

If we hold to this model we can answer this question thus:

> *Yes, human knowledge is more subtle and sophisticated, but it is not more direct.*

The development here is only a development of complexity. Careful consideration reveals that none of these developments in any way change the closed self-referencing nature of the organism's knowledge system.

The extraordinary specialisation and power of especially, our own visual organs, and the extraordinary development of our sensual memory, tend to mislead us into thinking that *my world* is more than a construction *within myself*. It is helpful, in trying to imagine this model as a model of your own experience, to consider the elaborate role that sensual memory plays in your own construction of the physical world. This sensual memory is especially developed in relation to our sense of sight. Recent advances in the understanding of visual perception reveal just how little of what we *see* at any one time is *sensed at that time*, and how much is constructed from memory.* However, we do not have to rely on recent science to remind ourselves of the importance of perceptual memory in our

---

* See, for example, Gordon [11].

experience. One worthy reminder is in finding your blind spot (see opposite, Figure 5.1). Another helpful experiment is to enter a familiar room blinded (by darkness or by a blindfold) and disorientated, and then to reach out and touch some familiar objects. Successful reorientation is often achieved by merely grasping two related fixed objects (say, a table and a couch). This can be enough for your mental image of the room to orientate and flood back in, sufficient to allow its safe navigation. When you remove the blindfold, or switch on the light, consider the objects now *visually* present as mental constructions prompted by visual 'touching'.

When we take away the patterns we find in our sensation we are left with incomprehensible white noise. Even when we learn to distinguish some patterns they can still remain incomprehensible like the sound of an unknown language or the scrawl of an unknown script. Babies born to this noise rapidly learn to make sense of familiar and general patterns of sensation. For we who are not babies any more, our normal experience is full of familiar forms that we long ago learnt to distinguish. Lots of noise still remains, it is just that we have learnt to ignore it.

Remember it is not only this sensual memory that is entirely internal. The sensual prompts to my memory—those immediate sensual references—are also *of* my being and *in* my being. Even the original white noise is the noise *of* my being and *in* my being. All my primary sensual experience, however orderly or disorderly, is *internal* experience. It is *experience of conditions of myself*. Just as touch is an experience of the distortion of the nerve endings in my skin, likewise, sight is an experience of changes in the state of my retina. My entire sensual experience is only a communicative activity of my *being* within my skin. In fact, what we normally call 'knowledge,' or 'cognition,' is only particular types of activities within my nervous system. The implication of this finding is that the objects of my world are—they can only be—real and present in my internal world. This is where they have their *being*. My world of independent things is *my* construction within *me*.

Solipsism

Many a philosopher has come this far. Perhaps they have come by way of different streams through different domains of knowledge, yet still they have arrived at what is formally the same familiar place where we have arrived just now. It is a place that can appear as a vortex of self-reference

Figure 5.1: Find Your Blind Spot

First Blind Spot Experiment
1. Hold the page upright about 30 cm from your eyes.
2. Cover your left eye and stare at the cross.
3. Slowly move the page away from you until you find a position where the black dot 'A' disappears from the right field of your vision. This 'blind spot' corresponds to the place on your retina where the optic nerve departs.
4. Keep your left eye covered and look around you. Notice how there is no gap in your visual field.

Second Blind Spot Experiment
1. Rotate the page so that the black dot 'B' is in the position where 'A' was.
2. Conduct the experiment again. When the dot disappears this time, notice what happens to the line that crosses it. You see what you cannot see.

from which there is no escape. Indeed, escape is required because only then can *I* propose a world of things independent from *my* experience of them. And only then can *I* propose others with whom I share knowledge of this common world. With this appraisal of this place, the leap to Representationalism is made. Those who make the leap look back on those who hesitate and see prisoners to an illusion detached from any ontological ground. When both Kant and Russell made this leap they were explicit as to the predicament they felt, and the choice they made. Kant chose Representationalism because otherwise we shall be landed in the absurd conclusion that there can be appearance without anything that appears. Russell chose Representationalism because otherwise we will be left alone in the desert. For those seen trapped in this vortex, the brotherhood of Representationalism allows extraordinary concessions in order to help them out. For each one of them has been there before, and none would want to undermine the grounds of their own refuge through the criticism of others. Thus, it has become permissible to take a leap of faith otherwise scandalous in modern philosophical systems. This leap of faith is no less than a leap from *my* consciousness to *our* shared world. This world we share is a world of unknown and unknowable objects from which all our empirical knowledge is derived and to which all our empirical knowledge corresponds.

We will not make this leap. We will not make it because there is no need. This place we have arrived at is not a vortex of solipsism. One of the main tasks of the next four chapters is to show how this realisation—that knowing is an entirely self-referencing process—is not a trap, but only the first step towards a complete understanding of the world in which we live and know and have our being.

That solipsism is not an outcome of our model is due to the fact that while *cognition* is entirely self-referencing in biological systems, this does not entail the denial of external *causation*. This biological systems model is all about how the environment of a system affects the closed internal communication of the system. Just think, if there were no external effect then our amoeba would not have been able to respond to the pressure on its cell wall and so avoid being crushed. Likewise, *my* environment affects the nature of the objects constructed in *my* world, in that it perturbs my world; and it is only by distinguishing these perturbations that I ever came to construct *my* objects in the first place. What is important to grasp here is that in a formal systematic sense, this is quite another thing from saying that the *objects-in-my-experience*—those that are not illusions—are those that *correspond to* some essential set of objects beyond my experience.

In this biological systems model, external causation on our internal cognitive systems also permits communication between us: it allows *me* to show *you* how to have the experience I am having. Once I have learnt the conventions of perturbational behaviour (be it pointing or language) I can then show you how to make the distinctions I am making. It is through successful communication that we do in fact have a correspondence of objects. This correspondence is not between the subjective-apparent and an external-objective, but, rather, it is between two (or more) subjective domains. It is between my sets of distinctions and yours. In our story of the introverted machine-tinkering boy, the father and son commune by showing, aligning and naming their distinctions together. Language, culture and the entire social domain is built on the communion of such distinctions between participating individuals. And it is no different in scientific communication. A specialist scientific community is like any other community—a group of people united in sharing more or less the same distinctions in this way.

Autopoiesis

Self-referencing Biological Systems Theory is sometimes also called evolutionary systems theory in order to suggest its compatibility with the Darwinian model of causal communication and differentiation. This name is evocative of attempts early in the 20th century to overcome the contradictions of Representational epistemology through a biological model. In *L'Evolution creatrice* (1907) Henri Bergson (1859-1941) tries to bring theory of knowledge to an evolutionary theory of life, and then extend evolutionary theory into a general principle of *being-as-process*, of being as change, as a Platonic *becoming*, and so a conquest over nought. [12, p. 291] His Creative Evolution was popular on continental Europe up until World War II. After the war, interest in Bergson collapsed and there is little in the way of historical continuity between his philosophical evolutionism and the development of recent bio-cognitive models. Theoretical difficulties aside, there were external reasons for the fall from favour. One was the cloud that hung over any attempt to take evolutionary theory into the human domain after the eugenics program of the Nazis. Another was because Creative Evolution proposes a mystical foundation to the original impetus to life. As such it directly threatened Logical Empiricism, and was consequently subject to sustained and effective attacks from Russell and the increasingly powerful Analytic movement. (See above, page 23.)

In acknowledging Bergson's work, we recognise that what I am introducing here is in the very least a 'second wave' of the bio-cognitive approach. This second wave emerged out of a movement across various fields of theoretical science called Systems Theory. The aim of this movement was to shift the focus of analysis towards the organisation of whole working systems rather than their individual components. With this approach now so entrenched in many fields of science, it is easy to forget that Systems Theory only really took off after World War II. The development within Systems Theory of the self-referencing model was in the revolutionary idea of taking the notion of system 'feedback' and making it the absolute rule. Key developments in self-referencing Systems Theory were advanced by two neuro-biologists, Humberto Maturana and Francisco Varela, in Chile during the years preceding the coup of 1973.*

In their work as biologists, Maturana and Varela found that in conventional models, living organisms were always referentially orientated to their environment. Yet these models were at odds with the organism's apparent autonomous nature. As Maturana reflects:

> ...any attempt to characterize living systems with notions of purpose or function was doomed to fail because these notions are intrinsically referential and cannot be operationally used to characterise any system as an autonomous entity. Therefore, notions of purpose, goal, use or function, had to be rejected...
> [14, p. xiii]

However, initially he did not know just *how to* reject these models and *for what* alternative. So he started exploring other ways of thinking about organisms. In his lectures he started to speak about living systems...

> ...in a manner that would grasp their autonomy as a phenomenon of their operation as unitary systems. Thus, eventually, I made a distinction between what I called self-referred and allo-referred systems, a distinction that separated systems that could only be characterized with reference to themselves, such as living systems, from systems that could only be characterized with reference to a context. I did this in order to emphasize that whatever took place in living systems as living systems, took place as necessarily and constitutively determined in relation to themselves because their being defined as unities through self-reference was their manner of autonomy;...
> [14, p. xiii]

---

* See [13] translated as [14]. Also in English, see [15].

Chapter 5: The Knowing Being is a Self-Referencing System

Through extensive discussions with his student Francesco Varela, there soon developed a new self-referencing theory of the organism, which they came to call *autopoiesis*.*

Autopoiesis is a model of a living organism as autonomously self-organising, and in this way self-distinguishing. The organism defines through its properties the space in which it exists. One of the key findings of Maturana's empirical work on the cognition of organisms was that there is no possible distinction between internally and externally generated states of nervous activity. [14, p. xix & p. 23] In other words, to distinguish between an organism's *knowledge-about-itself* and its *knowledge-about-its-environment* is, in effect, spurious. External *knowing* is only a self-*knowing*.

A direct comparison of the self-referencing systems model with the 'general systems' model is helpful at this point.

The General Systems Model

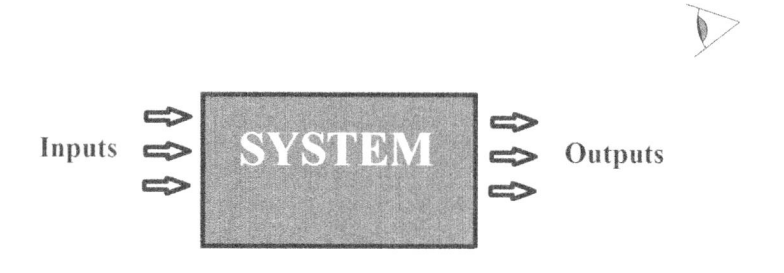

Inputs ⇨ SYSTEM ⇨ Outputs

The general systems model is an input-output system.# The inputs come from, and the outputs go to, an absolute context of the system. This could be a model for a factory, where the inputs are the raw materials and the outputs are the manufactured product, by-products and waste. If we consider a living organism in this way then we would see, for example, a hen generating eggs from the input of its feed. In this model the system is seen primarily as consisting of a linear causal component in greater chains of causation. It is helpful to consider Aristotle's ontology in this model. Remember the sculptor again: in applying the form of Hermes he produces

---
* '*Poiesis*' is from the ancient Greek, 'to create'. With the Greek prefix 'auto-', we have 'self-creation'. '*Poiesis*' has artistic connotations, referring to poetic creation in the same way that we are in the habit of using 'composition' specifically in reference to musical creation. For how Maturana came to coin *Autopoiesis*, see [14] p. xvii.
\# Pioneered by Ludwig von Bertalanffy. See in German [16] and later in English [17].

the statue of Hermes (output) from the wood (input). As a general analogy with Aristotle's form/matter metaphysics we can see how the *system* is like the form applied to the material *inputs*. It is the predicate applied to the subject. Or the logical 'operator' acting upon its 'operand'.

Self-Referencing Systems Model

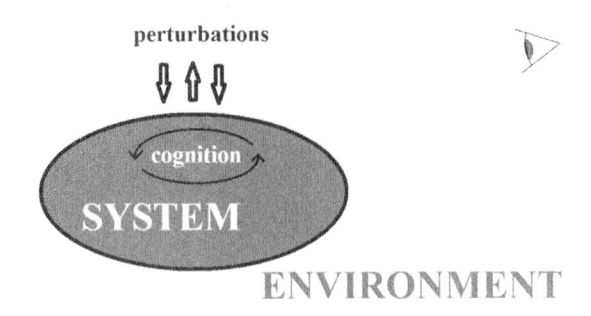

The self-referencing system is a system/environment unity. The system /environment is a complete identity. The environment is not some absolute context in which all systems fit. Rather, it is only *relative* to the system, as *the-environment-of-the-system*. For example, if the system were an amoeba, the system would be the amoeba within its cell wall and the environment would be all that is effectively outside. A universe, the universe of the amoeba, is complete and unique in this inside/outside distinction. From the point of view of an observer we can say that *the-environment-of-amoeba-A* is different from the environment of its neighbour, amoeba-B, if only because it contains amoeba-B.

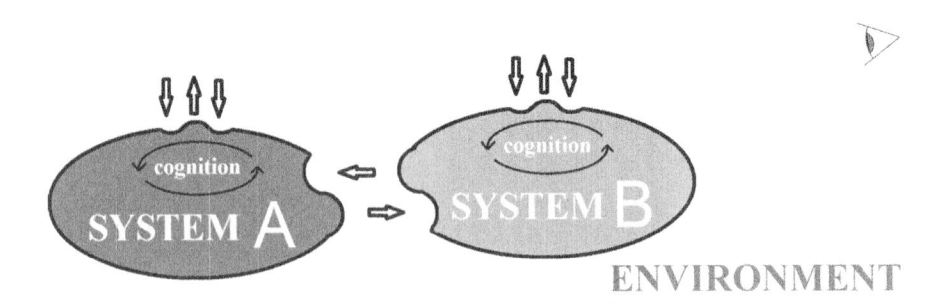

From the point of view of the system, the environment is what it knows it is not. The system's knowledge of the environment is entirely negative: it only knows its environment as its negation, and it only knows it in the way that it affects its knowing of itself. In terms of logic, the operator is the system and that which it operates upon, the operand, is the system. Its functionality (and the cognition that supports it) is entirely self-referencing.

If you think of yourself as just such an organism you now have the beginnings of a model for a self-referencing epistemology. What is radical about this model is that the object of knowledge has been redefined. In Representationalism, *knowing* refers to the *being* of objects *external to* the knower whereas, in this model, *knowing* refers to the *being* of the knower. It is a shift from *other-reference* to *self-reference*—where *know-your-other* reduces into the Delphic *know-thyself*.

This model purports to do what Berkeley never could: to eschew external reference and yet still allow independent and external causation. But does this model ring true as a model of our everyday sensual *knowing*? Have we really addressed the incredulity expressed by Voltaire, Johnson, Boswell and Kant in their various ways? Perhaps we are only presenting another *reality-is-illusion* thesis. I am the first to admit that it does sounds rather strange to say that while 'the tree' does exist wholly in my mind, my mind does not cause it to exist, nor when it falls, does my mind cause it to fall.

An Aside to the Reader

This is a point in the narrative where the bond between the reader and the writer is most likely to break down. It is where the task of writing is so much easier than the task of reading, and so I am compelled to give the greatest encouragement to my reader. It is easy for me to say these things. It is not so easy for you to accept them. I am not presenting a particular arrangement of things that can be accepted or questioned, but rather, I am introducing by a series of steps, a new way of thinking the way things are. Not surprisingly to our common ways of thinking, this new way is inconceivable. The first response is typically incredulity. This reaction characterised the reaction of the Enlightenment fathers who instructed the view that overwhelmingly prevails today. And mostly they were incredulous in good faith. They just could not see it any other way.

Burchard de Volder (1643–1709) was a Cartesian genuinely trying to understand Leibniz's ontology. After a long correspondence, Leibniz was finally very explicit with him:

> It should be said that there is nothing in things except simple beings, and in them perception and appetite. Matter and motion, however, are not so much being or things as phenomena of perceivers, the reality of which is situated in the harmony of the perceivers with themselves (at different times) and with other perceivers.

De Volder was shocked:

> You now clearly seem to me to eliminate bodies completely, inasmuch as you consider them merely appearances, and substitute mere forces for things, and not even corporeal forces but perception and appetite.*

This genuine incredulity continues. In a recent popular text, the great mathematician Roger Penrose footnotes a dismissal of the pressing subjective suggestions of quantum mechanics by saying that he takes for granted that any 'serious' philosophical viewpoint should contain at least a good measure of realism.

> It always surprises me when I learn of apparently serious-minded thinkers, often physicists concerned with the implications of quantum mechanics, who take the strongly subjective view that there is, in actuality, no real world 'out there' at all! The fact that I take a realist line wherever possible is not meant to imply that I am unaware that such subjective views are often seriously maintained—only that I am unable to make sense of them.
> [20, p. 299]

Whatever problems Realism has with the evidence about the fundamental nature of matter, the only conceivable alternative to the reality of the world out there is an idealism where the object of knowledge is no more real than...*let's say it*...the illusions of a lunatic. An appearance (the sense of an absence) corresponding to its objective reality (an absent presence) may be abandoned (for it is unknowable), but if it is abandoned then this can only be for an appearance that is not so grounded in reality and so unreal. Captives to this way of thinking cannot make sense of any theory of the known object where its existence is internal—i.e., real and present in subjective experience. What I hope my readers can now see is that this typical assessment of the limitations of any 'serious' epistemology is only a limitation from the standpoint of Representationalism.

In attempting to escape this view of the relations of *being* to *knowing*, it helps to keep reminding oneself that it is precisely the failure of modern Empiricism that it is unable to give an account of objects as presented *real* in experience. And it helps to remind oneself of this after

---

* [18, Vol II, p. 270–2]. Translated by Antognazza [19, p. 424–5.] except where I use 'being' for '*substantia*'.

engaging in some unthinking experience. Now is a good time to put down this book and engage with the physical world around you. Pick up some objects, a cup, a stone or a ball; feel yourself sitting in your chair; look at a candle flame. Does your experience of your world warrant any anxiety about its immediate reality? To call an object 'an appearance', or otherwise 'an illusion', is only to call it by another name. It is in a naïve state of observation that the perversity in the thinking of the fathers of modern epistemology is most evident. Fixed in a way of reasoning where the object of their experience must be forcibly removed from their experience, they find it inconceivable that another approach could retain its naïve, apparent reality.

Identifying the perversity of the old way still leaves us with the strangeness of the new. While we do begin and end with the self-evident presentation of our world in our experience, there remains a strangeness in applying this biological model to our philosophical problem. All that is required of the reader at this point is to consider whether this cognitive self-referencing model has the potential to lead us out of the perversity of modern logical Empiricism, which, while denying self-reference, is yet continually led into it, and fatally threatened by it.

Crypsis in Complexity

In contemplating the potential of this strange hypothesis, a common consideration concerns complexity. There is no doubt about the complexity (and the subtlety and sophistication) of human cognition. The question is whether the only difference between the cognitive form of our simple amoeba and the sum of human cognition is the complexity of the latter. At this point it may help to consider how in conventional science we find that the development of complex systems often leads them to mask their elementary form.

Take for example, the problem of the cause of differentiation in organic life, and the application of the Darwinian principle of natural selection. We can see how all those amoebas that don't respond quickly enough to avoid being crushed will die, and how all those that do survive improve their chances of reproduction. All that is required, in principle, is a mechanism for differential reproduction (that is, reproduction susceptible to mutation). Yet, can this really explain the development of proteins? Eyes? Wings? Cities? The pathways of differentiation involved in the development of these phenomena are inconceivably complex and almost entirely unknown, yet this is not in itself a reason for abandoning the Darwinian model.

The tendency of a complex system to mask its underlying principles is perhaps more easily envisaged where the developmental timeframe is shorter. Consider contemporary cybernetic technology. In writing this book I use a computer word-processing program. This program presents me with a linguistic world in which I create words on the screen by tapping a keyboard. Furthermore, the program identifies spelling mistakes and even unconventional grammar. I can 'cut' and 'paste' text, and when I am finished I can leave 'documents' on my 'desktop' or 'file' them away in 'folders'. *What do we know about the system that presents this world?*

We know that this world is an elaborate development of programming designed to mimic and assist conventional modes of linguistic communication. What I see on the screen only 'monitors' what is going on in the machine's internal communication. Furthermore, the program structure, the 'memory' and the coding of the information, are all generated from the principle of binary opposition. The opposing values in this system are often described as '1' and '0', but we know that in the computer this opposition of *presence* and *absence* is actually expressed in the gating of electrical current, and so the values are better described as 'open' and 'closed'. We also know that the computer is a closed self-referencing system. We *know* that the computer does not *know* my mind and it does not even know my fingers that fall on the keys. It only knows their effect at this interface. The only input is perturbations on its internal cognition of itself. Yet, in a way it does know my fingers falling on the keys in that it records these events through very specific changes in its internal state. And, in a way, it does know my mind; for instance, when I spell a work incorrectly, as if to say: *Don't you mean this word? If you do, you spell it this way....*

Is the Biological Model an Idealism?

If we are to propose that applying this biological model to epistemology can achieve what Berkeley couldn't, we should pause to consider how it fits with Berkeley and the post-Enlightenment epistemological debates discussed in Part I. In the first place, is it an Idealism? The claim that everything *I* know is ideas in *my* mind, and, furthermore, that these ideas are only ever ideas about *my*self, this sounds like Idealism. Certainly, it rejects reference to an external material reality. So it is with Berkeley in his 'Immaterialism'. And it is also with him in his Empiricism: it claims, in a fairly strong way, that what I know about things is derived from my senses. Where it departs from Berkeley is in rejecting reference to an external reality—remember that his system retains external reference, even if it is to a reality immaterial and divine. Thus, we can say in this context that we have here an Empiricism that is 'idealistic' and non-Representational.

In recognising the possibility of a non-representationalist empirical science, we should be careful not to presume implicit representationalism whenever we consider advocates of empirical knowledge in other times and other cultures. Nor should we presume a lack of interest in empirical science among those who try to avoid representationalism. This is especially important for our historical re-evaluation of philosophy of science, and the problem is most pronounced when we come to the mathematical 'idealism' of the likes of Dee, Kepler and Leibniz in Part III. Sometimes their work is difficult to interpret in this way because we lack the right interpretative tools. In the next chapter we explore an elementary way of thinking and working that is sympathetic with non-representationalist, self-reference science.

Chapter 6

DISTINCTION
The Mathematical Element

The Dao that can be told is not the eternal Dao.
The name that can be named is not the eternal name.

The nameless is the beginning of Heaven and Earth.
The named is the mother of all things.

Ever desireless, one can see the mystery
Ever desiring, one can see the manifestations.
Laozi

One, the wise, is unwilling and willing to be named God.
Heraclitus

We must begin our non-Representationalist account of knowledge prior to the subject/object distinction of sensual observation and linguistic communication. In this primitive situation we will introduce a mathematical (i.e., mystical) element that is self-sufficient in that it is compete in itself without the need for external reference. This methodological element has already been casually introduced as 'distinction'. It is now formally introduced and given careful consideration over the next three chapters: in this chapter we evoke its static unity; in Chapter 7 we introduce its multiplicity; whilst Chapter 8 moves to consider its dynamics in a generative principle and motive. This returns us to the ontological foundations of knowledge and readies us for the radical and sympathetic engagement with the Pythagoreans in Part III.

Chapter 6: Distinction: the Mathematical Element

Laws of Form

'Distinction' as the name for the mathematical element, is derived from a singular and remarkable account of mathematical Form, called *Laws of Form*, published by George Spencer Brown in 1969. There is no attempt here to alter or emend Spencer Brown's account of Form, so where doubts arise, his book should be consulted. Note that while Spencer Brown aims at a systematic and complete account, my aim is persuasion. The consequence is that my exposition is necessarily applied and interpretative. Should the reader develop her own vision of the Form and thereby find my account sometimes inaccurate or misleading then despite myself, I have achieved my goal. *Cast down this rickety ladder when you have climbed up it!* In part, the aim is to persuade some readers to make the effort (and effort is indeed required) to consult Spencer Brown's brief but difficult account. If you do, then remember when you have finished with it, you may cast down that ladder also, and express the Form as you know how.

Distinction cuts a space in two just as a circle drawn on a plain surface cuts that space in two and generates two situations, the inside and the outside.

Distinction is a binary opposition. In this domain, the inside is inside in that it is not outside, and the outside is only outside in that it is not inside. This graphic expression has a lack of precision in that it presents a third situation, which is on the line of Distinction itself. I could place the point of my compass on the line of the circumference, and this point would be neither inside nor outside. In order to achieve a better expression of Distinction as a differential *cut*, we can use a chromatic difference.

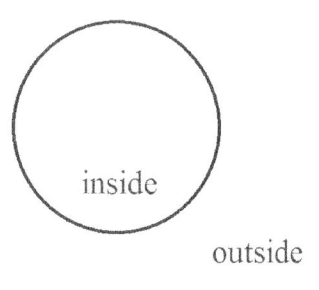

This dot better expresses Distinction as difference. There is now only inside and outside. The difference between inside and outside is a difference of value. We will call the shaded space (the inside) the 'marked space' and the unshaded (the outside) the 'unmarked space'. Thus, when a Distinction is made, a differential value marked/unmarked is generated where there was no such difference. The unmarked space is just as much a part of the Distinction as the marked. Our tendency is not to recognise this, and so it is worth dwelling upon.

The Figure/Ground Analogy

Those who work with images recognise the importance of the background to the presentation of figures. The plainer the ground the more the figure stands out. According to this rule, an entirely plain ground makes the figure most distinctive. Thus, a plain background is often required for photographic identification portraits. And a plain white page sets off black letter type. Let's take figure/ground as a graphical analogy for our Distinction where the marked space is the figure and the unmarked space is the ground.

Now consider this road sign. It is designed to be seen in difficult visual conditions with a reflectorized yellow background readily illuminated by headlights. The question to consider is this: *How is the figure of the kangaroo made distinct?* Is the marked space the black inside, or is it the reflectorized yellow outside?

What is peculiar about such signs is that the ground (outside) dominates. The figure (inside) is only negatively defining, as though it has been cut out and removed. Such a negative presentation of figure is sufficient, indeed in this case it is most effective: the negative definition causes the figure to visually leap off its ground. Thus, despite the dominance of the ground, in this graphic Distinction the black is our marked space. What this sign helps us notice is the complementarity of marked and unmarked and the importance of the unmarked space to the distinction as a whole. Let's explore this further.

Chapter 6: Distinction: the Mathematical Element

Consider this image. It is a classic example of figure/ground ambiguity. Depending on how you view it, it appears as a black vase or two faces. When the vase is perceived, the black is the figure. When the faces are perceived, the black becomes the ground. While the sensual information remains the same our perception can switch between two complementary distinctions: the vase and then the faces. The images below also have figure/ground ambiguity.

Vase / Two faces

With this figure/ground analogy in mind, consider the following characteristics of our Distinction.

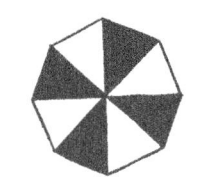

Unity in difference
The trinity of marked, unmarked and their mutual border are only three in that they are one. The unity of Distinction is the difference marked/unmarked. It has no independent parts and is nothing other than one.

Black cross / White cross*

Indicating and naming
Whenever we indicate something we are making, or repeating, a Distinction. One way to indicate a Distinction is to name it. Names are used to encode shared distinctions into our language.

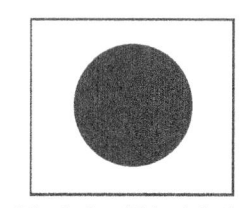

Yang rising / Yin rising

The importance of the unmarked space
A Distinction generates its own unmarked space, and the unmarked space should not be forgotten because it is as important as the ground for the figure. Consider the following scenario:

Black dot / Black hole

---

* After Wittgenstein [2], p. 207.

White hole / White dot

97

MATHEMATICAL EPISTEMOLOGY

There is a great inland plain. A house is built on it. A child comes to live in the house and is told, as she looks out the window: *never go outside*. Before the house was there, there was no *outside* because there was no *inside*. Later the family moves away, termites attack the house and it collapses into the dust. There is no inside any more. There is no outside any more.

There is no great outdoors in a country without doors. There are no unmarried in a society without marriage. The **unmarked** space of the Distinction does have the same value as the space prior to it being made, but there is a difference in that it is now part of the Distinction. Leibniz interpreted the first line of *Genesis* in his binary image of *creation-from-nothing* (see Chapter 13 below) such that before Earth was created there was no Heaven. Light is only light in that it is not dark. Light generated the darkness as an absence of itself. The Distinction of happiness implies sadness. The shore implies the sea.

> *And God divided the light and the darkness, and God called the light day and he called the darkness night.*
> *Genesis 1*
>
> "
> It did not say here,
> 'God *made* the darkness',
> because darkness,…is the absence of light.
> Yet God made a distinction
> between light & darkness.
> So too,
> we make a sound by crying out
> and we make a silence by not making a sound
> because
> silence is the cessation of sound;
> still in some sense
> we distinguish between sound & silence
> and call
> the one sound and the other silence.
> "
>
> Augustine
> *On Genesis*

The tendency to neglect the unmarked space

It is understandable that because the **marked** space by nature is to the fore, we tend to forget the **unmarked** space. The trouble is that if we don't take into account the **unmarked** space, we don't fully appreciated the nature of things. And if in a methodology of science, we ignore the **unmarked** space we are led into a mire of confusion and contradiction. Consider a conception of the universe as all that is contained inside a sphere. Such a universe immediately implies a non-universe, which is the space outside it. Here is Plato's mathematics mentor, Archytas, explaining the problem:

> If I were at the outside, say, at the Heaven of the fixed stars [the outermost sphere of a universe of concentric spheres], could I stretch my hand or my stick outwards or not? To suppose that I could not is absurd; and if I can stretch it out, that which is outside must be either body or space...We may then in the same way get to the outside of that [body or space] again, and so on, asking on arrival at each new limit the same question, and if there is always a new place to which the stick may be held out, this clearly involves extension without limit.*

Clearly, the notion of a closed universe emerged in the West well before Aristotle, but it was dogmatised in Aristotle's model, and prevailed in this model despite the criticism that preceded and followed it, and at least until Descartes. Some two centuries before Descartes, the first to turn the tide was Nicholas of Cusa (1401-64), the Christian Platonist, when he offered an *a priori* case for the unbounded universe. The error of a closed universe is not empirical but conceptual, it is in the very idea of universal containment. This conceptual error would continue after Descartes, and even after Einstein, in such notions as the *class-of-all-classes* and the universal set.# Of course, a *set-of-all* indicates the inside of a universal inside/outside complementary unity in much the same way that our house on the plain indicates the inside of an inside/outside Distinction where the child must play. Another case of universal containment is monotheism's *All is God*:

> *Is God good?*
> *- Yes.*
> *And God is all?*
> *- Yes*
> *Then God must also be not-good. And if he is powerfulness, he must also be powerlessness, and unwise as well as wise, and so forth. He must be whatever he is and also his negation because if he is <u>all</u> then he can never be the negation of, or other to, anything.*

And so we rehearse a familiar prelude to the various monotheistic mysticisms. The Islamic chant *There is no god but God* has a mystical interpretation such that it expresses a recognition of the absolute negation within the unity indicated by the affirmed of the absolute: 'God!' This same

---

* Translated by Heath [21], Vol I, p. 214. Plato's *Parmenides* [p 137c-138b] provides a more conceptual presentation of the issue. Archytas' stick has become a dart for Lucretius (99 – 55 BC) in *De rerum natura*. [22, Bk I, Line 921-83]

\# See Nicholas' *De Docta Ignorantia* [Bk II Ch 11 p. 156] translated in [23, p. 114] and the discussion in Jasper Hopkins' introduction [p. 16-17]. For a historical overview of the topic, including discussion of Nicholas, Descartes, More and Newton, see Alexandre Koyré's *From the Closed World to the Infinite Universe*. [24] For the universal class and universal set, see the discussion of Russell and Cantor above p. 33ff.

recognition is found in Nicolas of Cusa's mystical coincidence of contraries.* In one dialogue he defines God as 'not-other': in that God is the same as himself, he is not other to anything, and most generally, he is not other to himself. In the discussion, the reader is led to see beyond the apparent contradiction that all otherness, including the otherness of God, is contained within God.# His implicit critique of the Aristotelians comes to a head in the realisation that the coincidence of contraries at the very Godhead can only be envisioned: logic cannot arrive at the absoluteness of God, if only because of its prohibition of contradiction.

Nicholas' way of showing the mystical unity of the Godhead was in the Christian method of *via negativa*. For Medieval theology, the epitome of this 'negative way' was a mere few pages of late Hellenistic Platonism called 'The Mystical Theology', which was attributed to the Biblical 'Dionysius the Areopagite' and then further assimilated into Medieval Christianity as 'St Denis'. Other mystical traditions have other ways of overcoming the apparent contradiction in any 'positive' affirmation of the principle unity. For our current purposes we need to say that, in the element that we call 'Distinction', a thing is *itself-and-its-other* in such a way that it being *itself* is it being *not-its-other*. I will express this duality, however inadequately, by introducing a typographical convention '*itself(not-its-other)*'. For example, the indication of God expresses the distinction '*God(not-not-God)*'. The calling, or recalling, of a Distinction—in this case by calling its name—indicates its **marked** space but also negatively implies its **unmarked** space.

Both sides of a Distinction cannot be simultaneously marked

A Distinction is sufficient with one side **marked**. This is reflected in our naming. We don't say 'light-not-dark' because it is sufficient to say 'light' to indicate the distinction that negatively implies darkness. Furthermore, it is impossible for both sides to be **marked**. This is because a Distinction is only a differentiation of a single difference. In our figure/ground images, if both sides are shaded the figure disappears. Consider photographic film:

---

* In the Islamic tradition, see Gerhard Endress' commentary on Yaḥyā Ibn'Adī [25, p. 318] and as discussed by Janos [26, p. 260–2]. See Ali on the creator-God's transcendence, without associates; and then on our knowledge of God *via negativa*, by the negation of all attributes. [27, pp. 27–30] According to Nicholas, in God at his absolute maximum, opposites coincide, or contradictions coincide ('contradictoria coincidunt'). He says God is beyond all opposition...beyond both all affirmation and negation. [*De Docta Ignorantia*, Bk I, Ch 4, p.12] Related is the doctrine of enfolding, where God is the enfolding...of contraries. [Bk I, Ch 22, p. 67]. See Hopkins' commentary on his translation [23], p. 6 & 13. See *De Coniecturis* for the emanating of otherness that generates multiplicity by and in the godhead. [28, pp. 36–53]

De li non aliud translated by Jasper Hopkins [29]. Compare this with the discussion of unity in Plato's *Parmenides*, where on page 139c the conclusion is reached that One cannot be other than anything; only other, and nothing else, can be other than another.

Chapter 6: Distinction: the Mathematical Element

place a positive slide upon its negative and the image disappears. Draw it apart and it is as though a form is drawn from the blackness.

The ambiguous figure/ground images illustrate a number of characteristics of Distinction that I am pointing to here. They show in the first place, the essential asymmetry of Distinction (only one side can be marked). Secondly, they show the possibility of the positive/negative complementarity of two distinctions. They also show how the marking in a single Distinction can switch. What is striking about our perception of these images is not that two figures present *simultaneously*, but rather, that two figures present *alternatively*. We can think of this phenomenon as one Distinction alternating its marking, or else as two complementary distinctions. They are like the Distinctions of *light(not-dark)* and *dark(not-light)*, or the two shoreline Distinctions of *island(not-sea)* and its complementary opposite *sea(not-island)*. So, while it is common to find both the complementarity of two Distinctions and also the switching of marking within a Distinction, we should always remember that the element of knowledge—the basic unit of our method—demands two sides to everything, but only one at the fore.

The confusion that gives an elementary opposition of two **marked** sides leads to the dynamic of an elementary 'warring opposites'. The pun 'duelism' is apt, and the paradigm of such dual affirmatives in our tradition is that which underlies the struggle between good and evil. St Augustine (354-430 AD) famously found this an error of monotheism. He concluded that if God is all and God is good, then evil is negation and nothing.*
Since early Christianity, form/matter dualism is often viewed in this way. While Aristotle sometimes came close to defining his matter as mere absence, later Graeco-Christian sects (Gnostic and Manichean) often saw it as positive, oppositional and conflated with evil. The most famous challenge to a positive account of matter came before Augustine, at the height of Hellenistic Platonism, when Plotinus (204-70) found agreement with a view criticised by Aristotle that did reduce matter to absence.#

---

* Against the Manicheans and against the tendency in Christianity to ascribe an 'efficient cause' to evil, Augustine often argues that the original cause of evil is the *nothing* of creation. In *creation ex nihilo*, all being arises from (and so consists of) the absolute *being-of-God* and nothing. Thus, evil only subsists as the privation of Godly goodness (as not-good). Just as there is no cause for silence or darkness, except the absence of sound or light, likewise, there is no separate cause of evil. Evil can be a defect in the creation of goodness, and so *it can contain goodness*, but such a distortion of goodness is only possible due to the involvement of nothingness. See Augustine's *City of God*, Bk XI, Ch 22, Bk XII, Ch 6-7 & Bk XIV Ch 11. The *evil-as-privation* argument against the Manichean tendencies has its roots in an argument against a version of emanationism involving Aristotelian primary matter. This argument against the *being* of primary matter emerged prior to the Christian Manichean controversy in the Neo-Platonists (including, famously, Plotinus).
\# Aristotle comes close to defining matter as privation in *Physics*, Bk I, Ch 7-10. [191a ff] For Plotinus on matter as absence or void, see Enneads, *Ennead* II, Tractate 4, Ch 11-16. For Aristotle

The mystical other: the silence of the unmarked

The unity of the Form is in the Distinction of the marked from the unmarked. A Distinction shows its mark and only implies the unmarked in a negative way. I have begun to express this typographically in the form, '*marked(not-unmarked)*' as in '*God(not-not-God)*' or '*light(not-dark)*'. This is only an attempt to *show* the two sides of the Form using language and type, but these media are misleading. For this reason it is advisable to give more attention to the graphic figures when attempting to envisage the Form. The words tell you *what to do* with the images, and the images themselves are only guides to the Form. What is important to see, but difficult to describe, is that the unmarked is only unmarked in that it remains in the background, or, as we say, it remains 'unsaid'. *It must be silent.* When it is 'spoken', then the marking in the Distinction switches. So the unmarked becomes the marked (the faces appear, the vase retreats). Or else a new Distinction is made. Once you can envisage with some clarity the asymmetry of marking, you have arrived at another aspect of the mysticism in this mathematical method.

Remember that we came to the first way of mysticism with the example of the cardinal number **two**, noticing that it is only ever *expressed* by example (whether in notation or in things) and that *two-in-itself* is insensible, yet knowable and immediate to the mind. This led us to Platonic dualism, where the *experienced* world is found to be particular expressions of the *formal*. (See above, page 76-8.) The other aspect of this mysticism is, then, that in every expression of the Form, in its static unity, only one of its sides is present. Perceptions, thoughts, and things only present one of their sides. The other side is unspoken, invisible, hidden. It is absent. Unmarked is absence.

Point of view in complementary shared Distinctions

In our culture, in our language, we share Distinction in such a way that my Distinctions come into some sort of synchronicity with yours. However, sometimes my point of view on a shared Distinction will differ from yours such that the marking differs. Also, those Distinctions that are more fundamental may differ. This is especially the case when my *situation* in the distinction is different from yours. In the distinction of *sex*, I am on the male

---

arguing against matter as void see *Physics*, Bk IV, Ch 7. [p. 214a13] Note that while there are inconsistencies in Plotinus, the *Enneads* contain the elements of Augustine's emanationist theodicy. This includes the view that matter is the source of evil, see *Ennead* I, Tractate 8, Ch 7.

side. *Female* is the unmarked space for the male. In regard to *sex*, it is what *he* knows he is not. The male has a Distinction indicating *female*, but it is secondary and complementary to the Distinction indicating *male*. To a greater or lesser extent, the *negation-of-his-sex* (female), is matched by the primary Distinction of *female*, made by women. In the figure/ground ambiguity we can think of masculinity as the vase and femininity as the faces. Female is Yin. Male is Yang. This complementarity works with all forms of cultural identity. My Distinction of a *Cretan*, if it is any good, will be in sympathy with a Cretan's Distinction of a *Cretan*. At a more basic level: for you and me to converse, *my* distinction of *you* must more or less correspond to your distinction of yourself as *me*.

The fidelity of the correspondence of my distinctions with yours, and also our differing point of view on our shared Distinction, affect the way we communicate. It is one thing to recognise differing points of view but it is another to transcend them. Sometimes it is impossible to see from the other side, and other times this is only achieved with great difficulty. Fish must grow legs and lungs in order that they may contemplate the sea from the shore. It is a mistake when recognising a difference in viewpoint to think that by its very recognition, it can be transcended. This would be like my accusing you of Euro-centrism, and in so doing suggesting that my own point of view transcends my European cultural situation. The danger is that all I am doing is relativising a former universalism by calling it 'Euro-centrism', and then reaffirming another Euro-centric view as the new universalism. This in turn could serve to justify a higher form of 'cultural colonisation', which might be exactly the opposite of my intention.

A Distinction is complete in itself
If we draw our Distinction as a circle on a page, this Distinction is bounded by the edges of the page. But what if we draw our Distinction on a sphere? If we are in an unbounded space, as lines are on the surface of an object, a graphic distinction is unbounded and complete. Paint a circle on an orange and colour it in. If you don't have an orange, draw your Distinction on the Earth with a stick. In this space there is no limit other than the limit which is the Distinction itself. The surface of the sphere (or any object) expresses the unbounded relativity of Distinction to itself, but we have, here, arrived at one of the inadequacies of our graphic analogy. Put aside your markers for the moment and consider, directly, objects in our three dimensional reality.

MATHEMATICAL EPISTEMOLOGY

Take a spoon from the kitchen draw. Consider it as a Distinction. The **marked** space is the spoon. The Distinction is its limit—the surface you see and feel. The **unmarked** space surrounds it. Now consider: where does this **unmarked** space end? It is true that this space is more intensely felt close to the surface, but all the same, it has no outside limit, and so it extends indefinitely beyond it, to the limit of the kitchen…and out the window…and beyond the house. Even beyond the house we are still in the space that is not that spoon. What is remarkable is that the Distinction of the spoon is unbounded and yet it is a finite identity. It is unbounded yet still not everywhere—it is *not-everywhere* but *where-it-is*. It is a unit, clear and distinct (I can say *what it is* and *what it is not*) and yet it is absolute and complete in itself. In the same way, the amoeba that we invoked in Chapter 5 is absolute and complete in its distinction from its environment.

Distinctions are usually contained in others, but it is useful, in order to envisage their form, to imagine a Distinction complete and unbounded in its own dominion. The completeness of more conceptual Distinctions is often easier to imagine. Consider these conceptual Distinctions:

Married(not-unmarried)
Inside(not-outside)
God(not-not-God)
System(not-its-environment)
Present(not-absent).

Platonic complementary opposites are conceptual complete in this way. Plato's *Phaedo* (the dialogue about the *psyche* that depicts the last of day of the condemned Socrates) builds to consideration of the complement *living(not-dead)* from the opening consideration of the pleasure Socrates feels in having the shackles removed from his leg:

> What a strange thing, my friends, that which men call pleasure! How wonderfully it is related to that which seems to be its opposite, pain, in that they will not both come to a man at the same time, and yet if he pursues the one and captures it, he is generally obliged to take the other also, as if the two were joined together in one head.*

Distinction is the form of the universe and the form of the unit. It is both the set and the individual member of the set. Distinction is the very nature

---

* [30], p. 60b. See also discussion of one/not-one and same/other in *Parmenides* from p. 145e.

of identity in this method. This identity should be compared with the attempts to conceptually define and contain things using other methodological elements such as *predicate* or *class* or *sign*, as discussed in Part I. What we find is that these elements of knowledge require reference and require containment, whereas, our Distinction is sufficient to contain itself.

Finally, if you still have your spoon, then imagine it as a planet. It is the only planet. If it is a planet it is inconceivable without space. What defines this space? What measures this space? What gives the space shape? It can only be the planet. The *planet(not-its-space)* is its own universe. No vessel or medium is required.*

The topological similarity of inside and outside

Imagine a globe covered with an ocean but for one small island, an atoll in its vastness. Imagine the fishy point of view on this Distinction. A fish can swim wherever it wants. It experiences no horizontal limit except at the Distinction that is the shoreline of the atoll. Now imagine the atoll growing larger, even as a large continent. This continent covers one entire hemisphere. Imagine it larger still, until our fish is in a small lake (a mere pond) on a globe covered entirely (almost!) by a land mass. The difference between the island and the continent is only a difference of relative scale. In showing the topological similarity of the small island and the great continent we can see that when we graphically express Distinction, the inside is the same as the outside, except in the way it is marked. A distinction marking the inside (the shore of the island in the ocean) is similar to a distinction marking the outside (the shore of the pond), and it is just as unbounded and complete. The island surrounds the ocean as completely as the ocean surrounds the island. Likewise, in three dimensions, the Earth surrounds the sky as the sky surrounds the Earth. Our spoon surrounds its space as much as its space surrounds it. A single atom surrounds its universe and, as its negation, the universe completes it.

---

* The notion of unbounded finite space came with the non-Euclidean geometry of Bernhard Riemann (1826-66) and the 'Riemann Sphere'. Einstein's space-time continuum introduced the unbounded yet finite universe. However, this conception may be found much earlier obscured beyond a mystical principle in the writings of Nicholas of Cusa. According to Nicholas, the world is not infinite, yet it cannot be conceived as finite, since it has no limits between which it is confined. While this must be so, we cannot fully understand it because such understanding implies the comprehension of God who is the centre and the circumference of it. See *De Docta Ignorantia* [23] Bk II, Ch 11 p. 156. The translation is after Koyré [24], p. 3.

Chapter 7
A CALCULUS OF DISTINCTION

> *[A]rithmetic is a kind of statics of the universe by which the powers of things are discovered. ....But perhaps no mortal has yet seen into the true basis upon which everything can be assigned its characteristic number. ...And, although learned men have long since thought of some kind of language or universal characteristic by which all concepts and things can be put into beautiful order, ...yet no one has attempted a language or characteristic which includes at once both the arts of discovery and of judgement, that is, one whose signs or characters serve the same purpose that arithmetical signs serve for numbers, and algebraic signs for quantities taken abstractly. Yet it does seem that, since God has bestowed these two sciences on mankind, he has sought to notify us that a far greater secret lies hidden in our understanding, of which these are but the shadows...*
>
> *Leibniz*

Now that we have explored in a variety of ways the character of the Distinction as our element (also our 'unity' and our 'identity'), we can move towards considering a notation designed to express its multiplicity. This notation is a conventional derivation of the graphic expressions we have already been using—only modified to suit a calculus. To be precise, what we are doing here is expressing Distinctions—non-specifically, purely and formally—in a notation design for calculations which can express the arithmetic aspects of topology.

Chapter 7: A Calculus of Distinction

Number

Consider again the dot which we first used to indicate a Distinction on the unmarked page:

This mark of a Distinction could be duplicated (e.g., photocopied) and so repeated on another page, giving now two distinctions represented thus:

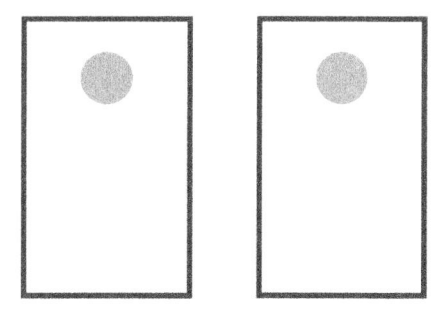

Here we have made a Distinction, 'marked' it and then 'recalled' it and marked it again. Each mark indicates a Distinction complete in itself yet identical to the other. Thus, we present the cardinal number **two**. While these two Distinctions each have their own **unmarked** spaces, for convenience of notation (but without affecting their values) we can present 'tokens' of these two Distinctions in the same background space. From the observer's point of view (i.e., from outside this 'notational space') these distinctions can be imagined as like one…then two…islands presented in a global ocean.

MATHEMATICAL EPISTEMOLOGY

Such an 'arrangement' of two Distinctions can be notated thus:

● ●,

which is the 2 distinctions now presented together.

If the Distinction is recalled again and mark with another token we get:

● ● ●,
and so we have 3.

Add another, giving 4:

● ● ● ●,
...and so forth.

We can present any number as,

●...[n]...●,
where 'n' represents a number of dots.

Each of these arrangements are similar in that they present simple Distinctions ('islands') against an **unmarked** background (their 'sea'). Their difference is their 'number' (of islands). Cardinal number is value neutral, which is to say, in Spencer Brown's language, the value of a call (an island) made again (another island) is the value of a call. [4, p. 1] Brownian 'number' is better understood by comparison with 'order'.

Order

Now, to continue the analogy, consider this image as presenting the form of a volcanic island containing a crater lake.

Whereas with cardinal number, the tokens expressing multiple Distinctions as distinct 'recalls' of the first, here a Distinction is made within the space of the first. This creates a new 'depth' of space. Remember that with number there was always only *outside* and *inside* (i.e., 'ocean' and 'island'). In this 'arrangement' of 'order' there is *outside, inside* and *inside-inside*

Chapter 7: A Calculus of Distinction

(i.e., 'ocean', 'island' and 'lake'). The depth of space is expressed by alternating differential values. Due to our analogy, the outer space remains **unmarked** ('sea') and the deepest space, the *inside-inside* (the 'lake'), is also **unmarked**. We could extend our analogy to give an island in the lake, and so add a further depth. This is just about the limit of this analogy, not so much due to the incredibility of further concentric lakes and islands, but rather because it does not make clear how the 'Re-Entry' of a Distinction into one of its own spaces affects the values of its spaces.

When a Distinction 'crosses' itself and repeats itself within itself, we say that it 're-enters' itself. This can be interpreted as self-negation. To understand what we are talking about here, try comparing these two iterative expressions:

> *One god*   *...and another god...*   *and another god...*
> *God*   *...and not-God...*   *and not-not-God...*

The first expression starts with one god and progresses to two and then to three gods, as though they are three independent Distinctions. The second expression starts with one absolute God and progress, *within his domain*, and *through his negation*, to an expression, which, as a double negative, is of equal *value* to the original affirmation. This monotheistic analogy presents the commencement of the ordinal series.

In proceeding towards a graphic notation for our calculus we must make a switch of convention. Until now it has been convenient to present the First Distinction on the page as a dot, like ●, which is a marking of the *inside* space. However, the convention of our calculus is to always take any **mark** as indicating its *outside*. In this convention the 'First Distinction' on a page always marks (shades) the whole page around its marking (leaving a dot of unshaded space). Actually, in the calculus there is no shading, but if we continue for the moment with the shading and yet avoid the inconvenience of a dark page, we can use a smaller shaded square to depict the **marked** background page (which was, remember, only standing in for the Distinction's own unbounded space—think of the circle on the sphere). One advantage of this notational convention is that the value indicated by an arrangement of marks can be determined by noting the value of the outermost space, the space of 'zero depth'.

Following this convention, Table 7.1 graphically commences the ordinal series, where a Distinction (marking its outside) re-enters its inner negative space. That new Distinction then re-enters its own inner

MATHEMATICAL EPISTEMOLOGY

space...and so forth. In this process, each Re-Entry alters the value of the arrangement so that the 1st, 3rd and so the 5th and all the odd ordinals will have their outer-most space shaded, which is to say their 'zero depth' will be marked. Alternatively, the 2nd, 4th and all the even values will be unmarked as shown in Table 7.2.

Table 7.1: The Ordinal Series

1st Distinction or 'God'
An arrangement of depth 1
The outside space (the zero depth) is marked, so the value indicated is marked or 'God'

Order: 2nd or 'Not-God'
The 1st Distinction repeats by re-entering its own negative space.
Depth: 2
Value: unmarked or 'Not-God'

Order: 3rd or 'Not-not-God'
The 2nd Re-entry into the unmarked space of the 1st
Depth: 3
Value: marked or 'God'

Order: 4th or 'Not-not-not-God'
A 3rd Re-entry.
Depth: 4
Value: unmarked or 'Not-God'

Table 7.2: Analysis of the Ordinal Arithmetic Series

Place in the order	N° of Re-entries	N° of spaces	Depth of space	Value of the arrangement
1st	0	2	1	Marked
2nd	1	3	2	Unmarked
3rd	2	4	3	Marked
4th	3	5	4	Unmarked

Thus, in this ordinal counting, we note the following binary values:

Odd = Odd = Marked
Even = Even = Unmarked
Odd ≠ Even or Marked ≠ Unmarked

Chapter 7: A Calculus of Distinction

The Primary Arithmetic

This finding presents the second law of the arithmetic, the *Law of Order*. The first law, the *Law of Number* we already have, but let's now consider it again.

The Law of Number is where the repeating of a distinction (to 're-call' it) in the same space *does not* affect a change of value. In our counting dots the following equation is true in terms of value:

● = ●● = marked

In our convention of marks indicating the outside, the same equation is:

⌐⌐ = ⌐⌐⌐⌐ = marked

At one depth deeper the equation is:

◯ = ◖◗ = unmarked

With these two laws we have all we need for the primary arithmetic. But to aid the presentation of more complex arithmetic arrangements, we require a simpler notation.

The Notation

Our topological way of expressing number and order is cumbersome but it has a critical advantage that we don't want to lose. Consider that if we were to revert even to the Pythagorean topological notation, it would not allow us to differentiate number and order.* Thus, the cardinal number 2, expressed as ●●, would be confused with the 2nd ordinal. That is, dot notation does not distinguish...

⌐⌐⌐⌐ from ◯ .

To use a more solid analogy, dot counting cannot distinguish a set of Russian dolls displayed on a shelf from these same dolls packed away inside each other. For our notation we need a simple way to express ordinal 'depth' in *two* dimensions.

---

* In fact, the Pythagoreans had a way of expressing ordinal depth, as we shall see in Chapter 10.

MATHEMATICAL EPISTEMOLOGY

One way to do this typographically is (by using brackets (we could even nest brackets (within brackets (to express multiple depths)) as we do when working with computer mark-up code). However, a great disadvantage with brackets is that two characters are required to express a single limit and this can cause depth confusion in complex expressions :-)

Another way of expressing depth is less adaptable to the technology of moveable type, yet it is retained in conventional mathematical notation.

$$\sqrt{2}$$

This is to utilise the second dimension of the page to express containment as with the square root sign.

In a similar way, George Spencer Brown uses incomplete closure to express full containment in the notation he designed to indicate Distinctions in his calculus of Form. In place of our circles he substitutes a right angle character.

Spencer Brown calls this character simply 'mark'. It indicates a Distinction where the 'inside' is the bottom left. The 'outside' is the top right.

Note that in the Brownian mark we have done away with the shading of the spaces, but we follow the convention that the First Distinction marks the outside, and the outside always expresses the value of the mark.

Here are two Distinctions notated at the same depth.

This is the notation for a *Distinction-within-a-Distinction...*

...which is equivalent to the 2nd term in the ordinal series expressed given above.

Marking inside a mark negates the value of the first mark and so this simple arrangement has the value of the unmarked page.

We can now express our two laws in Brownian notation.

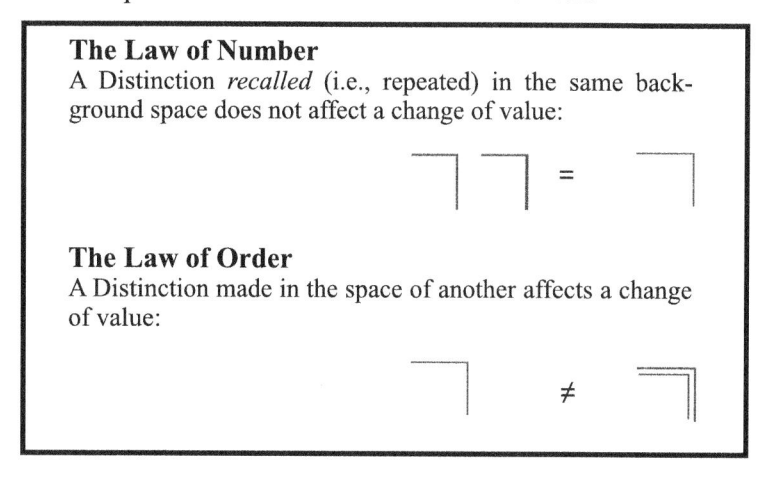

> **The Law of Number**
> A Distinction *recalled* (i.e., repeated) in the same background space does not affect a change of value:
>
> $$\overline{}\,\overline{} = \overline{}$$
>
> **The Law of Order**
> A Distinction made in the space of another affects a change of value:
>
> $$\overline{} \neq \overline{\overline{}}$$

To mark a distinction in the space of another is to negate it. Ordinal marking can be seen as negating, or better as 'crossing'. [4, p. 5] So, while *to recall* a distinction does not affect a change of value, this 'crossing' does. We have previously expressed the Law of Order as a law of the ordinal series thus: odd = odd, even = even, but odd ≠ even. In this notation, the Law of Order can be expressed positively in terms of odds:

$$\overline{\overline{\overline{}}} = \overline{}$$

Or positively in terms of evens:

$$\overline{\overline{\overline{}}} = \overline{\overline{}}$$

And, in a still simpler expression, in terms of evens:

$$\overline{\overline{}} =$$

which is to say, *a mark in a mark* = unmarked.

Here, instead of marking an absence with a cipher, as we do by the numeral '0', *the absence of a character indicates an absence*. By doing away with the notational zero, Spencer Brown has liberated arithmetic notation from a confusion of indication that has long inhibited its advance towards elegant clarity of expression.

MATHEMATICAL EPISTEMOLOGY

By resisting the temptation to mark the unmarked we are able to give expression to the elementary difference of the arithmetic in what is the simplest expression of the Law of Order:

⌐| ≠

Which is only to say: **marked ≠ unmarked**.

What is remarkable about these laws is that they seem as trivial as they are self-evident...and yet they are the foundation of the arithmetic. Now that our laws are expressed in the notation, we can begin to calculate.

Calculation

The simplest type of calculation in the arithmetic is to transform an arrangement through substitutions according to the two laws. In this way the value indicated by an expression can be determined. In our analysis of simple ordinal series above, we used shading to determined the value of each arrangement by starting from an **unmarked** deep space and alternating out to give the value of the zero space, which is the value of the arrangement. However, this method does not always work with complex arrangements. The way to find the value of any arrangement is to reduce it to the root expression of its value. Arrangements are analysed in this way by starting from the deepest spaces (the empty marks) and applying the laws in order to reduce the number of marks until you are left with a single mark...or no mark at all.

For the purpose of such manipulation, we can now summarise our two laws:

Law of Number	Law of Order
⌐|⌐| ⇔ ⌐|	⌐|⌐ ⇔

The two-way arrow meaning 'can be replaced by'. It is bi-directional because the transformation can be an expansion or a reduction, even though when analysing down to the root expression it is always a reduction.

For example, consider the arrangement:

Which can be expressed as:

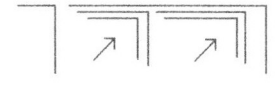

The arrows indicate the deep spaces.

Apply the Law of Order gives:

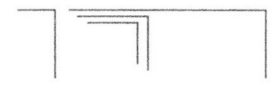

Apply the Law of Order again:

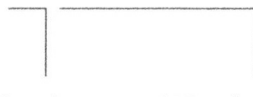

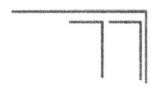

Applying the Law of Number gives:

The value of the original arrangement (and all the intermediates) is found to be **marked**.

Now consider this arrangement:

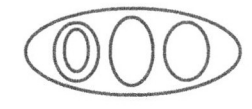

Which can be expressed as:

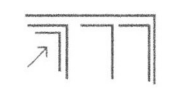

The arrow indicates the deepest space.

Apply the Law of Order:

115

...ply the Law of Number:

⌐

Finally, if we apply the Law of Order again we find the value to be **un-marked** as expressed by the blank page:

By successive application of the two laws, any arrangement (that consists of a finite number of clearly marked Distinctions) can be reduced to either the **marked** space or the **unmarked** space. By using the laws expansively (i.e., right to left) as well as reductively (i.e., left to right), it can also be shown that there is such a path of transformation from every arrangement of the same value to every other arrangement of that value. What this means is that all expressions in this calculus of the arithmetic, no matter how complex, can be evaluated as either **marked** or **unmarked**, and that within each of these value classes, each expression is a tautology of every other.

We leave the development of this arithmetic analysis at this basic outline. The necessary proofs, the further developments and applications to various fields of mathematics are readily available elsewhere.* What will be helpful at this stage is to show how this type of analysis can be advanced by introducing an algebra.

An Algebra for the Arithmetic interpreted for Logic

Algebra is a way of expressing relations between terms that hold irrespective of the value of the terms. For thousands of years algebras have been used to express *arithmetic* relations. Consider for example the equation:

$y = ax$

If **a** is 2 then the relation is **double**. If 12 couples will be attending a wedding feast then 24 dinner settings are required. The number of settings (y) is a 'function' of the number of couples (x), and that function is **double**.

---

* See *Laws of Form* and also, for example, Kauffman [31]

Chapter 7: A Calculus of Distinction

In the 1840s a self-taught English schoolteacher George Boole (1815-64) invented an algebra for logic. In this algebra the values are logical binaries, usually interpreted as **True** and **False**, and the principle functions (or 'operators') are AND, OR and NOT. Boole also incorporated the arithmetic values **1** and **0** into a calculus for logic. What Boole called the *Laws of Thought* soon found application in symbolic logic and set theory, where it served the efforts to reduce mathematic to logic. By the 1960s, Boolean Algebra had found what would be its most powerful application in the design of electronic switching circuits and languages for electronic computing. It was while developing switching circuits for railway safety design that Spencer Brown discovered that Boolean algebra is, after all, an algebra of arithmetic. An appendix to *Laws of Form* shows how Boolean logic (and its algebra) is but one interpretation of a most elementary arithmetic—a 'Boolean arithmetic' if you like—which is our arithmetic of Form. Working the other way around, we can now show how our arithmetic of Form can be interpreted for logic, and so we close this chapter with a brief introduction to a Formal algebra interpreted for logic.*

If we let **a** represent an unknown expression in our arithmetic, then we know at least that this expression will be valued as either **marked** or **unmarked**.

Now consider the simple algebraic expression: $\overline{a}$.

If **a** is **marked** then by substitution we get the expression: $\overline{}$.

Thus, the value is **unmarked**. Alternatively, if **a** is **unmarked** then it does not modify the mark containing it, and so the value of the expression is **marked**.

Every algebraic expression can be tested in this way with two possible substitutions for one unknown, four possible combinations for two unknowns, and so forth. The algebra has been found to have some remarkable symmetries that the reader is recommended to explore, but for now we consider only how it is interpreted for logic.

---

* For a fuller introduction see *Laws of Form* [4], Ch 6 and Appendix 2; & also see Kauffman [31].

If we interpreted marked as True, and unmarked as False, then we can say:

If **a** is True then $\overline{a}$ is False.
If **a** is False then $\overline{a}$ is True.

This simple algebraic expression can thus be interpreted for logic as a case of the Boolean 'NOT', and so 'Not-**a**'.

Now consider **ab**:
The possibilities are: ⌐⌐ , ⌐ , ⌐ and .

Each of these expressions are in the marked state except the last, where **a** and **b** are both unmarked. In the interpretation for logic the values are True, True, True and False respectively. Placing two arrangements beside each other like this can be interpreted as the Boolean 'OR'. That is, if either or both of the unknowns are True then the whole expression is True.

The Boolean 'AND' finds a less obvious expression as equivalent to Not-(Not-**a** or Not-**b**):

$$\overline{\overline{a}\,\overline{b}}$$

Try the four possible combinations for the two unknowns and you find that logically the expression is True only if both **a** and **b** are True.

Now finally consider the logical implication. If **a** then **b** can be expressed as:

$$\overline{a}\,b$$

By substitution we can see how this expression is only False if **a** is True and **b** is False. That this conforms to the nature of logical implication can be seen by example. In the implication *If a man, then mortal*, the first possibility is the direct implication of men's mortality, and so in the case where **a** (a man) is True and **b** (mortal) is True, then the expression is True. The statement also allows for a mortal non-man (i.e., it might be an animal) and an immortal non-man (i.e., it could be a god). What the statement does not allow is an immortal man, and this is the case of a True **a** and a False **b**, which is the only combination to give a false outcome.

Chapter 7: A Calculus

We are now able to translate into this algebra of arithmetic the logism considered in Chapter 2:

*If Socrates is a man, and all men are mortal,
then Socrates is mortal.*

Let Socrates = S, man = m and mortal = M.

The two implications that together imply a third can be arranged:

((S implies m) and (m implies M)) implies (S implies M).

Substitute the algebraic expression for the three primary implication:

($\overline{S}$|m AND $\overline{m}$|M) implies $\overline{S}$|M.

Finally, substituting the AND and the secondary implication gives a complete expression of the syllogism in Brownian algebra:

$$\overline{\overline{\overline{S|m}\ \overline{m|M}}\ \overline{S|M}}.$$

Chapter 8
THE DYNAMICS OF FORM

The hidden and the manifest give birth to each other
Laozi

The first to be sent in motion is the self-moved
which is the link between the unmoved
and the things which are moved extrinsically...
Everything originally self-moving
can turn in regard upon itself.
For if it moves itself, its motivation is directed upon itself,
and mover and moved exist simultaneously as one.
Proclus

You know who I am
You've stared at the sun
For I am the one
Who loves changing
From nothing to one
Leonard Cohen

Re-Entry of the Form

So far, all we have considered is arrangements of distinctions as presented statically, and as equal or unequal in terms of their elementary value. Now we will move beyond tautology to consider the dynamic principle of the Form, which is its self-generation. This principle is 'the re-entry of the Form into itself', and its effect has already been seen in the ordinal series, where marking in the space of another affects a negation of value. We will now consider 'Re-Entry' as the generator of such a series. It is introduced by analogy using a familiar mathematical actor, the recursive equation.

Chapter 8: The Dynamics of Form

Consider again the simple algebraic expression of the **double**:

$$y = 2x$$

For every value of x, y is **double**. Thus, for example: if x is 2, y is 4; and if x is 3, y is 6; and if x is 1.25, y is 2.5 .

Now consider what happens when I replace the y with x:

$$x = 2x$$

This equation is a contradiction because something cannot equal double itself. However, we could think of it as a 'recursive equation' which gives a sequential result:

$$x_{n+1} \Leftarrow 2x_n \qquad \textit{where } n \textit{ and } n+1 \textit{ indicate place in a sequence.}$$

If we start with $x_0 = 1$, then the next x, x_1, will be the **double** of 1 or 2. And if x now equals 2, then the next x, x_2, will be the **double** of **double** 1 or 4, and so forth. A recursive equation can be seen as an operation repeatedly acting upon its result to produce a series. And so the equation can be seen to hold different values depending on how many times it has iterated. Otherwise it can be seen to have the infinite series of values that it has the potential to generate. In this case the series is called the 'geometric double':

x_0,	x_1,	x_2,	x_3,	...
unity,	*double*,	*double²*,	*double³*,...	
1,	2,	4,	8,	...

'Geometric' series are series where the ratio between each consecutive term is the same. In this geometric series, the ratio is **double**, but it could be **triple**, or ½, or have any value we like. In each case, a recursive equation can be formulated to express the generation of the series.

We can think of such equations as 'operations' expressed thus:

$$\text{Operation(value)} \Rightarrow \text{Result}$$
e.g., $\quad \text{double(1)} \quad \Rightarrow \quad 2$

MATHEMATICAL EPISTEMOLOGY

Notice that I have turned the equation around so that the motion is now from left to right, which is more comfortable to read. This expression of the operation is incomplete because, if the equation is recursive, the result is re-entered into the equation as the next consecutive value. We can now present this feedback:

$$\text{operation (value)} \longrightarrow \text{result}$$
$$\uparrow \underline{\qquad\qquad}\rfloor$$

Here, the long arrow indicates the re-entry of the result back into the equation as the next value…and so giving the next result. In recursive equations, an equation that is contradictory in its 'static' form is interpreted as the generator of a series of values by a circular motion, a self-differentiating temporality, a self-referencing *dynamics*.

Recursive equations can be thought of as an iterative rule of transformation, or a rule of 'becoming'. For example, our recursive **double** could be the rule of **halving** that helps answers the question: *How do I divide a pie evenly into 8 pieces?* Or it could be a rule of periodic cellular division, or of bifurcation. In all these cases we can express the series:

	1st	becomes	2nd	becomes	3rd	becomes…
e.g.,	1	becomes	2	becomes	4	becomes …

Now consider the equation:

$$\overline{}\ =$$

This is also a contradiction. **Marked = unmarked** directly contradicts our Law of Order. But if we consider that **unmarked** is the value of one of the sides of a **mark**, then it can also be regarded as a recursive equation where the mark re-enters its own **unmarked** space. It might be easier to grasp what this equation is expressing by applying our monotheistic analogy and stating it as:

God = not-God

Now we can take this contradiction as a recursive equation or iterative rule:

Chapter 8: The Dynamics of Form

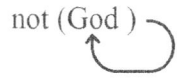

not (God) ↻

This gives the series:

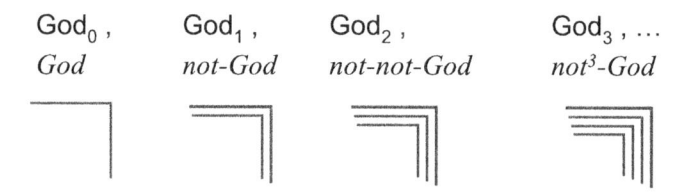

God₀,	God₁,	God₂,	God₃, ...
God	not-God	not-not-God	not³-God

The series generated is the ordinal series 1st, 2nd, 3rd,... and so this simple rule can be seen as the rule for generating the ordinal series in this arithmetic:

1st becomes   2nd becomes   3rd becomes...

⎤ *becomes*   ⎤⎤ *becomes*   ⎤⎤⎤ *becomes*...

We can now express the ordinal series, 1st, 2nd, 3rd,..., in our notation as:

[figure: nested marks with ...]

And the generator of the ordinal series, which we previously expressed as a recursive equation, can be expressed in our notation with a new character:

[Re-Entry character]

This character for Re-Entry expresses the negating of a Distinction as the operation of the Distinction repeating itself on one of its sides.* This character also shows that our contradictory equation could be re-stated as *the whole equals the part*, or, as the recursion, *the part becoming whole*. In

---

* Re-Entry of the Form was first introduced by Spencer Brown in [4], Ch 11. In 1975 a calculus for self-reference was developed by Varela [32], and in 1980 by Varela and Kauffman [33]. Spencer Brown's original notation of Re-Entry, which he called a 'marker', does not include the arrow head. This was introduce later with various notational styles developed by Kauffman [31] and is retained to make clear that this is a dynamic expression and to clearly indicate the direction of its motion.

each step, one side of the mark becomes a full mark and thereby changes the value of the entire expression. Such an equation is inexpressible in common mathematical or logical notations because they do not give expression to the implicit containment of the negation (or **unmarked**) in every affirmation (mark). Nor do they express how the marking of a Distinction in the space of another is, itself, a negation of that space.

Consider the contradiction also expressed as:

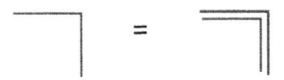

$$\overline{}|\ =\ \overline{}\overline{|}$$

This could be read as an instruction to make a mark in the space of another.

The elementary nature of this operation may cause confusion. Not only are the operator and the operand one, but, also, operations that we normally consider distinct and separate are, at this level, only different ways of understanding the same. Once we can see this, however darkly, the primitive nature of the arithmetic (and the elegance of its notational expression) begins to become apparent.

Re-Entry is the generator of the primary ordinal series but it is also the generator of all ordinal series in the arithmetic. Consider that here we have the Re-Entry of a singular Distinction into itself, but we could just as easily re-enter an arrangement of Distinctions into one of its inner spaces, and Re-Entry could occur simultaneously at a variety of levels in the same system. The great explorer of 'Form Dynamics' Louis Kauffman has revealed many fascinating patterns resonating through many fields of mathematics. [31] Our introduction to the Pythagoreans in Chapter 10 gives examples of some simple ordinal series in this arithmetic, and the reader may wish to pause and examine some of these now. Otherwise, it is sufficient to consider the examples in Table 8.1.

In principle, all generation of value must be a distinction acting upon itself in this way. This is because there is nothing else but *distinctions-made-in-distinctions*, and the only transformative action is to enter (or 'cross' into) a space, which is to say, to mark it. *Re-Entry is the generative principle of our formal method.* I have introduced it here in a particular way and expressed it in a new notation, but, of course, it is arrived at by various paths and it is expressed in innumerable ways. What we will do now is make a new beginning with our generative principle by reintroducing the 'First Distinction', otherwise called 'the Form.'

Table 8.1: Generation by Re-entry

⌐ which generates: ⌐, ⌐, ⌐, ...

i.e., a counting by 2s giving the even ordinals

⌐ which generates: ⌐, ⌐, ⌐, ...

i.e., a way to count by 2^2

⌐ which generates: ⌐, ⌐, ⌐, ...

i.e., a way to counting by 2^3

⌐ which generates: ⌐, ⌐, ⌐, ...

i.e., two Re-entries at the same level giving a doubling

⌐ which generates: ⌐, ⌐, ⌐, ...

i.e., the Fibonacci series. See [31], p. 57.

⌐a which generates: $\overline{a|a}$, $\overline{a|a|a}$, $\overline{a|a|a|a}$, ...

i.e., where a can stand for any formal expression

MATHEMATICAL EPISTEMOLOGY

The First Distinction

We may think of a science as having a First Distinction. For example, the First Distinction in geology might be the *geo*, 'the Earth', as in its rocks and their soils. Geology is founded on the distinction of what is its subject—*what-it-is-about*.

> *First of all came the Gap,*
> *Then wide-bosomed Earth,*
> *the seat of all.*
> Hesiod

So the Distinction *rock(not-not-rock)* is fundamental to this science that gives an account of rocks, just as the Distinction *mind(not-not-mind)* is fundamental to psychology, the science that gives an account of the mind, and the Distinction *social(not-not-social)* is fundamental to the science that gives an account of the social, namely, sociology. If, through the progress of the science, the distinction of the subject were to come into question then the science can come into crisis. *What about meteorites, and can we talk about the geology of the moon?* The First Distinction of the science must be redefined so as to head-off its fragmentation or collapse. Many sciences have come through such a crisis with a revolutionary new notion of what they are about (e.g., astronomy as to the nature of the heavens; physics as to the elementary nature of physical things). Other sciences divide for a time into schools that differ in the determination of this defining Distinction (e.g., psychology in dispute over whether or not the mind can be reduced to physical brain function; sociology in dispute over whether the social is reducible to the material relations of social classes).*

Let us now retreat from the defining Distinction of a science to a more fundamental Distinction, the Distinction of science itself. If we move from the First Distinction of a particular science towards consideration of science in general, we see that *science is about things-in-general*, and so we are now considering the First Distinction of knowledge. It is from our experience that we build our knowledge of things, and we can broaden our notion of experience beyond the experience of sensation to also include our experience of thoughts, memories and all that is seen by—to use the Platonic analogy—the mind's eye.# The eye of the mind can have in its sight

---

* A language may also be seen as a Distinction in a broad sense. In a multilingual environment the Distinction is often made, and then agreed upon, in the first exchange, if only, *Parlez-vous français?* and *Oui*.
# For the use of this term in Plato, see e.g., *Parmenides*, 132a, *Republic* 511a, 527e and 533d. See also Descartes *Rules for the direction of our native intelligence*, Rule 5, [34, p379]. Note that my account does not consider unconscious experience but it does not exclude it.

both thoughts and feelings, and note that in terms of sensations, its primary observation does not concern whether the feeling is caused externally (a perturbation of the body) or internally (a pinched nerve, an hallucination, hunger). The *observed* is the mere feeling itself. It is of this field of experience (defined in this broad way) that mind may proceed *to give an account*. That is to say, the Empiricists are right in this most elementary sense: *experience* is the subject of science, from which all knowledge proceeds.

In order to find the First Distinction of knowledge, we can now ask:

What is common to all that is experienced?

The mind's eye is more correctly called the '*experiencing-I*' or the '*observing-I*', and when we consider all that it observes, we find that what all these things have in common is that they are *not-I*. Each Distinction that is made, or *recalled*, is always in the first place distinguished from the observer, as *not-the-observer*. When I report that I hear a sound or I have a thought or I feel hungry, in each case the sound, the thought and the feeling of hunger is distinguished by my *I* as *not-I*, as *something else*. To put it another way: a contemplation of the activity of one's own *observing-I* shows that its First Distinction is the Distinction of its negation, *not-I*. Knowing is first and foremost a *no-ing*. To put it another way: *all observations of things are based in a mark negating the observing-I*. We can now say:

- The First Distinction is the distinction *not-I*.

- The act of perception is the *I* observing itself as other.

- All perceived objects are in the first place Distinctions of the *I* from the *I* through the act of observation.

While considering this foundation of knowledge *in knowing*, it is important to recognise that the *observing-I* is only known to itself as the generator of its Distinctions: *it is only known, or 'shown' through its very activity of distinguishing*. And it is only known negatively—it is experienced as *not-what-it-experiences*. It is necessarily hidden to itself in the unmarked state of its knowledge. Furthermore, while I can talk about it here, I am only talking from my experience, and, just as when describing a zebra as like a horse with stripes, there is no proof in my statements and no descriptive adequacy. The only purpose of this account is to encourage the reader to have a go at discovering this for herself. I make no excuses: the foundation of knowledge in the First Distinction is not something that can be known as an ordinary object of knowledge; it is mystical in every sense of mystical that we have considered so far.

Meditations on First Philosophy

This outcome has a number of resonances and affinities in the history of modern philosophy, some of which are worth considering at this point. Consider first the Cartesian *cogito*. In an account of an exercise in regressive scepticism the great pre-Enlightenment mathematical Intuitionist René Descartes tells us that he found a ground to his *knowing* and a confirmation of his *being* in the very act of thinking. This is usually quoted as *I am thinking therefore I am* or *Cogito ergo sum*. But in *Meditations on First Philosophy* Descartes avoids the suggestion of logical implication by reducing the principle to the very affirmation of being.

> After considering everything very thoroughly, I must finally conclude that this proposition, *I am, I exist*, is necessarily true whenever it is put forward by me or conceived in my mind.*

From this ontological ground, Descartes proceeds to the elementary nature of the known objects of this *being* as clear and distinct ideas.

> I observed that there is nothing at all in the proposition *I am thinking, therefore I exist* to assure me that I am speaking the truth except that I see very clearly that in order to think it is necessary to exist. So I decided that I could take it as a general rule that the things we conceive very clearly and very distinctly are true; only there is some difficulty in recognising which are the things that we distinctly conceive.
> [34, p. 36]

Descartes' account of his meditation was quickly subject to logical analysis by his follower Antoine Arnauld, who found the argument circular and thereby brought Descartes' foundation for truth into doubt. However, the

---

* Second meditation [34, p. 81]. See also in the *Discourse*: I noticed that while I was trying to think every thing false, it must needs be that I, who was thinking this, was something. And observing that this truth, *I am thinking therefore I exist* [in the Latin version '*Cogito ergo sum*'] was so solid and secure that the most extravagant suppositions of the sceptics could not overthrow it, I judged that I need not scruple to accept it as the first principle of the philosophy that I was seeking. [*Discourse*, Pt IV, p. 32]

author of the Port Royal *Logic* may have missed the lesson in Descartes' guided meditations. For Descartes, who distrusted the direction of logic in such matters, the lesson of his progressive doubt might have been a simple *showing*.* If you conduct Descartes' experiment yourself, and you are able to reach the level described by Descartes, then you may find yourself descended to a truth quite evidently more fundamental than logical proof. Try thinking without predication. Think: *I am*. It may be that the very act of distinguishing makes you aware of your *being*: *I am*: I am the *I* that had been thinking. The *cogito*, the *thinking-I*'s thought of its own *being* led to its unthinking *being*: *sum*.

Correspondence: Internal and External

It is also rewarding at this stage to ascend into the realm of thought occupied by John Locke's *Essay Concerning Human Understanding*, the classic of Enlightenment philosophy destined to reshape the landscape of dispute when it was first published in 1689, half a century after Descartes' *Meditations*. You will recall that our principle objection to Locke is to his notion of a correspondence between one's experience of an object and the external, unknown object itself. We do not admit this correspondence, which gives an epistemological representationalism, and yet we do admit other correspondences that tend to be confused with this one.

In our biological systems view of cognition there is a correspondence between *my* arrangements of Distinctions and *your* arrangements of Distinctions. This correspondence is built up through our common experience and it is synchronised by way of our semiotic communication. The extent of this synchronicity, and the extent of this correspondence, is the extent to which our individual worlds are our common world. Now, there

---

* 'Objections' and 'Replies' were published with the first edition of *Meditations on First Philosophy* in 1641. The circularity of the argument is raised in the Fourth Objection by Arnauld and also in the Second Objection by Marin Mersenne. For extracts of the objections and replies that deal with logical circularity, see [34], p. 139, 142–3. Regarding Descartes' distrust of logic, earlier, in the *Discourse*, he notes: I observed with regard to logic that syllogisms and most of its other techniques are of less use for learning things than for explaining to others the things one already knows or even, as in the art of [Ramon Llull], for speaking without judgement about matters of which one is ignorant. And although logic does contain many excellent and true precepts, these are mixed up with so many others which are harmful or superfluous that it is almost as difficult to distinguish them as it is to carve a Diana or a Minerva from an unhewn block of marble. [*Discourse*, Pt I, in [34], p. 28] Regarding the limits of linguistic reasoning: But as I reach this conclusion [that my perception of objects is a case of pure mental scrutiny] I am amazed at how prone to error my mind is. For although I am thinking about these matters within myself, silently without speaking, nonetheless the actual words bring me up short and I am almost tricked by ordinary ways of talking.... [Second Meditation, in [34], p. 85] Regarding the method of exposition as *showing*, not *saying*: My present aim, then, is not to teach the method which everyone must follow in order to direct his reason correctly, but only to reveal how I have tried to direct my own...I am presenting this work only as a history or, if you prefer, a fable.... [*Discourse*, Pt I, in [34], p. 21]

is also another correspondence that we recognise here. It is the correspondence between *my experience* and *my world*. This correspondence needs to be clearly differentiated from the internal/external correspondence as imagined by Locke, and in Representationalism generally.

Earlier, I suggested an exercise for considering the power of sensual memory where you stand blinded and disorientated in a familiar room. (See above on page 82.) The exercise is to feel for some familiar objects in the room and notice how this information is sometimes sufficient to orientate your sensual memory. Now, if you continue the experiment and while remaining blinded you reach out to touch those objects again, before you touch them you will have an expectation of the sensation (of the texture of the surface, of the position of your arm, etc.). This expectation is due to your sensual memory and it can then be confirmed (and re-enforced) by the actual sensation in touching. There is a correspondence here between the sensually remembered object and a particular sensual experience. This correspondence is very important to our sensual life. When a sensation does not correspond to expectations we are naturally alarmed. When, say, I feel not a table but a toad, I am consciously awakon from habit and called to pay attention to the sensation that is incompatible with expectation based on a mentally constructed reality.

In recognising the importance of this correspondence we should also remember that while both my world and my sensations of it are *other to* the *observing-I*, neither *my-world* nor *my-sensations-of-it* are in any way or part external to my mind. What is external is the *cause* of particular sensations. This causation affects the feedback in my closed system of *knowing* that allows me to construct and modify my reality in such a way that this external causation 'makes sense' and is predictable. Contrast this with the classic accounts of representationalism found in Locke and his followers, where each mentally constructed (apparent) object is taken as containing its own essential *external* (insensible) reality, to which particular sensations correspond, and from which they are derived.

Motives of Re-Entry

There is another way in which this account of our knowledge as generated by the *observing-I* has resonances with Locke. *The Essay Concerning Human Understanding* begins, in the very first sentence, with an appraisal of the understanding as a faculty unique to man among all sensual beings,

Chapter 8: The Dynamics of Form

and a faculty that gives him advantage and dominion over them. Yet, while this commends the understanding to inquiry, such inquiry is not without its difficulties:

> The understanding, like the eye, whilst it makes us see and perceive all other things, takes no notice of itself; and it requires art and pains to set it at a distance and make it its own object.

Locke admits that self-observation presents a problem, yet he considers that whatever it be that keeps us so much in the dark to ourselves still some light can be let in upon our minds. What we have found seems to contradict Locke's initial assessment of the possibility of a self-inquiry of the understanding. We have found that the mind's eye—which seems to equate here with Locke's understanding—*cannot* make it its own object. We find that the mind's eye can only *show* itself to itself, in its act of Distinguishing, and only negatively. The analogy of the eye is helpful. I can know what it's like to see by seeing particular things, but I cannot see myself seeing. The eye of the mind is *always* in the dark to itself. If I do attempt to see myself seeing I can only see myself seeing myself seeing myself seeing…an eternal regression. Hold a mirror in front of you and observe something beyond the mirror. Now try to observe yourself observing that object by looking into the mirror. All you see is yourself observing yourself. *What is the object of this self-observation?* It is yourself observing yourself observing yourself observing yourself…. It is as though there is a mirror behind as well as in front.*

Observing something is observing it *as not*. The *observing-I* can distinguish part of itself from itself and observe that *as other*, but observing itself *as observer* can only be an endless *not-ing* of itself. If the *observing-I* does try to set it at a distance and make it its own object, the action is as though to *re-present* itself as *other-to-itself*. Such an act is formally analogous to the generator of Re-Entry. Such an act would initiate a Re-Entry *of the First Distinction*, or what Spencer Brown calls the re-entry of the Form. And so, cryptically and inadvertently, Locke provides us with our first analogy for the '*motive*' of Re-Entry. It is an analogy for the *motive* to generate knowledge and to generate thing. This motive is the impetus to self-observation: the desire of the *observing-I* to observe itself.

---

* This analogy of facing mirrors is often found in recent literary 'deconstruction', where relentless signification is related to the technique of painting known as *mise en abyme* ('placed into abyss'), where a copy of the painting appears in the painting.

MATHEMATICAL EPISTEMOLOGY

Syncretism

That this account of the generator and motive of knowledge is analogous to accounts in previous mystical traditions is to be expected, although each analogy will, of course, reflect its own cultural situation. Consider firstly how, in this view of the Form of Re-Entry, we are able to see that monotheism's *God entering his void* is equivalent to *God becoming other to himself*, which, in turn, can be seen as motivated by his desire to observe/know himself, which is, at the same time, God's will to create.

In Platonism the motion is usually expressed in more mathematical terms. Remember Xenocrates, the head of the Academy in Aristotles' time, who defined *psyche* as a self-moving number, *the-One-that-moves-itself*.* We know precious little else of the teachings of the Academy at the time, but at the other end of Hellenistic Platonism we have a number of extant texts by Proclus (410-485), the penultimate head of the revived Athenian Academy, which had been re-established in 410 and continued until an ascendant Christian hegemony finally forced closure in 529 AD.

Proclus' *Elements of Theology* is a systematic account of the emanation of form. All but incomprehensible to modern ears, it now finds some resonances with our own account. Following Plato, Proclus identifies the principle of *being*, the One, with the Good. The principle of becoming is the self-moved [*autokineton*] which is the first autonomous generator [*autarkes*] in an emanation where the mover and the moved are One. It is the first to be set in motion as a negation of the One, and it is seen as the link between the unmoved and the things which are moved. All creation that emanates from the *singular-good* through the activity of the *self-moved* is *other-to* this *principle-One* and consists of a mixture of both One and 'not-One'. The motive, as the motion, is entirely reflexive. Proclus describes it as the regard of the *self-moved* towards itself, its self-observation [*epistreptikos*]. Whereas this singular-Good lacks nothing, since it has no desire for other, the motive of the autonomous generator is desire towards the Good.#

'Desire' is a common analogy for the motive of the *becoming*. It can be seen as the will to know/have/love oneself as *other-to-oneself*: the

---

* See above, p.50. Note that this definition of the soul is also cited in Dr John Dee's famous Preface to the first English translation of Euclid's *Elements* (1570): And in our Soul, Number bears such a sway, and has such an affinity therewith: that some of the old Philosophers taught, Man's Soul to be a Number moving itself. [35, p. 152]

\# See *Elements of Theology* [7], Prop 1-17, and specifically Prop 14 & Prop 17 where *epistreptikos* is translated as 'turning upon itself', but could be to 'regarding itself'. See also Plutarch's *Isis and Osiris*, where he says the Egyptians belief in Isis expresses something akin to 'I came by myself' which is indicative of autokinesis. [36, p. 376a-b]

Chapter 8: The Dynamics of Form

desiring-self wants to be its own object. It can be a self-regard, a self-possession or a self-love. This *desire-for-the-other* is formally found to be a desire for the same, as the desire for *the-same-as-other*. In this way all 'otherly' love is self-love: the love of the figure for the ground; the love of the presence for its absence. The elementary form of the expression of otherly love is the activity of *entering-other*, even when it is a *being-entered-by-other*. The man wants to come inside the women. The women wants to be 'comed'. The motive is this rude and this crude. The women allures, entices, tempts a presence into her absence. Coitally they are the lover and the beloved. The lover's motive extends to a desire to plant the seed of himself within himself on his other side. He wants to become in his other. The sexual analogy is old. A version of the Egyptian creation story has the father of becoming masturbating an ejaculation into his own mouth (i.e., a vagina-like absence within himself) and then spewing out all creation.*

The crude characterisation of sex in this analogy—with the male as presence and active, and the female as absence and receptive—is often taken as unbecoming of woman. Here we have yet another example of a failure to recognise the mystical value of the **unmarked** state. Denying this basic sexual difference in a pretended equality of the present-active, is to deny precisely the feminine value. And in so doing, it blocks a deeper understanding of the generative principle. The space prior to the First Distinction is **unmarked**. If the First Distinction is seen as the self-generation of this space, then its **unmarked** side suggests the underlying *being* prior to the activity that begets all becoming via the becoming of the First Distinction.

In this view, the true coincidence of opposites—the Platonic One beyond *becoming* and even beyond the absolute *being* of *One-and-its-opposite*—is arrived at via this absolute feminine void.# And in this view, this primary naught, this absolute zero, is the source (mother) as well as the object (beloved) of Re-Entry. The source is reached through *desirelessness*, while *desiring-the-source* serves to negate it, to violate it, in a desire-driven transgression that is the very creative principle. All masculine desire has shades of Oedipus re-entering his mother. And so in this deeper mysticism, this principal absence is recognised to be, by desire, the mother of all.

---

* There are various versions of the Egyptian self-creation myth involving 'Altum', the self-creator, and 'Khepri', the *becoming*. See Pritchard [37] p. 6 & Lamy [38] p. 8–9.
\# See *Republic* p. 508e-509b, a passage that served as one of the key sources for the 'negative way' in Proclus, Pseudo-Dionysus and the Christian tradition of Mystical Theology.

MATHEMATICAL EPISTEMOLOGY

This feminine origin finds expression in the Christian myths of Mary the *mother-of-God* beautifully assembled and recounted by Archbishop Jacob Varagine in the penultimate Medieval textual authority, *Legenda Sanctorum* (later *'The Golden Legend'*). Mary's great attribute is her virginity. Born immaculate, without a mark, the empty purity of her womb is a worthy tabernacle of God. It is unto this place that God spirits down to conceive himself in flesh. The son, so born, is the original first-born Son-God, the *Logos*, now incarnated as Jesus Christ for his special duties on Earth. After their heroic completion he ascends bodily into Heaven and takes the place of the Father as ruler of the universe. But seated in his lofty throne this Son-King still yearns for his mother, eventually proceeding down with angels and virgins and calling to her:

Figure 8.1: The Mother-Bride
A mosaic of 1140 AD in the central apse of Santa Maria in Trastevere, Rome, shows Christ embracing his mother as bride with the caption: Come my chosen one I shall place thee on my throne. Surrounded by a proud party of contemporary church leaders, the Mother-Bride already wears her crown while her Son's wreath of victory is spirited from the Father above. This is not the first Roman church dedicated to the Mother-Goddess, and Charlemagne had long before so dedicated his palace church in Aarchen, but it does appear just before great cathedrals were to rise up across Europe in her hallowed name.

> Come, my chosen one, and I shall place thee upon My throne, for I have desired your beauty!

And She answers:

> My heart is ready, O Lord, my heart is ready.

And then the chorus sings:

> This is she whose bed was free of sin, and who shall have fruit in the reflection of holy souls!

Jesus Christ in Heaven appeals to his unmarked mother not as a son but as a suitor. He wants to make her his queen. And his wish commands Mary's

Chapter 8: The Dynamics of Form

Figure 8.3: Vierge Ouvrante

The Virgin statue above left (ca. 1300) opens to reveal that the Mother of God contains her Son holding his cross. The crucifixion of her Son is pre-eminent among the seven stations of *her* life—the others forming a triptych on the open wings. A common variant of these popular medieval icons opens to reveal the entire Trinity inside (see on the right where the winged Spirit is now lost). The Russian-doll topology unambiguously presents the unmarked, feminine god-mother all-encapsulating. While these icons were declared to be depicting the mother of salvation, not the mother of creation, it was due to the overpowering suggestion of supreme priority that they were destroyed after the Reformation, even on the Catholic sides. Rome reined-in the cult of the *virgin-mother-of-all* by declaring her as only the material cause, in the Aristotelian sense, of the *generation-by-the-Spirit* of the god-man saviour.

soul to arise for her Heavenly coronation. Next is the scene of Mary's carnal assumption. Miracles thwart the efforts of the (anti-Christian Jewish) townsfolk to burn the body that bore the seducer, and this seducer so accused indeed gushes:

> Arise my dear one, my dove, tabernacle of glory, vessel of life, Heavenly temple...*

At this Mary's body is united with her soul and she is assumed into the Heavenly bride chamber. Mary becomes the bride of Christ. The Son-God's love

---
* *The Golden Legend*, Ch 119, in [39], p. 465–8]. The canonical sources for the divine king's sexual desire are 'Song of Songs' and Psalm 45. The Immaculate Conception of Mary, a feast day since 1476, became Catholic dogma only in 1854. The Assumption of Mary was formally accepted into Catholic doctrine in 1950, but only after 3,387 cardinals, patriarchs, archbishops and bishops petitioned for its proclamation during the preceding 100 years. [40, p. 92] For more on the development and variations of this myth see Warner [40], Ch 6.

MATHEMATICAL EPISTEMOLOGY

for his mother matures into a desire that is unmistakably sexual and unmistakably physical. The majestic archetype of Christian love is a perfect unadulterated incest of the Oedipal kind. But there is no trick of fate and no eye gouging, only an exulted affirmation of the desire of the first-begotten to re-enter the place, the unmarked space, of his birth.

This flamboyant depiction of Mary as the object of desire contrasts with Mary, peaceful, passive and pure, the epitome of invocation. This is the Madonna of the side chapel, and of all the annunciation icons. Depictions of Mary passively awaiting spiritual coitus were sometimes painted in meditation cells and often also depicted in stone with the spiritual trajectory crossing the arches through which one enters the magnificent wombs of Our Lady's own dedicated cathedrals, as though passing through the scene of the Virgin's spiritual visitation would help the emptying of the soul and open the way for divine grace to visit its single mark of absolute plenitude.

This allegory of Mary became so overpowering in both Byzantium and Western art that just as the Son

Figure 8.2: Mother-Goddess

a) *Coronation of the Virgin*
Fra Angelico ca. 1432

b) *Annunciation*
Fra Angelico, 1426

c) *Christ in majesty*, Royal Portal Notre Dame, Chartres, France

---

The Royal Portal at Chartres (8.2.c) presents the quintessential Romanesque symbol of the Christ as ruler and creator. The son is within the mandorla—symbolising the mother from whom and in whom he creates and rules. Sometimes he holds a book or globe—signifying his universal rule. Other times he holds a geometer's compass to guide his orderly creation. Here he is surrounded by the symbols of the four canonical accounts of his acts and sayings. Elsewhere these four are within a square signifying the four directions and the four corners of the world.

Chapter 8: The Dynamics of Form

had supplanted the Father as the king in Heaven and creator of the physical universe (and it is mostly the unmistakable young face of Jesus that we see), this story of the Mother, in turn, came to overwhelm the story of Jesus. It is not Our Saviour (and his mother), it is the Madonna (and her son). In many parts of Europe, from England to Tuscany, and up until the Reformation, the New Year was celebrated on the Annunciation, 25 March, despite all the difficulties this date caused for the celebration of her son's great work, with the New Year arriving sometimes before, sometimes after and sometimes during the movable feasts of Easter.

In her supreme exultation, Mary is not only *Queen-of-the-Universe* but also the *Mother-of-Creation* as *Mother-of-(the-Creator)-God* [*Theotokos*], a doctrine that remains alive and well in Eastern Churches. In the West, before the Reformation, the Son's divine mother-wife is also hard to avoid in surviving art and architecture. Yet this mysticism of the feminine origin is never so commanding and never so finely expressed in Christianity as it always has been in Asian religions.

Consider only Daoism. The Dao itself is this *absence-of-becoming* that is also its sufficient origin. The Dao begets a binary Yin/Yang, interpreted in the static as absence/presence and in the dynamic as receptive-/active. Some translations of the 5th and 6th propositions of *Dao De Jing* ['Tao Te Ching' ca. 5th century BC] seem to point the way to the undifferentiated *being*, and then to its *becoming*:

> Ever desireless, one can see the mystery.
> Ever desiring, one can see the manifestations.

The Dao *desireless* is the mystical absence; the unmoved unnameable, which is yet recognised as the indistinct origin of the first distinction, Heaven, in the negation of which all Earthly things come to be. The Dao *desiring* is the dynamic form, particular in its name, distinguished and distinguishing, the mother of all things.*

In Platonism, Sufism, and Christian mysticism there is a tradition of mystical ascent from profane desire towards a desire for the divine and a complete sexual union with the divine as lover and beloved. Beyond this, the mystic reaches a *union-without-distinction* when the lover becomes the

---

* Translation of *Dao De Jing*, by Laozi, Ch 1 by Gia-Fu Feng [41]. Compare with Nicholas of Cusa's discussion of the Triune origin: For in the case of God we must, as far as possible, precede contradictories and embrace them in a simple concept. For example, in God we must not conceive of distinction and indistinction as two contradictories but [must conceive of] them as antecedently present in their own most simple Beginning, where distinction is not anything other than indistinction; and then we will conceive more clearly that the Trinity and the oneness are the same thing. For where distinction is indistinction, Trinity is oneness; and, conversely, where indistinction is distinction, oneness is Trinity. *On Learned Ignorance*, Bk I, Ch 19 [23, p. 73]

beloved in an unbounded love.* This union is described as a death of desire (or death of wilfulness) which allows union with the *will-of-the-Creator*, and thus with all Creation. For Marguerite Porete, a Beguine mystic burned alive by the inquisition in 1310, it is 'Lady Love' [*Dame Amour*] who guides one to this divine love by renouncing self-will and knowledge. [44] I leave it here for the reader to find other analogies of these two principles in other mystical traditions. For now, we will consider only the motive for Re-Entry as it appears in modern Empiricism and its scepticism. I want to show here how the confused application of this principle of 'manifestation' within this non-mystical tradition has led to its inevitably self-contradiction, and, thereby, to its scepticism.

The Motive of the New Scepticism

You will recall the argument in Part I that the fundamental contradiction of representational epistemology, as noted by George Berkeley, is an inevitable outcome of the elementary methodology of modern philosophy. Whether the element be *predication* or *signification* or some other type of code, the consensus in modern method is a methodological element that is *other-referring*. That is to say, whatever is the object of knowing is *other-to* that which marks it. The subject refers to the predicate, the sign to the signified, the code to the encoded.

Consider the sign. It consists of the **signifier** and the **signified**. The **signifier** refers to the **signified** and, in the act of signification it is equated with it. Yet, in the sign, what is signified is exactly *not* the **signifier**. The 'motion' of the sign can be presented thus:

Signifier $\Rightarrow$ **not-Signifier**

The operation of signification is of the form *something-becoming-its-other* familiar to us as the form of Re-Entry. Our formal method finds that the sign is indeed elementary, but it is elementary *dynamics*. We find that, in semiotic elementism, *the elementary dynamics is taken for the elementary identity*. We can now see how, due to this elementary error, every attempt to use the semiotic method tends to regress into paradox and scepticism.

Our formal method has brought us to understanding why the semiotic element is indefinite, incomplete and incontinent. The Distinction by

---

* For Plato, see *Symposium*. For Sufism, see the poetry of Rumi. For Christianity, see Ramon Llull [42] & [43].

comparison is definite and complete in its very marking of itself. Distinction is the sufficient form of every object and of every unit of experience, and it is the form of the very knower itself. By contrast, when the unit of knowledge is the sign, then, in its very attempt to signify, we find a motive for Re-Entry. This is the difference between a Distinction indicated and a signified signified. The first is in itself a static unity, while the second is a generator of a dynamic process. Signification is an operation that produces signifiers. As the Port Royal *Logic* explained back in 1662, there is no inherent way of stopping this process. The motion from word to meaning, to *meaning-of-meaning*,…or, otherwise, from signifier, to signified, to *that-signified-by-the-signified*,…can now be seen as another way of expressing our simple ordinal series:

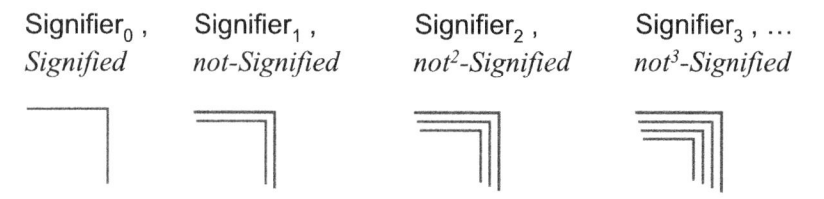

$Signifier_0$, $Signifier_1$, $Signifier_2$, $Signifier_3$, …
Signified   *not-Signified*   *not²-Signified*   *not³-Signified*

Let us now consider the act of external reference in epistemological representation itself. In Chapter 3 above, simple external reference is reduced to the propositional form A is B_{not-A}. In the reference of the word 'table' to *the-table-in-itself*, what I know (*the-table-in-itself*) is, in my perception of it, exactly what I do not know. In other words, whenever *the-table-in-itself* is defined in words or given in sensations, it is always materially and necessarily beyond these words and these sensations. This reference to the represented object can now be seen as of the form *something-becoming-its-other*. The elementary form of representational epistemology is revealed a potent generator of Re-Entry. In general we can say: driven by its *other-referring* elements, Representational Epistemology can only affect a self-referencing loop, where the external reference is only a *becoming-other-of-the-same*. Jacques Derrida's notion of deferred difference (différance) points to the devastating sceptical consequences of this use of this formal dynamics. In an environment where mystical foundations are unacceptable, and where the consensus of the code is all pervading, this devastation is total.*

---

* See above, p. 61. Compare Derrida's semiotic analysis with the logical analysis in Plato's *Parmenides*, p. 137ff. Plato and Derrida provide invigorating re-reading in the light of formal Re-Entry.

In the context of French philosophical semiotics, Derrida had discovered the same motive as Spencer Brown at roughly the same time. But there is a striking contrast in the epistemological consequences they each saw in it, and also in the attention their accounts each received. Re-Entry appeared at another pivotal point in recent philosophy and the response was different yet again. Sixty years before the publications of both Derrida and Spencer Brown, Russell discovered that his *universe-of-classes* required a class that is one of its own members. Russell was forced to deal with a class whose wont is to re-enter itself, as part of itself, and to do so again and again without end. The motive to Re-Entry here can be interpreted as an initial misunderstanding of the nature of identity. The whole is taken for its expressed part. The **marked** space is mistaken for the Form. This elementary error eventually expresses itself as a Re-Entry at the outer limit in the equation:

Universe = Universe(not-not-Universe)

This initial and elementary confusion of the part with the whole goes unrecognised in logical method, and so when the logician discovers Re-Entry by way of this confusion, it is taken as a monstrosity. In general, throughout the history of positive linguistic method, we witness successive discoveries of elementary self-reference and the horror with which the discovery is almost universally met. And so too, we witness it hurriedly denied, forcibly terminated, quietly suppressed or pointedly outlawed. What we now recognise as a principle of sound method was rejected every time due to a misunderstanding of its elementary role. And we now find the truth in Poincaré's mock celebration of Russell's discovery of the Logical Paradox. (See above on page 57.) He said that with the paradox, logic can at last go beyond tautology, and so it is no longer barren. For us, the paradox expresses perfect self-reference as the very generator of knowledge; it is the fertile principle in the foundations of arithmetic outlined by George Spencer Brown.

Having pointed to this error in the prevailing post-Enlightenment accounts of science, it is worth stating explicitly what is already implicit, that is, that this account of science does not at all discount the importance that a *belief* in the external referent can play in the *generation* of knowledge. Consider the paradigmatic example of 'matter' in Aristotelian form/matter dualism. Where this dualism persisted in the physics of the last 150 years, we could, in hindsight, define its 'matter' as the name for the elementary form of things one step beyond the scale at which technology permits its observation. A belief that the essential *being* of matter is at this one step beyond our knowledge has undoubtedly motivated research up to Heisenberg's Uncertainty Principle and beyond. If one is striving to know the external material *object-in-itself*, belief in its existence serves to motivate the generation of knowledge. Desiring *the-other-as-the-same* is the same as desiring *the-same-as-the-other*. In both cases, the desiring *in its striving* is necessarily *never satisfied*, and so may continue apace unless scepticism intervenes. The persistent belief that the end of physics is just beyond the horizon of knowing has tended to encourage the scientist to strain more keenly at the glass, to pull harder on the oars and so hasten towards the perpetually promised land. In this way, our 'ever desiring' to know the unknowable has helped us, as the *Dao De Jing* would say, to see the manifestations.

The contradiction between this motive of knowledge and an appreciation of its truth condition is much like the contradiction of capitalism, where the *desire-for-more* generates wealth, but only in the quiescence of this desire is one able to truly appreciate its value. On the Sabbath one would rest and reflect upon the true source and creator of all the wealth. Likewise, with science: we need rest from the generation of knowledge in order to reflect on its creation. Philosophy of science is not another science but only ever a discourse for contemplation upon our day of rest.

Being and Being Known

Our account of science is now complete but for a clear statement of the relationship between *being* and *knowing*. I have described a self-referring epistemology where the ontological objects of my *knowing* are *present* in my experience, *constructed* in my experience and *other to* my experiencing—but in no way beyond, or external, to my experience. This is our 'Idealism'. It is an ontology *internal* to its epistemology. Yet, this is not the whole story of the relation between *being* and *knowing*. There is, in the mystical approach to science, *being* that is not constituted within *knowing*. This is the 'feminine' *being*, the unknowing *being* of the knower that I invoked above (page 133). It can be experienced negatively in *knowing*, as per the Cartesian *cogito*, but it can also be experienced positively in *unknowing*, as the very void of *knowing*.

In our account of Form, the First Distinction is *being-generating-knowing*. It does this by distinguishing itself and re-entering itself. All knowledge begins with such a Distinction, and so knowledge can be defined as the self-differentiated *being* of the knower. Where we have said that *things-of-the-world* are 'in the mind,' we can now see them as in the being of the knower. Known objects are Distinctions of the knower's *being*. We could turn this statement around by calling this primary ontology 'my world,' or 'the world,' and then present the knowing of things *as the world distinguishing itself from itself and observing itself as other*.

This account of the relation of *being* to *knowing* would not amount to much unless the reader considers it in terms of some direct experience. In order to consider this view of science it is helpful to have experienced an unthinking state of sensible awareness where the observer/observed distinction has collapsed. Pathways beyond this to an 'unknowing' enlightenment are found in every mystical tradition, including Christian mysticism, but all these paths have been alienated from Western science and its philosophy since the 18th century Enlightenment. The liberation of natural philosophy and science from any theological foundations was undertaken by the Enlightenment advocates of science in rejection of the renaissance of theosophical science begun in the 15th century. Nicholas of Cusa's doctrine of learned ignorance, was an early (if flawed) attempt to project the monastic *via negativa* methodology back into its mathematical context. Much later was Descartes' method of turning the sceptic's regressive doubt toward this ontological ground. With mystical method all but extinguished in our tradition, the reader will find it easier to seek out popular Eastern pathways to this unknowing source of knowing (e.g., Hindu, Buddhist, Daoist). In the meantime, and especially for readers not of a religious bent, I will continue by taking a 'common sense' secular route towards a complete account of the foundation of knowing in the *being* of the knower.

For the secular scientist it is a practical truism to say that the experience and knowledge of an organism are epiphenomena of its *being*. For the neuro-psychologist, when the rat dies, so too does its perceptions, its thoughts, and its learning. Now, if we see humans as organisms, we can infer that when my colleague dies she also stops seeing and thinking. Common sense tells me that being alive is a precondition for cognition. And common sense tells me that my feelings, visions and thoughts happen within me—they are aspects of *my* being.

Chapter 8: The Dynamics of Form

This common sense path takes us so far, but it leaves us in a contradiction which can be questioned thus:

How do I know, in the first place, the <u>being</u> of my colleague as anything other than <u>being</u> in <u>my</u> knowing?

The answer comes indirectly. Let us call 'my colleague' '*you*', as though '*you*' were someone familiar to me. I know *you* through my experience of you, including my experience of our linguistic and other semiotic communication. The *you* I know is not the you that is your *I*, but the you presented in my experience. I also know that I also present myself in our mutual experience when I communicate with you. Through this communication I infer that behind the *you* that I know is an *I* that I don't know, but which is similar to my *I*. So, while I may act on a basic assumption of your *knowing-I*, I only suppose its existence *indirectly* through my knowledge of myself.

Second Order Observation

This indirect knowledge of other knower-observers is a case of what has been called Second Order Observation.* Below Second Order Observation is First Order Observation, which is my *being* distinguishing itself from itself and observing itself as other. Below this is what we might call Zero Order Observation, where experience remains undistinguished from the observer. How we advance from this pre-knowing state to our ordinary social realm of Second Order Observation now warrants a clearer presentation.

Zero Order Observation is unthinking experience sometimes called 'being at one with the world' or 'in a state of presence'. It is a state of consciousness but not of self-consciousness. *I am the world (but I don't know it)*. There is no recollecting, anticipation, analysis, judgement or interpretation of what is experienced. The world may be distinguished but it is not marked-up in a indicative system. It is pre-thought, pre-linguistic and, in fact, entirely pre-semiotic.

In First Order Observation the *observing-I* is awake to experience the world as other. And the observer may think about what it sees. *I* judges, compares, and remembers as *I* takes in experiences, and so *I* can be

---
* This account of Second Order Observation is derived from that of Niklas Luhmann in [45].

actively constructing the world. *Is this real or is this an illusion? Is that a gunshot or a backfire?* (Signs and language, as tools of communication operating at the next level, may aide this process.) I am conscious of myself as having experiences, but I am not conscious of myself as other observers might observe me. This is naked Adam and Eve before they fell into a self-consciousness of their appearance. Self-consciousness only comes through Second Order Observation.

Second Order Observation occurs within First Order Observation when I observe other observers observing our common experience from their point of view. It is through this Second Order Observation that I know what I don't experience, and it is how I know what I *cannot ever* experience. It is the order of semiotically *mediated* knowing. It is the realm of the social—the semiotic communication between observers. It is like there is a big event—say, the Fire of London long ago, or a protest rally yesterday—and every participant experiences it differently. In the rally, some are up front and can hear the speakers, while others are up the back. Some stand near the drumming ferals, others are near where the scuffle starts. A speaker knows what its like to speak, but not what its like to be in her audience, and so she asks *How did I go?*, which means *How did I appear to you?* Every experience of the event is unique to every participant, and yet, by sharing accounts of experiences after the event, participants, observers and historians come to develop a common picture of the event and where they fit into it. But this picture is never absolutely independent. In Second Order Observation there is no absolute, or 'objective', view. There is only ever an amalgamation, accord or communion of various accounts of subjective observations.

One set of relative Second Order Observations that are important to each of us as members of society are those upon which the *I* infer the *observing-I* behind *you*. Another is *my* observations of the observations others make of myself. This is important because it is essential for my communication and participation in society to know how I appear to others. From this feedback is constructed the self-conscious '*me*', a projection of my *I* into my world generated to correspond with how I perceive your observations of myself as '*you*'. In other words, self-consciousness is about surmising what I can never know about myself directly: how I appear to you. It is both Adam's shame and Narcissus' pride.

We now have an account of the persons of speech: '*I*' as the 'first person' observer and generator of my world; '*you*' as my observations of you generated in my world; and '*me*' as my projection of myself as another 'second person singular' in my world. Our speech can show the way. Consider the nature of the observation expressed in, and indicated by, this parental imperative to Second Order Observation: *Look at me while I am talking to you!* Consider also reflexive statements. We might say *I look at myself* but we never say *I look at my I* because the experience, or 'awareness', of the *I* as itself is not an observation (not an *observation-of-other*) and so cannot be expressed in the subject/predicate form.

If we return again to the Zero Order of Observation, then this retreat from observation into the *absolute-being-behind-all-knowing* is a retreat into the pre-logical, and yet it can find expression linguistically in a very special sentence that is without predication, that is, the affirmation *I am*. The great *I-am* of the Jews.* The foundational *being-of-all* may also be found through the Yogic mantra *So hum*, or *I am that*. It also arrives in the Sufi self-affirmations: *Subhani!* and *Ana al-Haqq!* In Sufism, the way to the principle unity of the soul is in finding, then dissolving, the principle opposition (not-God/God or I/you or lover/beloved). In Descartes, the retreat is from an awareness of my knowing (cogito) to an awareness of my unknowing being (sum). The simplest sentence. The pre-logical affirmation. Sum.

Conclusion

This account of knowing revolving around the *being* of the *self-observing-I* challenges two principle assumptions of scientific practice. The first is the assumption that there is an absolute world of objects beyond all points of view. This assumption is behind the notion that good experimental scientific practice is the striving for the 'objectivity' of data rather than, say, the predictability of results. This assumption is sometimes presented as a striving for the 'God's eye view'. The other assumption is, to continue the analogy, as though the scientific observer is this Godly *eye-in-the-sky* that sees everything happening below but is not himself part of it.# In order to perpetuate this pretence to the external neutrality of the observer, the young scientist is taught how to rigorously remove all subjectivity from her written accounts.

---

* Yahweh said to Moses I am who I am and This is what you must say to them: 'The one who is called I AM has sent me to you.' [Exodus 3, 14] Note that the Hebrew word for 'I am' has close associations with 'Yahweh', and so here in the name of the father is the Cartesian 'Sum'.

\# Note that, while we may call our *observing-I* a 'god', this 'god' generates the world through observing itself, it is therefore not an *independent* observer of the world as is envisaged here.

Another way to characterise this independent observer is as Gilbert Ryle's 'ghost in the machine', and this leads us to one of the most striking and resilient legacies of theology in our ostensibly atheistic science. The *I* observes from the point of view of the soul, which is not bodily, but enters the body and inhabits the body and controls the body. Ryle's ghost is not *the-other-side-of-the-being-of-things*, as we would have it, but it is, instead, in a place of observation *independent* from that which is observed. Sometimes in this doctrine the soul is also considered to leave the body upon death, and so this 'ghost' is often associated with doctrines of the immortality of the soul; but the notion of immortality is not exclusive to this doctrine, as 'immortality' could otherwise refer to, say the immortality of Form in a Platonic dualism. What we are talking about here is not *I* 'participating' Form, but *I* inhabiting body. This vision of a *ghost-inhabiting-body* is the source of the mind/body problem often associated with Descartes, but it was only brought into crisis by him, while it can be traced back in a continuous line through the Western tradition and beyond the Christian era.*

Again I remind the reader that philosophy of science often has a life somewhat independent from the practice of science itself, and so these two assumptions are often limited to the account/justification/propaganda of science. Moreover, even where these dogmas do influence scientific practice, their effect is not always negative. One time when this sort of 'objectivity' did have a great impact on practice came with a push towards establishing a sound scientific foundation for psychotherapy in the latter half of the 20th century. This foundation was sought in the empirical observations of the behavioural signs of the mental activity of humans and rats. This was undertaken in an explicit rejection of more direct means derided as 'subjective'. In the name of science, 'experimental psychology' rejected its role as the first science—i.e., the introspection of the knowing mind—to instead, place itself most exposed to the Berkeleian critique. That is to say, no matter how much it tries to found itself in objective facts, the science of mind can only ever be a product of mind, and therefore entirely subjective. The prevailing subjective approach of this time, Psychoanalysis, did not make this error, although, indeed, it was imploding due to schismatic dogmatism, lack of clinical success, and perhaps even due to its

---

* This 'ghost' appears most explicitly in Descartes' *Discourses* directly after the 'Sum' ontology is confirm, and it leads the discussion towards the mind/body problem: ...this 'I'—this 'I' that is, the soul by which I am what I am—is entirely distinct from the body, and indeed is easier to know than the body, and would not fail to be whatever it is, even if the body did not exist. [34, Pt 4, p. 33].

Chapter 8: The Dynamics of Form

insistence on a subjective epistemological foundation. For Sigmund Freud [1856-1939] the epistemological foundation of Psychoanalysis is in self-analysis. The analyst's direct investigations of his/her own psychology is an essential prerequisite for investigations (via Second Order Observation) of the psychology of others.*

The recent and monumental failure of a psychotherapy founded in a 'subjective' epistemology does nothing to encourage attempts to rebuild the foundations of science upon this much maligned ground. If calling it 'subjective' is misguided, then we prefer 'mystical' or 'enthusiastic'. But a better name for our introspective means might be *'in-quiry'* and its results *'in-sight'*. And so it can be said that we are now armed and ready to engage with the long tradition of *in-quiry* in our scientific history, if only by reviving the *in-sights* of the Pythagoreans.

---

* On knowing the consciousness of others only by inference, see Freud's 1915 essay 'The Unconscious': the assumption of a consciousness in [others] rests upon an inference and cannot share the immediate certainty which we have of our own consciousness. [46, p. 171] On the necessity of self-analysis to Freud's teachings, see his Preface to An Outline of Psycho-Analysis: The teachings of psycho-analysis are based on an incalculable number of observations and experiences, and only someone who has repeated those observations on himself and on others is in a position to arrive at a judgement of his own upon it. [47, p. 9]. For Freud discussing his own self-analysis see his letters to Fleiss, and also see James Strachey's commentary [48, p. 19–20]. The importance of self-analysis to therapy is given in Freud's recommendations to physicians practising psycho-analysis. See [49], p. 360.

PART III

ENTHUSIASTIC MATHEMATICS

Let no Greek ever be afraid that we ought not at any time to study things divine because we are mortal.... God...is of course perfectly aware that he does teach us, and that we learn, the very subject we are now discussing, number and counting; if he fails to know this, he would show the greatest want of intelligence, the God we speak of would not know himself.
Epinomis

Why ever did God bid Socrates...act as midwife to others but prevent him from himself begetting?

...What Socrates held to be alone wisdom, which he called passion for the divine and intelligibles, is for humans a matter not of generation or of discovery but of recollection. For this reason Socrates was not engaged in teaching anything but by exciting perplexities as if inducing the inception of labour-pains in young men he would arouse and quicken and help to deliver their innate conceptions; and his name for this was 'obstetric skill', since it does not, as other men pretended to do, implant in those who come upon it intelligence from without, but shows that they have it native within themselves but undeveloped and confused and in need of nurture and stabilization.
Plutarch

Today the depth of Pythagorean thought cannot be perceived except by using a sort of intuition. And one cannot exercise such an intuition except from inside; that is to say, only if one has truly drawn spiritual life from the texts studied.
Simone Weil

Introduction to Part III

The aim of these chapters is to offer a sympathetic interpretation of the Pythagorean attempts to find the mathematical emanation that is elementary to science. This interpretation is made in the light of *Laws of Form*. The premise is that the Pythagorean mathematical investigations offer an historical context to this work by George Spencer Brown, and, at the same time, *Laws of Form* opens up a means towards understanding Pythagorean emanationism.

The style of this presentation is in the development of an hypothesis. This development has three simultaneous layers. The first layer is an account of the nature of arithmetic. The second layer is a projection of how the Pythagoreans understood this nature. The final layer is the fragmentary evidence we have of this understanding. Such a hypothetical approach has always been controversial because it puts the theory before the evidence. It tries to match the evidence to a preconceived theory. The defence of hypothetical method often points to moments in the history of science where great leaps of understanding seem to have come about only by stepping out of conventional ways of understanding the evidence and trying on new ones. This is what is required for a better historical understanding of the project and the achievements of the Pythagoreans. The main problem with conventional scholarly interpretations of the evidence, from Aristotle onwards, is that they have little sympathy with the underlying mysticism. And if you are blind to the mysticism then, while you can still see much of the action, you miss the main game.

During the late 19th and early 20th centuries, extraordinarily thorough philological examinations of the remaining evidence allowed, as never before, a clear evaluation of the developments of Greek science; and it is upon this foundation that some excellent 20th century histories are based.* That these histories reflect the prevailing attitudes to number, and to the role of mathematics in philosophy, is quite natural; a history of the formal sciences can't help but write about prior discoveries and developments as steps towards (or away from) the truth as viewed in the present. The result is that these interpretations are, at best, strained in their

---

* Hermann Diels' *Die Fragmente der Vorsokratiker* includes a collation of authenticating fragments of pre-Platonic authors first published in 1903. The 5th edition, edited by Walther Kranz, ([1] & [2]) remains the standard reference and we use it here. Other results of the scholarship upon which our study is heavily reliant are Heath's edition of Euclid [3] and his History [4].

appreciation of what these first mathematicians were trying to do, and the extent to which they achieved their goal. Furthermore, recent attempts to re-evaluate the Pythagorean legacy as a mystical mathematics of generation remain marginal to scholarly controversy, and so lack the refinement that can be the fruit of such controversy.*

In these chapters then, I take a familiar although less travelled path, carrying with me *Laws of Form* as an interpretative guide. My attempt thus far to persuade the modern reader towards finding the foundations of science in a mathematical emanation provides the necessary introduction to this re-evaluation of the Pythagoreans, and so these chapters seem well placed here. However, there is no doubt that they lack the refinement of work within a scholarly context. I decided to persist with this study, despite my concerns about its scholarly rigour, in the hope that its very sympathy, if not its accuracy, will awaken the reader to a reconsideration of what these early scientists were trying to achieve and how close they came to achieving it.

---

* See for example *Sacred Geometry* by Robert Lawlor [5] and, earlier, Simone Weil's *Intimations of Christianity among the Ancient Greeks*, Chapter XI [6]. Influential on 20th century 'esoteric' scholarship in English was Thomas Taylor [1758–1835], especially his *Theoretic Arithmetic of the Pythagoreans*.[7]

Chapter 9
THE MATHEMATICI

[The Phythagoreans] consider number to be the principle, both as the matter for things and as forming both their modifications and their permanent states. The elements of number, according to them, are the just and the excessive. Of these the former is limited and the latter unlimited; The One consists of both; numbers are derived from The One; and numbers, as we have said, compose the whole heaven.

Aristotle

Number has a treble state: One, in the Creator; an other in every Creature (in respect of his complete constitution); and the third, in Spiritual and Angelical Minds, and in the soul of man. In the first and the third state, Number is termed Number numbering, but in all Creatures, otherwise, number is termed Number Numbered. And in our Soul, number bears such a sway, and hath such an affinity therewith: that some of the old Philosophers taught man's soul to be a number moving itself....Number numbering...is the discretion discerning, and distincting of things. But in God the Creator the discretion in the beginning produced orderly and distinctly all things, For his Numbering then was his Creating of all things. And his continual Numbering, of all things, is the conservation of time in being.

John Dee

What kind of science is Pythagorean science?

Pythagorean science is not an empirical science. Nor is it aimed towards technological advance. We should think of it more as a theology, and compard it with our Christian theories of the Creator, of his Creation and of the way by which he creates. Its orientation is entirely towards the formal or mystical realm. As a cultural phenomenon, Pythagoreanism is thoroughly religious. In fact, its original moral teachings, its rites and rules, had a strong affinity with the ancient cult of Orphism. The first Pythagorean *'mathematici'** lived a cloistered communal life, taking vows and following codes of behaviour that covered all aspects of daily life. They worshipped at temples, and Pythagoras is even said to have made a sacrifice upon the discovery of a new mathematical law. The Academy founded by Plato was different in many ways from the commune founded by Pythagoras. In the first place it was a non-residential institution within a cosmopolitan city, and yet it was exclusive and its teaching had an entirely religious character. The other great centre of mathematical research in the ancient world was the huge Greek temple complex in Alexandria, the *Serapeum*. Here the *mathematici* of Alexandria conducted their sacred investigations in a continuous tradition of monastic seclusion for seven centuries; this began at least from the time of Euclid (fl. 300 BC), and marvellous progress was made right up until Hypatia (375-415), who was eventually torn to pieces by a Christian mob during the difficult years after the final sack of the *Serapeum* in 389 AD.

The theological orientation of these mathematicians did not at all mean that their insights found no application in the world. The application of their advanced geometry in classical architecture and engineering is still evident today. Even more significant for us is that the celebrated advances in natural science of the 17th century emerged out of the context of a Pythagorean revival. For Leonardo da Vinci, Galileo and Kepler the world presented as expressing mathematical formulations emanating from the Creator. It was their sacred duty, and their act of worship, to explore and reveal the mathematical nature of his Creation.

The Historical Development of Pythagorean Science

Pythagorean science flourished in the ancient world in a continuous tradition for more than a millennium, starting with the founding of the commune by Pythagoras in the middle of the 6th century BC, and only foundering with the demise of the independent Greek schools of learning in the face of a rising Christian hegemony during the 4th and 5th centuries AD. In our examination of the Pythagoreans, the tradition divides

---

* The original *'mathematici'* were the early Pythagoreans. However *mathemata* and *mathematica* could translate more generally as 'science' and 'scientist' respectively. After Aristotle, there was non-mathematical sciences that were referred to as *mathemata*, however a narrower meaning was emerging restricted to the mathematical sciences especially as promoted by Platonists and Pythogoreans. See [4], Vol 1, p. 10–11. When Hellenistic natural science contracted to astrology, those who calculated horoscopes were *'mathematici'*.

Chapter 9: The Mathematici

historically into four main periods:

1. The pre-Platonic or 'early' Pythagoreans (5th century BC)
2. Plato and his contemporaries (late 5th and 4th century BC)
3. Hellenistic Platonism (334 BC to 5th century AD)
4. The Christian Platonic revival (15th, 16th and 17th century)

As to the originality of Pythagorean mathematics, this is of little interest to us here. Many of the theories and formulations we discuss are evident in the previous civilisation of the Phoenicians, the Sumerians and the Egyptians. There is no attempt by the Pythagoreans to hide these sources. On the contrary, they boasted them. The ancients were 'closer to the gods' and so had better access to the elementary principles if not their technical elaboration.* Greek science would be on sound footings if it began where the oracles and priests of these older civilisations left off, although it was the Egyptians who tended to receive most of the credit. Iamblichus (fl. 300 AD) claims that Pythagoras spent 22 years in the shrines throughout Egypt where he studied with the priests and prophets and instructed himself on every possible topic before spending a further 12 years in Babylon, where he consorted with the Magicians, a willing pupil of willing masters.# Similar credentials are attributed to Thales, the founder of Greek science before even Pythagoras, and to Plato, as well as other masters.+ What is of interest for us here (and this goes for the Christian Platonists as much as the ancients) is not any priority in the discovery of particular theories and formulation, but, rather, the progressive attempts by successive generations of Pythagoreans to theorise the significance of these formulation towards a complete mystical emanation. What follows is only an historical overview designed to orientate the reader to the later discussions and elaborations.

If as we are told, the Greek cult of mathematics began in the 6th century BC when the first Pythagoreans gathered around Pythagoras in Croton (Italy), then we know almost naught of it. While later writers tell tales of his life and the moral code of the commune, there are no mathematical innovations that are conclusively traced back to Pythagoras and his

---
* I use 'technical' for formulations and theories as though this is the 'art' [*techne*] of mathematics and not its underlying theology. The view that science began with the Greeks emerged in the Enlightenment against the prevailing view of the Renaissance, against the espoused view of the Greeks themselves and against the available evidence. That this view persisted into the 20th century is apparent in Burnet's account, [8], p. 4–7.
\# Iamblichus, *Life of Pythagoras*, Ch 4, translated by Heath in [4], Vol I, p. 5.
+ Others include Eudoxus, who is said to have studied in Egypt. [4, Vol I, p. 322] Plutarch in *Isis and Osiris* [p. 354e], lists Solon, Thales, Plato, Eudoxus, Pythagoras, who came to Egypt and consorted with the priests. See also Diodorus, *Library of History* Bk I, p. 96 & p. 98. See also Clement of Alexandria, *Stromateis*, Bk I, p. 69. The first book of Proclus' commentary on Euclid gives a summary of the history of geometry whereby the origins of its study are taken back to the measuring of land (*geo* = earth *metry* = measuring) in Egypt. See Heath's discussion in [4], Vol I, p. 4 & p. 121–2.

contemporaries. The first known testament to Pythagorean philosophy was written late in the 5th century BC, only after the commune had been destroyed and the members dispersed. This was almost in the time of Plato, and, in fact, the young Plato is said to have met and revered its famous author, Philolaus. Of this text only a few metaphysical fragments remain, and the earliest reliable descriptions of any specific technical work by these, the first *mathematici*, are found in Plato, Aristotle and Euclid.

After the 5th century there was a dramatic shift in the orientation of the whole philosophy. This was towards an emanation by way of the '*Logos*', or ratio, acting in continuous 'geometric' series. This revolution seems to have come about as an outcome of the crisis of 'asymmetry' in the arithmetic analysis of geometry—that is to say, it came via the solution to the problem of the irrationality of surds. The drama of this revolution occurred in and around Plato's Academy in Athens. Prominent figures in this story are: Archytas and Theodorus, older influences on Plato and his Academy; Theaetetus and Eudoxus, the two famous Academics who worked towards the solution of the problem of *asymmetrical* magnitudes; and Plato himself, who attempted to reformulate the Pythagorean philosophy in accord with this new understanding.

The work towards a new formulation of the emanation is evident in a number of passages in Plato's dialogues, but we should be careful to remember that the nature of the dialogues is discursive not affirmative, and by no means thoroughly Pythagorean. The dialogues are mostly inconclusive, interwoven accounts of various philosophical approached, including those of Heraclitus, Protagoras, Parmenides and Socrates, all of whom Plato evidently held in high esteem. The influence of these philosophers is made plain in the dialogues, but their influence is often viewed, in hindsight, within the context of a progression in Plato's thought towards a total mathematical reduction. Even if we grant that there is this tendency in the dialogues, what is truly remarkable in the doctrines of Plato's followers is not so much the complete dominance of this mathematical reductionism but the pervasiveness of a new dogma of the elementary emanation. In Platonism the Logos is elementary to the emanation from the original one, and often we find two new terms introduced to define this emanation, viz., the '*Monad*' and the '*Dyad*'. These two principles come to characterise Platonism, and yet they are barely even suggested in any of the surviving texts of Plato. Furthermore, this Platonism is what Pythagoreanism became in the Hellenistic period—the Platonic revolution in mathematical philosophy was as complete as it was irrevocable.

The best evidence we have of a proper theoretical connection between this broad movement of Platonism and the teachings of Plato is through contemporary account by Aristotle (and a few others) of the oral teaching of Plato in the Academy. It is Aristotle who is the first to announce to us the innovation that Plato made to the core doctrine of the Pythagoreans. [*Metaphysics* p. 987a29–988a15] There may well have been some long lost Academic texts giving a full account of the Dyadic emanation from the Monad, but equally likely, there may not have been any such writings. The surviving evidence suggests that the whole tradition of Platonism took off from 'unwritten' esoteric teachings of Plato and from the teachings of the 'Old Academy'. For this to have been the case is not at all surprising. A demarcation between esoteric and exoteric teachings is common in cults across the ancient world. From Egypt to China secret teaching that would be incomprehensible to outsiders, and open to misinterpretation, distortion and ridicule if published, were kept precious to those initiated by a lineage of masters. One of the most familiar such movements in ancient Greece is Orphism, with which some of the surviving descriptions of the cult of Pythagoras could easily be confused. The Orphic 'mysteries' were taught only to initiates, or through a rite of initiation.

It is likely that this secrecy is the primary reason that the high teachings of the Academic masters are lost to us, but to increase our difficulties even more, any exoteric writings of Plato's early successors have also been lost. Of these, Xenocrates' output seems to have been very influential. Indeed, he is said to have written hundreds of books, yet none have survived, and we have precious few sympathetic contemporary accounts. Aristotle's accounts are at best unengaged, at worst incredulous, even hostile. We must rely upon the more forthcoming exoteric writings of later Platonists to project back upon this period, and of these we have a more plentiful supply, including whole philosophical treatises by Plotinus (205-270 AD) and Proclus (410-485 AD). But when reading back in this way we should be cautious not to project later modification (refinement or decay) in what was very much a living tradition; and we should keep in mind that Proclus, for example, is further in time from the unwritten teachings of the Old Academy than we are from the extant writings of St Thomas Aquinas. In the face of all these difficulties, it is the doctrines concerning the elementary emanation developed in the Old Academy by Plato and his immediate followers that are of particular interest to us here.

Within a century of Plato's death, around about the middle of the 3rd century BC, the Platonic teachings of the Academy were eclipsed by a controversy over materialist epistemology. At least it appears that this controversy had this impact: there may only be an eclipse in our record while in fact the old teachings continued to flourish in the background. The extent to which that was the case is a question that we should continue to pose. Nonetheless, there is a long period, of three centuries and more, when Platonic philosophy all but disappears from our view. Where it is evident, it is mostly in a degenerate form or presenting through an Aristotelianism or Stoic glass. By this time Epicurus (341-270 BC) had already advanced a complete materialist ontology of external things known to the mind via our senses. A similar Representationalism was developed by the Stoics. An attack on this Stoic epistemology was launched by Arcesilaus, Plato's successor in the (revived) Academy and it descended into scepticism. Whether this scepticism was at times an exoteric defence of continuing esoteric teachings of Platonic mysticism is a point of speculation. However, we do know that besides their empirical epistemology, the Stoics retained and developed the Platonic doctrine of the mystical emanation by way of the divine Logos, and this doctrine would continue to evolve in its adoption by Christianity. In this way at least, Platonic emanationism survived, even thrived.*

But materialism, at least in a form/matter or spirit/matter divide (often with Gnostic good/evil overtones) prevailed to such an extent that we find in this period the beginnings of a very un-Platonic cosmogony given as the doctrine of Plato. As a *generation-from-primary-matter* it is as though this is the cosmogony that Aristotle would have offered if he did not reject the very idea of a creative emanation. It is based spuriously on a *generation-from-disorder* (not a primary disorder) presented in one of Plato's dialogues featuring a cosmologists called *Timaeus*. This interpretation of this dialogue had reached such prominence by the Christian Middle Ages that Plato was counted not as the source of the monotheistic doctrine of *creation-from-nothing* but as its opponent.# Not until the third century

---

* The discussion of the doctrines of the previously neglected period between Plato and Plotinus is opened up by John Dillon in his *The Middle Platonists*. [9] Harald Tarrant follows Dillon's careful reconstruction and manages to transcend one prevailing misconception, viz., that scepticism (of materialism) is incompatible with (mystical) Platonism. [10]

\# Cicero was important in privileging *Timaeus* and its cosmogony in the Western tradition. Indeed, his Latin translation of the cosmological section of *Timaeus* remained important through the Middle Ages. Ficino's translations and interpretations opened up a more rounded view of the Platonic legacy, but the Medieval interpretation of *Timaeus* continued to characterise Platonism at least until the time of Kepler. Plutarch's attention to, and interpretation of, the doctrine of generation presented in *Timaeus* was more broadly influential, East and West. For a taste of this interpretations see his 'Platonic Question 2': Why did [Plato] call the supreme God the father and maker of all things? (*Moralia* p. 1001a-c). In Question 4 he explains that the bodily universe is generated by the *psyche* from disorderly and shapeless body (1003a-b). See also 'On the Generation of the Soul in the Timaeus' (*Moralia* p.1014a-b & 1014e-f). Plutarch presents an early version of a doctrine of generation that is heavily reliant on *Timaeus* and which stood in sympathy with Aristotelian ontology. This doctrine is in direct conflict

AD, during the great revival of Platonism, did Plotinus famously expel materialism from Platonic physics, winding back this primary matter to an absence of qualities. He concludes that what is called matter is the principle of difference; it is 'the other' and otherness, and at the same time it is pure negation.* Later still, well into the Christian era, Proclus would reconnect the formal emanation with its mathematics. Prior to this 'neo-Platonic' revival there is meagre evidence of continuing Platonism untainted by materialist influences. But that is not to say it is entirely absent; and in fact the mathematical theology that has survived from around the beginning of the Christian era is not only suggestive of what might be lost, but its very content is important to the story I am about to tell. In fact, if it weren't for the survival of two mathematical textbooks from this time—one attributed to Theon of Smyrna, the other to Nicomachus of Gerasa— then this story could hardly be told.

In the locality names of 'Smyrna' and 'Gerasa' there is a hint as to what might have happened during this time. Athens retained a status as the founding centre of Platonism right through the Hellenistic period, but the Old Academy was gone forever. Successive attempts to revive it were disrupted by political instability. There were even times when warfare emptied the city of all its philosophers; indeed, Roman Stoicism and Epicureanism was largely built upon the teachings of Greek masters fleeing to Rome. This disruption at its home accelerated a diaspora of Platonism across the expanding Roman Empire, which is evident in the locality names attached to the personal names of the authors of the surviving texts: Smyrna, Gerasa, Rhodes, Syracuse, Gades (Cadiz) and so forth. However, there is one locality that stands out from the rest. This large, wealthy, cosmopolitan port city became a new world centre of Platonic philosophy and theology.

Sited in Africa on the Nile delta, Alexandria grew rapidly to become the quintessential Hellenistic city. As such it also became the most important site of mathematical research and the teaching of Platonic philosophy. Already at the beginning of the 3rd century BC, when materialism was first on the rise, we find Euclid in Alexandria consolidating and systematising Pythagorean mathematical discoveries. And then it may have been Eudorus of Alexandria who was instrumental in reviving the teaching of

---

with the more Pythagorean modes of generation that were prevalent throughout the Hellenistic Platonism tradition, that were revived in the Renaissance and that are of interest to us here.
* See Plotinus, *The Enneads*, 2nd Ennead, 4th Tractate.

the Dyadic emanation in the decades just before the time of Christ.* What is clear from the record is that it was here more than anywhere else that Platonic philosophy overflowed into other traditions. Famous and historical important examples include: the *Sophia*, or Jewish 'Wisdom' books, and the writings of the Alexandrian Jewish philosopher, Philo (20 BC–40 AD); the Christian philosophy of the Alexandrian Church fathers, especially Clement of Alexandria (150-ca.215 AD) and Origen (185-254 AD); and the accounts we have of the Alexandrian heretic, Arius (fl. 300 AD), who was supported by the Eastern Church bishops after his disgrace at the Council of Nicea (325 AD).# Later came the Egyptian, Augustine of Hippo (354-430 AD). Although not Alexandrian and not proficent in Greek, Augustine's assimilation of Christianity was deeply Platonic in the Alexandrian way. His beautifully structured Latin prose tranmitted Platonic theosophy into the Western Church. In these Jewish and Christian Platonists we witness the development of the early Christian theology of the Creator-God out of a background of Platonic mystical creationism that dominated Alexandrian theology of the day; and this explains why Christian theology would remain sympathetic with remnant Greek theosophy long after the final destruction of the rival pagan institutions.

The final demise of the non-Christian Hellenistic traditions under the increasingly powerful Roman state church was soon followed by the final demise of the Roman state itself. In the Dark Ages of European culture, political instability and impoverishment left little room for the higher arts. The classical Greek texts (and Greek readers) disappeared, little was translated into Latin, and less mathematics was actually taught. During this time the legacy of mathematical theosophy was conserved in the Eastern Church, from where Islamic scholars gained access to some key texts during their mathematical renaissance. This renaissance began in Baghdad in the 9th century, but it quickly spread across the Arab world—not the least into southern Spain, where the potential for wise communication with Christian Europe was occasionally realised.+

---

* See Dillon [9], Ch 3, especially p. 126-7.
\# Philo wrote in Greek and did not know Hebrew. His views are similar to those in the Jewish *Sophia* texts, which he may have authored. Some of these writings are preserved in the Bible's Old Testament, its *Apocrypha*, and as fragments incorporated into the 'synoptic' Gospels. For discussion of the Christian Platonic theology of the anti-Nicean Church fathers and the Arian controversy, see below p. 275ff.
\+ Caliph Ma'mum ruled Baghdad from 813 to 833, where he established a 'House of Wisdom' for the preserving, translating and teaching ancient philosophy. The translations from Greek into Arabic sometimes went via Cyrillic. This Arabic renaissance that continued through the 10th century seem to have been an early medium of transmission to the West, although informal and obscure. We do know that by the early 12th century some Latin translations via Arabic appearing in Toledo. After that came the iconic figure of Ramon Llull of Majorca (1232-1316). Using his fluency in Arabic, Latin and Catalan, Llull opened up avenues of communication in his attempts to show Islamic (Greek) wisdom harmonious with Christianity.

Chapter 9: The Mathematici

The situation in Christian Europe improved sporadically with the first significant attempt to revive the old spirit when Charlemagne established his court in Aachen and negotiated a politico-religious power-share with the Patriarch of Rome; this was marked in the year 800 AD by his coronation by the 'Pope' as Holy Roman Emperor. Then, on the cusp of the 2nd Christian millennium, we find the Platonist Pope Sylvester II, promoting mathematical education armed with the Arabic numerals and abacus to aid computation. As the new millennium progressed, the Platonic quadrivium of arithmetic, geometry, astronomy and music came to be taught in the new universities, guided by the writings of the late-Roman Christian Platonist, Boethius (480-524), and by early translations of Euclid into what became the new scholarly *lingua franca*, Latin.* Throughout the late Middle Ages elementary mathematical education continued. But, almost from the beginning of the university system, and especially after St Thomas Aquinas, any residual mathematical theology would be discredited, and the Platonic 'forms' became the 'universals'—a more or less real framework abstracted from the observations of an external material world. Controversies between competing 'schools' over the 'real' (or otherwise 'nominal') status of these 'universals' heralded the arrival of Aristotelianism, and it dominated the economy of ideas in the university system for its first three centuries.#

Meanwhile in the East, a continuity of scholarship in the Greek language across 2,000 years finally ended in 1453 with the fall of Constantinople. The demise of Christian civilisation in the East during the first half of the 15th century came at the same time as destabilisation in the Western universities that eventually led to the fragmentation of 'scholasticism'. The one may even have influenced the other. And the exodus from Byzantium might even have brought some high quality ancient Greek manuscripts to the attention of an increasingly wealthy and secular Europe. Even before the final fall, it was a delegation from the imperilled East that brought a charismatic teacher of ancient Greek theosophy to seed a passion for ancient paganism among the Florentine business elite. Whatever the source, soon after Constantinople fell we find that manuscript hunters had

---

* The most common and influential Platonic text of the monastic Middle Ages was *Timaeus*. While it contains some famous cryptic mathematical passages it was not very helpful in fostering the mathematical approach. See above the note on p. 158.

The ontological status of the so-called 'universal' was the great controversies to emerge with the new universities of the 12th century. While the notion of universals is derived from the teachings of Plato, this is very much an Aristotelian derivation. Even today, in Analytic Philosophy and elsewhere, Plato continues to be viewed through just such an Aristotelian lens, and so this scholastic legacy continues to deflect his modern reception.

successfully retrieved the complete works of Plato, and the Platonic *Hermetica*. These were received with delight by the powerful Florentine banker and industrialist Cosimo de Medici, who then directed their careful translation. The translations by Marsilio Ficino were eventually set for the newly invented printing press, and the printing of other translations followed (with the more difficult graphics included), thus preparing the beds for a renaissance of ancient mathematical philosophy.*

Pythagoreanism and the Rise of Empirical Science

One peculiarity of the reception of Greek mathematical theosophy in the Christian revival still casts a shadow upon us today. This is that the theological doctrines of Platonism are alienated from the mathematical elaborations. One mark of this separation that persists is in the distinction we continue to make between Hellenistic 'Platonism' and Hellenistic 'Pythagoreanism'. While there were revivals of ethical and cultural Pythagoreanism (sometimes espousing a degenerate mathematical dogma), for the *mathematici* the Platonic revolution was all-pervasive.# After Plato, Pythagorean science could never be the same again. That is to say, the Platonic revolution in mathematical philosophy is better compared with Darwinian revolution in the biological sciences than with say, the Christian break with continuing Judaism. To the extent that we can say that modern biology is Darwinian, we can say that Hellenistic Pythagoreanism is Platonic. Despite the evidence for this, it became conventional in Western philosophy to consider separately theosophical Platonism *detached from any technical elaboration* and call this 'Platonism', while any theosophical Platonism that is *continuous with the mathematical elaborations* is often lumped in with a continuing Hellenistic 'Pythagoreanism'.

There were moments in the Renaissance when this awkward demarcation between the theosophy and its mathematics completely dissolved, but yet it soon reformed, and as a consequence modern accounts of Renaissance science tended towards blindness even to these exceptions. To some extent this distortion was redressed during the second half of the 20th

---

* It was not widely acknowledged until the 17th century that the *Corpus Hermeticum* and other most anciently attributed texts were of a Hellenistic Platonic milieu. Thus, during the Renaissance, Platonism was project back into the earliest antiquity. See discussion below from page 311.

The Pythagorean, Moderatus of Gades is perhaps the exception that proves the rule: his attempted to turn the tide of Hellenistic philosophy was overwhelmed by the Platonic and Aristotelian revolutions. He held that Plato and the Platonists were nothing but followers of Pythagoras, although not in good faith. He saw Plato, Speusippus and Xenocrates appropriating for themselves what was fruitful in the preceding Pythagorean while setting up for ridicule what was not. [9, p. 346]

century, but not entirely.* Our difficulty in trying to understand Kepler's genius is a case in point.

Any casual reader of the history of astronomy is familiar with Kepler's interest in Pythagorean motifs, but the picture we paint is often that this interest was obsessive, dogmatic and inhibitive of his genius: he *succeeded* by abandoning the Platonic dogma of circular orbits because it did not fit the data; and he *failed* by clinging to his hypothesis that the 'Platonic' regular solids spaced the planetary orbits, despite all the evidence to the contrary.

Is it Kepler, on the cusp of modern science, with one foot still dragging in the mud of ancient dogma and one foot rising to the solid ground of modern Empiricism? Or was he only progressing ancient mathematical astronomy by sometimes challenging a degenerate dogma and trying on various innovative hypothesis—but yet never abandoning the underlying principles of Platonism? There is a lot at stake here because Newton's realisation of the Copernican revolution is inconceivable without the work of this single man; and the 18th century Enlightenment had so quickly and endurably claimed Newton's success to the practice of modern Empiricism.

However we might interpret the reasons for Kepler's successes, Kepler himself presented his mathematical work as thoroughly within the tradition of theosophical Platonism. Kepler's *Harmony of the World* (1619) is presented as a completion and extension of the job begun by Proclus in his *Commentary on the First book of Euclid's Elements*, from which he quotes freely.# Only after extending Proclus' commentary by elaborating

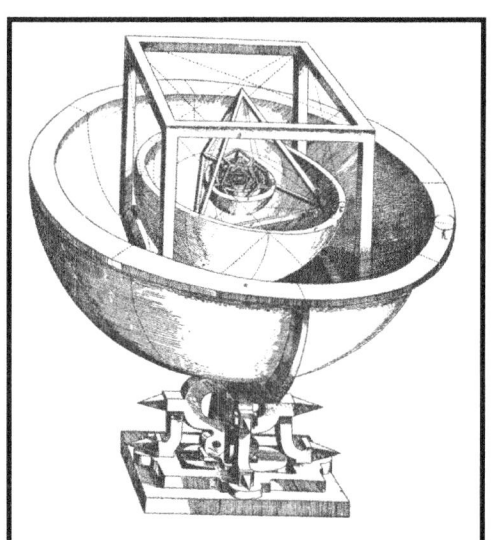

Figure 9.1: Kepler's model of the solar system with the five Platonic solids giving the key to the planetary orbits around the sun, from his early publication *The Cosmographic Mystery* (1596), which was also the first published defence of the Copernican system.

---

* In Newtonian studies the text of a tri-centenary speech that J M Keynes never presented, 'Newton the Man,' marks a turning point. [11, Vol 10 Ch 35] Other popular contributors to this turnaround were Frances Yates (see for example [12]) and Alexander Koyré (see for example [13]).
\# See [14], especially the introduction to Book I, and Bk IV, Ch 1.

harmonic proportions, does Kepler at the beginning of Book IV choose to place his 'metaphysical discussion'. Thus, it immediately precedes the fifth and final book, the famous account of planetary motion. This metaphysical discussion is primarily a defence of Platonic ontology against the Aristotelians. To this end Kepler saw fit to translate and insert almost an entire chapter of Proclus' *Commentary*. This extract opens with the question, whether mathematical forms should be regarded as abstractions from sense objects or…

> …should we rather assign to them an existence prior to sense objects as Plato demands, and as the emanational order of things indicates?

Proclus answers with a beautiful defence of the Platonic position which Kepler then affirms against prevailing scholastic Aristotelianism and its overt tendency to outright Materialism.*

For Kepler to emphasise the mathematical foundation of the natural science in his book about the world was entirely in keeping with the spirit of the Platonic revival. We might recall Galileo's famous use of the analogy of the universe as a grand book, giving it as a book of mathematical expression. (See above page 77.) Half a century earlier we find John Dee's popular Elizabethan *Preface* to Euclid. This is a gushing Renaissance invocation that follows Proclus by situating the geometry compiled in Euclid in the theological emanationism of the Divine Plato and his followers.

> The great and godly Philosopher Anicius Boethius said… *All things (which from the very first original being of things, have been framed and made) do appear to be formed by the reason of Numbers. For this was the principal example or pattern in the mind of the Creator.* O comfortable allurement, O ravishing persuasion, to deal with a Science, whose subject, is so ancient, so pure, so excellent, so surmounting all creatures, so used of the Almighty and incomprehensible wisdom of the Creator, in the distinct creation of all creatures: in all their distinct parts, properties, natures, and virtues, by order, and most absolute number, brought, from nothing, to the formality of their being and state. By numbers properties therefore, of us, by all possible means, (to the perfection of the Science) learned, we may both wind and draw ourselves into the inward and deep search and view, of all creatures' distinct virtues, natures, properties, and forms, And also, further, arise, climb, ascend, and mount up (with speculative wings) in spirit, to behold in the Glass of Creation, the Form of Forms, the Exemplar Number of all things Numerable: both visible and invisible: mortal and immortal, Corporeal and Spiritual.
> [16, p. 151]

---

* See Kepler quoting Proclus in [14], p. 298–301. The translation of Proclus is by Morrow [15, p. 10] except where 'emanational' for the Greek *'pro-odos'* is more in sympathy with our reading.

Later in the *Preface*, Dee enthuses upon a science of actual experience sensible, what Nicholas of Cusa termed...experimental science. [16, p. 195] It wasn't until the next generation of *mathematici* that the likes of Galileo and Kepler overcame conceptual difficulties—difficulties almost impossible for us to imagine in hindsight—and found some leads in the darkness that thereby allowed them to extend the ancient mathematics in systematic accounts of the phenomena. And they achieved this (despite how later generations felt about it, and however we might think it might have been done better) while viewing the objects of their empirical science as expressions of mathematical form.

Remember that Dee was writing in 1570, Kepler in 1619, Galileo in 1623. This was in the time of Francis Bacon, who unlike Dee and Galileo was not brought into disrepute by his state religious authorities, and whom the Royal Society was to (posthumously) elect as their (politically acceptable) Elizabethan prophet. But Bacon and his contemporaries were a few generations before the Restoration, which was when the London Society finally gained its Royal charter and when John Locke was elected as a member. The tendency of modern history has been to fudge the fact that the great pre-Enlightenment scientists did not leap from Aristotelian dogma to modern Empiricism, but that modern Empiricism arrived late, after many of the great riddles had been solved during a remarkable renaissance of mathematical philosophy.

Those mathematical philosophers who lived into the 18th century were themselves caught up in the appropriation of their achievements by the champions of the Enlightenment vision of science. Among them was G W Leibniz, who wore his colours bright and to his peril; and Isaac Newton, who extracted the clues buried in Kepler's work sufficient to solve the riddle of the universe, but who was also ever secretive, cautious, and then complicit in the 18th reinvention of his own genius. It wasn't until the 1940s, when John Maynard Keynes described the young Newton as the last of the magicians, that the spell finally broke and our eyes were open to the activity of an altogether unfamiliar mind. [11, Vol X, Ch 35]

For so long we obscured the theosophical foundations of the very best of the science of the 17th century so as to honour the demarcation of theology, placing it beyond the inquiry of science. This guarding of the dogma was professed and policed throughout the development of Western science; that is, before, during and after the Renaissance of theosophical mathematical science. This is why we have found it so difficult to come to terms with an aspect of the history of science that is as important as it is evident, which is the underlying agreement between, for example, the theorist Proclus, the evangelist Dee, and the astronomical pioneer Kepler; who, themselves all found a seamless continuity between, respectively, the technical mathematics found in Euclid, the theosophy of Plato, the tradition called Platonism, and the ratio of the world.

The alienation of Platonism from its mathematics was challenged during the Renaissance, this challenge was obscured by the Enlightenment, but the separation of Platonism from its science began in the 13th century with the advent of Christian Aristotelianism. This is when St Thomas positioned mathematics as the science that *abstracted* the formal nature of *material* things in a natural philosophy that was distinct from, and sometimes contradictory to, Christian theology. By cutting pagan science off from its theology, and then positioning it as an abstraction from the non-theological material object, this meant that the Medieval revival of interest in the pagan legacy was thereby rendered permissible because its threat to the revealed dogma of Christianity had been diminished. To use a later term, coined for a similar political purpose, science was positioned *a-gnostic* (unknowing) of the sacred knowledge of the divine Creator. Euclid's *Elements of Geometry* fitted comfortably into this epistemic structure, as it preserved much of the technical achievements of the Pythogoreans, and yet the archetypal style—with its definitions, propositions and their proof—stripped out the theosophical context. In contrast, other sources where the mathematics is inseparable from the theology—including, no less, Proclus' commentary on Euclid—were much more difficult to assimilate because they directly challenged the revealed dogma about the creator-God.

Prior to this Aristotelian revolution in Medieval Christian ideology we find Romanesque architecture, Gothic architecture and Gothic art resonating with a mathematical theology of the creator-God, himself symbolised as a geometer setting a compass on the face of the deep.* In fact, episodic Platonic revivals are evident throughout the scholastic period—albeit soft, vague and never fully formed. And where the mathematics of

---

* Proverb 8. *Timaeus*, the most important of Plato's texts in the Middle Ages gives an account of the Creator as a mathematician. The Christian traditional of a creator-geometer can also be traced to Plutarch quoting Plato saying God is for ever playing the Geometer. See *Convivial Questions* VIII, 2.1 in [15], Vol I, p. 386.

Boethius continued to be taught, it seems to have been taught as the text presented, that is, as mathematics fully integrated with the theology of the creator-God. Boethius' Hellenistic sources were even more theosophical. It turns out that Boethius' mathematical works are bare Latin paraphrases of a 2nd century textbooks of Nicomachus of Gerasa. Both authors are thoroughly Platonic, yet we still tend to class Boethius as a (Christian) 'Platonist' and Nicomachus as a (pagan) 'Pythagorean.' Along with his introductions to Arithmetic, Geometry and Music, Nicomachus also wrote a *Theology of Arithmetic*, which has only survived in fragments. What has survived complete is Proclus' theology, which exacts a thoroughly mathematical monotheism. In fact, most of the Hellenistic writers who have always served as the great elaborators of the Greek mathematical legacy, when you consider their work as a whole, would best be describe as mathematical theologians. Consider finally, Theon of Smyrna. We only have his mathematical textbook (which bares striking similarities to Nicomachus's Introduction to Arithmetic), but it expresses its deferral to Platonic theosophy in its very title: *Mathematics useful for understanding Plato*.#

Figure 9.2: *Christ-the-creator* creating by means of geometry*

---

* Frontispiece of *Bible Moralisee* ca. 1220 AD.
\# This forced demarcation continues in the best scholarship of the period. For Dillon, those who have the Monad and Dyad as the first principles are classed as Pythagorean or as 'Pythagorised' Platonists. [9, p. 141–2] Theon occupies the border regions as 'an enthusiastic Platonist of Pythoagorean tendency'. [9, p. 397]

ENTHUSIASTIC MATHEMATICS

In contrast to these European sources of the technical mathematical, the main sources of theosophical Platonism (Boethius exempted) are almost entirely non-technical, and so they fitted comfortably on the theological side of the Thomist theology/philosophy divide. As theology, this Platonism was destined forever to contention between its identification with Christianity and its rejection as a pagan threat. And it was often comfortably identified with Christianity because Christian theology was always already Platonic. If we look beyond the redemptive power of the resurrected God-incarnate and consider the doctrines of the creator-God found in the early Fathers of the Church—especially the Alexandrian Fathers before Constantine's conversion—these are difficult to distinguish from the doctrines of contemporary Platonists. However, none of the Church Fathers were mathematicians, and their Platonic theosophy is always a step removed from any mathematical elaboration. This is also true of the great Hellenistic influences on Medieval Christian mysticism, *The Mystical Theology*. This short but powerful 6th century statement of Platonic 'negative theology' (attribution to 'Dionysius the Areopagite') is heavily reliant on Proclus. But, whereas Proclus himself moves freely between the technical mathematics and the theosophical, there is no explicit mathematical content in *The Mystical Theology*. Likewise Plotinus (who became the model of Platonism in the European revival) gives very few explicit mathematical references. But the problem is as much in our reading as in the sources themselves. Even where the dialogues of Plato slip into the technical, there is a tendency among modern students (many with a literary non-mathematical bent) to skip over these mathematical passages. This tendency, which Theon had set out to circumvent so long ago, is not discouraged by modern introductions and commentaries. The command reportedly inscribed above the entrance to Plato's Academy——that no one unversed in geometry may enter—is often neglected in our modern textual gateways. [17, p. 386]

The result of all this is that in the modern reception of Platonism, the Monad and the Dyad, and the generative power of the Logos, are left hanging as vague mystical concepts unconnected with the technical elaboration of the emanation for which they were originally invented. And we find various movements of 'Platonism' where there is little interest in the mathematics preserved in Euclid, in the textbooks, or in Plato himself. An early example of this is found in the 17th century with the 'Cambridge

Platonist'—liberal theological rationalists with little interest in mathematics—who stand in sharp contrast to contemporaneous mathematical philosophers like G W Leibniz. As we shall see, what is extraordinary about Leibniz is that during the very twilight of Renaissance Platonism he was able to bring Christian Platonism back to its obscured mathematical roots in a theological arithmetic that is no less than an analogy of divine creation.

Chapter 10
FOUNDATIONS OF ARITHMETIC

> *To crown it all, we must go on to the generation of things divine, the fairest and most heavenly spectacle God has vouchsafed to the eye of man...Every geometrical figure, system of numbers, composition of harmony and the regularity in the revolution of the stars must appear to one, who properly learns, to be one in principle in all cases; and it will so appear, if, as we say, one learns correctly, looking to one thing. For it will appear to them on consideration that there naturally exists one bond of all these things.*
>
> *Epinomis*

We now recount the foundation of arithmetic. In the first place, this will bring attention back to the basics of mathematics that we know so well, but in such a way that is sympathetic to Pythagorean arithmetic emanationism. Because this approach to arithmetic (and to the formal sciences generally) varies from the conventions and presumptions underlying modern interpretations of this tradition, it will allow us to see how the modern view of the formal sciences can serve to obscure the insight of the ancients.

1. Shape and Similarity

Two figures are identical in shape if they have the same proportions. Relative size is not considered. This notion of similarity is fundamental to visual perception: by it we establish the identity of objects experienced both near and far.

Chapter 10: Foundations of Arithmetic

In one dimension, in the straight line, all lines are identical in shape.

2. Dimensions

Remember that when we consider a line we do not consider its width (we treat it as though a cut in the surface upon which it is drawn) and we are yet to consider its length, so a straight line can be defined, after Leibniz, as a curve each part of which is similar to the whole.* Self-similarity is also found in (non-straight) curved lines and linear figures. One of the most basic examples is the very simplicity of the circle, where we may follow Leibniz again and consider that each point in a circle is in the same place. [20, p. 73] Every point in the circle is in the same place in relation to its centre. The neutrality of places on the circle makes it the most neutral linear closure to illustrate our Distinction in the plane. Now, if a curved line is not one-dimensional (call this '1-D') then what is its dimensionality? This has not been codified until recently. Any curved line drawn in the plane utilises the freedom of that plane and so, to the extent that it does, it is two-dimensional (call this '2-D'). Consider a child scribbling a page black, or an artist shading a drawing with a pencil. The pencil line gradually acquires the dimensional characteristics of the surface upon which it is drawn. Thus, a curved line in the plane can be considered to have a fractional, or 'fractal', dimension somewhere between 1-D and 2-D.#

3. Limit and Situation

Limits define spaces. They create closure. A limit generates two spaces, one on each side. When we are considering limitation, or topology generally, shape and size do not matter. Closed lines may create limits on surfaces, thus generating differential spaces like those presented here.

---
* [18], Bk V, p. 185; quoted in [19], p. 419.
# A natural example of a line verging on 2-D is the convoluted coastline of Norway. Examination of

4. Order of Situation and the Alternation of Value

In the above example the three figures that are identical in terms of limit have two limits generating three spaces: the outer; the inner; the inner-of-the-inner. Thus we can say that there are 3 situations:

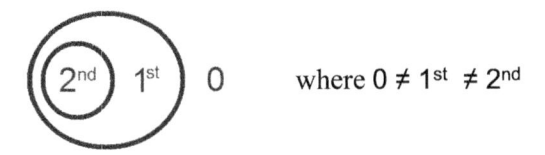

$$2^{nd} \quad 1^{st} \quad 0 \qquad \text{where } 0 \neq 1^{st} \neq 2^{nd}$$

The orders of situation, or 'depth', expressed in this figure can be seen as generated by successive limitation of the space of the page; they are successive distinctions from, or negation of, that space. If a double negation is seen as a return towards the 'value' of the original, then the ordinal series $1^{st}, 2^{nd}, 3^{rd},...$, expresses a primary alternation in value between its 'odd' and 'even' members. The ordinal value of the odd members, in its identity, is opposite to the value of the even members; while the value of the evens is identical to the value of the original (zero order) space. As we saw in Part II, *Laws of Form* shows how such a process of negation is sufficient to generate all arrangements of limitation by its self-limiting principle ('Re-Entry').

In the line, only one limit is possible and this is a break in the line.

Limitation in 1-D has no depth of situation but only the binary situations of line and break, or 1st and 0. This corresponds to the presence and absence in electronic computing, where the sequential arrangement of linear segments is used to communicate depth.

---

such an example can lead to the conclusion that any measurement of natural limit-lines is dependent upon the scale of the instrument used to measure it, and that in fact they have no length and no tangent. Examples of 2-D verging on 3-D are the absorption 'surface' of the large intestine or the lung. On coastlines see [21], p. 167–8, & [22]. On fractal dimensions generally see [19].

5. Number (Cardinal)

The counting of things presupposes limitation, as it requires the indication of discrete units. These units can be distinguished by their position, shape, colour, size…, or in any way whatsoever distinguishable. Depth of situation need not matter in counting, but number is usually exemplified by identifying distinctions at the same depth. A simple expression of number is a collection of distinct limits (ignore shape and size) each generating a depth of the 1st order in a neutral background, such as the pebbles on sand represented figuratively here.

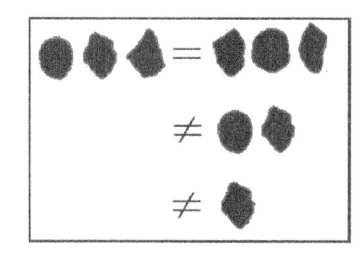

In the line, where there is no depth of situation, number is generated by limitation.

6. Dimension as Limit

The line can be defined as the 'limit' of the surface. This can be expressed on the page as its very edge, or by a cut in the page, or otherwise, as a distinction between two surface spaces marked by a chromatic difference.

In this way the first dimension, the line, is negatively defined as the limit of the second dimension, the surface. This relation of limit also holds between the second and third dimension. Thus, the surface is the 'limit' of the solid. And, we can go back to the line and find its limit in the point. In summary the regression is: the solid is limited by the surface, the surface is limited by the line, and the line is limited by the point. The point is the limit of all dimensions, but itself has no dimension, and so is pure limit. If the point is pure limit, and if we define limit as dimension, then the zero dimension is the essence of all dimensionality. This is, in fact, precisely how the Pythagoreans saw it. But that is jumping ahead of ourselves…, but only a little, because we now have five of the basic aspects of geometry: shape, limit, situational order, number, and dimension. And while we have not yet arrived at geometry as such, we can already start to engage with Pythagorean mathematical doctrines.

Limitation in Early Greek Philosophy

As far as we know, limitation was of elementary interest from the beginning of the Greek tradition of natural philosophy. We find this interest first in Anaximander, a pupil of Thales of Miletus, who is thought to have foundered Greek philosophy and natural science in the 6th century BC. Thales may not have left any writings at all and it is Anaximander who is said to have provided the first written account of nature, although this is long lost and all that remains are secondary accounts and hearsay. What we are told is that he was the first to abandon the idea that a particular nature—i.e., one of the natural elements, Earth, Water, Air or Fire—is the basis of all things, and to declare that a 'principle' is elementary.* The Greek word for 'principle' is *arche*, which also has the meaning of 'beginning' or 'origin', and so I will sometimes use 'origin' or 'principle-origin' to express its meaning. Anaximander called this principle-origin the 'unlimited' or *a-peiron*. The root of this term *'pera'* is a Greek word for 'limit' as in our *peri*meter, and it has a meaningful affinity with our word 'about', as, for example, in the standard title given (often retrospectively) to the written accounts of nature [*physios*] by the early philosophers: *Peri Physios*, 'About Nature'. The *apeiron* that Anaximander gave as the first principle in his, the first *Peri Physios*, would denote, then, an origin--without-limit. It has nothing *about* it. It is an uncontained origin. From this *apeiron* all the heavens and worlds come into existence.

In his own book about nature, Aristotle provides a summary explanation of the doctrine of a fundamental and elementary unlimited principle.

> For everything is either origin [*arche*] or derived from an origin. But the unlimited [*apeiron*] has no origin—for then it would be limited. Again it is ungenerated and indestructible and so is an origin...[The unlimited origin] has no origin but, itself, is regarded to be an origin of everything else and to govern everything....And it is also divine; for it is 'deathless and unperishing', as Anaximander and most of the natural scientists say.
> [Physics p. 203b6-14]

---

* For Thales liquid is elementary, for Heraclitus it is fire, and for Anaximenes it is gas. Note that the narrative is perhaps a little anachronistic as the latter two philosophers came *after* Anaximander.

Chapter 10: Foundations of Arithmetic

Who is Aristotle referring to when he includes most of the nature scientists? It is usually understood that he at least includes the early Pythagoreans, whom, so he explains, also had an elementary interest in limitation. In support of this view we find preserved in Diogenes Laertius (fl. 3rd century AD) the first line of the first Pythagorean *Peri Physios* written in the 5th century BC by Philolaus.

> Nature in the world was connected from the unlimited and limiting, both the whole world and everything in it.*

Alternation in Early Greek Philosophy

In the early Pythagoreans this principle interest in the unlimited, limit and limiting is associated with the doctrine of alternation as a principle of generation, and this seems to have some precedence. In our accounts of Anaximander's emanation of the heavens and the worlds from the *apeiron* we are told that the end or destruction of things is a return to the things from which they came. Perhaps the only surviving words of Anaximander's *Peri Physios* are contained in a commentary by the Hellenistic philosopher Simplicius.

> And the things from which existing things come into being are also the things into which they are destroyed, in accordance with necessity; for they give justice and reparation to one another for their injustice in accordance with the ordering of time.#

This fragment, which Simplicius assesses as somewhat poetical, could be interpreted in many ways, but other evidence suggests that the generation is some kind of temporal movement to a state of injustice, and that the justification of this injustice is the destruction of that which has been generated. Furthermore, this generative process could also be a process of negation, where the destruction of one thing is the generation of another.

Just such a *generation-through-destruction* is more apparent in another early philosopher on the Ionia coast, Heraclitus of Ephesus. His book about nature was written perhaps 40 years after Anaximander's death, and around the time that Pythagoras (also Ionian) had his commune established over in Italy. Although his book is also lost, we know that Heraclitus profoundly influenced later Pythagoreans, if only through his admirer Plato.

---
* [23, Bk VIII, p. 85]. Diels B1. Translation by Barnes [24], p. 216.
# Simplicius, *Commentary on Physics* 24, 13-25. Translation based on Barnes [24], p. 75.

ENTHUSIASTIC MATHEMATICS

Heraclitus is said to have giving various 3-term and 4-term formulae for natural generation that have inherent in them both alternation and *becoming-through-destruction*. In Heraclitus we find alternations between two extremes via intermediate terms, where the way up and the way down are one and the same.* Few direct quotes of Heraclitus remain, but this may be one.

> For Psyche it is death to become Water
> For Water it is death to become Earth
> Since
> From Earth is generated Water, and
> Out of Water Psyche.#

The transmutation from **Earth** through **Water** to **Psyche** is the reciprocal of the movement from **Psyche** to **Water**, and on to **Earth**. Inherent in this out-and-back dynamics is a generation by way of destruction. The becoming of **Water** is the destruction of **Psyche**. The becoming of **Earth** is the destruction of **Water**. This can be expressed in the form:

not-Psyche = Water
not-Water = Earth

That is is to say, *The negation of Psyche gives Water* and *The negation of Water gives Earth*. The generation is an *alter*-ation, an *othering*, and it might even be interpreted as the successive *cumulative othering* of opposites—that is, an *alter-nation*. In this interpretation, not only is there an alternation between the extremes, **Psyche** and **Earth**, but in the steps between them also. Thus, **Earth** is not-**Water**, but also not-not-**Psyche**.

Two other ancient accounts suggest that Heraclitus saw this form of becoming in the transmutation of all the four elements into each other.+ This time we present the sequence in a flowchart.

---

* Hippolytus, *Refutation of All Heresies*, 9.10.4. Diels B60.
\# Clement, *Stromateis*, 6.17.2. Diels B36. My translation. See also Diels B48, which seems to be saying that that which we name 'living' is death-ing.
\+ Diels B76. Variations include one in Plutarch *Moralia*, 392c, and another in Marcus Aurelius *Meditations*, 4.46. See Robinson [25], p. 46–7. Another version (Diels B76) gives Fire living the death of Earth. See also Plato *Timaeus* p. 32b, where this sequence is related to the two mean proportions required in the solution to the problem of the doubling of the cube as discussed below p. 234.

Our main interest here is in the pure formality of these formulae, but we might pause to find some sympathy with this alien scheme in our own understanding of nature. If the four physical 'elements' of the ancients are likened to what we now call the physical 'states' of our chemical elements, then we have **Earth** = solid, **Water** = liquid, **Air** = gas (*psyche* was associated with breath, and so with air). As for the fourth element, **Fire**, it is the transmutative element and, for Heraclitus, the principle about which all change revolves. In this interpretation, consider how our chemical elements (e.g., water) are observed responding to fiery heat by altering states from solid (ice) to liquid (water) to gas (steam), and then, in cooling, returning back toward solid.

Perhaps with a Heraclitean formula in mind, or something similar, Simplicius continues his discussion of Anaximander:

> It is clear that [Anaximander] observed the change of the four elements into one another and was unwilling to make any one of them the primary matter, but rather chose something else apart from them. He accounts for *coming-into-being* not by the alteration of the elements but by the separating off of the opposites by an eternal motion.

According to Simplicius, Anaximander, at least, saw generation as, in principle, a motion that generates by the distinguishing of opposites.

Arithmos: the Excessive and Just

The surviving accounts of Anaximander and Heraclitus were written many centuries after their deaths, but they may be enough to suppose that at the very beginning of Greek science an elementary unlimited principle was under consideration, and that these first philosophers were at least very close to the idea that the elementary process of generation from this *principle-origin* involves the alternation of opposites. However, there is too little evidence for us to ever know for sure whether *generation-by-alternation* preceded the 5th century Pythagoreans. As for these followers of Pythagoras after his death, the evidence that they upheld just such a principle of generation is much more convincing.

If we return to Philolaus' opening affirmation of the elementary ontology of 'unlimited' and 'limiting' (quoted above on page 175), our interpretation is helped by another passage in Aristotle's *Physics* (213b) where he is expounding the various prevailing doctrines of the void. According to

ENTHUSIASTIC MATHEMATICS

Aristotle, the Pythagoreans teach that the heavens inhale the void as though an unlimited breath, and that its vacancy is what comes to separate and distinguish objects in nature. He reports that this natural process of involving void is given principal expression in numbers, since it is this void that delimits their nature. So the unlimited does its limiting according to the nature of arithmetic delimitation. This suggests that the key to the understanding of the *emanation-by-limitation* is in understanding the delimited nature of number. And in fact Philolaus' opening affirmation of the unlimited/limiting ontology is directly followed by the introduction of number [*arithmos*] as an epistemological principle:

> And all the things that are known have number—for without this nothing could be thought of or known.... Now number has two proper forms, odd and even (and a third, even-odd, a mixture from both); and of each form there are many shapes which each thing-in-itself signifies.
> [Diels B4-5]

The most basic classification of number throughout the Pythagorean tradition is the binary **odd** and **even**, which are reciprocally woven in harmony as they alternate in the progression of the natural numbers, 1, 2, 3, 4, 5,....*

Today, binary counting is often considered to be newly invented and yet there are resonances of *counting-by-alternation* across culture and time, ancient and modern, including in the most primitive counting systems which are often based on an elementary pairing. Sometimes this counting does not extend beyond **one** and **one pair**, before arriving at 'many', but if it does proceed then it often takes this form:

> one, a-pair, a-pair-and-another one, a-pair-and-another-pair,...

Also common across time and place is the notion that the first is masculine and the second is feminine.

Wherever the universality of this counting 'two-by-two' might reside, we can be more precise about how it relates to the delimited nature of number as given by the Pythagoreans. The word for 'odd' is *perissos*, which literally means 'excessive' in the sense of 'exceeding a limit'. The word for 'even', *hartios*, is closer in meaning to our 'even'. It means 'just'

---

* The quote is from Nicomachus [26], p. 190. In his textbook, there persists the euphoria over the wonderful and divine nature of these two fundamental species that embrace the essences of quantity. As D'Ooge notes, there is a similar passage in Theon of Smyrna's arithmetic textbook regarding the alternating progress of even and odd. See [27], p. 23.3 for the Greek, and [28], p. 15 for a translation.

in the sense of 'equal' or 'level' and in the sense in which we use 'justify' to mean 'bring to the same level'. This *excessive/just* alternation was often expressed in Pythagorean dot notation by a progression in pairs:

•	•	••	••	•••
•	•	•	••	••
Excessive,	*Just,*	*Excessive,*	*Just,*	*Excessive,*

And, yes, the *excessive* was identified with male and the *just* with female.

Evidence is plentiful as to the elementary importance of the *excessive* and *just* right through the Hellene and Hellenistic Pythagorean tradition. Firstly, in the early Pythagoreans: in the famous passage about them in the *Metaphysics*, Aristotle says that they assumed the elements of number to be the element of every thing in all nature, and then that the elements of number are the just and excessive. [p. 986a2 & 986a19] Secondly, when Plato is drawing a distinction between numbered things and *numbers-in-themselves*, he tends to refer to numbers in their pure form as simply the just and the excessive.* That is to say, Plato uses the phrase 'the just and the excessive' as his synonym of preference when evoking numbers with the sacred mystical significance given them in the old Pythagorean teachings. And thirdly, in Platonism: the importance of the *excessive* and *just* to the whole of the mathematical sciences is expressed powerfully in a canonical passage of *Epinomis*, an appendix to Plato's *Laws*, often taken as written by Plato himself. Its cryptic message has attracted attention and interpretations in recent attempts to understand the elementary principles of Platonist theosophy. It is now generally agreed that *Epinomis* was written shortly after Plato's death by a sympathetic Academic contemporary but this does not lessen its value to us, and we shall return to it again.#

---

* See in *Gorgias* p. 451a-c where Socrates presents the difference between *arithmos* and *logistic* (as discussed below, p. 180). Also see *Theaetetus*, 198a-b, were the art of arithmetic is presented as knowledge of all the just and excessive. In *Republic*, 510b-c, the *just* and *excessive* are presented as the fundamental principles of arithmetic. In *Statesman*, p. 262e, we are told that the division of number into *just* and *excessive* is true to the Form.

\# See below, p. 258. For recent interpretations, see for example A E Taylor [29] and Simone Weil [6, Ch 11] . For an earlier treatments, see the textbook of Theon of Smyrna [28, p. 6]. While he and Nicomachus presumed that *Epinomis* was written by Plato, some later Greek authors (such as Diogenes Laertius and Proclus) were not so sure. Diogenes Laertius proposes that it was written by the Academic Philippus of Opus, and modern philology agrees at least that it is a text of the Old Academy. Nevertheless, the presumption of Plato's authorship held out through the Renaissance, and John Dee considered it the treasury of all Plato's doctrines. [16, p. 160] More recently, A E Taylor finds the evidence against this presumption not so strong. [29, p. 420] If it were not written by Plato, then this makes it the most substantial surviving text of his followers in the Old Academy.

This rare document of the Old Academy gives a hierarchical account of the mathematical sciences starting with the most elementary:

> The first and most important of these is the study of *numbers-in-themselves* [*arithmos auton*]; not of those which are corporeal, but of the whole generation of the excessive and just, and the powerfulness of their influence on the nature of reality [*onton physin*].
> [p. 990c]

Thus, the first science is the study of arithmetic *taken as* the study of the generation of the *excessive* and *just*. Before we consider how the generation of this basic, alternating, arithmetic series might be understood as a process of limitation, it is helpful to first consider what is meant by *numbers-in-themselves* in Plato and Platonism. Here the distinction between the sciences of *arithmetic* and *logistic* is important.

Arithmetic and Logistic

This difference between *arithmetic* and *logistic* is a difference between the pure and applied science of number. *Arithmetic* concerns *numbers-in-themselves*, their purely formal character, what we would now call 'number theory'. The passage in *Epinomis* follows on from a famous passage in Plato's *Republic* which heralds this study of numbers as the first among the sciences and as a gateway to understanding the formal nature of things. Of interest to the *mathematici* was the nature of the principle-origin, how it generates plurality and how it can be, simultaneously, both one and multiple, the same and yet different.* This is theory of number but understood as theory of differentiation through emanation.

Later ancient commentators are more explicit on how such investigations differ from the applied science called *logistic*. They tell us that *arithmetic* investigates, in and by themselves, the species of number as they are successively evolved from the unit, whereas *logistic* is concerned with the counting of things and calculation in relation to this counting.#

---

* For the discussion about *arithmetic* (numbers in themselves) and *logistic* (the counting of things), see *Republic*, p. 522-526. See also Plato's *Philebus* 12c-17
\# For a summary of the evidence see Heath [4], Vol I, p. 13–15, from where I have taken a quote of Heath paraphrasing Geminus as presented by Proclus. For more direct (but less explicit) evidence in Plato, see *Theaetetus*, p. 198a-b, where *arithmetic* is presented as knowledge of all the just and excessive, and *Gorgias* p. 451b-c.

Chapter 10: Foundations of Arithmetic

Greek logistical counting and calculations were advanced quite early, due perhaps to their evident borrowings from Egypt. Techniques of calculation, like addition, subtraction, multiplication, division and so forth, were advocated in Platonism as skills important for farmers, military commanders and merchants. The initial counting of things, upon which these calculations are made, begins with a one-to-one correspondence between unit numbers and the individual things counted: *one finger/stick/pebble corresponds to one cow*. *Logistic* is the manipulation of such numbers through calculation.

Powerful aids to *logistic* were the abacus and the counting board. The counting board is similar to the abacus, except that instead of rows of beads on rods they places markers like pebbles in columns on a board. Each rod/column represented units, tens, hundreds and so forth. Base-10 counting was not always used, but our modern decimal place-value notation is derived from such calculators, which were in use right across the ancient civilised world. The ancients had no need for a place-value *notation* because they did not calculate on paper.* Only when the calculations was completed would they write their results in words or numerals on the tablet or page. Because they did not use place-value notation they did not need to mark the empty place. The **zero** on the counter *is* the empty place. It is only when calculating on the page (where there are no pre-defined columns or rows) that the problem of marking an absence presents itself. As *Laws of Form* makes evident (and against the modern heroic saga of, and controversy over, the invention of the notational **zero**) the obscuring of the very contradiction inherent in *marking-an-absence* has in fact retarded modern number theory. The cardinal **zero**, the **zero** of *logistic*, was never a problem for the *mathematici*. This is, however, in striking contrast to the ordinal **zero**, which they lacked, or at least confused with the ordinal **one**, and, as we shall see, this had crippling consequences for the development of their mathematical philosophy.

Anyway, the *mathematici* warned against confusing *logistic* with *arithmetic*. Logistical numbers might be derived from *arithmetic* but then they are placed in correspondence with the things counted, and so the subject matter of *logistic* is these pre-distinguished things. Such counting

---

* Our word 'calculate' is derived from the Latin for the small 'stones' use as counters. 'Place-value' refers to the use of position in a sequence to indicate degrees of value. For example, using our decimal system, in the number '1010', the first '1' indicates the value '**one thousand**', while the second '1' indicates the value '**ten**'. Techniques of adding and subtracting in notational columns mimic the techniques used on counting boards.

is by reference to these objects *as they appear*. By contrast, the interest in the Pythagorean science of *arithmetic* is in the insensible reality of numbers—the form of their generation from the *principle-origin*. And this elementary generation is an alternation of the *excessive* and *just*. So, as *Epinomis* says, the elementary science of *arithmetic* is the study of this elementary emanation, the whole generation of the excessive and the just. Thus, it is ordinal self-generating alternation that is elementary to *arithmetic*. The natural arithmetic series 1, 2, 3, 4, 5, ..., is seen by the Pythagoreans as the ordinal, 1st, 2nd, 3rd, 4th, 5th,..., whereby the 5th (*excessive*) is derived from the 4th (*just*), the 4th is derived from the 3rd (*excessive*), the 3rd is derived from the 2nd (*just*), and the entire series is derived from the principle origin via the 1st to exceed it.

Affinities with Laws of Form

What is striking when we consider the Pythagorean dogma of *arithmos* in the light of *Laws of Forms* is that as far as we can tell, from the earliest times the Pythagoreans were looking at a generative principle that conforms to the process of 'Re-Entry' described by George Spencer Brown. Firstly, *Laws of Form* is all about limiting. In Spencer Brown, the Form is a principle-origin that is an unlimited limit, and its generation by Re-Entry is an unlimited limiting. The generation is a *sameness-becoming-other-to-itself* by exceeding its *limit-self* and entering its own *otherness*. This *otherness* as a negation of the *same* is its perfect opposite. In Re-Entry, this elementary *othering* generates an elementary alternation between the *value negating the origin* and the *value of the origin*—between a value *exceeding* the origin and a value *just* with it.

However much this guiding insight inspired the marvellous advances in mathematics across the ancient world, it was never fully reconciled with any of them. As far as we know the Pythagoreans failed to explicate this dogma at the most basic level: they could not formulate the mechanism by which the natural arithmetic series was generated out of the original unity according to this alternating principle; and they failed to fully reconcile this numeration with geometrical generation. And yet, if they did not achieve their final unifying goal, they did nonetheless expend a great deal of energy towards revealing the fundamental mechanisms of mathematical generation, and in doing so, they made significant progress. Some of their achievements seem quite quirky and of limited use, while

Chapter 10: Foundations of Arithmetic

others are altogether obscure. However, when they are examined in the light of *Laws of Form*, we gain a deeper appreciation of these achievements, and also a better appreciation of their situation in the grand unifying project of the Pythagoreans. In considering some of the products of their investigations of the mathematical emanation, we come at last to consideration of the familiar medium between shape and number that is 'magnitude'. We have only now arrived at the science they called 'geometry'.

Magnitude

I have not yet mentioned one other aspect of the differentiation between the higher art of *arithmetic* and the low art of *logistic* that was long upheld by the Pythagoreans. Upheld that is, until it was finally successfully challenged by advances in Alexandrean mathematics quite late in the day. This is that *arithmetic* is limited to the treatment of number as it relates directly to shape.* Numeration was always considered to be a *geometrical* activity. Their sacred investigations of plane and solid figures were essentially about trying to find either the natural geometry of number or the arithmetic nature of shape. They were searching for the natural medium between number and shape in a unified account of their generation.# This explains why they eschewed *logistic* and also why they ignored the Babylonian algebraic techniques for solving equations with unknown values. These were applications of arithmetic with no apparent relevance to their interest.+ To put their interest in our terms, they were primarily concerned with Brownian order (i.e., *arithmos*), they had a secondary interest in Brownian number, but the extension of their ordinal arithmetic was towards the expression of magnitude.

Magnitude is the quality that is generated through the analogy of ordinal arithmetic with relative size. Magnitudes are arithmetic values assigned as lengths, widths, areas, volumes and so forth. The science of magnitude is what the first Pythagoreans called '*geometry*'. Remember that an unmeasured straight line has no length, and so all that is linear,

---

* See again Heath's summary [4], Vol I p. 14–16.
# For a discussion of the principle of mathematical *being* as a whole, see Proclus [15], p. 4, where he declares the limited and unlimited to be the all-pervading principles that generate everything from themselves.
+ The Egyptians worked with problem of equations involving unknown quantities that were clearly derived directly from geometry, but the Pythagoreans showed no interest in algebra until the work attributed Diophantus in the 2nd century AD.

183

ENTHUSIASTIC MATHEMATICS

including the parts of a whole, are identical (in shape). One way to move towards magnitude is to compare two (or more) lines by their length. However, this does not give a magnitude, only the relative binary of greater and smaller. The simplest way to begin a geometry of the line is to, in the first place, *generate* the magnitudes using a standard unit of length. We can call this unit a 'measure' or 'meter', and count out different lengths as we would by counting feet or steps. Such counting generates linear magnitudes that are all in ratio to the unit. If we duplicate the meter and add it to itself we get 2 meters, and if we add another duplicate we get 3 meters, and so forth. Thus, 2 meters is double 1 meter, 3 is triple, and 7 meters is 7 X 1 meter. All lengths have a ratio to the unit length and thereby also to each other, thus 3 is $3/7$ths of 7. In this way it is easy to see that because all (natural) numbers are in ratio, and all (finite) fractions are ratios of numbers, then all magnitudes so generated can be related. In fact, to be in ratio *is* to have an arithmetic value and the two sciences united in the concept of ratio. On account of this identity common to their generation there is always a path of multiplication or division from one arithmetic value to the other.

Geometry begins in the analogy with arithmetic value in this way, as a pure constructive science, and not as an applied science. The first step in geometry is not *to measure* a pre-existing shape (e.g., a length) but, instead, to generate one. This is why the author of *Epinomis* considered the name 'geometry'—literally, 'earth measuring'—ridiculous. [p. 990d] And it is why critics continue to call Pythagorean science fantastic.* Here, as elsewhere there is no reference to an external reality, or a pre-existing reality other than itself. Geometry measures itself; it is a purely intellectual self-referencing science only *expressed* by marks on the page. All lengths that are generated by the unit length are similar in that they are 'scale models' of each other. They are said to be 'rational'—of the same ratio—because they are generated '*sym-metric-al*'—of the same measure.

Beyond linear magnitudes, plane and solid magnitudes are also rational. But the ratios of the higher degrees of magnitude are generally given in terms of the first. Let us consider for the moment two dimensional square space. Placing metered lengths at right angles to each other generates spaces that are reducible to squares, and, in this way, we are able to count surface magnitudes:

---

* For a contemporary indictment of Pythagorean mathematics as fantastic, see the Chapter on the Pythagoreans in John McLeish's book *Number* [30], which is entitled: 'Ancient Greek Fantasies about Number'.

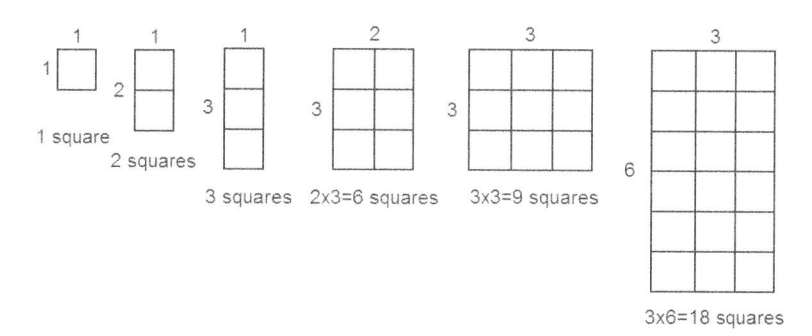

The surface 'area' of these rectangular figures is found by counting the squares which constitute them, or by the calculation **Length X Width**. If the length is the same as the width, the area is **Length X Length**, or length 'squared'. The numbers expressing the magnitude of such square and rectangular spaces (as well as those expressing any surface magnitude) were called 'plane' numbers. If we are considering square space in relation to lines then **Area = Length^2 [y = x^2]** is a fundamental relation between the line and the plane. This thinking is extended by degree to the cubic magnitude of solids, where we now have 'depth', as well as length and width, and so the equation **Volume = Length^3 [y = x^3]** gives the relation between linear and solid numbers.

Figured Numbers and Gnomic Generation

All lines that are in ratio are also similarly proportioned to each other, but this is not so for plane and solid figures. Consider that to generate two lines in the proportion of double is easy, but to find a way to double the size of a given square or cubic is a problem worthy of the genius of the ancient mathematical masters. As we shall see below (page 232), it can be done but only in terms of the linear. In higher dimensions, magnitude and proportion are not identical. Consider again the squared figures above. Adding together two unit squares gives a rectangle with an area of 2, but this 1 X 2 rectangle is clearly not the same shape as the unit square. While the 1 X 2 rectangle is not in proportion to the 1 X 1 square, a 3 X 3 square is proportional. We can express this difference of proportions numerically by saying that the ratio of the width to the length in the 1 X 2 rectangle is not the same as the ratio of the width to the length in the unit square, which is to say, $1/2 \neq 1/1$. The 1 X 2 rectangle is, however, in proportion to a 3 X 6 rectangle because $1/2 = 3/6$. And this relation of similarity can be extended

ENTHUSIASTIC MATHEMATICS

to all areas that measure their length as double their width. Thus, for example:

$$\frac{1}{2} = \frac{3}{6} = \frac{27}{54} = \frac{32}{64}$$

In general this relation of similarity between rectangles can be expressed:

$$\frac{\text{Width}_1}{\text{Length}_1} = \frac{\text{Width}_1}{\text{Length}_2}$$

And this relation need not only hold between rectangles but between any two pairs of magnitudes (or any two pair of numbers) where *the ratio of the first to the second is the same as the ratio of the third to the fourth.** What we have here is the '4-term proportion' expressed algebraically as:

$$\frac{a}{b} = \frac{c}{d}$$

Now consider these squares:

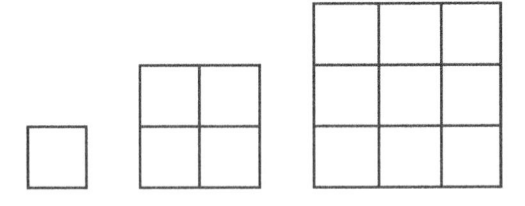

They are all in the same proportion because they are all clearly squares, with length in a ratio to width of 1:1. The sides of the second square are proportion to the sides of the first as 2:1. The sides of the third square are in proportion to the sides of first as 3:1. Furthermore, the sides of the second square are in proportion to the third as 2:3. The ratios of sides of each square and between the three squares can be summarised:

$$\frac{1}{1} = \frac{2}{2} = \frac{3}{3}$$

Now, while the ratio of the sides between these squares is 1 : 2 : 3, the ratio of the areas are different, they are 1 : 4 : 9. The areas are in propor-

---
* Compare with Theon's account [28], p. 25.

Chapter 10: Foundations of Arithmetic

tion to the square of the sides delimiting them:

	Sides: 1	:	2	:	3
	Area: 1^2	:	2^2	:	3^2
or	Area: 1	:	4	:	9

The question arises as to how these plane magnitudes might be given as directly related to, or even generated from, each other.*

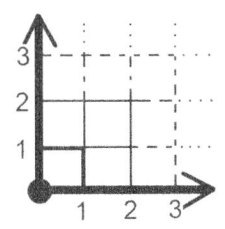

This figure helps us envisage such a generation simultaneous in two dimensions.

Pythagoreans expressed this series using their dot notation:

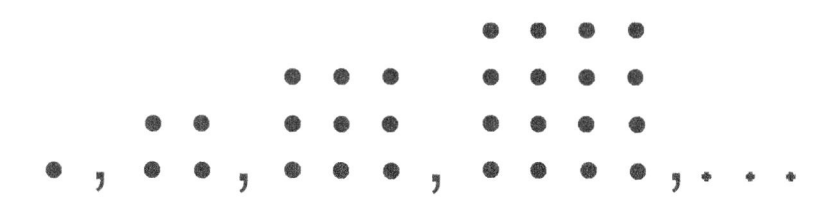

We don't know exactly how they envisaged the mechanism of generation, but only that they saw it as producing successive lines of points along two sides. Each successive addition they called a *'gnomon'*, meaning 'set-square', on account of its shape. Starting from the point origin, the series of square numbers is thus found to be generated by the successive application of 3, then 5, then 7 dots according to this *gnomic* rule.

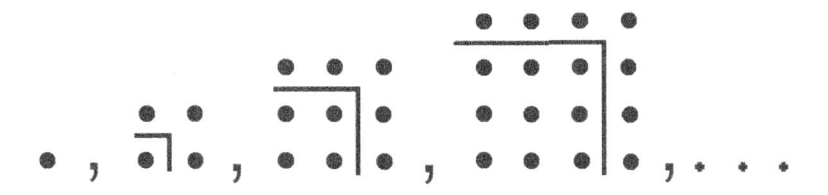

---

* For the definition of plane numbers and solid numbers in this rectilinear presentation of the dimension, see Euclid Bk VII definition 16 & 17. See the commentary in [26], p. 55.

ENTHUSIASTIC MATHEMATICS

These ancient diagrams do not yet tell the full story of their generation, and so what follows is only an hypothesis.

Consider the all-important first generation from the point. The generation of the *first-born* square number from the original point could be expressed using arrows. The original dot becomes 4 dots by duplicating itself in three directions and thereby marking the 4 corners of the square.

The generation of the 2nd and 3rd squares in this series could be envisaged in a number of different ways, but here is the simplest:

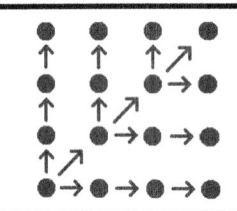

The quadrupling that generated the first-borns is repeated with every new generation as a kind of 'nodal' growth on the diagonal. These nodes then sprout left and right branches of simple duplication.

We now have a picture of the causal paths in the generation. This causation could also be expressed as containment. That is, the generation of each dot is contained within the generation of the dot from which it came.

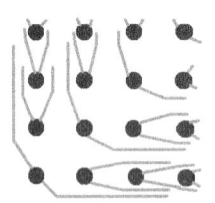

To express the generation in this way the arrows are removed and containment lines added.

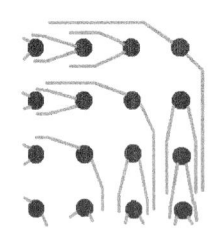

If our 'containment' diagram is rotated 180° (so that the original point is now in the top right corner) then we have a diagram that is close to the Brownian notation.

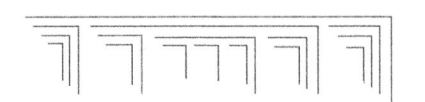

Remove the dots and straighten the lines and we arrive at an expression of the square numbers in the notation of *Laws of Form*.

188

Chapter 10: Foundations of Arithmetic

The generation that produced this third generation square number can now be expressed in both notations. Here, arrows are used to show the paths of growth:

Pythagorean Notation (modified)	Brownian Notation (modified)
←● ↙↓	
←●←● ↙↓ ←● ● ↙↓ ↓	
←●←●←● ↙↓ ←●←● ● ↙↓ ↓ ←● ● ● ↙↓ ↓ ↓	
●←●←●←● ↙↓ ●←●←● ● ↙↓ ↓ ●←● ● ● ↙↓ ↓ ↓ ● ● ● ●	

The square shape is lost in the Brownian notation but the arithmetic form of the square number series is preserved. The relationship of the odd series to the squares series (i.e., as its *gnomic* additions) remains apparent. And the self-similarity found in the Pythagorean notation is even more apparent in the Brownian notation. The principle generator of this self-similarity is found in our generative expressions of the *first-born* square. The Re-Entry formula for the series is a 2nd degree Re-Entry notated thus:

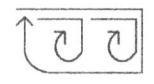

This generator of the square numbers will be explained when higher degree arithmetic is introduced below.

Compare our conventional numerals with the Brownian and Pythagorean notation and you notice that they inhibit the proper *expression*, or even the proper *representation*, of this series of plane numbers. The main problem is that conventional notation does not express Brownian order. Consider the *first-born* square number. How can it be expressed in our numerals? It is 4, but it is a 4_{planar}, not 4_{linear}. It is also 1 + 3 and also the 3_{gnomon}. Consider that if we call this first square number simply '4', it could be confused with other numbers, including the following:

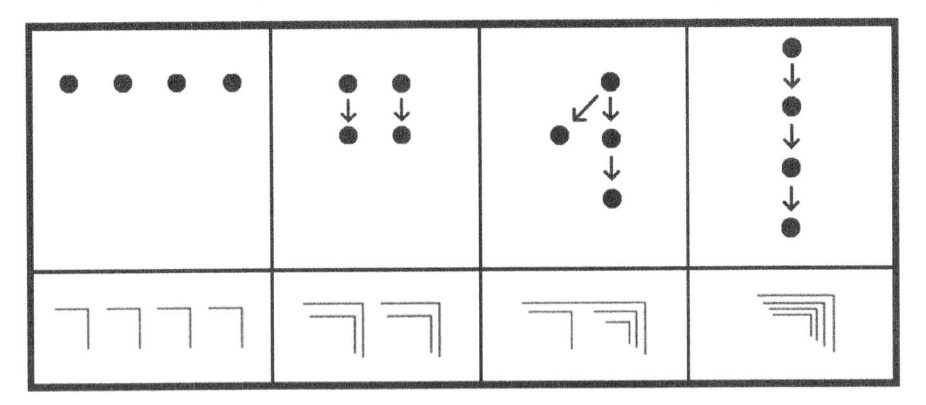

In *logistic* there is no confusion here because four is four is four is four. Thus, we can already see that the Pythagoreans were using their arithmetic notation to explore the mathematical emanation in ways that are obscured by logistic numeration.

The Pythagoreans offered various other figured number series, and in their jargon, the term *gnomon* generalises to refer to the additions made in any such expansion, whatever its shape. These *gnomic* expansions seem to be amongst the oldest (and most original) teachings of Pythagoreans. And from the early times one of them was exulted as first among the rest. This is the expansion using a simple straight-line *gnomon* to produce the triangular numbers. Its elementary nature is suggested in a number of ways. In the first place, the *tri*-angle is the first of the plane figures in that it has the least number of angles (and sides). Arithmetically we notice that while the *gnomic* series for square numbers is [1], 3, 5, 7, 9..., or the odd series, the *gnomic* series for the triangular numbers is simply [1], 2, 3, 4, 5..., or the elementary number series.*

One member of the triangular series was seen as expressing all the essential qualities of the entire series, and by implication it expressed the essence of all figured numbers. This very special triangular number is the third-born, or the fourth in the series if you count the origin. They called it

---

* The name *'gnomon'* has a special significance for early Greek science. It was the name for the builder's set-square but also for the vertical rod in the sundial—which has been called *gnomon* from the earliest times to this day. Legend has it that the sundial, one of the earliest scientific instriments, was brought from Babylon by Anaximander. And this may have been the first derivation of the term for figured number generation, as the *gnomon* for the triangular numbers (including the sacred *Tetraktys*) is a straight rule. See Heath [4], Vol I, p. 78.

Tetraktys. In the mystique surrounded it, its generation held the key to the generation of all numbers and all numerical relations. It was upon this number that the Pythagoreans swore their oath:

Figure 10.1: The Tetraktys with the third *gnomon* indicated

> By him who handed to our generation the Tetraktys, source of the roots of ever-flowing nature.*

What are the characteristics of the Tetraktys? It is four (hence *tetra-*) because it is the 4th in the series, because the *gnomic* addition that completes it is 4, and because it generates an equilateral triangle with sides measuring 4. But it is more that this. A satire by Lucian (2nd century AD) mocking Pythagorean arithmetic reductionism is nevertheless instructive. Pythagoras tells a potential 'buyer' of his philosophy that it would help him in the practice of music, geometry and counting. The buyer protests that he already knows how to count and starts counting, 1, 2, 3, 4…. Pythagorus interrupts:

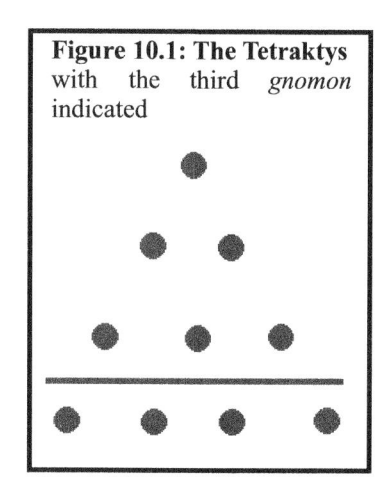

> 'Don't you see? What you take as four is ten, a perfect triangle and our oath.' #

The intervention *What you take as four is ten* is telling of the relation in the *Tetraktys* between the successive *gnomic* additions and the triangular numbers. Pythagoras uses the $4_{ordinal}$ to invoke an identity of the 4_{gnomic} with the triangular number, $1 + 2 + 3 + 4 = 10$. The *Decad* was important to the early Pythagoreans if only for the same reasons it is important to us. The base-10 counting that we use for ordinary arithmetic is inherited from the Greeks, who in turn followed the Egyptian system. Most historians related the evolutionary stability of this convention to the ever-ready digital computer on our hands. Throughout the Pythagorean tradition the *Decad*—as expressed in the *Tetraktys* and by base-10 counting—offered some competition to the elementary interest in the binary opposition of same/other, female/male, *just/excessive*, and so forth. However, the *Decad* is of little interest to us, and whatever its importance may have been to the early Pythagoreans, we do know that this receded dramatically with the advent of the Dyad in Platonism. (See below, Chapter 13.)

---
* Iamblichus, *On the Pythagorean Way of Life*, p. 162, [31, p. 177]. Translation by Barnes [24, p. 113].
# Lucian *Philosophies for sale*, p. 4. Quoted in Heath [4], Vol I, p. 77.

ENTHUSIASTIC MATHEMATICS

The exulted status of the *Tetraktys* itself never receded. And it was recognised to have a multitude of other attributes, including the harmonic ratios of the octave (1:2), the 5th (2:3) and the 4th (3:4). [4, Vol I, p75–6] So, from what we know, we can at least say that this triangle number expressed the $4_{ordinal}$, the 4_{gnomic}, a 10_{planar}, and it also expresses the ratios of its constitutive *gnomons*, [1] : 2 : 3 : 4.

Now, let us consider how the *Tetraktys* and the triangular numbers might be generated. The simplest way to express this *gnomic* expansion is by inserting arrows.

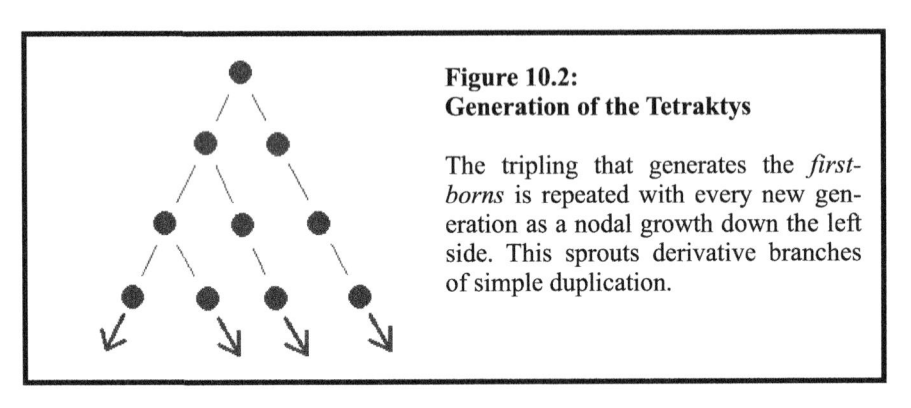

Figure 10.2: Generation of the Tetraktys

The tripling that generates the *first-borns* is repeated with every new generation as a nodal growth down the left side. This sprouts derivative branches of simple duplication.

We can express the Tetraktys by containment as follows:

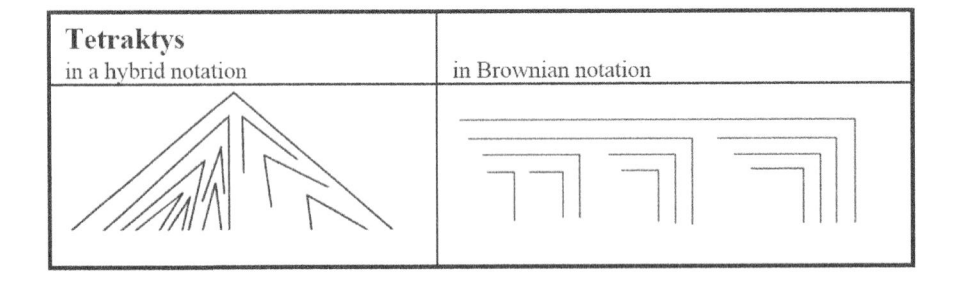

Tetraktys in a hybrid notation	in Brownian notation

Note that in the three types of notation used here, the arithmetic form of the *Tetraktys* is directly expressed. In the Brownian notation we can easily see the following: the *tetra* ('four') both in the four ordinal depths and in the number of characters at the 4th depth; the natural number series is counted by the number of characters at each deeper depth; and by count cumulative we arrive at the Decad. Finally, the harmonic ratios are found by relating the number of characters at each depth.

Chapter 10: Foundations of Arithmetic

How impoverished our conventional numerals are! There is no translation of the *Tetraktys* into our notation. We can only describe its various features as 4 and 10 and 1 + 2 + 3 + 4 and 1 : 2 : 3 : 4. But we cannot express the arithmetic form of the *Tetrkatys* as it is. When instead we use Brownian notation, it is apparent to the eye why the triangular numbers attained a sacred significance in Pythagorean emanationism. What is special and revealing about the triangular series is that it counts Brownian order by Browning number; that is the ordinal depths 1st, 2nd, 3rd, 4th are counted 1, 2, 3, 4 by the numbers of marks at each new depth. This leads us to a new insight into Pythagorean emanationism. It turns out that the triangular series is a straight *Re-Entry-of-a-Re-Entry*, or Re-Entry in the 2nd degree, expressed simply as:

Thus we have found that the elementary and sacred 2-D figured number series is but an analogy of the 2nd degree of infinite ordinality in the Formal arithmetic.

We now have two expressions in the 2nd degree Formal arithmetic, one for the square numbers (see above, page 189) and now the most elementary 2nd degree number as an expression of the triangular number series. The 2nd degree Formal arithmetic differs in two important respects from our 2nd degree of square counting notated algebraically as x^2. Firstly it is triangular and secondly it is infinite. These characteristics of the 2nd and higher degree arithmetic will become clearer as we now consider the generation of dimensional magnitudes.

The Generation of the Dimensional Magnitude

A fashionable reflection of futurists at the time of writing is that they operate in the rarefied domain beyond the simple unknown: it is not just that they don't know what is going to happen, but they *don't know what they don't know*. This predicament is often called 'don't know squared'. The half-comic analogy with mathematical degree works fine, but what is curious is how we naturally fall into pronouncing this degree as a degree of the square. In this unquestioned leap to degrees of finite square space, there might just be a silent lesson on our tendency not to think outside the square.

Since ancient times, higher degree arithmetics have generally been expressed in terms of the degrees of square magnitudes. Thus, plane numbers are expressed in terms of squared numbers, and solid numbers in terms of cubed numbers. We do this no matter what shapes we are working with. Thus, the area of the circle is given as πr^2, and the hypotenuse of a unit right angle triangle is given as the square root of 2. Independent of this geometry we find that repeated multiplication—a common *logistical* process—conforms to this geometry so that a number multiplied by itself is 'squared', and multiplied again is 'cubed'.

That this convention of reducing geometric degrees to terms of the square has proved very useful is beyond doubt. There is no suggestion to abandon it. But it does obscure another way of thinking higher degree arithmetic, a way that was elementary to the Pythagorean understanding of the generation of dimensional magnitude. This doctrine was put in place by the founders of our mathematical systems, and then respectfully disregarded. In order to engage with it now we must leave the finite square for the infinite triangle; but in doing this we will see how its infinite form is able to generate the finite Euclidian-Cartesian square space in which, despite any reservation, we still mostly prefer to think.

The Pythagorean doctrine of the order of dimensional magnitude begins with their basic vision of the emanation that gives our 3-D world. We already touched on this with the lower dimension given as *the limit of* the higher. This limit is at the same time the beginning [*arche*] of a motion. The dimensions arise as degrees of an original linear dynamics of the point. When the point moves it generate the line. When the line moves it generates the plane. Likewise, when the plane moves it generates the solid. Just as the point is the stasis of the line, so the line is the stasis of the plane and the plane the stasis of the solid. Each high dimension is the realised 'power' (*dynamis*) of the previous ones. The lower dimension is also called the root [*riza*] or stock [*pythmen*] of the higher one, just as though a tree root or trunk might be regarded as potentially its branches. The geometric point, the primary limit and the potential of all dimensions they saw as the 'seed' or potent origin of all geometric forms.*

When this doctrine of the emanation of the dimensions is applied to the generation of magnitude, planar magnitude is given as emerging from

---

* For '*pythmen*' see Nicomachus Bk I, Ch 19, 6 [26, p. 216]. Theon uses this term in the same way [27, p. 80], although this is lost in the English translation [28, p. 53]. Prime numbers had an importance in this regard because they are unambiguously linear. They were called 'linear' and 'incomposite' because they are geometrically one dimensional (see [4, Vol I, p. 72–3] and Aristotle's *Metaphysics* p. 1020b4-9).

Chapter 10: Foundations of Arithmetic

the linear in *triangular* (not square) form. The triangular numbers are first, and from them are derived the square numbers. After the square numbers are pentagonal numbers, hexagonal numbers and so forth, sequenced by the increasing number of angles in the figures each series generates. From these figured numbers, all other plane numbers are derived. From the plane arises the solids, and here in 3-D it is the triangular pyramid numbers that are the first. After the triangular pyramid series come the square pyramids, the pentagonal pyramids and so forth, sequenced by the increasing number of angles in the base of the pyramids each series generates. The most expansive surviving account of this doctrine of geometric emanation is in Nicomachus' *Introduction to Arithmetic* Book II, Chapter 6 to 14, and his organization of the figured numbers is summarised below in Table 10.1.

By way of explaining the order and degree of this arithmetic emanation, Nicomachus does give some justifications. For example, he shows how all the other polygon numbers in the plane are found to be made up from elementary triangular series. He also shows how the *gnomon* (or interval) increases by 1 in the triangular series, by 2 in the squares, by 3 in the pentagonals, and so forth. He shows how the stacking of the successive triangular numbers can generate the triangular pyramid numbers, and how the stacking of the square numbers gives the square pyramids, and so forth. However, in all this discussion there is still a sense that he is justifying a dogma not fully understood. What I want to do now is present a clear picture of the formal symmetry of this scheme using Brownian notation. The remarkable outcome of this interpretation is that the Pythagorean vision of dimensional generation directs us towards a hierarchy of degrees in the ordinal arithmetic naturally arising within the Form.

Table 10.1: The emanation of figured numbers according to Nicomachus	
0-Dimension	*The point* corresponding to the original One or 'Monad'
1-Dimension	*The line* corresponding to the natural number series i.e., [1], 2, 3, 4, 5…
2-Dimension	*The triangular* number series is elementary. From it are derived the square number series, the pentagonal numbers, the hexagonals, the heptagonals and so forth.
3-Dimensions	*The triangular pyramid* number series is elementary. From it are derived the square pyramid numbers, the pentagonal pyramids, the hexagonal pyramids, the heptagonal pyramids and so forth.

ENTHUSIASTIC MATHEMATICS

Firstly, consider plane figured numbers. They are arranged in Table 10.2 according to the Pythagoreans scheme and notated to show the form of their generation. The first column presents the linear numbers, which are the origin of the plane numbers and analogous to the Formal ordinal series generated by a simple re-entering mark. Next are the triangular numbers, which are also a self-generating line, but this time generating offshoot lines at every period. In the Brownian notation this is found to be a Re-Entry re-entered into itself, thereby giving the unitary form of the 2nd degree ordinals. In the square numbers, we have two offshoots, and this is expressed in the Brownian notation as two primary Re-Entries re-entered at the 2nd degree. For the pentagonals there are three offshoots and so three primary Re-Entries. There are four for the hexagonals, and so forth. The number of iterating branching is thus express in the Brownian notation as the number of Re-Entries. And here we have an expressions of Brownian number—this time not the *number of marks*, but, instead, the *number of re-entered marks re-entering at the 2nd degree*. That is to say, the plane figured number series organised by increasing number of 'angles' is an analogue of Brownian number in the 2nd degree of Re-Entry.

Table 10.2: The generation of plane figured numbers

	[Lines]	Triangles	Squares	Pentagonals	Hexagonals
The primary generation					
Expressed as Re-entries					
Number series	1,2,3,4,5...	1,3,6,10,15...	1,4,9,16,25...	1,5,12,22,35...	1,6,15,28,45...
Gnomon series	1,1,1,1...	2,3,4,5...	3,5,7,9...	4,7,10,13...	5,9,13,17...
Gnomic interval	0	1	2	3	4

Of course, the Pythagoreans did not put it this way, but they did recognise the importance of this number to their scheme. The 2nd degree Brownian number that each series expresses is also found as the constant difference of the gnomon series. This is *the-difference-of-the-difference-of-the-successive-numbers-in-the-series*, or the 2nd 'derivative'. In Table 10.2 we call it the 'gnomic interval'. Nicomachus explains in his *Introduction* how to find this number for each series and then gives the rule: it is always two less than the number of angles in the figure that the series is generating. Thus for the square numbers it is 4 - 2 = 2. [26, p. 246]

The pattern continues by degree with the solid numbers as shown in Table 10.3. Firstly, consider the expression for the triangular pyramid numbers. In Figure 10.3 the first few iterations are presented graphically using a simple computer program designed to explore Form dynamics.* The labelling shows how this 3rd degree Re-Entry is made up of a 1st degree Re-Entry and a 2nd degree Re-Entry at its first depth, and then, with the 3rd degree repeating, so do these 1st and 2nd degrees repeat at every subsequent depth. These three ordered components correspond, respectively, to the three dimensions of the figured numbers so generated.

Now, read the Brownian expressions in Table 10.3 from left to right and see, respectively, 0, 1, 2, 3 and 4 first degree Re-entries in the two inner depths. This matches the Brownian number at the 2nd and 3rd degree. Finally notice how this count matches the count in the 3rd derivative.

Table 10.3: The solid numbers in Brownian notation with derivative analysis

	[Triangular]	Triangular Pyramid	Square Pyramid	Pentagonal Pyramid	Hexagonal Pyramid
Number series	1,3,6,10,15,...	1,4,10,20,35,...	1,5,14,30,55,...	1,6,18,40,75,...	1,7,22,50,95,...
Gnomon series	2,3,4,5,...	3,6,10,15,...	4,9,16,25,...	5,12,22,35,...	6,15,28,45,...
2nd derivative	1,1,1,...	3,4,5,...	5,7,9,...	7,10,13,...	9,13,17,...
3rd derivative	0	1	2	3	4

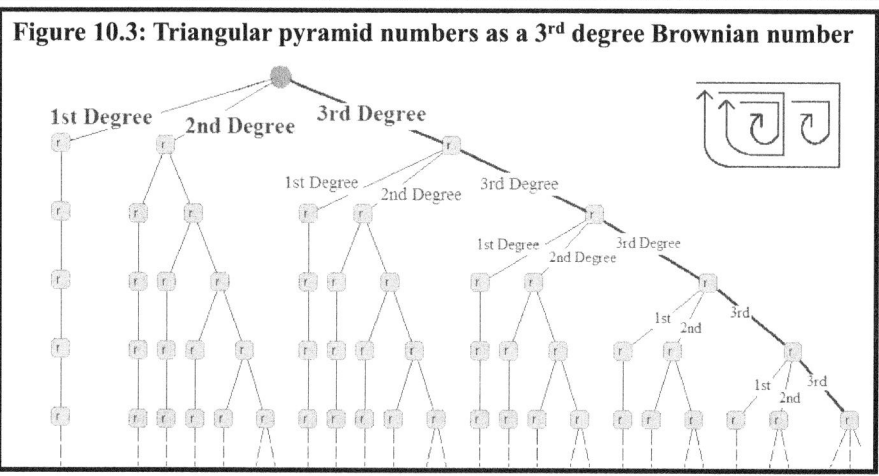

Figure 10.3: Triangular pyramid numbers as a 3rd degree Brownian number

---

* The Java program 'Dynamics of Form' developed by Bernie Lewin and Ben Hughson was launched on Github in April 2018.

ENTHUSIASTIC MATHEMATICS

Let's leave aside Brownian number for now and consider only the unitary value in the degrees of Brownian order. This returns us to the elementary figured numbers given by Nicomachus for the 1st, 2nd and 3rd dimensions, that is, the linear, triangular, and triangular pyramid numbers. Table 10.4 presents these unitary values in various notations. The dot notation expression of the series is purposefully arranged to show how these very simple formulae can be use to generate a grid of chequerboard Cartesian space in 1 or 2 or 3 dimensions. The Pythagoreans did not use it in this way but it pays to consider how this infinite arithmetic hierarchy can be used to generate the space of analytic geometry.

Table 10.4: The three dimensional magnitudes according to the Pythagorean emanation

Number Type	Point 0-D	Line (1-D)	Triangle (2-D)	Triangular Pyramid (3-D)
Pythagorean dot notation (the first 5 periods modified to show the alternation of *excessive* and *just* values)	●	● o ● o ●	[dot triangle pattern]	[tetrahedral dot pattern]
Brownian notation	⏋	[nested brackets]	[nested brackets]	[nested brackets]
Re-entry formula		↷	↷	↷↷
Derivative Analysis Number: Gnomon: Gnomic interval: 3rd derivative:	1	1st 2nd 3rd 4th 5th 1 2 3 4 5 1 1 1 1	1 3 6 10 15 2 3 4 5 1 1 1	1 4 10 20 35 3 6 10 15 3 4 5 1 1

Consider the plane space (2-D). Conventionally it might be generated in an advance of squares, according to our sequence above on page 187. If, instead, this space is generated by the advancing triangle series, then it can generate infinitely extended square space upon which all sorts of figures may be represented, including squares, triangles, circles and other curves. However, for analytic geometry the background space must also be infinitely divisible. Such a 'continuum' can be imagined by applying additional degrees of our arithmetic. Thus, to imagine the potential infinite

Chapter 10: Foundations of Arithmetic

divisibility of the real number line, an additional degree could be utilised for the infinite division of each discrete space marked by the dots in the second column of Table 10.4. To imagine the potential continuum in 2-D, an additional two degrees are required for the infinite subdivision of each discrete square in the plane. In 3-D, three extra degrees are required. In this way, each dot in Table 10.4 (metering each discrete space) is imagined re-entering itself by 1, 2 or 3 degrees. (Further dimensions could also be added, the most obvious being the temporal). The subdivisions might be made in a variety of ways, but to imagine uniform divisibility in the line a 'double' generator could be embedded.

Thus, insert ⌐⌐ into ⌐ to give ⌐⌐.
Iterate the double generator a few times, then remove the 'legs' of our marks and we get the progressive division of linear space into alternating marked/unmarked units. (Compare with 'Cantor dust' below on page 212.)

The Pythagorean never developed such *representational* (i.e., analytic) techniques in geometry, and if we return to their basic hierarchy, we should harbour no illusions about its novelty or sophistication. It is after all, only the degrees of cumulative addition—one series is the derivative of the next. This gives the following recognisable pattern of numerals in the unitary values:

1	The cardinal value of the origin
1, 1, 1, 1, 1...	Each generation of the linear series
1, 2, 3, 4, 5...	The summing of the linear generations, or the generations of the triangular series
1, 3, 6, 10 15...	The summing of the triangular generations, or the generations of the tri' pyramid series
1, 4, 10, 20, 35...	The summing of the tri' pyramid generations or the generations in the 4th degree series

This pattern is recognisable as that of Pascal's Triangle, where order is one axis and degree the other.

ENTHUSIASTIC MATHEMATICS

In our version of Pascal's Triangle, as the series in successive *degrees* build by cumulative addition, so too the series in successive *orders* build across the degrees, thus giving a table symmetrical about a central vertical axis. In this symmetry, we can see how the *Tetraktys* of the 2nd degree (boxed) provides a neat summary of the first three degrees of the arithmetic through its similarity with the series at the 1st ordinal depth (boxed and shaded). That is, the 1, 2, 3 and 4 across the first order are the *first-born* numbers for the unitary values in their three degrees of arithmetic, starting with the 1 for the 0-D point, through the first linear number (2), plane number (3) and solid number (4).

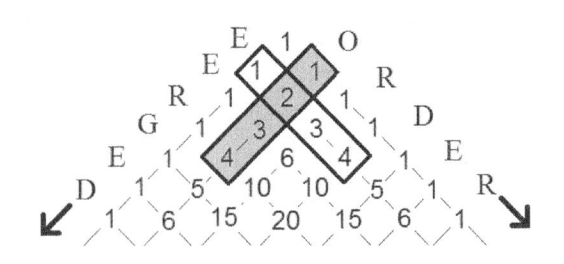

Already we have taken this arithmetic emanation beyond the analogy with the three physical dimensions and we can see how the hierarchy builds according to pattern whereby each higher dimension contains all the previous ones added together and re-entered. Thus:

The plane ⌐⌐⌐ re-enters the line ⌐ .

The solid ⌐⌐⌐⌐ re-enters the plane ⌐⌐⌐ and the line ⌐ .

And this could be extended to a fourth dimension where

⌐⌐⌐⌐⌐⌐ contains ⌐⌐⌐⌐ and ⌐⌐⌐ and ⌐ .

The orderly generation of this structure is more elegantly expressed in a variant of the flowchart notation introduced by George Spencer Brown in Chapter 11 of *Laws of Form*. Table 10.5 presents unity in the successive degree, whereby the flow across a thick vertical line indicates the crossing of a mark.

Chapter 10: Foundations of Arithmetic

Table 10.5: The Pythagorean hierarchy expressed as flowcharts					
0-D [Point]	1-D [Line]	2-D [Triangle]	3-D [Tri' Pyramid]		4-D

In this notation, the crossing of the vertical line presents a marking, where all crossing subsequent to a crossing are within that cross. The zero degree of Re-entry is a single crossing, the making of a Distinction. First degree Re-entry is expresses by a cycle of repeated marking inside the previous mark. In 2nd degree, after every marking in the outer cycle, the flow bifurcates to produce a 1st degree offshoot. In 3rd degree, after every outer cycle mark, the flow trifurcates to produce 2nd degree and 1st degree offshoots. And so forth for the higher degrees, where in each period, offshoots are produce in each lower degree.

A Hierarchy of Arithmetic in Itself

We have seen how a hierarchy of infinities develops according to this *geometric* generation. But yet is the geometry misguiding us here? Is there an *arithmetic* hierarchy more elementary than this? Remember that we have found geometric mensuration to be only an *application* of arithmetic. And this is in accord with Nicomachus who prefaces the discussion of these figured numbers by noting that the seeds of these ideas are taken over into arithmetic, as the science which is the mother of geometry and more elementary than it. [26, p. 237] Throughout his discussion he reminds us that while we can discover these numbers as we do by their geometric expression as figured numbers, they exist nonetheless in themselves in an absolute arithmetic form prior to and independent from their particular expression in the figure form by which they are named. The question then arises whether arithmetic in itself has a more elementary hierarchy? Whether or not any Pythagoreans ever found this to be so, then we certainly do.

In the pure arithmetic form, higher degree unity builds directly as *Re-Entry of Re-Entry of Re-Entry*.... Table 10.7 gives this hierarchy of infinite number in itself. Compare Table 10.7 with Table 10.6 to find the similarity of the infinite hierarchy with the hierarchy of finite order. The notation in both tables is purposefully distorted to show the empty **zero**

ENTHUSIASTIC MATHEMATICS

values in each order/degree. Finally, compare row 3 in Table 10.7 with Table 10.3 (page 197) to see how it is only with the solid pyramid numbers that the Pythagorean hierarchy of dimensional magnitudes diverges from our hierarchy.

Table 10.6: Finite Number

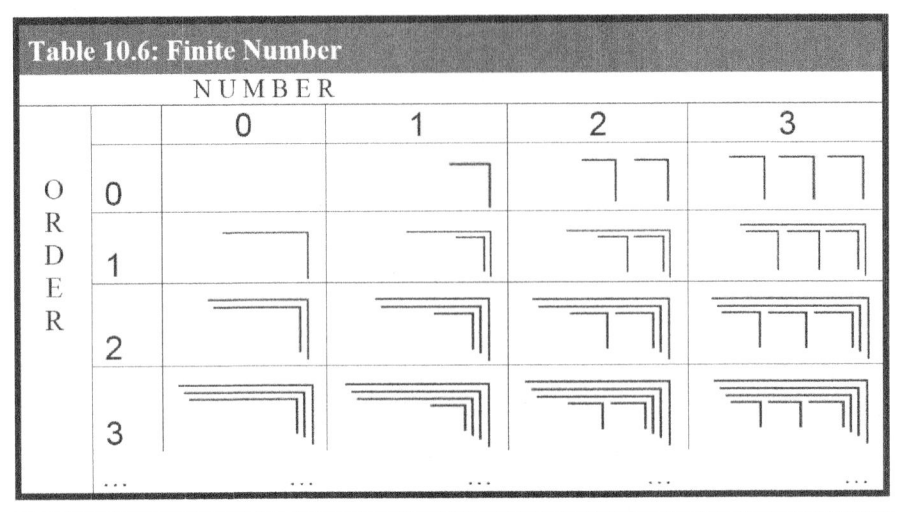

		0	1	2	3
O R D E R	0		⌐	⌐⌐	⌐⌐⌐
	1	⌐	⌐	⌐⌐	⌐⌐⌐
	2	⌐	⌐	⌐⌐	⌐⌐⌐
	3	⌐	⌐	⌐⌐	⌐⌐⌐
...					

Table 10.7: Infinite Number

		0	1	2	3
D E G R E E	1		↺	↺↺	↺↺↺
	2	↑⌐	↑⌐↺	↑⌐↺↺	↑⌐↺↺↺
	3	↑↑⌐	↑↑⌐↺	↑↑⌐↺↺	↑↑⌐↺↺↺
	4	↑↑⌐	↑↑⌐↺	↑↑⌐↺↺	↑↑⌐↺↺↺

The significance of the divergence with the Pythagorean hierarchy should not be overstated. The Pythagorean solid number series are but a variant form of the Brownian number. Consider for example 2^{D-3} with some of its variants given here with their derivative analysis:

Chapter 10: Foundations of Arithmetic

		Square Pyramid	
2^3-D			
1, 3, 8, 18, 35, 61...	1, 4, 11, 24, 45, 76...	1, 5, 14, 30, 55, 91...	1, 6, 17, 36, 65, 106...
2, 5, 10, 17, 26...	3, 7, 13, 21, 31...	4, 9, 16, 25, 36...	5, 11, 19, 29, 41...
3, 5, 7, 9...	4, 6, 8, 10...	5, 7, 9, 11...	6, 8, 10, 12...
2, 2, 2...	2, 2, 2...	2, 2, 2...	2, 2, 2...

Note how each number has two primary Re-entries at the 3rd degree while they differ in the number of primary Re-entries at the 2nd degree. But notice also how this variation does not affect the number as expressed in the third derivative. They are all 2 in the 3rd degree. They only vary in their 2nd degree values. The difference between the pyramid numbers and the 'pure' form of the 3rd degree number might be compared with the different between the following two equations in the conventional hierarchy of finite square degrees:

$$y = 2x^3 + 2x^2 \quad \text{and} \quad y = 2x^3$$

Both equations express a third degree doubling. The additional value at the lower degree (or any value at a lower degree) has a consequence on the relationship, but this consequence is a minor variation on the principle relation at the highest degree. Similarly, in our infinite arithmetic, all the above numbers are variations of 2 in the 3rd degree.

I will leave the reader to explore the reason why the Pythagorean dimension hierarchy must differ from the arithmetic hierarchy.* As for our 'pure' form of the arithmetic hierarchy, one of its remarkable characteristics is the relationship across the degrees between 0, 1 and infinity.

Zero, One & Infinity

In our higher degree arithmetic, **infinity** in one degree is **unity** in the next and **zero** in the next. This relationship is evident in Table 10.8 and can be summaries thus:

$$\infty^{Dn} = 1^{Dn+1} = 0^{Dn+2}, \text{ where } x^{Dn} \text{ is a number to the n}^{th} \text{ infinite degree.}$$

---

* This can be explained metaphorically thus: To make solid pyramids requires 1st degree branching at every depth on the 3rd degree trunk, whereas in the pure form of each higher degree number the 1st degree branching only arises from 2nd degree branches.

ENTHUSIASTIC MATHEMATICS

Curiously, this relationship has some resonances with the Pythagorean dogma. Remember their description of dimensional generation (see above on page 194). This is were the point is the beginning of the line but not a part of it, and the line the beginning of the surface but not part of it, and likewise for surface with the solid. If we recognise that their concept of *limit-as-starting-place* corresponds to the ordinal **zero** then this relationship between 0, 1 and infinity also corresponds. Thus, for example, the singular line (infinite in one direction) is the zero of the plane.

Tree Notation

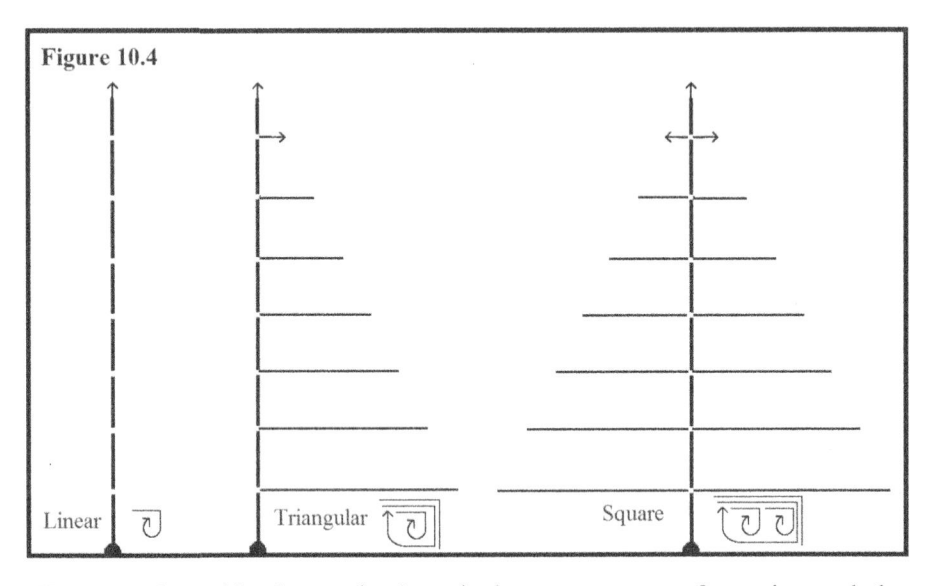

Figure 10.4

Linear | Triangular | Square

We now close this chapter by introducing a new type of notation to help visualise the emanation at higher degrees. This notation follows the Pythagorean analogy with the growth of plants and their 'seed', 'root' and 'stock'. Figure 10.4 gives expression to the linear, triangular and square numbers as trunk and branches. Here the celebrated triangular numbers look rather lopsided! But now consider a common variation of this 'pinnate' branching, found especially in foliage, where the branching alternates right-then-left at each node. If a right branch is identified with a Re-Entry at an even depth, and a left branch with a Re-Entry in a odd depth, then we have a symmetrical analogue of unity in the 2nd degree.

Often this 'alternate pinnate' branching is repeated upon these branches—every branch is itself the 'stock' for finer branches. This 'alternate bi-pinnate' structure is an analogy of Re-Entry to the 3rd degree.

Table 10.8: Zero, One & Infinity

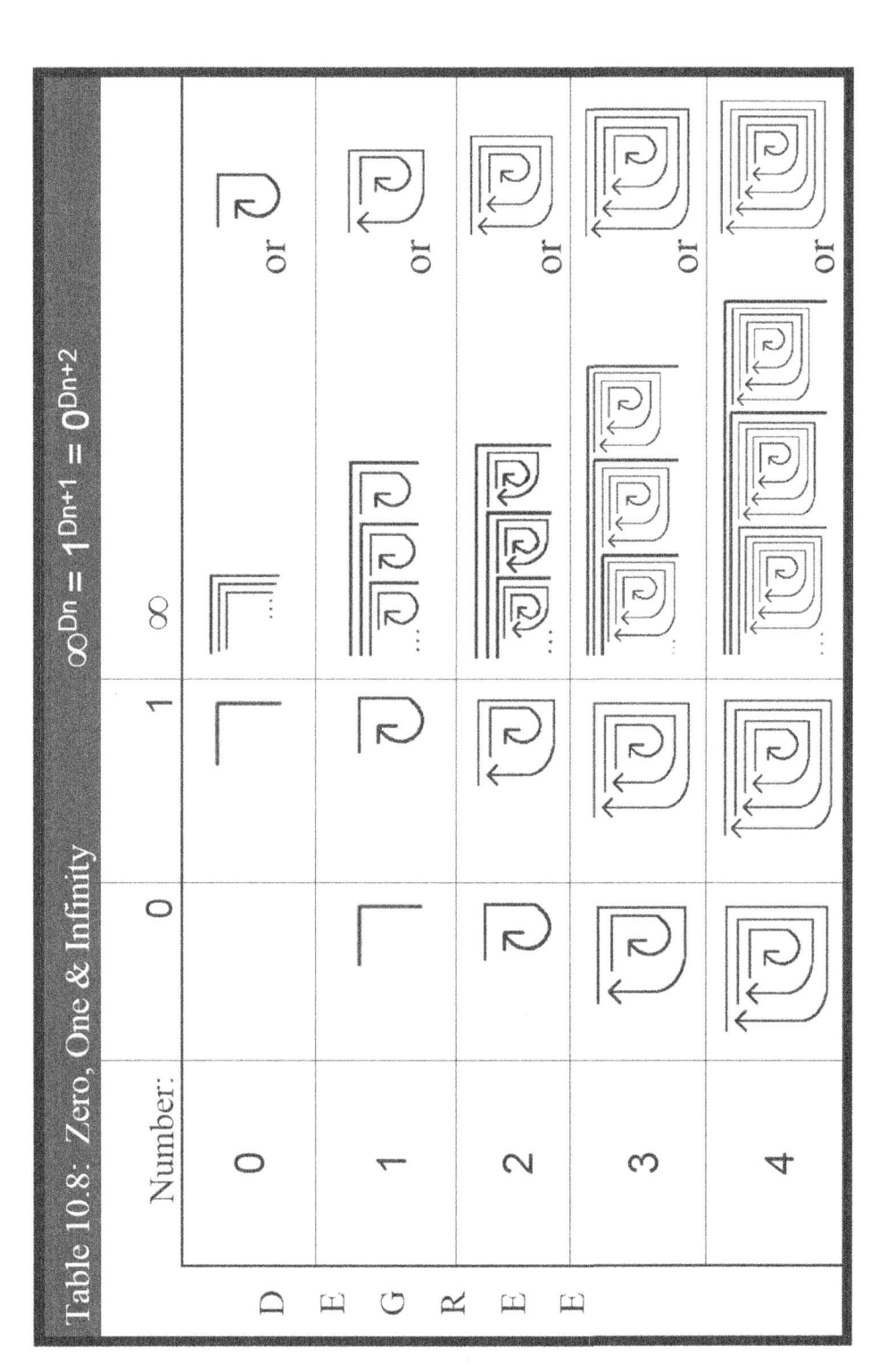

$$\infty^{Dn} = 1^{Dn+1} = 0^{Dn+2}$$

Number:	0	1	∞	
0				
1				or
2				or
3				or
4				or

DEGREE

ENTHUSIASTIC MATHEMATICS

The fronds of the Australian tree fern (as many other ferns) express this hierarchy in their branching down to the 3rd degree in their leaflets—upon each segment of which it seasonally produces packages containing thousands of copies of the program to do it all again.

Actually, in the generational structure of the tree fern, the fractal at the 3rd degree of the iteration completes itself in leaflets which are definite terminal structures branching right and left on a 3rd order 'trunk'. An expression for these terminal structures can be embedded into the formula by adding a mark in the deepest space as shown. This gives final branches that are only one generation long in a complete expression of frond branching.

***

Thus completes our exploration of the *Tetraktys* arithmetic. The *Tetraktys* and all it represented in the emanation of geometric form remained an icon of Pythagorean science throughout the entire tradition. But, at the time of Plato, a breakthrough achieved along another line of research resulted in a revolution unequalled in the entire tradition. A consequence of this revolution seems to be that the *Tetraktys* was left aside in the advance of new research. If there were one word to describe the Platonic revolution it would have to be '*logos*'. And, if in hindsight (and with the help of Brownian notation) we can find a connection between the generation of figured numbers and generation by the Platonic Logos, then there is no evidence that any Pythagoreans ever found it. Therefore, we now treat it separately.

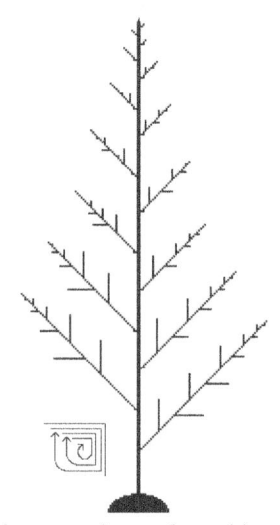

Alternate pinnate branching

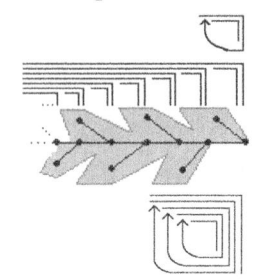

The Barnsley fern is a fractal pattern generated by a simple computer program to mimic the fern structure that is also expressed here in Brownian notation.

Chapter 11
LOGOS AND ANALOGIA

Of this Logos, which holds forever, people forever prove uncomprehending, both before they have heard it and when once they have heard it. For all becoming moves down according to the Logos.

The Logos is common.

Listen not to me but to the Logos it is wise to agree all is one.

The soul possesses a Logos which grows itself.

Heraclitus

We say that one-and-many are generated by Logos, and always, both now and in the past, circulate everywhere in every thought that is uttered...All things that are said to exist are sprung from one-and-many and carry inherent in them the limit and the unlimited.

Plato

The Pythagorean teaching on the generation of the dimensions, just now discussed, begins in the first dimension with an arithmetic series proceeding by common difference. That is, the linear series 1, 2, 3, 4, 5... proceeds by the common *gnomon* of 1. We call any series proceeding by common difference an 'arithmetic series' in order to distinguish it from a different type of series that proceeds by common ratio, called 'geometric series'. These series generated by ratio appear altogether different from those generated by difference, and they are usually treated separately—as they are in most Pythagorean texts. Whether or not *generation-by-ratio*

ENTHUSIASTIC MATHEMATICS

was important to the early Pythagoreans is unclear, but we do know that by the end of the 5th century BC it began to bear more fruit and so command more attention. In fact, research into *ratio*-nal generation advanced so dramatically that around the time of Plato it came to be seen as the very principle of the emanation. Why it rose to such prominence is not hard to appreciate, but some explanation is now required. I will also speculate on how the Pythagoreans then attempted to commensurate elementary arithmetic generation with this powerful geometric mode.

Geometric Expansion

When earlier we considered the similarity of rectangular plane figures, we met with the 4-term proportion, where for example a 1 X 2 rectangle is in proportion to a 3 X 6 rectangle because 1 is to 3 as 2 is 6 (see above, page 185).

Now, let's consider a special case of the 4-term proportion where the two ratios share a mean term. This relation can be expressed with rectangles where the width of a second rectangle is the length of the first. In our example the side measuring 2 is the length of the smaller rectangle and also the width of the larger one.

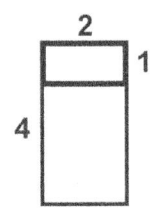

This relation can be expressed numerically as:

$$\frac{1}{2} = \frac{2}{4}$$

The 2 is in the same ratio with 4 as with 1, which can be expressed: 1 : 2 *as* 2 : 4. It is said that 2 is the 'mean proportional' of 1 and 4. The number of terms have reduced to three, which are in continuous ratio. This so-called '3-term proportion' can be expressed algebraically thus:

$$\frac{a}{b} = \frac{b}{c}$$

In our example, in the double ratio, the way to get from 1 to 4 is *by means of* the 2. The 3-term proportion can be seen as expressing a continuous generation proceeding by ratio. Thus, the series 1, 2, 4 can be extended as the 'geometric' double series:

1, 2, 4, 8, 16, 32, 64, ...

This series can be generated by continuing the substitution of length-for-width in successive rectangles according to the rule of substitution where...

$width_2 = length_1$
and $width_3 = length_2$

and in general...

$width_{n+1} = length_n$.

This last equation expresses the geometric series where every term is related to every other term in the series by the double ratio. In such a series, any two consecutive terms can be related to any other pair of consecutive terms to give a 4-term proportion. Here are two examples:

$$\frac{2}{4} = \frac{16}{32} \quad \text{and} \quad \frac{4}{8} = \frac{64}{128}$$

So, while I introduced the 3-term proportion as a special case of the 4-term proportion, we can now start to see how both proportions can be found to be derived from a basic geometric series—in this case the geometric double.

The 3-term proportion and the geometric series find their identity in the idea of ratio. Ratio is the Latin translation of the Pythagorean term '*logos*', and the word for this proportional relation between two (or more) ratios is '*ana-logia*'.*   In the strict use of this term, *analogia* refers to the generative process by means of a *logos*. The value of the *logos* in an *analogia* could be double, triple, half, 1½ or any value whatsoever. The nature of the generation is determined by the *logos*, but also by the original term. If the double series were begun with 15, then the series would be 15, 30, 60,.... However, a special significance was given an *analogia* that starts at

---

* Boethius and others translated *analogia* as *proportio*, hence our 'proportion'.

ENTHUSIASTIC MATHEMATICS

1 because it expresses an emanation by *logos* from original unity. And a special significance was given to the term that followed the 1 in such an *analogia*. This is because, while the *logos* is only implicit in the rest of the series, this '*first-born*' of the series manifests the *logos*. Thus, in the series double, 1, 2, 4, 8, 16…, the 2 is a manifestation of the double ratio, which is the hidden medium of the whole series starting from unity—and entirely hidden in those double series not starting from unity. In the series triple, 1, 3, 9, 27, 81, 243…, the 3 manifests the triple ratio that is the generator of the entire series. This *logos* is the key to the emanation out of the original One, the power-potential of the entire series.

This thinking survives in our language and notation where the geometric double series is given as the powers of 2 thus:

$[1], 2^1, 2^2, 2^3, 2^4,…$

The original 1 can be shown as potent with the double *logos* by recognising that $x^0 = 1$, thus $2^0 = 1$. Thus, the geometric triple series is:

$3^0, 3^1, 3^2, 3^3, 3^4,…$

And similarly, the ten-fold series that gives the powers of the columns on the counting board is:

$10^0, 10^1, 10^2, 10^3, 10^4,…$

As a generative principle, *analogia* need not be restricted to relations of magnitude. It could refer to the common ratio between similar things in a chains of causal relations. And in Platonism, in Stoicism and in Christianity, it came to express a physical, and even a metaphysical, principle. In Plato's *Timaeus*, soon after Timaeus establishes that the emanation of all living beings is from one living being, he considers the bond between all things:

> …the most beautiful is one that brings perfectly unity to itself and the parts linked; and this is most beautifully done by *analogia*.
> [31c]

Centuries later, Theon quotes Eratosthenes of Cyrene (fl. ca. 250 BC) saying that the logos is the principle which gives birth to the analogia, and that this *logos* is also the primary cause of the creation of all orderly things. [28, p. 54] The

Chapter II: Logos and Analogia

standard expression of the geometrical *analogia* (as first found in a fragment of Archytas, a teacher of Plato) is in the formula for the geometric mean:

1st *is to* 2nd *as* 2nd *is to* 3rd .*

It is not hard to find such relations in mathematics, philosophy, and nature. And we now consider a variety of examples (some Pythagorean, others not) as this might help awaken our minds to how these ancient mathematical reductionists envisaged the expression of this mathematical relation in natural realms yet unexplored.

Already we have seen the formulae of Heraclitus, where the generative relation between the terms is negative. Consider again:

For Psyche it is death to become Water
For Water it is death to become Earth

If the *logos* is 'death' then this can be expressed as the proportion:

Psyche *is to* Water *as* Water *is to* Earth.

Now consider the geometric paragon of *analogia*, the relation of the dimensions of 'square' space:

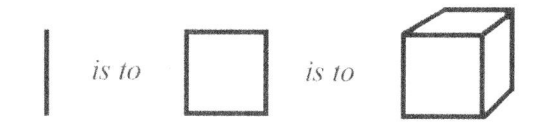

Line *is to* surface *as* surface *is to* solid

When magnitudes are applied to this ratio we see why this mean was call 'geometric':

2_{linear} *is to* 4_{planar} *as* 4_{planar} *is to* 8_{solid}
3_{linear} *is to* 9_{planar} *as* 9_{planar} *is to* 27_{solid}
$½_{linear}$ *is to* $¼_{planar}$ *as* $¼_{planar}$ *is to* $⅛_{solid}$

---

* In *Greek Mathematical Works*, Vol I (Loeb #335), p. 112; and Deils B2.

ENTHUSIASTIC MATHEMATICS

If we take the relationship between length, area and volume as but a fragment of a geometric series, then each of these series could regress back to the 1, analogous to the point-origin. But what about the series starting with the unit line? The ratio of the unit line to the unit square and to the unit solid is a ratio of equality, 1 : 1 : 1. Measurably there doesn't appear to be any generation at all. Yet the Hellenistic textbooks by Theon and Nicomachus instruct that this *analogia* of identity is primary to all ratios. Consider Theon: after quoting from Adrastus of Aphrodisias (a near contemporary) and another Pythagorean authority (Erathosthenes), Theon says that the *logos* of equality is the principle and the element of all analogia.* We shall soon see how the seemingly non-generative relation could come to be regarded as the generator of all.

Two more recent geometrical examples of *analogia* are Cantor Dust and Koch Island.

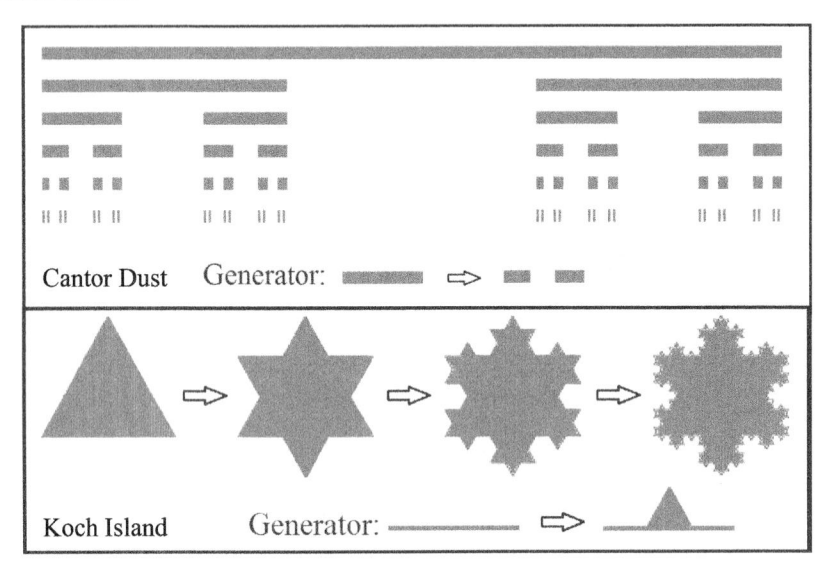

What is remarkable about these figures is perhaps most evident when considering the 'coastline' of the Koch Island. With each iteration in its generation, the length of the coastline increases and continues to increase

---
* [28, p. 70–71]. Lawlor translates thus: Adrastus shows that the ratio of equality is the first in order and that it is an element of all the ratios of which we have previously spoken and of all the proportions they give, for it is from it that all others take birth, and in it that they are all resolved. After quoting Erathosthenes, Theon continues by saying that he will show that all mathematics consists in the proportion of certain quantities, and that equality is the principle and element of proportion. See also on p. 54 of the same translation another quote from Erathothenes saying that the ratio is the principle which gives birth to the proportion and it is also the primary cause of the creation of all orderly things. Every proportion is indeed composed of ratios and the principle of the ratio is equality. In a similar vein, Nicomachus says: all the complex species of inequality and the varieties of these species are produced out of equality, first and alone, as from a mother and a root [26, p. 226]; and in the realm of inequality, advance and increase have their origin in equality. [26, p. 230]

Chapter II: Logos and Analogia

without tending to any particular value. It has an infinite length (or better, it has no length) and no tangent. Its position is ultimately indeterminate and yet it is definitely situated as the shoreline limit of the island delimited by the 'sea,' that contains it.*

Analogia is not restricted to the formal sciences, rather it is found in all fields of knowledge both scientific and traditional.# Culturally it is expressed in all sorts of ways. Consider the nursery rhythm 'The old women who swallowed the fly'...

> She swallowed the frog to catch the spider
> She swallowed the spider to catch the fly

Here the *logos* 'to catch' expresses the predatory relationship, and the absurdity is that, while each new predator catches the previous one, it still must contain it, and this eventually kills the old woman who contains them all!

A similar containment *analogia* is the expression of the matriarchal relation of Russian ('Matryoshka') dolls:

> Grandmother *is to* Mother *as* Mother *is to* Daughter.

The meaning of our modern word 'analogy' is derived from the Pythagorean *analogia*, and in some senses the original meaning has been retained, although it tends to hark back to the more common use of *analogia* as for the similarity between two pairs of relations (the 4-term proportion) rather than the more proper Pythagorean meaning as the continuous rational series itself. Word meanings themselves are often derived by analogy in this way. Consider how the radio station 'broadcasts' its signal *just as* the farmer once broadcast his seed. Allegory is just such an analogy. But in some instances we do have analogies that are the comparison of two continuous proportions. Consider the first generative lesson of the Russian Dolls: as the smaller doll *is to* the larger, *so too* a daughter *is to* her mother (i.e., the one comes out of the other). And likewise, the first lesson for the bureaucrat: the lines of authority above and below you are continuous relationships of power *just like* the pecking order of hens.

---
* The indeterminacy of this Koch coastline is analogous to the indeterminacy of natural coastlines where the measured length is determined by the scale of the rule. See Mandelbrot [19] Ch 5, Ch 6 & Ch 8.
\# For some Pythagorean examples of relationships that are non-arithmetic 4-term proportions see Theon [28], p. 54.

ENTHUSIASTIC MATHEMATICS

If *analogia* can be seen as a powerful medium of generation, organisation and communication, this suggests that some primary *analogia* may be the elementary principle of the emanation. In order to investigate this hypothesis the next step would be to find the *logos* elementary to all these species of *logos*. Just such a *logos* (which we will now call 'Logos') attained divinity and pervaded Hellenistic theology from the beginning. Its entry into Judaism is evident in the writings of Philo of Alexandria (see above page 160). That was around the time that Christianity was emerging as a Jewish sect. Before it made its break with Judaism, Logos entered the Christian canon via the Gospel of John.

In this Gospel, *God-the-father* is identified with the original **One**, while the first-born Son is the Logos, such that this Logos is the medium of, and the medium back to, the **One**. In this first passage the medium is called 'love':

> As the father has loved me so I have loved you, remain in my love.
> If you keep my commandment, you shall remain in my love;
> Even as I have kept my Father's commandments, and remain in his love.
> [John 15, 9-10]

Here the medium is speaking as the Son, the Logos manifest:

> Holy Father, keep them in your name whom you have given me, that they may be one as we are. ..
> Sanctify them by thy truth; the Logos is truth. As you sent me into the world I sent them into the world...
> That they all may be one as you father are in me and I in you, that they also may be one in us...
> And the glory that you have given me I have given them; that they may be one as we are one. I in them and you in me that they may be perfect in one. *

The name of the father is the mystical **One** marked. Followers of the Father's commandments (elsewhere called '*sons-of-God*') become **One** through the Logos. The Christian theology of Logos (that was merged with the story of the Jewish messiah and God-man Jesus) bares a striking resemblance to the contemporaneous theology of the Stoics. For them the Logos is the medium of all generation; it is the 'seed' of all in the origin,

---

* Excerpts from *John* 17, 11-23. See Weil's discussion [6], p. 157–8. See also *Matthew* 7:12, and *John* 13:34: As I have loved you so you must love one another. See also John Dee: Our neighbour's *proportio* is also prescribed of the Almighty lawmaker: which is to do to other even as we would be done unto. [16], p. 129.

and thereby it is the law of *being* and of *knowing*.* Later, in the Roman Christian church, the meaning of Logos would be lost in the translation as *verbum* (thus 'the Word'), while in the Eastern Church the Logos continued with its Hellenistic meaning as the principal ratio and medium of *being* (ontology), *knowing* (epistemology) and *loving* (sociology).

We cannot say for sure how Logos came to such prominence in Stoic and Christian theology, nor the extent to which it was derived from (and remained true to) the Logos that came to prominence among the *mathematici* centuries earlier. There are huge gaps in the evidence. We can only observe the similarities of these Logos doctrines with the contemporaneous and remarkably pervasive Platonic doctrine of an elementary medium and generative principle. Claims for the origins of the Platonic Logos priory to the 5th century Pythagoreans must also remain speculative. Logos as a principle of generation and mediation bares a striking similarity to the common and mediating logos of Heraclitus, but only vague elaborations of his Logos have survived.#

Less obscure is the progress of Logos towards the heart of Pythagorean science during the 4th century BC. In fact, the story to which we now turn is the story of the emergence in Plato's Athens of the idea that there is a *principal-logos* elementary to the emanation.

The Golden Section

The ascendency of the Logos was by no means easy or painless. To begin with, there is a characteristic of the geometric series that presents them as most unsuitable for this elementary role in the emanation. This is because, in *analogia*, the Logos is not presented *immanent* in the original **One**. It is not a potential of the **One**, but it is apparently a second and independent cause of the generation. The original **One** is potentially the double series but, just as well, it is the potential of the triple, or any other such series. It is only when the Logos is *applied*, that the series is determined. Thus, in the geometric series we have a model of generation that conforms more to the Aristotelian *form-applied-to-matter* mode.

Remember Aristotle's insistence that all generation must be *from something* and *by something* (see above, page 49). The *from something* is the 'material cause' and the *by something* is the 'formal cause'. Things are

---
* For the Stoic doctrine of *Logos* see Dillon [9], p. 80.
# The earliest evidence of philosophic doctrine of *Logos* is found in the saying of Heraclitus. See some examples at the head of this chapter. For a discussion of the Heraclitean *Logos* see Guthrie [32], p. 419–434.

brought into being by two independent powers [*dynamis*]. The Pythagorean *analogia* is thus described in the language of Aristotle such that the One is the 'primary matter' to which a formal *logos* (e.g., the double or the triple) is repeatedly applies so as to generate the terms of the series. In modern logic these two 'causes' are called 'operator' and 'operand'. In his *Fractal Geometry of Nature* Mandelbrot calls them 'initiator' and 'generator'. In the generation of Cantor Dust, the initiator (material cause) is *the line* and the generator (formal cause) is the *breaking-of-the-line*. In the generation of the Koch Island, the initiator is the equilateral triangle and the generator is the *triangular-kinking-of-the-sides*. But in a true and elementary expression of the emanation, the generator would be identified with the initiator; the Logos would have to be seen not just as a *potential of* and *within* the origin, but as the potency of the origin itself. This is how it is famously put in the prologue to the Gospel of John:

> In the origin was the Logos
> And the Logos was with God
> And the Logos was God
> [The Logos] was in the origin with God
> All things came into being through him
> And without him not even one thing that came into being came into being.

The Logos was God at the beginning of creation. In a self-generating emanation, the generator must be immanent in, and identical with, the initiator. *How could we envisage such a self-generating origin in a geometric series?*

Imagine a line divided so that the first part *is to* the second part as the second *is to* the whole. This would give what Euclid called 'the division of extreme and mean', or what came to be known in the Renaissance as the 'Golden Section'.

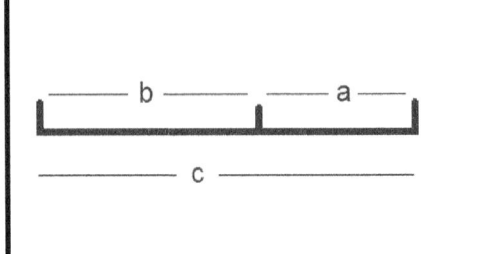

This division of a line by extreme and mean gives the parts a and b of c such that a : b *as* b : c. The series can be continued where d is generated by duplicating the mean term, b, and adding it to c. So, just as c = b + a likewise d = c + b, and a, b, c and d are in continuous ratio.

Chapter II: Logos and Analogia

This special 3-term proportion is expressed algebraically thus:

a *is to* b *as* b *is to* c, *where* c = a + b

In the geometric series generated by this ratio, the ratio of the origin, c, to the *first-born*, d, is implicit in the origin itself. Thus, if the origin is regarded as *the-line-divided-in-exactly-this-ratio*, then *the origin is already the Logos*. The 'generator' is the potency of the 'initiator'.

Euclid, Book II, Prop 11, shows how the Pythagoreans could generate this ratio, and its procession, geometrically.*

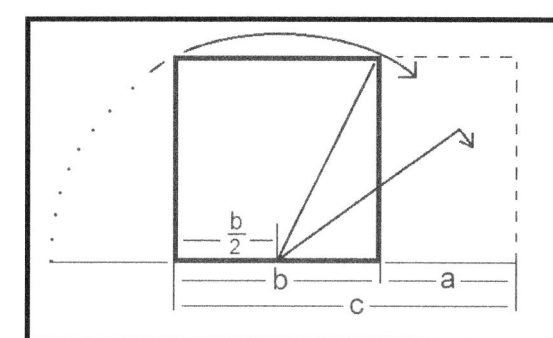

The 'Golden Ratio' can be generated geometrically by extending line b by a to give c. This also generated 'Golden Rectangles' a X b and b X a, where length and width are in the Golden Ratio.

Once constructed, Golden Rectangles can expand (or contract) by *length-for-width* (or *width-for-length*) substitutions.

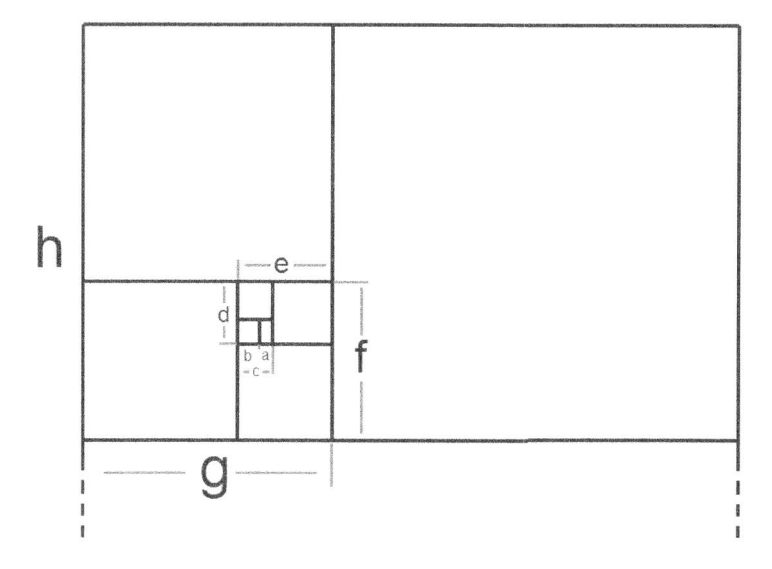

---

* For Euclid's specific instructions on how to make the cut, see Bk VI, Prop 30.

217

ENTHUSIASTIC MATHEMATICS

Euclid also shows how the Golden Section can be used to construct the pentagon in which a star exhibiting the ratio can be inscribed. Once the first pentagon is generated, pentagons and stars can built through expansions, or contractions, recursively. The pentagon is also the shape of the 12 sides used to construct the fourth regular solid, the dodecahedron, and so the Golden Section was seen as elementary to its form.*

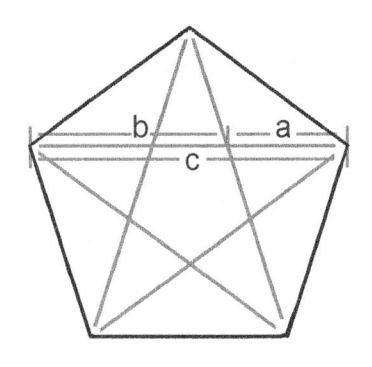

---

* Euclid, Bk IV Prop 10 & 11; Bk II, Prop 11. On the construction of the star pentagramme, see Bk IV 10-14. See Heath's discussion [3], Vol II, p. 99. The star-pentagon is found in Babylonian art and there are examples of the dodecahedron with 12 pentagon sides dating back to Neolithic times. See Boyer [33], p. 50] and Lawlor [5], p. 96–7.

Chapter II: Logos and Analogia

If the early Pythagoreans investigated the Golden Section then they left barely a trace. Indeed, it is rare to find a Pythagorean text discussing it beyond the lemmas and proofs recorded by Euclid in Alexandria around 300 BC. But the lack of evidence may be due to the secrecy under which this sacred ratio was shrouded. What we have from outsiders is most suggestive. They say for example, that the star-pentagon (or *'pentagramme'*) was used by the ancient Pythagoreans as a secret symbol of recognition, as though a password, and that it was given the cryptic name 'health'. [3, Vol II, p. 98–9]

Discovery of the Golden Ratio and its significance may have even preceded the Greeks. But while natural exhibitions of the ratio are well documented and accepted, this acceptance is in contrast to the controversy over the supposed usage of Golden Ratios and Golden Rectangles in ancient human artefacts. In the greatest of all the ancient sacred artefacts, the Great Pyramid of Giza, the square base and the sloping sides are in this ratio. Closer to the Pythagoreans are the Golden Rectangles found in the structure of the Athenian Parthenon designed by the famous Phidias, who was active in the 5th century BC—before Plato, but around the time of Philolaus. Late in the European revival, the first letter of Phidias' name, Φ, came into use as the algebraic symbol for this ratio, which had already featured in Renaissance art, architecture and mechanical design. The most famous book on this subject, *De divina proportione*, was published in 1509, with text by Luca Pacioli and illustrations by Leonardo da Vinci. This book identifies 'The Divine Ratio' with the creator-God, who expresses his triune nature as a unity in three terms.*

For the rest of this chapter we will consider this ratio, its expansion and mensuration, in as much as it served the search for the elementary arithmetic emanation.

---

* For the identification of the ratio with the Trinity, see in *De divina proportione*, the dedication to Ludovico Sforza and Ch 5. See also the discussion in Livio [34], p. 131–2. For a contemporary discussion of the Golden Ratio in nature also see Livio [34], p. 109–123. For an early discussion, see D'arcy Thompson [35], Ch 11 & 14. On the controversy over early human knowledge and uses of the ratio, see Livio [34], Ch 3. In the great Pyramid, in cross-section, a vertical line from the summit gives a right triangle, the so-called Egyptian Triangle. The ratio of the slant height of the pyramid (hypotenuse of the triangle) to the distance from ground centre to the side (i.e., half the lengths of the square base) very closely approximates Φ.

Linear Expansion of the Golden Section

Once a line has been sectioned by 'extreme and mean', the simplest geometrical expansion to generate the Golden Series is in linear geometry, where the mean is added to the length, and then this is repeated recursively:

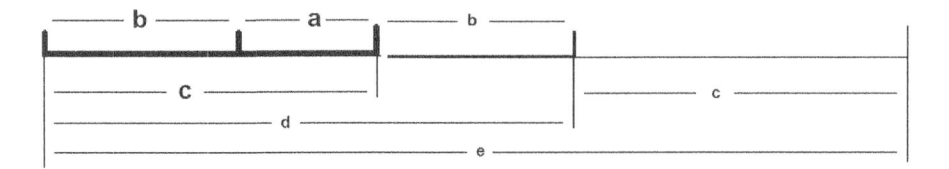

If b = 1 and c = c/b = Φ, then d = Φ + 1 and e = Φ + 1 + Φ, and so forth:

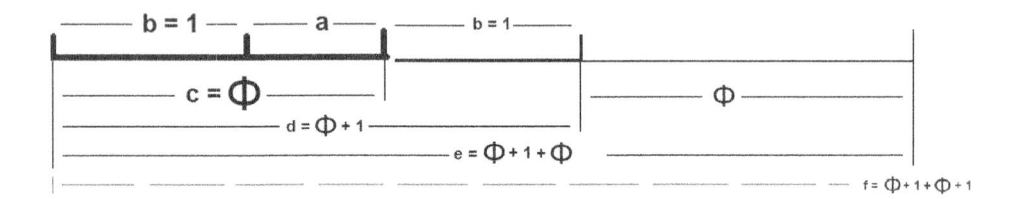

Starting from the original ratio, Φ: 1, each value in the series is the sum of the two previous values:

```
b =   1
c =   Φ
d =   (Φ + 1)
e =   (Φ + 1) + Φ
f =   (Φ + 1) + Φ + (Φ + 1)
...
```

Because this series *proceeding by summation* is in continuous ratio, it can also be generated by repeated *multiplication* and presented as the power series:

1, Φ, Φ², Φ³, Φ⁴...

If the series were contracted rather than expanded, the first step would give b = a + (b − a), and so a is now the mean part of the line b, just as b is the

Chapter II: Logos and Analogia

mean part of c. So, while a and b are the original parts of c, the contraction shows that a is also a part of b. The contraction then begins 1, a, (1-a)..., which can be converted into an inverse power series such that $a = 1/\Phi$ and $(b - a) = 1/\Phi^2$.

Φ^0 $\quad$ $1/\Phi \quad \Phi^1$ $\quad$ $1/\Phi^2 \quad\quad \Phi^2$ $\quad$ $1/\Phi^3 \quad\quad\quad \Phi^3$ $\quad$ ... $\quad\quad\quad$ ...	This bi-directional series can be expressed as a 'lambdoid diagram' (see below on page 252) symmetrical about the mean, $b = 1 = \Phi^0$. This symmetry is also found in arithmetic approximations: $\quad\quad \Phi = 1.618...$ and $1/\Phi = 0.618....$

Asymmetrical Magnitudes

In all these expansions and contractions we have measured the ratio in terms of itself but yet have not given it arithmetic expression. In fact, the difficulty in dealing with this geometric series is that Φ has no arithmetic expression. That is, it is a geometrically generated relation of magnitudes that cannot be expressed in the ratio c:b, such that c and b are whole number values. This is then, the first time in our story that we have come to discuss what are now call 'irrational numbers'. And there might be another reason for us to pause here to consider them, because there is some evidence to suggest that the interest in *this* (irrational) ratio was even greater than the interest in the (irrational) ratio of the diagonal in the square ($\sqrt{2}$)—or of the circumference embracing the line (π)—and that the Golden Section was the first irrational to be discovered and investigated by the Pythagoreans.[*] Yet, while the proof of the irrationality of Φ would have been quite within the skill of the early Pythagoreans, no such proof—and no direct discussion of its irrationality—is found preserved in the record.[#]

What we do know is that the early Pythagoreans did discover that elementary geometric procedures could generate magnitudes that are inexpressible arithmetically in terms of the original unit magnitude from which they were geometrically derived. They knew that this occurred especially in relations across the dimensions, and they did at least have a proof of the

---
[*] For discussions of this possibility see Boyer [33], p. 51 & 73, and Livio [34], p. 35–6.
[#] For a proof, see Livio's Appendix 2 [34], p. 256–7. See also [33], p. 51. The first six propositions of Euclid Bk XIII concern the Golden Section. There is evidence that Prop 1-5 originate with Eudoxus. However, the proof of Φ's irrationality in Prop 6 is widely regarded as an interpolation. See Heath [3], Vol III, p. 441 & 451.

irrationality of √2. It is from their '*a-logia*' that we get the Latinised '*ir-ratio*-nal'. Other terms were also used to identify and distinguish irrationals. These included 'inexpressible' [*harreton*], and the term preferred by Plato, '*asymmetrical*'. While this latter term has a variant meaning in modern language, its meaningful construction, '*a-sym-metric*', retains for us the Pythagorean meaning, 'without-common-measure', and so there is no need for us to move beyond this transliteration to the conventional translation (after Boethius) as 'incommensurable'.*

Observers of Pythagorean science have long recognised the gravity with which the problem of *asymmetry* presented itself. When an arithmetic value can no longer be obtained, the science of magnitudes—which is to say, *geometry* itself—comes to a grinding halt. The analogy of arithmetic to the relative size of figures collapses. In the Golden Series we have found an *analogia* that is an analogy of a self-generating origin—the *logos is* the origin—and yet this *logos-origin* is itself inexpressible arithmetically, and so, thereby, is the entire series. It is true that approximations of the value of Φ can be found by direct measurement, and that these are sufficient in applications of the Logos to art and architecture. But this will not do for pure mathematics. Once we step into approximation, this application of arithmetic to figure loses its generative harmony. When we generate a magnitude inexpressible as an arithmetic ratio then we can express no medium to the arithmetic from which it was derived. In essence, the problem is that the ratio Φ:1 cannot be expressed in terms of the arithmetic duplication, 2:1.

It is important to recognise here the exact nature of the problem of irrationality. It is that Φ cannot be reduced to an arithmetic ratio. But the relation called 'Φ' is still a ratio. The Golden Ratio is rational in the sense that it has a ratio to 1, and this ratio is expressed in the *analogia*: 1 *is to* Φ *as* Φ *is to* $Φ^2$. This *analogia* generates the 'geometric series' 1, Φ, $Φ^2$, $Φ^3$, $Φ^4$,..... It's just that this ratio cannot be expressed in terms of the arithmetic ratio of 2:1 from which it is apparently derived. This is why it is better to say that Φ, and π and √2 are 'inexpressible' or 'asymmetrical' rather than 'irrational'. They are inexpressible as arithmetic ratios because they do not share the ratio that all arithmetic values (i.e., rational numbers) share with 1. It is as though the ratio Φ:1, √2:1 and π:1 generated three separate emanations; three entirely new species of magnitude, the terms of which

---

* Boethius translated *asummetros* into the Latin as *incommensurabilis*. See *summetros* and *asummetros* used in this sense in Plato's *Theaetetus*, p. 147d, and in Euclid, Bk X, Def 3 and 4.

Chapter II: Logos and Analogia

clearly express similarity to each other, and yet each species has no relationship to ordinary arithmetic magnitudes. Just as any square is *similar* to all squares and *dissimilar* to all circles; likewise the geometric '√2' is similar to 2√2, √2², 1/√2, etc., and dissimilar to the ratio π and the linear arithmetic ratio 2.

It seems that at first the Pythagoreans struggled with this discovery of these 'irrational rationals' precisely because their geometry was founded in the analogy with arithmetic. Consider that by definition, in the Golden Series the ratio of line b to line c is equal to the ratio of line c to d. We expressed this identity of ratio as $1/\Phi = \Phi/\Phi^2$. But, as Φ has no arithmetic expression then we cannot say that the ratio of line b to c is equal to the ratio of line c to d—because neither term has a definite value. In other words:

> *If geometry is about magnitude and magnitude is always reduced to arithmetic value then neither term has a magnitude, and so neither term has a definite value that can ever be identified.*

The consequences of this outcome is crippling for geometry because it makes the expression of proportional relations (continuous or otherwise) impossible whenever irrationals are involved. And most often they are—the exceptions are very special cases. Consider that a right-angle triangle with an irrational hypotenuse could not be regarded as in the same proportions to a similar triangle of different size because its hypotenuse has no definite value.* Nor could a circle of diameter 1 be considered similar to a circle of diameter 2 because in each case the circumference is inexpressible arithmetically. This is why it is thought that the discovery of the irrationals sent Pythagorean geometry and the entire project of an arithmo-geometric emanation into crisis.

Just when the Pythagoreans first faced the problem of the irrationals, and for how long they suffered it, remains obscure. There are various stories recorded later that suggest they suffered the crisis long and deeply. Whether or not there is any truth behind these stories, we do have a much clearer picture of how and when the crisis was overcome such that the search for the elementary medium of the emanation could continue.

---

* The exceptions are 'Pythagorean triples', the first being 3, 4, 5, where $3^2 + 4^2 = 5^2$. They have been known and were utilised well before the Greeks by the Babylonians. We don't know that the Babylonians had any proof of incommensurability for the rest, but the fact that they seemed to calculate from these special cases suggests that they also knew that all the others were (at least for all practical purposes) incommensurable.

What was required to circumvent this crisis was to abandon the notion that the arithmetic ratio is elementary to the emanation. This does not necessarily mean abandoning the mathematical model. It could be that there is a more elementary means of generation, of which arithmetic and *asymmetrical* generators are but particular modes. If we refrain from reducing proportions to their expression in terms of arithmetic values then similarity between figures could be expressed simply in *the identity of ratio*. The identity of the ratio is the ratio in itself. This would be Logos *qua Logos*, not Logos *qua arithmetic*. Such a view of the nature and significance of proportion could only be considered in a unified theory of mathematical generation if it were proposed that Logos were elementary to arithmetic; that is, only if the ratio 2:1 in ordinary arithmetic were consider but a particular form of a more general Logos. Just such a theory of proportion is preserved in Euclid Book V Definition 5, and its invention is attributed to Eudoxus, the Academic contemporary of Plato.

That this new theory of proportion represents a breakthrough in the crisis of *asymmetry* has long been argued by modern scholars. [3, Vol II, p. 112-3, 116–8 & 20–22] That it was part of a revolutionary realignment of geometry—such that an elementary *logos* took centre stage—is not always granted by sober historians. However, this revolution has been celebrated by the enthusiastic Christian Pythagorean, Simone Weil (1909-1943). For Weil, this new theory of proportion is a key element in the foundation of the Platonic versions of Pythagoreanism, and as such it is a pre-Christian intuition of the Christian theology of Logos. While the reader may take or leave the Christian frame of reference of this fanatical convert, it is Weil's view of the Eudoxan revolution that we follow here. In Platonism, geometry is no longer the science of magnitude but the science of Logos—as the ratio elementary to both symmetrical and asymmetrical terms.

The revolutionary theory of proportion attributed to Eudoxus allowed a way of dealing with the rationality of irrationals, but as such, it only served to define the problem of *asymmetry*. The various species of *asymmetricals* could each be treated in their own symmetrical self-similarity, but they needed to find the underlying similarity of all species in an *analogia* that is also elementary to arithmetic. A celebrated passage of Plato's *Laws* says as much. The anonymous Athenian (usually taken to be Plato speaking for himself) implores that we must continually put this problem to each other and give our love of victory a pastimes worthy to us. The problem, the desired victory, is to know…

> ...the generative nature of the symmetrical and the asymmetrical in relation to one another.*

In *Epinomis* (the addendum to *Laws*), plane geometry is redefined as the manifest assimilation to one another of numbers which are naturally dissimilar, effected by reference to areas. [p. 990d]

Plato's Academy had brought the project of mathematical emanation science to this clearly defined juncture, after which some magnificent progress would be made towards finding the relations between the different species of number revealed in plane geometry. But alas, the victory that Plato envisaged was never attained. The problem of finding the underlying symmetry of the emanation remained the central problem in Pythagorean science right through the Christian revival, through Kepler and on to Leibniz, as we shall see.

Kepler's Divine Numbers

If we now return to the Golden Section, we can see that the problem of its *asymmetry* is particularly acute. This is after all the geometric ratio investigated as its own self-generating origin, but instead of finding it to be the higher Logos mediating arithmetic with shape, it is discovered to exemplify geometry's utter alienation. One can imagine a scenario, perhaps repeated more than once in our history: in the search for a basic principle of mathematical self-generation the idea of the Golden Section emerges; a way is discovered by which it can be geometrically generated; applications for it are found in the generation of other important figures and relations in geometry; excited investigations are undertaken to determine its exact arithmetic value; but finally, it is discovered that this ratio has no value. How can this impasse be overcome?

It turns out that a way forward is via the geometric expansions itself. This remarkable technique involves giving Φ the nominal value of identity, that is, 1:1. We can do this by letting $a = 1$ and also $b = 1$. So, whereas in the Golden Series proper $(b - a) + a = b$, where $(b - a)$, a and b are in continuous proportion, here we are equating the whole (b) with its 'mean'

---

* p. 820c. The context of this injunction is a discussion of the problem of the relation of line and surface to solid or of surface and line to each other (p. 820a-b), thus, the problem of geometric incommensurability. The stranger explains that the essential nature of the symmetrical and asymmetrical is closely related to the problem of geometric incommensurability and that the errors arising are similar.

part (a). The whole equals one of its parts. If we allow this contradiction, then a + b = c = 2, giving the ratio between the second and third term as the arithmetic ratio of duplication, 2:1. We can now substitute arithmetic values for all the terms in the geometric expansion of Φ:

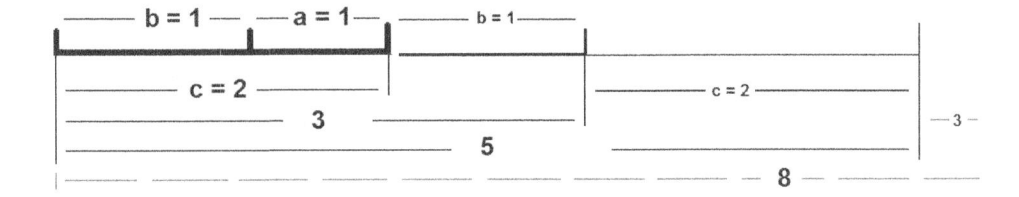

```
——— b = 1 ——  —— a = 1 —      ——— b = 1 ———
|————— c = 2 —————|            |————— c = 2 —————|
|——————————— 3 ———————————|                         — 3 —
|——————————————— 5 ———————————————|
                                    |——————— 8 ———————|
```

Starting with the original identity of 1:1 the first difference is 2 expressing the ratio 2:1 where we previously had Φ:1. The expansion continues with 2 now substituted for Φ:

1	= 1	After the identity, 1:1, each value in the series is the sum of the two previous values, and thereby the series is constructed from combinations of one and its double, the arithmetic 1st and the 2nd, the elementary *excessive* and *just*.
1	= 1	
2	= 2	
2 + 1	= 3	
(2 + 1) + 2	= 5	
(2 + 1) + 2 + (2+ 1)	= 8	
...	...	

While we have evidence of a similar technique used to find the values for √2 (see Chapter 12 below), this expansion is not found anywhere in the ancient record. The arithmetic series it generates first appears in the *Liber Abbaci* of 1202. This was one of the first texts by a European advancing the mathematical techniques coming to them from the Arabs. Its author, Leonardo of Pisa, was otherwise known as 'Fibonacci', and this is the name give to the sequence. No record of the Fibonacci sequence is found in any texts prior to 1202, and even then Leonardo did not present it in relation to the Golden Series. As far as we know, it was Kepler in 1608 who was the first to record the Fibonacci sequence as an arithmetic expression of the Golden Ratio. [34, p. 151–2] Seemingly independent from this Leonardo, but very much in the spirit of the other Leonardo (the illustrator of *De divina proportione* 100 years earlier), Kepler describes his derivation of the series from the 'divine ratio' much as we have above.

For Kepler this ratio is one of the two great treasures of Geometry (the other is Pythagoras' Theorem) and, with barely any evidence in the offing, the principle of organic pro-creation:

> It is in the likeness of this self-developing series that the faculty of propagation is, in my opinion, formed; and so in a flower the authentic flag of this faculty is shown, the pentagon.
> [34, p. 110]

This faculty of continuous, divine self-creation can be express both geometrically and arithmetically:

> The propagation of plants and the progenitive acts of animals are in the same ratio as the geometrical proportion, or proportion represented by line segments [i.e., Φ], and the arithmetic or numerically expressed proportion [i.e., in the Fibonacci sequence].*

According to Kepler, the pentagon in the flower announces the form of natural generation which is in the likeness of the self-generating (Fibonacci) series that gives expression to the Golden Mean.

The Fibonacci sequence is useful in the first place in applied mathematics for giving finite arithmetic approximations to represent Φ. The ratio of consecutive terms provide increasingly closer approximations to Φ. For example, the tenth ratio of **89/55** already provides an approximation accurate to three decimal places, that is, **1.618**.

In the series as presented by Kepler, the initial distortion of *equating-the-whole-with-its-part* is progressively diminished through osculations within osculation around the true but inexpressible geometry ratio. Kepler demonstrates this osculation by way of a law of the 4-term proportion that gives the product of the first and the last term as equal to the product of the second and the third term. In the case of the 3-term proportion, the second and third terms are identical, and so the 'square of the mean' equals the rectangle of these 'extremes'. Thus, in $a/_b = b/_c$, $b^2 = a \times c$. For example, in the geometric double: $2^2 = 1 \times 4$, $4^2 = 2 \times 8$, $8^2 = 4 \times 16$, and so forth. Now, while the Golden Series is a geometric series, with Φ as the common ratio, the Fibonacci sequence given to express this ratio is not itself in continuous proportion, that is, $1/_1 \neq 1/_2 \neq 2/_3 \neq 3/_5$....

---

* Quoted in Livio [34], p. 154.

ENTHUSIASTIC MATHEMATICS

However, the relationship of this series to the geometric series that Kepler knew to be both 'divine' and inexpressible, can be seen in the following equations relating the square of successive means to the 'rectangle' of their extremes:*

$1^2 = (1 \times 2) - 1$
$2^2 = (1 \times 3) + 1$
$3^2 = (2 \times 5) - 1$
$5^2 = (3 \times 8) + 1$
...
$89^2 = (55 \times 144) + 1$

The square of the successive means in the Fibonacci sequence alternates a unit below then a unit above the value they would be if the mean were in the same ratio with both extremes. As the series progresses to larger values, the variance of a unit diminishes exponentially in its proportional significance, and thus we can see how the ratio between successive terms quickly approaches that geometric mean hailed by Renaissance Pythagoreans as a principle of Divine Creation.

The significance of the Fibonacci sequence to the pure mathematics of the Golden Section is not that we can use it to generate arithmetic representations of Φ, but rather that it is itself the arithmetic form of Φ: as Kepler says, it is Φ numerically expressed.# The sequence is an infinite arithmetic expression of Φ. Here we have a geometrically generated ratio (the Golden Section) that is found to have no arithmetic expression (i.e., it is irrational) but yet, through an analogy of its geometric expansion we can generate an unlimited series of arithmetic values that does express the ratio. The consequence is that the analogy of arithmetic with relative size can be restored if the geometric ratio, Φ, is seen not as any particular arithmetic value, but rather as the unlimited series itself. That is, the arithmetic expression of Φ is like the geometrical generation of Cantor Dust and the Koch Island. There is never any last member of these generative series that is any more than an approximation to these objects. With each iteration the 'mass' of Cantor Dust approaches zero, and with every iteration the kinked length of the Koch 'shoreline' gets longer and longer without limit. No particular member of the series gives us the actual 'dust'

---

* If we start the series with 0 then it still works: $1^2 = 0 + 1$
\# The Fibonacci sequence is not the only series to converge on the golden ratio. Any series generated by adding the previous two numbers will converge on the golden ratio no matter what numbers it commences with.

Chapter II: Logos and Analogia

or 'shoreline'. Instead, the recursive rule itself, which gives the relation between consecutive members, is what defines these infinite geometric forms.*

As an infinite arithmetic form, Fibonacci self-similarity is hidden by our conventional numerals, but it finds direct expression in notation that distinguishes Brownian order from Brownian number. Moreover, in the Brownian infinite arithmetic Fibonacci symmetry is found expressed in a variety of ways. We have already presented one simple way to directly generating the series in Table 8.1 (page 125). At the end of Chapter 14 we will show how the same symmetry is found immanent in the emanation of 2nd degree unity—that is, in the same emanation that generates the triangular numbers and the sacred *Tetraktys*.

In his *magnum opus* on world harmony, Kepler went as far as to claim that God the Creator has shaped the laws of generation in accordance with this ratio. [14, p. 241] We can agree with Kepler only if the 'accord' is with something elementary to both its arithmetic and geometric expression. As for the Academic Pythagoreans, although there is no evidence that they found an infinite arithmetical expression for Φ, we do know that by Plato's time they had found just such an expression for the diagonal of the square. We are now ready to consider the paradigm case of $\sqrt{2}$.

---

* For a discussion of these series compared to the Greek 'method of exhaustion' and the infinitesimal calculus, see Chapter 14 from page 289.

Chapter 12
ALTERNATING ANALOGIA

*The strong and the weak displace each other
and produce change and transformation.*

Yi Jing

*...for they give justice and reparation to one another for their
injustice in accordance with the ordinance of time.*

Anaximander

The Geometry of the Diagonal

We now move to consider a problem of *asymmetry* that we know was solved by the early Pythagoreans. The diagonal of the square is special to plane geometry because it cuts across the plane generated by perpendicular lines. It cuts this plane in such a way that it is no more in one direction than it is in the other, and in this way it cuts the square into two identical right-angle isosceles triangles. The 'diagonal' is thereby a basic figure in trigonometry. Not only did the diagonal play a role in Greek attempts to find the relationship between *symmetrical* and *asymmetrical* magnitudes, it also has a special role in the relating of magnitudes within the higher dimensions (i.e., areas with areas and volumes with volumes). All of these aspects of the diagonal coalesce in the ancient problem of $\sqrt{2}$.

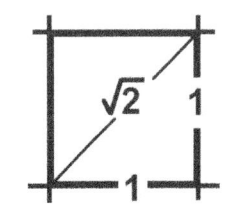

Chapter 12: Alternating Analogia

According to Pythagoras' Theorem the diagonal of the unit square has the value of $\sqrt{(1^2 + 1^2)}$ or $\sqrt{2}$. The early Pythagoreans recognised $\sqrt{2}$ as *asymmetrical* with its sides, and they even had a proof.* It is easy to see how this finding can be generalised to all squares with rational sides—their diagonals are but multiples of $\sqrt{2}$, and as such they all remain irrational.

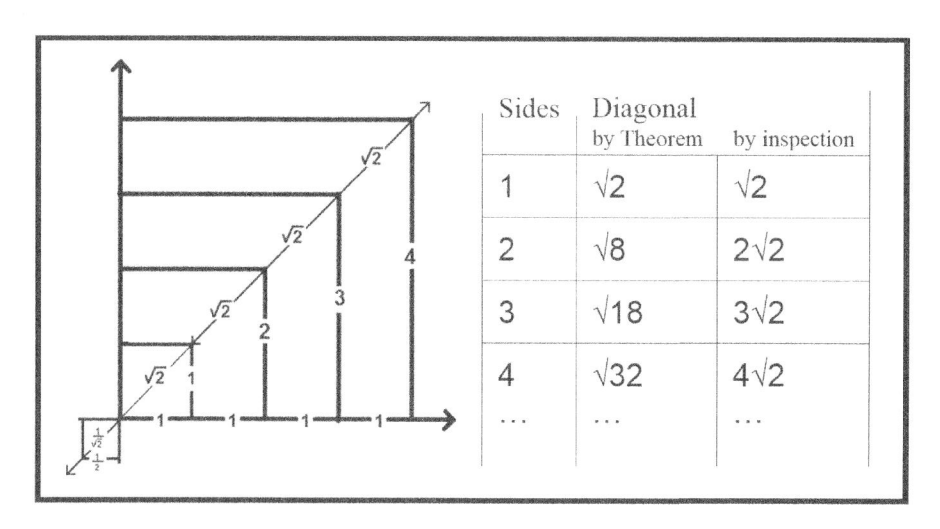

Sides	Diagonal by Theorem	by inspection
1	$\sqrt{2}$	$\sqrt{2}$
2	$\sqrt{8}$	$2\sqrt{2}$
3	$\sqrt{18}$	$3\sqrt{2}$
4	$\sqrt{32}$	$4\sqrt{2}$
...	...	...

All values for the diagonal of a square with rational sides have an irrational component, that is, $\sqrt{2}$. The similarity between the squares can be expressed as 4-term proportions:

$$\frac{\sqrt{2}}{1} = \frac{2\sqrt{2}}{2} = \frac{3\sqrt{2}}{3} = \frac{4\sqrt{2}}{4} = \frac{1/\sqrt{2}}{½}$$

Let's first consider the special role of $\sqrt{2}$ in the relating of magnitudes in higher dimensions.

The Doubling of the Square

We have already seen that the generation of the 2_{linear} from the 1_{linear} is a straight forward duplication, but that doubling (or any multiplying) in higher dimensions is more complicated, and so too are all relations of proportion in higher dimensions. (See above, page 185.) So far in our story,

---
* For the proof see Heath [4], Vol I, p. 215-6. See also below on page 239.

progressions in higher dimensions have been rooted in the first. Thus, the series of squares 1, 4, 9, 16, 25..., are derived from the series of their roots generated by the successive duplication of the linear unit: 1, 2, 3, 4, 5,.... But if we were to try, how would we perform a duplication directly within a higher dimensions? That is, how would we move from 1_{planar} to 2_{planar} or 1_{solid} to 2_{solid}?

In both cases we would need to know by what factor the lengths of the sides are multiplied. The problems of doubling the square and of doubling the cube both achieve great prominence in the Pythagorean tradition, the latter perhaps the more so because it took so long to solve. The doubling of the square was quite simple to solve but its importance was more to do with its elementary significance. Its solution not only pointed the way to a solution for doubling the cube, but it also provided further insight into the role of $\sqrt{2}$ in geometric generation by *analogia*. Let me explain.

This is the figure that provides the solution to the doubling of the square. If the sides of the unit square are duplicated to create a 2 X 2 square, then a square on the diagonal of the unit square can be created within this square. By counting the number of triangles in the unit square (area = 2 X ½) and the number of triangles in the square on the diagonal (area = 4 X ½) we can determine by mere inspection that the area of the square on the diagonal is double the area of the original. We can also see that the diagonal of this double square is the length of the sides of the 2 X 2 square, and by counting triangles again (area = 8 x ½) we see that its area is double again. This figure thus presents the first two steps of the geometric double series in the plane; a progression generated by the successive substitution: *diagonal-becomes-side*.

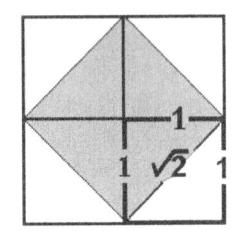

Analysis of the doubling squares			
	Unit ☐	Double ☐	Double-double ☐
Side	1	$\sqrt{2}$	$\sqrt{2}^2 = 2$
Diagonal	$\sqrt{2}$	$\sqrt{2}^2 = 2$	$\sqrt{2}^3 = 2\sqrt{2}$
Area	One	Double	Double²

The side-diagonal series can be expressed as follows:

$$\sqrt{2}^0, \sqrt{2}^1, \sqrt{2}^2, \sqrt{2}^3, \sqrt{2}^4, ...$$

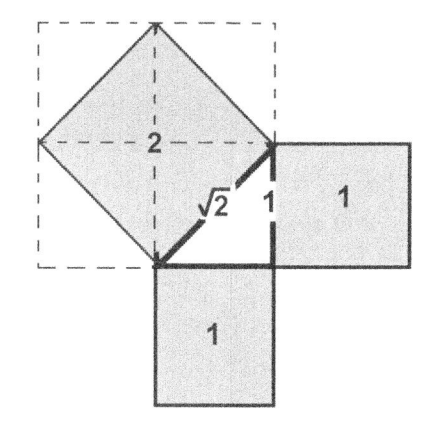

Chapter 12: Alternating Analogia

A modification of our diagram gives a demonstration of Pythagoras' Theorem as it applies to the right-angle isosceles triangle. It is *by mere inspection* that we know the area of the square on the hypotenuse will always equal the area on the other two sides. And this observation could lead the mind to consider that this rule holds for all right angle triangles. Thus, this diagram could be considered the paragon of Pythagoras' Theorem (and thereby of trigonometry). Remember that the determination of the value of the hypotenuse as '$\sqrt{2}$' can be made without the aid of the Theorem: It was by our method of counting triangles that the square on the diagonal was found to be 'double', and so, thereby, its side must be *the-square-root-of-double*.

This solution to the problem of doubling the square makes its first appearance in the historical record when Plato uses it to exemplify his theory of learning as 'recollection' [*anamnesis*]. In *Memo* an uneducated slave boy is prompted from self-evident first principles towards the solution.*

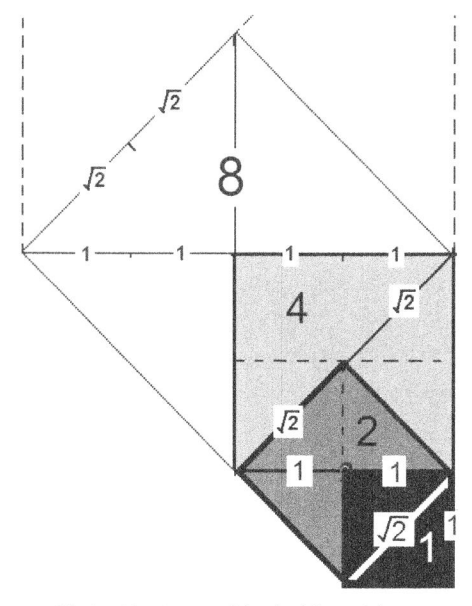

In this figure we continue the *diagonal-becomes-side* expansion, and consider the proportions involved. While the areas of the successive squares are in the ratio of double, the length of successive sides are in the ratio of its root. The diagonal is not only *the-square-root-of-double* but it is also the geometric mean between the double and the single. That is, 1 *is to* $\sqrt{2}$ *as* $\sqrt{2}$ *is to* 2. This series thereby finds the mean terms between successive members of the

---

* For the early discussion of recollection see above p. 78. For Plato's use of the doubling of the square to demonstrate *anamnesis*, see *Memo* p. 81-85.

ENTHUSIASTIC MATHEMATICS

double series:

$$1, \sqrt{2}, 2, 2\sqrt{2}, 4, 4\sqrt{2}, 8, 8\sqrt{2}, 16, \ldots$$

This finding leads to the general idea that the problem of finding the double of an area can be reduced to the problem of finding the *side-of-the-double* as the mean proportion between the two areas:

x_{planar} *is to* a *as* a *is to* $2x_{planar}$, where a is the sides length of 2x.

And this in turn leads to the reduction of the problem of the doubling of the cube to the problem of finding *two* mean proportionals between the volume and its double:

x_{solid} *is to* a *as* a *is to* a^2 *as* a^2 *is to* $2x_{solid}$

This breakthrough in the problem of doubling the cube is first found recorded in Plato's *Timaeus*, where this *analogia* is given as a principle of the creation of the 3-dimensional physical universe by way of the four elements in a formula reminisce of Heraclitus:

Fire *is to* Air *as* Air *is to* Water *as* Water *is to* Earth.*

An Arithmetic Expression for the Diagonal

We have already seen how the 17th century Christian Pythagorean Johannes Kepler found an infinite series of arithmetic values to express the geometrically generated ratio Φ. While there is no evidence of this series any earlier in the tradition, evidence in Plato and the Platonists indicates that this way of giving an infinite expression for an arithmetically inexpressible ratio was already known to the early Pythagoreans in the case of the diagonal of the square. The full account of this method has only survived due to the survival of Theon of Smyrna's textbook *Mathematics useful for Understanding Plato*.# In this very Platonic 2nd century account,

---
* *Timaeus* p. 32. See discussion of Heraclitus above p. 176-7.
# We know that Plato knew this formula for a passage in *Republic* (p. 546c). See Heath [4], Vol I, p. 92–93 and Taylor [29], p. 428–9.

Chapter 12: Alternating Analogia

Theon uses the term 'Monad' for the original **One** (and also for the units of its generation) and the *'seminal logos'* for the generative principle.* He begins:

> Even as numbers are invested with power [*dynamis*] to make triangles, squares, pentagons and other figures, so also we find side and diagonal ratios appear in numbers in accordance with the *seminal logos*. Therefore since the Monad is the principle-origin of all figures according to the *seminal logos,* so also in the Monad will be found the ratio of the diagonal to the sides.#

Here we find Theon starting his exposition by referring to the generation of figured number magnitudes 'powered' by arithmetic. This is already familiar to us. But then Theon invokes the *seminal logos* and launches into a different, specific claim about the ratio of diagonals to sides, that is about √2. In the first place this prefatory passage is of interest because it runs together (in the name of the Monad) these two modes of generation, which are otherwise found elaborated separately and are never presented as commensurate or as expressing the underlying unity that we propose. Theon's specific claim about the diagonal is that this *logos* is found as a potency in the Monad *principle-origin* in accord with the *seminal logos*. How can this be?

It turns out that Theon's account is contrived and romantically embellished in order to conform to the doctrine of rational emanation. This stylisation makes the passage difficult to follow, but the advantage is that it offers insight into the unity of the formal science that the Pythagoreans were straining to achieve by way of the Logos. Theon's answer is given in a geometrical expansion of the square like the one given above on page 233. However, Theon's expansion starts with an imagined Monad square with diagonal-to-side ratio in identity, 1:1. In sympathy with Theon, we could also express this identity as $\sqrt{2}^0:\sqrt{2}^0$, thus expressing it as the potent value of the ratio √2:1 in the seminal point-origin that emanates the unit square. In the series that Theon describes, the next two squares are

---

* The *spermatikos logos* is more commonly associated with the Stoics who considered that it is by way of this *logos* that all things come into being from the Divine Fire. That this same motif also appears in Nicomachus attests to the syncretism of the time. See the fragment from his *Arithmetic Theology* where he identifies God with the Monad since he is seminally all thing in nature, and then later, where this *seminal Logos* is the active principle that creates the world (translated by Dillon [9], p. 355]; for the Greek and a discussion, see [26], p. 95–6).

\# Translation from [17], Vol I, p. 132–137. Note that I often translate *diametros*, 'diameter', as 'diagonal'. See an interpretation of this passage by Taylor [29], p. 428–432. See Lawlor's translation [28], p. 29–30, and Lawlor's interpretation [5], p. 39–41.

ENTHUSIASTIC MATHEMATICS

generated by adding successive diagonal and side lengths as shown in Figure 12.1. As the expansion continues it builds the two series:

Sides: 1, 2, 5, 12, 29,...
Diag: 1, 3, 7, 17, 41,...

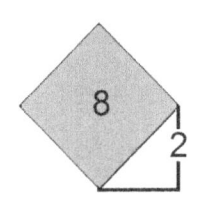

To understand how this formula works, considering a normal square of side lengths 2. According to the expansion we performed above on page 233, the square on its diagonal should be $(2\sqrt{2})^2 + (2\sqrt{2})^2 = 8$. But in Theon's series, the square on the diagonal is $3^2 = 9$. This is 1 above what it should be. In Theon's next square the side lengths are 5, and this should give a square on the diagonal with an area of 50, whereas it is $7^2 = 49$. This is 1 below what it should be. Theon explains that as the generation proceeds, the value for the square on the diagonal alternates now greater by a Monad, now less by a Monad than twice the square on the side, but each time giving a value that has an 'expressible' square root. Theon describes the generation as alternating *analogia* [*analogon enallae*]. As the squares get larger it can be shown that the arithmetically expressible ratios of *diagonal-to-side* alternate closer and closer around the true but arithmetically inexpressible ratio for the diagonal of a square.

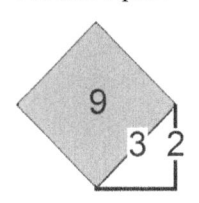

Iteration	0	1st	2nd	3rd	4th
Side:	1	2	5	12	29
Diagonal:	1	3	7	17	41
Ratio ($\cong \sqrt{2}$):	1	1.500	1.400	1.417	1.414

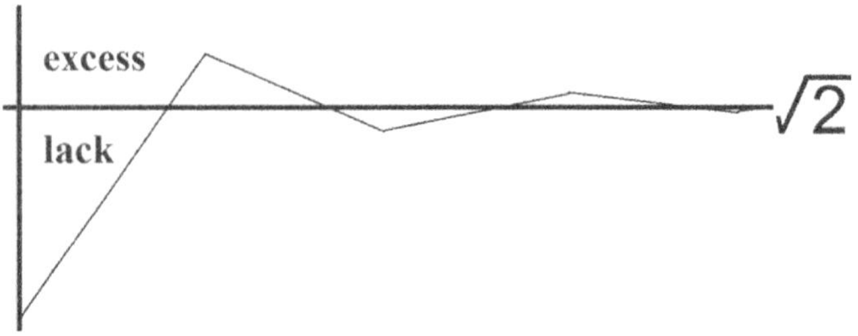

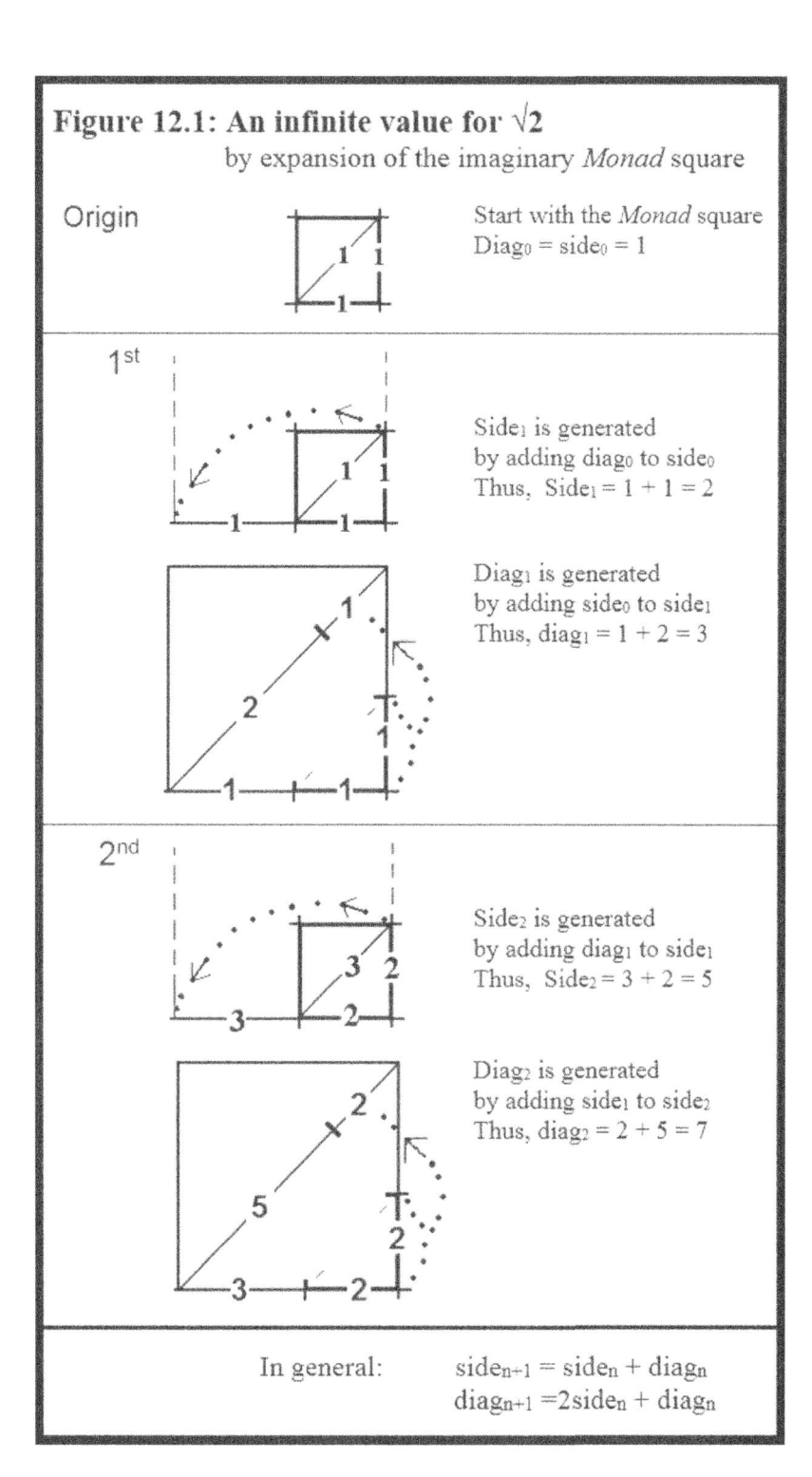

Figure 12.1: An infinite value for $\sqrt{2}$
by expansion of the imaginary *Monad* square

Origin

Start with the *Monad* square
$Diag_0 = side_0 = 1$

1st

$Side_1$ is generated
by adding $diag_0$ to $side_0$
Thus, $Side_1 = 1 + 1 = 2$

$Diag_1$ is generated
by adding $side_0$ to $side_1$
Thus, $diag_1 = 1 + 2 = 3$

2nd

$Side_2$ is generated
by adding $diag_1$ to $side_1$
Thus, $Side_2 = 3 + 2 = 5$

$Diag_2$ is generated
by adding $side_1$ to $side_2$
Thus, $diag_2 = 2 + 5 = 7$

In general: $side_{n+1} = side_n + diag_n$
$diag_{n+1} = 2side_n + diag_n$

ENTHUSIASTIC MATHEMATICS

Theon puts it that this alternation of 'excess' [*monadi pleon*] and 'lack' [*monadi elatton*] does not constitute an error, but that the lack of one iteration of the series is found in the excess of the next, and that this Monadic alternation compensates for itself so as to provide a measure for the geometry. Thus, just as Kepler presented the series of ratios in the Fibonacci series as the infinite arithmetic expression of Golden Mean, here we have a series of arithmetic ratios equated with the geometric ratio of the diagonal.*

Theon's presentation of this expression for $\sqrt{2}$ as a very peculiar geometrical expansion of the Monad square strains to extreme the analogy of relative size with number. We don't know if this was how the formula was envisaged when it was first discovered, or at the time of Plato. What we do know is that the Pythagoreans were resisting pure algebra, disciplining themselves to derive expressions of geometric relations directly from the geometric form. What we also now know is that the intuition evident in Theon's account is correct. Theon need not have strained the relationship between $\sqrt{2}$ and the emanation of squares if he had known of another, simpler infinite expression for $\sqrt{2}$. As we shall see at the end of Chapter 14, the square number series and $\sqrt{2}$ are two interpretation of the number 2 in the 2nd degree of Brownian arithmetic, and all the other diagonal numbers can be discovered in a similar way.

The Pythagorean proof of the asymmetry of $\sqrt{2}$

If in one sense Theon's account of this $\sqrt{2}$ series suggests a failure of the project for a complete account of the mathematical emanation, then the formula itself does at least provide a remarkable piece of evidence of early progress in the development of the infinite geometrical techniques that would later power whole fields of algebraic mathematics. Other evidence confirms that convergent infinite series had been introduced to the mathematical discussion by the time Plato and Eudoxus arrived on the scene. These include Zeno's Paradox of dichotomy, or repeated halving, which involves the equation:

$$1 - 1/2 - 1/2^2 - 1/2^3 - 1/2^4,\ldots = 0 \; ^\#$$

---

* This relationship between the sides and diagonals of this imaginary series of squares can be expressed algebraically as: $diag^2 - 2side^2 = \pm 1$. This technique amounts to finding all the integral solutions of the indeterminate equations $2x^2 - y^2 = \pm 1$. See Heath [4], Vol I, p. 91–2.

\# The 'dichotomy paradox', and the related paradoxical race between Achilles and the tortoise, are

And we know from Archimedes, who mastered it, that the method of exhaustion—the forerunner to the infinitesimal calculus—goes back at least to Eudoxus. Clearly the 4th century Pythagoreans were involving infinity in various ways, but this discovery of an expression for the diagonal may well have been the most significant of their infinite expression because this *alternating analogia* solved the problem of a key *asymmetricals* in a way that suggests a whole new possibility for the nature of the generation in the emanation.

We are now beginning to get a picture of the exciting stage that mathematical science had reached at the time when Plato and Eudoxus were at work in Athens around 400 BC. The evidence suggests that before or during Plato's lifetime, the advancing science of mathematical emanationism witnessed two revolutionary developments—both coming in the face of the discovery of the *asymmetricals*. The first was the abandonment of the reduction of *logos* to *arithmos* in order to allow for ratios *asymmetrical* with the ratio of 2:1. The second was the discovery of a way to express a key *asymmetrical* ratio as an unlimited series of arithmetic ratios. We know that the first development opened the way to the search for an elementary Logos in a higher science—a theology—primitive to both arithmetic and geometry. But what implications did the second development have for Pythagorean emanationism? The answer is in the realm of speculation, although there are some tantalising hints.

Consider for example not the resolution of the problem of $\sqrt{2}$ but its identification. An ancient proof of the irrationality of $\sqrt{2}$ is found first mentioned in our record exemplifying a logical technique where it also makes its first appearance. In Aristotle's explanation of his logic tool (his '*organon*'), this proof is the only example he gives when introducing the technique by which a proposition is affirmed by showing the impossibility of the implications of affirming its contrary. Here is how Aristotle introduces the technique commonly known after the Medieval Latin as '*reducto ad absurdum*':

> Everyone who carries out a proof *per impossibile* proves the false conclusion by syllogism, and demonstrates the point at issue hypothetically when an impossible conclusion follows from the assumption of the contradictory proposition. For example, one proves that the diagonal of the square is *asymmetrical* with its side by showing that if it is assumed to be *symmetrical*, *excessive* becomes equal to *just*. Thus he argues to the

---

both recounted in Aristotle, *Physics* Bk VI p. 239. For their contribution to mathematics viewed in a positive light, see for example Baron on the origins of the infinitesimal calculus [37], p. 22–24.

conclusion that *excessive* becomes equal to *just*, and proves hypothetically that the diagonal is *asymmetrical*, since the contradictory proposition produces a false result.*

This proof to which Aristotle refers begins by proving that the value for the side in the *diagonal-to-side* ratio must be *excessive*. And then it proves that the side must also be *just*. If the statement The diagonal and side are in ratio is true, then the value for the side must be both *excessive* and *just*. All agree that the classification of numbers into *excessive* and *just* is a mutually exclusive binary opposition—i.e., a number is either *odd* or *even*—and so this conflation of *excessive* with *just* is a contradiction. Therefore, there is no number for which this is the case.# This proves *reducto ad absurdum* that this ratio can have no arithmetic expression.

For Aristotle this ratio is impossible, for the Medievals it is 'absurd' (hence our 'surd'), but what significance might this contradiction have had for the Pythagoreans? Could they have regarded the implications of this proof in a more positive light? That is, could they have seen it as revealing the very condition of a type of number they were pitching every effort to master?

In leaving aside the Aristotelian interpretation of this proof let's return to the series we have just found preserved in Theon's *Mathematics Useful for understanding Plato*, namely the infinite series understood to give an early Pythagorean arithmetic expression of this *asymmetrical* ratio. Theon gives the side lengths alternating *excessive* (1), *just* (2), *excessive* (5), *just* (12), *excessive* (29), ... Could it be that this expression of √2 and this proof of its *asymmetry* led to a new speculation about the nature of *asymmetricals*? While continuing to affirm that the simultaneity of *excessive* and *just* is arithmetically inexpressible, these infinite numbers could have been seen as expressing *excessive* and *just* sequentially. Alternatively? Aristotle may have rejected as absurd the idea of a number as an infinitely alternating *analogia* even in his use of the very expression: excessive becomes equal to just.

This brings us to a reconsideration of the Pythagoreans elementary classification of number into the *excessive* and the *just*. Remember that when the first Pythagorean book of nature (attributed to Philolaus) gives the two proper forms of number as *excessive* and *just*, there is added a

---
* *Organon*, Prior Analytics Bk I, p. 41a 24-27. For the full proof see an interpolation in Euclid Bk X. See Heath [4], Vol I, p. 91
\# According to Aristotle, in the Pythagorean system, only the original one (or Monad) is both *excessive* and *just*, but as the origin of number, it was not considered to be one of them. See especially *Metaphysics* Bk I, p. 986a19-21.

third form 'just-excessive' [*artio-peritton*] as a mixture from both.* It might be that the proof of the *asymmetry* of √2 and the infinite expression of √2 had an obscured association for the early Pythagoreans that has so far eluded us. And that this is exactly the sort of association that the logical reductionist must refuse, namely generation by way of self-contradiction. After all, not only does Theon's series proceed by what we recognise as a self-referencing equation, but it begins with the outrageous self-contradiction of his Monad square with the diagonal the same length as its side. What would Aristotle have thought of that monstrosity?

We are long habituated to the significance of contradiction as proscriptive. Indeed, contradiction is illogical and absurd. It can be logically paradoxical (as per the Liar's Paradox) but also mathematically paradoxical (as per Zeno's Paradoxes). It is only in the last century that the generative power of contradiction (in recursive equations and so forth) has become acceptable in modern mathematics. It is only in the last decades that quantum computing theory has taken us beyond the bi-valued of 1 and 0 to legitimate a third value alternating 1↔0. And so now at last it is easier for us to take seriously, and respectfully, the following possibility: that before (and even after) Aristotle introduced contradiction as the first proscription of his analytic method, it may have had an altogether more positive significance for the Pythagoreans in their investigations of mathematical generation.

A Re-interpretation of the Natural Number Series

We are now approaching the heart of the matter and the nub of my hypothesis about what happened to the Pythagorean doctrine of emanation at the time of Plato. This is where we take the generative form of *analogia* and also *alternating analogia* to the problem of the natural number series.

If Logos were the principle of the emanation then it must be the principle of the elementary arithmetic series, the 1, 2, 3, 4, 5.... Clearly, on the face of it, this series has no common ratio. As the Pythagorean textbooks later taught, an 'arithmetic' series, proceeding by a common 'interval' or 'excess'. In the elementary series, where this excess is one, there are no 'geometric' means. It does not proceed by a common *logos*.# The

---

* As quoted above on page 178. For a discussion of possible interpretations of the fragment, see Heath [4], Vol I, p. 71.
\# See Nicomachus [26] Bk II at the beginning of Ch 23 when he says not in the same logos, and the earlier discussion in Bk II Ch 21. For a discussion of the issue see note 1 on p. 264. Also see Heath's discussion of Euclid Bk VII, Def 20 [3, Vol II, p. 292–3].

arithmetic series is so apparently not in *ana-logia*, and yet why do the Hellenistic textbooks call it such? It is striking that while these systematisers will point out that an *analogia* in the proper sense is a combination of terms with the same *logos*, they themselves continued to call the arithmetic progression an arithmetic *analogia*.* In fact, after giving this proper sense of the term, Nicomachus then makes a big fuss about the importance of treating the arithmetic *analogia* first. Is it not clear that nature shows it forth before the rest? This *analogia* gives the elementary natural numbers series beginning with one with no term passed over or omitted. Here Nicomachus provides a good reason for treating it first, but not, by his own account, a good reason for calling it an *analogia*. #

The standard explanation for this confusion in the meaning of *analogia* is that the word was used with less rigour as time went by. At first it was restricted to geometric means and series, while later it was used for other 'relations' [*schesis*], such as the arithmetic 'mean' [*mesotes*] and the harmonic 'mean'.+ This might explain why Euclid's axiomatic system only ever uses *analogia* for geometric relations, while centuries later in the textbooks and commentaries the terminology got confused. But this does not explain an apparently authentic 5th century BC fragment, where Plato's teacher Archytas presents the arithmetic mean in an apparent oxymoron, that is as an analogia of common excess [*huperochian analogon*]. Porphyry actually introduces the Archytas quote as an example of how the ancient masters regarded such relations of terms by 'interval' as also in ratio, despite the fact that it is clear that ratio differs from excess.++

An alternative explanation might be that later Pythagoreans were repeating a dogma that did not make sense to them. With the original understanding lost, the meanings of the word changed. In this view, the history of the usage of the term could be just like the history of our own word 'counter' in the retail setting. Just as not so many centuries ago the shop 'counter' was a proper counter (i.e., a counting board), likewise not so

---

* Nicomachus [26] Ch 21, 2. See also the beginning of Ch 24, when he finally comes to the geometric mean which he says is the only one in the strict sense of the word to be called an analogia. See also Theon [28] Ch 50 , p. 70, where, after earlier treating the Arithmetic analogia and mean, he quotes the Aristotelian mathematician Adrastus of Aphrodisias (fl. 2nd century AD) saying that the geometric mean is the only one which is a true analogia, and so it is the first, for all the others have need of it, whereas it has no need of the others. See also his Ch 56: ...the geometric mean, also called the proper analogia. (Translation from [28], p. 76.)

Bk II, Ch 22, 2-3, in [26] p. 267. Theon also begins with arithmetic mean in Ch 33, in [28] p. 56.

+ This view that the arithmetic *analogia* was original only an arithmetic 'means' or 'relation' was first presented in a footnote by Nesselmann [38], p. 210n.

++ The Archytas fragment (Deils B2) is found in Porphyry's *Commentary on Ptolemy's Harmonics* 1.5. Later Pythagoreans usually follow this passage from Archytas in presenting the minimum standard set of means, viz., the arithmetic mean with the geometric and harmonic. Euclid does not do this and he only ever uses '*analogia*' for relationships involving (what we now call) geometric ratios. He never uses it for relationship with the same 'excess' or 'interval', as is found in the elementary arithmetic series ($n_{next} = n+1$). Indeed, it is even suggested that what is called an arithmetic *analogia* is numbers

Chapter 12: Alternating Analogia

many centuries before these Hellenistic texts, the arithmetic *analogia* was (understood as) a proper *analogia*. That is, a *progression-by-common-excess* was at some early stage (or in some esoteric circles) understood as a *progression-by-common-ratio*. And perhaps all arithmetic relations were seen as reducible to the elementary arithmetic series regarded in this way.

The modern scholar would not trouble with such an explanation because an arithmetic series with a common ratio is absurd. When viewed from our conventional understanding of arithmetic, it would be to say that $1/2 = 2/3 = 3/4 = 4/5$ is both true and elementary. However, this is not so absurd when viewing the Pythagorean project through the glass of Brownian arithmetic, whereby Re-Entry of the Form gives the elementary contradiction generating the ordinal series in the continuous 'ratio' of Boolean negation. I will explain this more fully below, but if we permit this hypothesis as to a 5th century claim on the geometric nature of the arithmetic series, then a case could be made that either this were a vision of mathematical reduction never realised, or else that the textbooks were not privy to this knowledge for reason of secrecy and/or the degeneration of the teaching down through the centuries. Whatever the case, the consensus across the Hellenistic texts that the arithmetic series is not a true *logos* is an explicit rejection of the *principle-logos* hypothesis; an hypothesis that seemed to have emerged among the Pythagoreans by the 4th century BC, and which remained exulted, despite these statements against its expression in arithmetic relations. Exulted not only among these Pythagoreans but also across the Hellenistic theology of Stoics, Jews, and Christians. If all generation from the *original-One* is by means of Logos then, for the Pythagoreans at least, this Logos must surely have been seen as the medium of the ordinal 1st, 2nd, 3rd, 4th, 5th, ...

Let us then propose that aside from Euclid and long before the textbooks, the question of an elementary *logos-of-arithmetic* remained open, and that some groups in some ways progressed the investigations of the *principle-logos* hypothesis. To begin with, imagine that in the early attempts to solve the problem, one of the first hypotheses might have been that the one, two, three, four, five,... has a ratio through some

---

in geometric proportion. Here is a summary. In Euclid Bk V, on magnitudes, the definition of *logos* (Def. 3) in not clear, but Euclid generally uses the term to mean ratio in the modern mathematical sense. See Heath's commentary in [3], Vol II, p.116–119. Def 5 is Eudoxus' new definition of the 4-term proportion that tolerates *asymmetricals*. The expression for proportion is in the same ratio [*hen to auto logo*], which in the next definition is equated with *analogia*. Def. 8 to 10 introduce continuous proportions, including the least possible proportion in three terms (a:b *as* b:c). In Book VII, on arithmetic, numbers are made up of multiple units, arithmetic mean is not discussed, and a definition of *logos* is avoided. Finally, in Def. 20 we find the old definition of the geometric proportion (a:b *as* c:d) given as the case when numbers are in proportion [*arithmoi analogon eisin*].

symmetrical middle terms. Remember that the *asymmetrical* geometric mean, √2, was found between 1 and 2 in the solution to the *doubling-of-the-square*. (See above on page 334.) We know that the possibility of a *symmetrical* geometric mean between consecutive members of the elementary arithmetic series was investigated as early as the 5th century BC. Archytas not only gives us the first surviving account of the three means but he also provides one of the earliest surviving mathematical proof, which is the proof that there is no *symmetrical* geometric mean between any two terms in the relation n : n+1. [4, Vol I, p. 215]

If the natural number series cannot have a rational mean between any of its terms, then there is still another possibility: the arithmetic series could be an '*alternating analogia*' derived from an inexpressible *logos* primary to it. Remember that in the case of √2:1, an infinite *alternating analogia* of arithmetic terms was found to express a *logos* of geometry that cannot otherwise be expressed in arithmetic terms. In that Theon's series does express the inexpressible ratio, the ratio that it expresses is seen as primary to its generation. Here we witness a new way by which number can be derived from geometry, viz., as an *alternating analogia* emanating from a primary asymmetrical *logos*. Could this be a clue to the real relationship between number and figure? Remember how Plato presented the critical problem of mathematics as the need to find the generative nature of the symmetrical and the asymmetrical in relation to one another. (See above on page 225.) And could this be a clue to the generation of numbers in general? That is, a clue to their generation as from a seminal but inexpressible ratio primary to both arithmetic and geometry?

No direct evidence that they investigated these hypotheses can be found. But all the same, what I would now like the reader to consider is how the ancients might have investigated the arithmetic series for characteristics of both *analogia* and *alternating analogia*. And I would like you to make this consideration in terms that are sympathetic to the Pythagorean view of arithmetic, that is, in terms of the Brownian ordinals so that we can recognise the patterns that would have been both obvious and elementary for them. This will lead us to an interpretation of the Platonic doctrine of Dyadic emanation in the next Chapter. What follows then, is an interpretation of the generation of the Brownian ordinals, first as an *alternating analogia*—with the inexpressible geometric ratio primary to it—and then as itself an *analogia* with a common ratio between each term in the series. In both cases we rely heavily on the evidence for two prevailing interests of the Old Academy. The first is the old Pythagorean dogma of the odd/even emanation, which remained beholden in the Academy, at least according to *Epinomis*—remember it proclaiming that the study of *numbers-in-themselves* is the study of the whole generation of the *excessive* and *just*. The second is the interest in infinite series, evident not only in the discovery of an infinite expression for a key irrationals, but also in Zeno's Paradox of dichotomy and Eudoxus geometric method of exhaustion.

The Arithmetic Series as an Alternating Analogia

Let's begin by recalling in *Laws of Form*, the static Form as the 'Distinction' as discussed in Chapter 6 above. The Distinction that constitutes the origin of the ordinal series is both presence and absence, **marked** and **unmarked**. This condition is not entirely expressible. The Distinction is only expressed by its mark, while its other side remains hidden. When I distinguish 'male', female is only implied negatively. Whatever way we indicate a Distinction, the identity **marked (not-unmarked)** is the Distinction. It is no more and it is no less. But it is always more than what expresses it.

The Distinction is not only incomplete in its affirmation but it is also *asymmetrically* so. Something and nothing have nothing in common. There is no ratio of 1 to 0. The **marked** has no similarity to the **unmarked**, except their difference. And there is no difference in the Distinction other than the Distinction itself. An attempt to mediate the two sides of the distinction is an attempt to negate the difference, and this only results in the dynamics of the Distinction, called 'Re-Entry'. This generates a series of expressions in alternating values, where both the **unmarked** and the **marked** states are expressed in the ordinal series. The series is generated in the First Distinction but the First Distinction is not part of it. It is the original unmeasurable (geometric) relation of identity, and as such the origin of the arithmetic series, but it is not a member of that series.

In this way the ordinal series could be considered as an *alternating analogia* expressing the ratio of the Distinction analogous to the series given by Theon that expresses the ratio of the diagonal emanating from the Monad square. The original Form, the First Distinction, is a complete, sufficient and static unity, with no difference but the difference which is itself. In its Re-Entry, the origin emanates an alternation *between* its **marked** and **unmarked** states, which endlessly compensating for each other. This *alternating analogia* has two dimensions: the alternation itself and the convergence. The alternation is expressed when we consider the series in terms of the elementary values of **marked** and **unmarked**, *excessive* and *just*, or the binary 1 and 0. However, when we consider the ordinal series cumulatively (that is, as counted in the binary 1, 10, 11, 100, 101,..., or the denary, 1, 2, 3, 4, 5,..., rather than the elementary alternation of 1, 0, 1, 0, 1...), then we can see that the ratio of successive marked and unmarked terms approaches the inexpressible identity of the origin prior to its differentiation:

The Origin	The ratios in the ordinal series approaching the value of their Origin								
1 (not-0)	1/2,	2/3,	3/4,	4/5,	5/6,	6/7,	7/8...	$10,000/10,001$	
	0.50	*0.66*	*0.75*	*0.80*	*0.83*	*0.86*	*0.88...*	*1.00*

The series begins with the ratio of 1:2, but as the **marked**↔**unmarked** alternation progresses, the difference in the cardinal value of successive terms becomes less and less distinct, approaching 1:1, the ratio of identity and the value of the origin.* Considered visually, we could shade in black a crossing from **unmarked** to **marked**, while leaving white a crossing back to **unmarked**. By the time we got an expression for 10,000 crossings and for 10,001 crossings, there would be nearly the same number of black and white regions, which is half each, which is also the ratio of **marked** to **unmarked** in the origin.

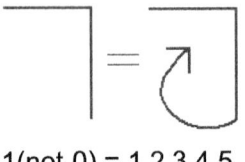

1(not-0) = 1,2,3,4,5...

Re-Entry of the Form might be seen as an infinite arithmetic expression of its asymmetry.

This analysis of the natural number series as Brownian ordinals suggests that their generation has some similarities to the generation of infinite arithmetic representations of √2 and Φ found in Theon and Kepler. Now let's analyse the series again, but this time to support the hypothesis that like the common geometric series, it has a constant ratio between its terms.

---

* Compare to Theon's analysis at the end of Ch 5, in [28], p. 15.

Chapter 12: Alternating Analogia

The Arithmetic Series as a Geometric Analogia

In something of a contradiction to what we have just said above, there is a sense in which we can regard the ordinal series as a simple *analogia*. The ratio between each term in the **marked** state (*excessive*) and the following term in the **unmarked** state (*just*) is the same as the ratio of each term in the **unmarked** state (*just*) to the following term in the **marked** state (*excessive*). This is because they are complementary opposites: **marked** is **not-unmarked** and **unmarked** is **not-marked** (the *excessive* is not-*just* and *just* is not-*excessive*). The interpretation of the Brownian ordinals as a geometric series is best expressed when Re-Entry is interpreted as successive negation:

One *is to* not-One *as* not-One *is to* not-not-One

The arithmetic series proceeding by a common interval (+1) is yet an *analogia* proceeding by a common ratio, the ratio of negation. This negation is of the nature of Boolean logical negation (a 'not-ing') rather than what we know as arithmetic negation (n−1). Numbers are indeed composed of units (or 'marks'), but in the arithmetic series the successive additions of these units, the 'n+1', is generated by a *logos* that is self-negation. We can find this 'generator' in the origin as the negation latent in the Form of the Distinction. When the mark negates its absence it becomes something as *not-nothing*. So there *is* a ratio of 1 to 0 after all. And this 'generator' is in the 'initiator'—the Logos is a potential of the origin, in the origin, as is all its generation. Number is then the manifest self-differentiation of the origin within the origin, and so we meet the demands of a self-sufficient emanation by way of a common Logos. We are now ready to consider the extent to which Platonic Pythagoreanism shows conformity to this hypothesis in the doctrine of the Monad and its Dyad.

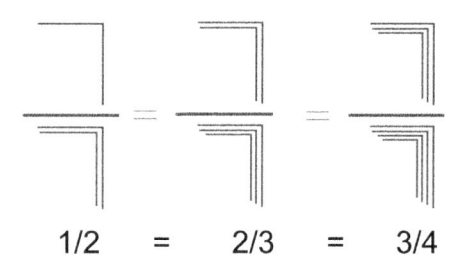

1/2 = 2/3 = 3/4

The Brownian ordinals in ratio as an elementary Pythagorean *analogia* where the ratio is a 'crossing' or a Boolean NOT.

Chapter 13

DYADIC EMANATION
A New Theory of Number

> The Pythagoreans [who, like other previous philosophers,] spoke of two principles, made this further addition, which is peculiar to them: they believed, not that the limited and the unlimited are separate entities, like fire or water or some other such thing, but that the unlimited itself and the One itself are the essence of those things of which they are predicated, and hence that number is the essence of all things. Such is the nature of their pronouncements on this subject.
>
> They also began to discuss and define the 'what' of things; but their procedure was far too simple. They defined superficially, and supposed that the essence of a thing is that to which the term under consideration first applies—e.g., as if it were to be thought that double and the two are the same, because two is the first number that is double another. But presumably to be double is not the same as to be two. Otherwise, one will be many—a consequence which actually followed in their system....
>
> The system of Plato contained certain peculiar features distinct from the philosophy of the Pythagoreans. ...Since the Forms are the cause of everything else, [Plato] supposed that their elements are the elements of all things. Accordingly, the material principle is the *great-and-the-small* and the essence is the One, since numbers are derived from the *great-and-the-small* by participation in the One. In treating the One as an essence [*ousia*] instead of a predicate of some other entity, his teaching resembles that of the Pythagoreans, and also agrees with it in stating that the numbers are the cause of *being* in everything else; but it is peculiar to him to posit a duality [Dyad], instead of the single unlimited, and constructing the unlimited out of *great-and-small*....He made the other principle a duality [Dyad] because the numbers other than the primes can be generated from it by a natural process as from a mould.
>
> Aristotle, *Metaphysics* Book I

Chapter 13: Dyadic Emanation

In his *Metaphysics* Aristotle says that in most respects Plato is in accord with the metaphysical doctrine of the early Pythagoreans, excepting his principle innovation, the 'Dyad'. The way Aristotle sees it, the doctrine of the One and the Dyad supplants the old Pythagorean emanation in terms of limitation. (See the extended extract at the head of this chapter.) Although Aristotle does not use the word 'Monad', it later becomes more or less synonymous with the original One. If we grant this, then it is here in Aristotle that we have the first surviving account of the Platonic emanation in terms of the Monad and Dyad.

The doctrine of Dyadic emanation seems to have developed in the Academy of the time of Plato and his immediate successors, but while this doctrine is referenced, recast, reshaped and undoubtedly corrupted endlessly down through the long Hellenistic period, we have a complete absence of any first hand accounts—save this one by Aristotle, alas, estranged and less than sympathetic. Perhaps it is because of the difficulties in determining the exact terms of the doctrine that little effort has been made in modern scholarship towards trying to determine its precise nature. The offering of an interpretation, as I do now, is both bold and precarious, and while I feel there is a case here, I am not sure how strong it is. What I hope is that discussion and debate will provide something of an answer. I don't have the powers (or the space in this book!) to make a thorough case that deals with all the apparent contradictions in the numerous versions of this doctrine. All I do here is (shamelessly!) pick out the accounts that best suit this hypothesis and briefly offer one explanation for some of the corruption and confusion that soon entered the tradition.

The Monad and Dyad

The word 'Monad' [*monas*] ordinarily meant the 'one-alone', the 'singular'. In Platonism it comes to be the term for the origin of the emanation, the 'singularity', and also the common mathematical unit. The word 'Dyad' comes from *duas*, or two, and ordinarily means duality or twoness. In Platonism it comes to mean becoming-two or the-becoming-two-ness-of-the-One. In this sense it means double and doubling, but not in the ordinary sense of double as the ratio in the geometric progression of double.

My hypothesis of the Platonic Dyadic doctrine is that it describes the ordinal generation by Re-Entry as described (using different terms) in *Laws of Form*. The analogy is in essence:

- The Monad is the Distinction in its static form, expressed as the Form, or First Distinction, and re-expressed in every mark of the Form.
- The Dyad was found to be the *principle-logos* of the emanation as expressed in the *first-born*, and as such it is the dynamics of the Form, its Re-Entry.

To begin, let's consider this account:

> The principle of all things is the Monad; from this Monad there comes into existence the indeterminate Dyad as matter for the Monad, which is cause. From the Monad and the indeterminate Dyad arise the numbers... *

'Indeterminate' and 'cause' are commonly used in descriptions of Dyadic emanation. In our hypothesis, the Dyad is 'indeterminate' [*aoristos*] because it is perpetually altering itself in an unending progression. The description of mathematical emanation in terms of 'causes', and especially the reading of a 'material cause', is due to the Aristotelian influence. But just as elsewhere other Platonists turned the Aristotelian language upon itself by concluding that the matter upon which Form acts is 'nothing' or 'not-one', similarly here: the 'material cause', the Dyad, is clearly nothing other than the Monad. It is a potency of the Monad and not an independent cause. The Dyad is a self-generation of the Monad:

> The Monad is the principle of existent things, by participation in which each of the existent things is termed one; and this, when conceived in self-identity, is conceived as a Monad, but when it is added to itself in virtue of otherness it creates the indeterminate Dyad. #

The Monad is the principle identity, the simple Distinction, it is **One**-*the-same*, while the Dyad is **One**-*becoming-other-to-itself*. Nicomachus says that the Monad is the principle of the same and sameness while the Dyad is the principle of other and *othering*.+ In his *Theology of Arithmetic*,

---

* Alexander Polyhistor's report of the Pythagorean doctrine dated to about 80 BC. Quoted in Dillon [9], p. 342.
# Sextus Empiricus' report of Pythagorean doctrine, where, according Dillon, he is borrowing sources from well before his own time. [9, p. 342]
+ Nicomachus [26] Bk II, Ch 18, p. 259; and, in the preceding chapter, p. 254-5, where, with reference to the doctrine of the ancient school of Pythagoras, the word '**one**' [*to hen*] is used instead of 'Monad'.

Chapter 13: Dyadic Emanation

Nicomachus also says that the Dyad is generated by the self-doubling—or perhaps we should say the 'becoming-two' [*diphoretheisa*]—of the Monad.* For Theon, the principle of arithmetic is the Monad which in seeking otherness made the Dyad different by its own doubling.# This *becoming-different* must be a negation, so it is one-*becoming-double* as one-*becoming-not-one*.

Here is another statement of the static and dynamic principles:

> Thus the principle of unity and sameness and equality, and the cause of the *sympnoia* and *sympatheia* of the universe and of the preservation of that which is always one and the same they call One, while the principle of otherness and inequality and of everything that is divisible and in the process of change and different at different times they termed the dual principle of Dyad. +

In his *Theology*, Nicomachus compares the Monad to God, who is in a seminal sense all things in nature. It has the character of Prometheus the maker of life (whose name is taken to mean 'never running forward'), because it generates all (differentiation) while itself always remaining the same.++ Throughout his *Introduction to Arithmetic*, Nicomachus explains or presumes that the Monad embodies *potentially* all numerical forms.+++

How did the Pythagoreans come to such a doctrine?

We don't know for sure. However, it is not difficult to have a pretty good guess if we just pause and make some small effort to get inside the problematic of emanationism as it presented to the first Academics. The biggest clue in the surviving accounts of Dyadic emanation is also preserved in the very word itself. It is that this solution to the problem of arithmetic emanation appears to have emerged from the investigations of the ratio that generates the **two**. That is, the generative principle evolving the **double**. The difficulty would be in finding how the Dyadic generator differs from ordinary doubling.

---

* Quoted in Dillon [9], p. 355.
\# [27], p 27. See also translation in [26], p. 255n1 and [28], p. 18.
\+ Moderatus of Gades quoted by Porphyry in Dillon [9], p. 346.
++ Quoted and discussed by Robbins in [26], p. 96 & 101.
+++ See for example [26], Bk I, Ch 16, p. 211–212.

ENTHUSIASTIC MATHEMATICS

Ordinary Doubling

For Plato at least, the problem of the nature of the arithmetic emanation comes down to the problem of the *'one-and-the-many'*, that is, the generation of multiplicity from singularity.* The simplest multiplicity is *'twoness'* and so the simplest generation is one-*becoming*-two. There are two different ways of becoming 2: by division and by doubling. These two ways are sometimes the two aspects of what the textbooks called the 'natural contrariety' of the parts to their division. Consider the division of 8. Its division into two equal parts produces 2 parts of size 4. Whatever the number of the division, the size of the parts vary in inverse proportion, and the multiplying of the number of parts by their size always equates with the original. Thus, the division into 4 produces 4 parts of size 2, and division into 8 parts gives 8 **units**.

This contrariety was sometimes expressed in the elementary 'lambdoid diagram'. Named after the Greek letter 'Λ', it gives the symmetry of the contraries of a division (i.e., a value and its inverse) around the **one**. The highest and most important contrariety is the division of **one** by two, giving 2 X ½ = 1. It is both 'the greatest' and 'the smallest'. Its parts are the greatest in size (½) and the smallest in number (2).# The act of *division-by-two* (often called simple 'division' but otherwise known as 'dichotomy') involves **doubling** and also complementary opposition (i.e., in terms of the whole, the one part is the *other* of the other), and our discussion so far has already given ample expression to the importance of these two aspects of elementary mathematics in terms both Brownian and Pythagorean. Now I would like to draw attention specifically to the nature of division itself by considering two ancient techniques: Platonic logical analysis and the 'Egyptian method' of multiplication and division.

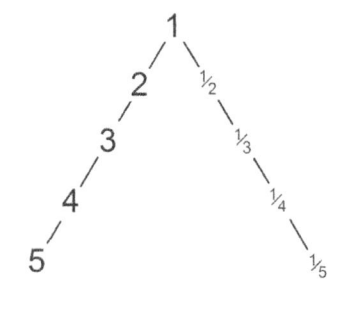

---

* For a Platonic introduction to the problem of the *one-and-the-many* see *Philebus* p. 13c–17a. For a more in-depth discussion around the topic see *Parmenides*, especially from p. 129.
\# For an explanation of natural contrariety of magnitude and quantity see the note in [26], p. 191n1.

The Platonic Method of Division

In Aristotle's early writing, which he may have composed while still associated with the Academy, there is evident a method for the analysis and classification of things that is more primitive than his linguistic method of predicate logic. This method is expressed most famously in his groundbreaking works on biological classification but is often called the Platonic method of division [*diairesis*]. It does seem to have been Plato's innovation although it also evidently answers Heraclitus when he commands us to follow him by making natural divisions [*physin diaireon*] of each thing and in this way indicate what *is*. Heraclitus might be only saying that we should strive to make distinctions in our knowledge corresponding to their existence in our experience. [Diels B1] As Plato put it in *Phaedrus*, the trick is to find the real 'joints' beneath the superficial, and then making the divides there. Finding the joints is about examining all the differences before making an informed decision about exactly where to make the divide. [p. 265d-e] Plato presents the method as a way of right thinking, but never a proof like a mathematical proof (although Aristotle came to see the method as failing in this regards and so rejected it in preference for his new method of analysis, which, as we saw in Chapter 3, itself constituted this same insufficiency). Rather than a tool for determining truth, it is a tool of scientific investigation that aids development of an orderly system of knowledge. Indeed, this method that is exemplified in Aristotle, explained in *Phaedrus*, and most extensively discussed in Plato's *Sophist*, is no less than our first surviving, explicitly proposed, methodology for empirical science.

The *Sophist* explanations the analytic aspect of the method. One begins by taking any object of knowledge that requires a definition and first situate it in a wider class of things. Then you narrow the definition by dividing the class into two mutually exclusive classes. The class containing the object is again divided, and such divisions are then progressively repeated whereby each new division is generated from one side of the previous, much as we saw in the Brownian Re-Entry. The dividing continues until one side of a Distinction contains only the object requiring the definition.

The method is illustrated in an idealised half-comic way with an attempt to develop a satisfactory definition of 'angling'. [p. 218e-221] The structure of this definition is summarised in Figure 13.1. [After Taylor, 39, p. 378–379] But this method is clearly not just about definitions. We can begin to appreciate the seriousness and power of the method beyond its use in taxonomy by considering the generality of its practical application: it is by finding the distinguishing characteristics of wheat that the ancients were able to separate it from the chaff; or the metal from the slag; and it is the finding of the distinguishing characteristics of invading or mutant cells that is a preliminary in modern medicine to the finding of a treatment that tends to destroys them more than normal cells. Science and its application has always been in a very great part about finding the right distinctions. The interest for us here is that Plato is giving ordinal distinguishing as the right form of empirical analysis, and that this methodological tool (which we now recognise to have an arithmetic form) was used successfully even by Aristotle himself prior to his realignment of metaphysics according to his new (linguistic) tool.

The Egyptian Method of Division and Multiplication

The 'Egyptian method' of division and multiplication was first found by modern scholars in an account of Greek *logistic*, and only later was it discovered in a much earlier Egyptian source.* Multiplication is effected by repeated **doubling**, while division is the inverse of multiplication, effected by doubling and re-doubling the divisor until the dividend can be obtained by summation of the appropriate **doubles**. In this method we find the product of 27 X 57 as follows:

27 x 57 is treated as:		
	1~	57
	2~	144
(16 + 8 + 2 + 1) x 57	4	228
~ indicates the orders of the	8~	456
doubling of 57 to be summed.	16~	912
		1539

The first task of this method is then to analyse the multiplier down into its expression in the **double** series (or for fractions, the inverse double series). Whatever the value of the multiplier, it will be expressed in this way, and so the universal applicability of this technique demonstrates that all natural numbers can be expressed as a sum of terms in the double series—a characteristic unique to this series among all geometric series (at least those involving whole number ratios).

---

* This account follows closely that by Karpinski in [26], p. 6.

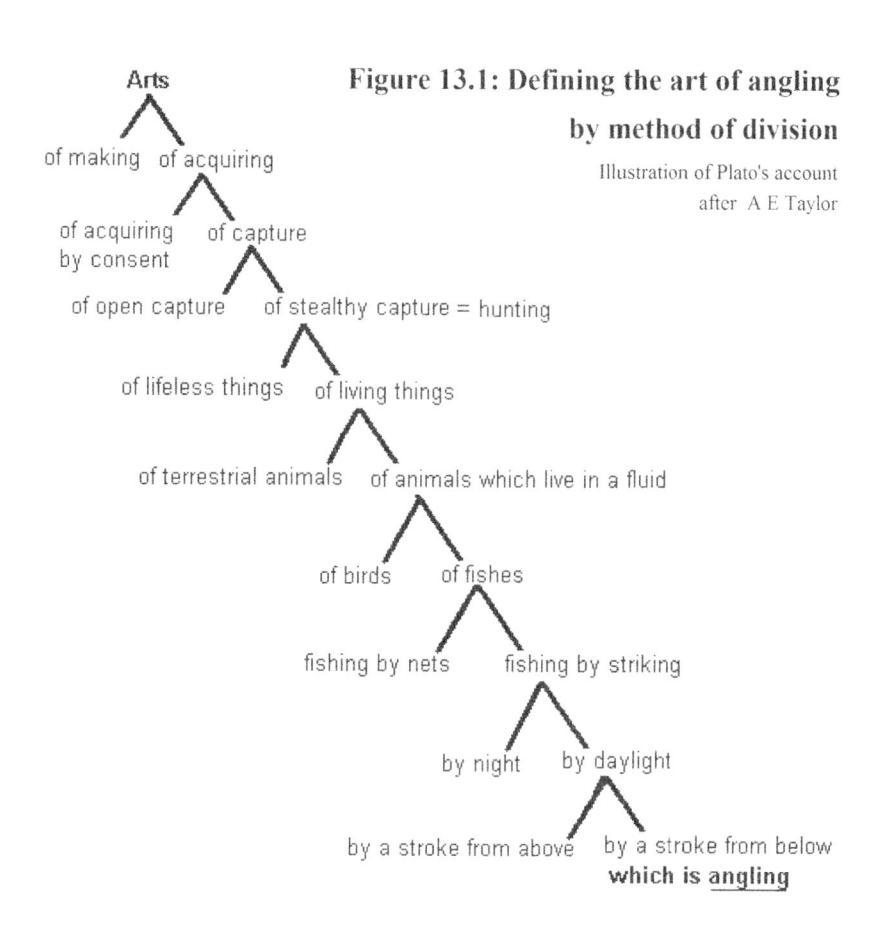

Figure 13.1: Defining the art of angling by method of division

Illustration of Plato's account after A E Taylor

```
                          Arts
                         /    \
                of making   of acquiring
                            /      \
                  of acquiring    of capture
                   by consent     /      \
                        of open capture   of stealthy capture = hunting
                                          /        \
                                of lifeless things   of living things
                                                     /         \
                                          of terrestrial animals  of animals which live in a fluid
                                                                   /        \
                                                             of birds    of fishes
                                                                          /      \
                                                                 fishing by nets  fishing by striking
                                                                                   /        \
                                                                             by night    by daylight
                                                                                          /       \
                                                                            by a stroke from above   by a stroke from below
                                                                                                    **which is <u>angling</u>**
```

The successive containment of each division on one side of the previous division is more evident when linear bifurcations (above) are replaced by concentric circles, or squares (below).

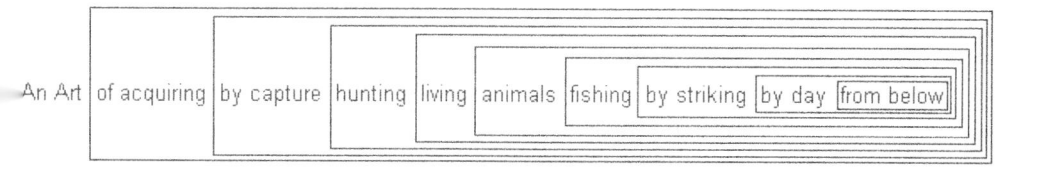

| An Art | of acquiring | by capture | hunting | living | animals | fishing | by striking | by day | from below |

The 'Egyptian method' does not appear in the Hellenistic textbooks, but much effort is spent there in analysing numbers according to their relation to the hierarchy of **double** implicit in this series. And the textbooks had a special name for the **double** series when the 'powers' of **double** are considered as a hierarchy of pairs in this way. Theon and Nicomachus both use the term justly-just [*artis artiakis*] narrowly to refer specifically to the members of this hierarchy, and they introduce this class of numbers at the beginning of their accounts of arithmetic—directly after the *excessive* and *just*. Nicomachus dedicates a small chapter to outlining their unique qualities and symmetries. He does not actually say that all numbers can be generated by a sum of terms in the **double** series, but he does point out that each term in this series is one more than the sum of the previous terms.*

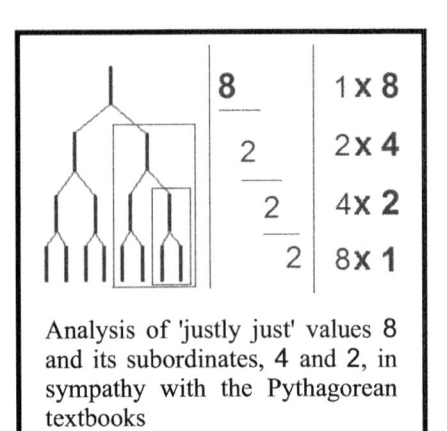

8	1 x 8
2	2 x 4
2	4 x 2
2	8 x 1

Analysis of 'justly just' values 8 and its subordinates, 4 and 2, in sympathy with the Pythagorean textbooks

The Arithmetic Progression in Degrees of Double

With these insights to the pre-Aristotelian landscape of Greek thought, let's now return to the problem of the arithmetic progression in the *principle-logos* hypothesis, and consider it in terms of the **double**. In the move from 1 to 2 the arithmetic progression and geometric progression are the same, only at the next term the divergence begins: 1, 2, 3, compared to 1, 2, 4. How can we find the harmony of this divergence?

The answer comes if we regard the arithmetic series as developing in the pattern suggested by the *justly-just* hierarchy. Consider firstly the number series as progressing arithmetically as successive pairs of *excessive-just* alternates. These *male-female* couples can be seen as complete units of complementary opposition viz., not-*just* and *just*. Call each couple a 'double'. Now, if we count the progression giving only this differentiation, then, while there is a distinction within each **double**, the **doubles** themselves are not distinguished from each other, and so we have only the

---

* See Nicomachus Bk I, Ch 8, text and commentary in [26], p. 192–6. See also Theon Ch 8, [28, p. 17] where the discussion is less elaborate. Generally *artiakis* means 'an even number of times', only in the textbooks does it have this narrower definition. In *Parmenides* [p.143e] Plato seems to use it in a less restricted sense, as does Euclid in Bk VII Defn 8. See Heath [4], Vol I, p. 71–2.

Chapter 13: Dyadic Emanation

primitive counting of pairs:

1st, 2nd, 1st, 2nd, 1st, ...

But, if the first two **doubles** are counted as the alternates of a higher order complementary unity, then we can distinguish the second **double** from the first **double**, and thereby count from 1 to 4:

1st of double$_1$, 2nd of double$_1$, 1st of double$_2$, 2nd of double$_2$.

When counting pairs of pairs in this way, the pattern repeats after the fourth term. But then again, these first two pairs of doubles can also be distinguished by counting them as alternates of a still higher order unity. Thus, if we count **doubles, double-doubles** and **double-double-double** according to the *justly-just* hierarchy, we proceed from 1 to 8.

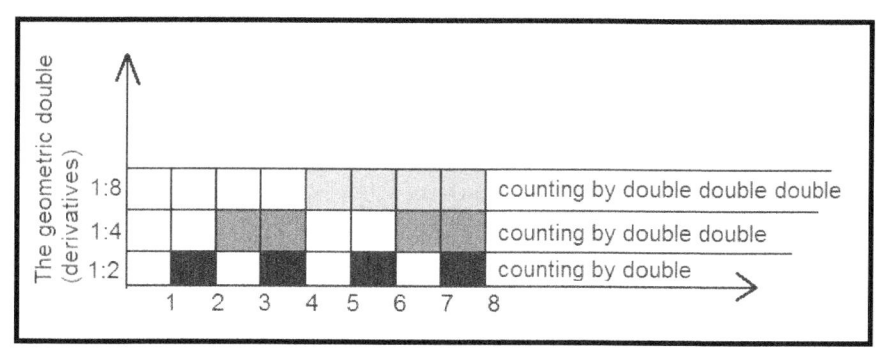

By counting this way all numbers are generated in order with no term passed over or omitted, and the geometric double series appears to arise naturally and symmetrically by degree of the arithmetic double. Another way to arrive at this arithmetic is in the reduction of a place-value system to its minimum form, which gives the pattern expressed in the modern notation of binary numbers made up of 0s and 1s—a pattern the power of which we only began to appreciate in the post-War development of cybernetics. But consider how this same pattern of generation would have given even more significance to the **double** for those ancients wanting to express the emanation of the dimensions in primitive arithmetic terms. Proceeding from 1 to 8 in this way gives an analogy of the generation of the dimensions of 'square' space as the movement around the arithmetic *excessive-just* **double** in three 'powers'. That is, double = the line [2], double-double = the plane [2^2], double-double-double = the solid [2^3]. But the ancients never had anything like this...*or did they?*

Could it be that there is evidence for a binary arithmetic that we have so far ignored or blindly misinterpreted? It may be that the technical advance of modern mathematics has engendered an arrogance that has blinded us to the fact that binary arithmetic is not at all advanced, but basic. Perhaps the ancients—who were less sophisticated than we are, but who were thereby closer to the gods—attained a clearer understand of elementary place-value arithmetic long before we rediscovered it. Already we have reawakened this lost symmetry in the doctrine of figured number generation. For the rest of this book we address what appear to be three accounts of the same binary element, except where the degrees are generated as powers of the **double**. The first account is a climactic passage in that rare text of the Old Academy, *Epinomis*; the second in the Dyadics arithmetic of Leibniz; and the third in the precedent to his Dyadics that Leibniz found in an ancient sacred notation of China.

Turning about the Double

The stated purpose of *Epinomis* (see above, page 179) is to outline the training required of the proposed 'Nocturnal Council', a topic left hanging in the last book of Plato's *Laws*. Plato had proposed the Nocturnal Council as a supreme council of judgement upon the law of his utopian community. The members of the council therefore need more than mere knowledge; they require wisdom [*sophia*]. So the question is: What is the science that trains a man for wisdom? I have sort the vision of it in the heights and in the depths says the Athenian stranger, and will now do my best to set it clearly before you.

Wisdom is best attained by honouring and studying the divine. Such piety is the highest virtue and its science is in fact astronomy. Astronomy is regarded as the study of the order of the motions of the gods, the order which Law—the divinest of things that are—has set before our eyes. [986c] In short, the author is asking that the divine law of the order of the planets be the model and guide for the law and judgement of society. But the planetary orbits are difficult to comprehend, says the Athenian...

> ...and to train capacities which can deal with them we shall have to spend a great deal of labour on providing preliminary teaching and training in boyhood and youth.
> [990c]

It is at this point that the mathematical sciences are nominated in a hierarchy accorded with the sequential advance of the dimensions and their corresponding powers.

A similar hierarchy of the mathematical sciences is found earlier, in *Republic*, Book VII. The hierarchy moves from *numbers-in-themselves* (generating the linear) to plane and then solid geometry. The account in *Republic* is more complete, starting with the study of the original One and extending to the study of moving solids, which is how Plato there defines 'astronomy'. Both accounts begin by pointing to the inherent opposition in number. In *Republic* Plato introduces the higher study of the One by distinguishing it from the study of units apprehended by the senses, as in finger counting (i.e., *logistic*). Unlike the cardinal one, the One that Plato's Socrates is talking about is the one that draws the mind to the apprehension of essence [*ousia*], where

> ...contradiction is always seen coincidentally with it so that it no more appears to be one than the opposite...
> [524e]

If the opposite of one is not-one, then in the Greek [*oud-hen*] it also means 'nothing' as per our 'not-one' compressed to 'none'. While this suggestion of the primary coincidental the opposites (one and not-one) is picked up by later Platonists, notably Proclus, it is absent from *Epinomis*. Instead, great emphasis is placed on the *excessive* and *just* at the first level of the hierarchy. The study of *numbers-in-themselves* must begin not with the cardinals [*somata echonton*], but rather with the whole generation of the excessive and the just. Their study is concerned with the powerfulness of the influence of this generation on the nature of physical reality.

After the linear numbers, plane and solid geometry are introduced and re-defined in the task of making similar numbers that are dissimilar by their nature, thus announcing that geometry—the science of ratio and the preliminary to astronomy—has come down to the problem of finding the symmetry of the *asymmetrical* ratios. Thus so, the three sciences are enumerated in the order of the three dimensions before the author then raptures:

> A divine and marvellous thing it is to those who envisage it and reflect how the whole of nature moulds off species [*eidos*] and genus, as power and its opposite continually turn about the double according to each *analogia*.
> [990e-991a]

ENTHUSIASTIC MATHEMATICS

How do we interpret this exulted passage that gives the mode of natural and universal generation as a turning about the double?

The key to my interpretation is to consider the double about which the power and its opposites turn, as formally equivalent to the *excessive* and *just* mentioned earlier in the passage: power and its opposite affect the alternation of the *excessive/just* double. And this power opposition conforms to the two aspect of power in Re-Entry: the active and the receptive: the marking (active) of the **unmarked** space (receptive).

The passage continues without proper grammatical structure something like this:

> The first analogia is the double moving by the arithmetic progression in the ratio of 1:2, next is double to the power [i.e., 1:2^2] and in doubling again we pass to the solid and tangible, having proceeded from 1 to 8.

What seems to be envisaged here is a **double** line, a double-*by*-double plane and a **double**-*by*-**double**-*by*-**double** cube. The three '*analogia*' of **doubles** are the three arithmetic series of **double** generated by degree in the geometric series of **double**. These arithmetic series are: the **double** series, moving by 2s; the **double-double** series, moving by 4s; and the **double-double-double** series, moving at a ratio of 1 to 8. This can be presented as a hierarchy of linear alternations similar to the chart above on page 257, or otherwise as a series of cubic building blocks:

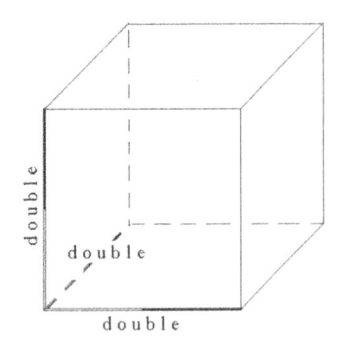

We could also express the 'turning' graphically by introducing a binary clock. Such a clock would have two phase-values, *just* and *excessive*, and note that in counting phases we would start with the *just* until the *excessive* value is reached at the halfway point. The clock would be geared such that

Chapter 13: Dyadic Emanation

the full turning of the circle by the 'second hand' (linear) is counted by a phase-value change of the 'minute hand' (plane), and, likewise, the turn of the minute hand is counted by a phase change of the 'hour hand' (solid).

This relative motion is not easily expressed on the page, but otherwise we could imagine a clock with only one hand but with the three ratios expressed on the face.

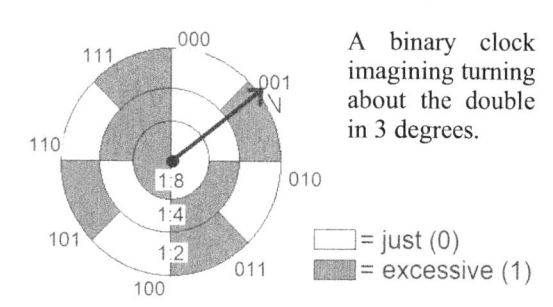

A binary clock imagining turning about the double in 3 degrees.

☐ = just (0)
■ = excessive (1)

Zero Origin, Zero Absence

There is no evidence that the Pythagoreans had anything like this binary notation. In the first place, they simply were not equipped to produce it. It is not that they lack a place-value system (see above, page 181), but rather as far as we know, they did not have a device of any kind to express their elementary values that alternated in excess and in justice with the origin. In this interpretation of power and its opposite turning about the double, we have applied modern binary notation that uses a character for **one**, which they had, but it also uses a character for **zero**, which they did not have. Even more debilitating for the understanding of Dyadic generation in Hellenistic Platonism was the confusion over the origin, the *ordinal* **zero**. This confusion extended beyond the problem of an expressive device.

The ordinal **zero** is seminal in Pythagorean mathematics. It is no less than the origin of an emanation. It is rooted in the doctrine of dimensional emanation, where the point is the origin of the line but not itself part of the line, and where the line is the origin of the plane, and the plane the origin of the solid. The point is the ordinal 'zero' of all dimensions at once, and we are now familiar with some of its other names, including 'limit' and 'potential'. In the analogy with arithmetic, the original **One** is identified with the point as the principle origin, the limit and potential of all numbers. It is the starting place of the series, the origin of the *excessive* and the *just*, and so the **zero** of the series. Yet it was called '**one**'.

261

The term 'Monad' seems to have been introduced to distinguish the arithmetic origin from its generation (as the 'one-alone' or the 'singularity'). But the confusion persisted because the *first-born*-one and every subsequent unit generated in the image of the Monad-*qua-origin* came to be called, and rightly so, a Monad. Indeed, *monad* is often found translated as 'unit', and, in the right contexts, rightly so. Thus, in Platonism the Monad-*qua-origin* often gets confused with the *first-born*-one and also with the cardinal one: our 'unit'. In this confusion where the Monad is identified with the number 1, as the first *excessive* numbers, the Dyad is identified with the number 2, as the first of the *just* numbers.*

In our interpretation, if the Dyad were aligned with any number it would be with the 1-*qua-first-born*, where it is manifest as the ratio of the series. It is the first *excessive* number, and as the very principle of 'exceeding' it is the principle of all the *excessive* numbers. But it is also the dynamic principle of all numbers in that they are all exceeding (and are '*other-to*') the Monad. This interpretation gives the Monad as the principle of justices and sameness, and so the principle of the *just* numbers, but it would also be the principle of all numbers as their very origin and their identity. In the face of great potential for confusion, we can at least agree with the Hellenistic Pythagoreans when they give the Dyad as an *othering* or the principle of *otherness*. Indeed, they usually identified the Dyad with the *first-born* as the Logos and as the generator of all numbers exceeding their origin. But we find this doctrine contradicted when in the textbooks the Dyad is identified with the number 2, and so aligned with the *just*.

At one point Nicomachus makes just this move against our interpretation, but then in the very next chapter, when aligning the old doctrine of limit with the Platonic doctrine of the Dyad, we find a list of opposites that is true to our interpretation, including the alignment of the Dyad with the *excessive* numbers:

> Philolaus says that existent things must all be either limitless or limited, or limited and limitless at the same time, by which it is generally agreed that he means that the universe is made up out of limited and limitless things at the same time, obviously after the image of number, for all number is composed of the Monad and the Dyad, *just* and *excessive*, and these in truth display equality and inequality, sameness and otherness, the bounded and the boundless, the definite and the indefinite. #

---

* Another confused approach was to follow the dogma and say that Monad and Dyad are not numbers but the origin of numbers, and then identify them with the 1 and 2, and then declare that the triad is the beginning of actual numbers. See Robbin's discussion of the treatment of the Monad and Dyad in the arithmetic emanation found in Nicomachus' *Theology* as well as his *Introduction* [26], p. 116–7.

\# [26] p. 259. Translation based on Dillon [9], p. 354. For the alignment of Dyad with number 2 in

Chapter 13: Dyadic Emanation

Just how the two new principles of arithmetic—the Monad and Dyad—should be aligned with the two ancient elements of arithmetic—the *just* and the *excessive*—seems to have developed into something of a controversy among the Hellenistic *mathematici*, as various positions have survived with varying justifications. What seems to have happened is that the original understanding behind the Dyadic doctrine of generation was lost, the doctrine became a dogma, and that this dogma was then defended or rejected in terms alien to the original understanding. There are hints in the textbooks that the authors had before them earlier accounts of this alignment that were in conflict with the contemporary thinking on the matter—but which yet makes sense in our interpretation. The above quotation from Nicomachus is a case in point. Another is in Theon. Just before he concludes his discussion by identifying the Monad with the *excessive* numbers, he dutifully points out that Aristotle in *The Pythagoreans* (a text now lost) reported that the One participates both natures, that is, the *excessive* and the *just*. That a 2nd century Pythogorean must use Aristotle as an authority for such an important point of difference with early Pythagorean opinion is telling, but then Theon seems to be pointing to more direct evidence corroborating Aristotle's witness when he adds that Archytas himself seems to concur with this account.*

The susceptibility of Dyadic doctrine to this misinterpretation can be traced back to the problems the Greeks had in identifying the Monad with the point, and thereby, to the confusion over a geometric **zero**-origin. A passage in Nicomachus provides insights into their confused (yet, rather advanced) thinking on this matter and so I quote it in full. It is directly after introducing Pythagorean dot notation that he proposes the Monad-*to-point* analogy.

> The Monad, then occupying the place and character of a point, will be the beginning of intervals and of numbers, but not itself an interval or a number, just as the point is the beginning of a line, or an interval, but is not itself line or interval. Indeed, when a point is added to a point, it makes no increase, for when a non-dimensional thing is added to another non-dimensional thing, it will not hereby have dimension; just as if one should examine the sum of nothing [literally 'not-one'] added to nothing, which makes nothing [0 + 0 = 0]. We saw a similar thing also in the case of

---

the previous chapter, see Bk II, Ch 17 [26, p. 255]. See also Heath's brief discussion in [4], p. 71.
* [28], p. 13–15. In his *Theology*, Nicomachus says something similar, namely, that the Monad embraces all things in potentiality and that it is *just* and *excessive* and *just-time-excessive* (quoted in [26], p. 194n). In *Metaphysics* [986a 19-23], Aristotle says for the Pythagoreans the One consists of both *just* and *excessive*, both limited and unlimited, and that all number is derived from the One.

263

equality among the relatives; for a proportion is preserved—as the 1st is to the 2nd, so the 2nd is to the 3rd—but no interval is generated in the relation of the extremes to each other [i.e., where x is to x as x is to x, x − x = 0], as there is in all the other relations with the exception of equality. In exactly the same way the Monad alone out of all number, when it multiplies itself, produces nothing greater than itself [1 X 1 = 1]. The Monad, therefore, is non-dimensional and elementary, and dimension first is found and seen in 2, then in 3, then in 4, and in succession in the following numbers; for dimension is that which is conceived of as between two limits. *

Attempts to clarify the nature of the ordinal original were not helped by the Greek way of enumerated magnitudes. The starting place would be called one, and not, as we would have it, zero. When we count a length, or interval, we count in the finishing point but not the starting point, whereas the way they calculated a magnitude they included both start and finish, and so three paces distance would be counted by the number 4.

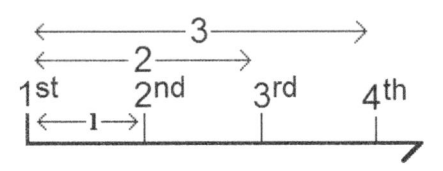

At first site this method may appears altogether erroneous, but not if you are familiar with our (Pythagorean) musical scale, where the divisions of the octave is still count in this way. Thus, the 2nd note is the 1st interval from the origin, itself called the tonic 1st, and likewise the 5th is only four notes up the scale. This convention is harmless in this context, but entirely dysfunctional when the Pythagoreans attempted an alignment with arithmetic generation. If the One is the non-dimensional point, then what is the linear 2? If the dimensions begin between two limits then the first case of this gives the interval 1 delimited by the 2nd. Otherwise, if the 2_{linear} is the interval 2, then it involving a two-point jump to the 3rd, leaving the interval 1 (and 1^n) confused with the One of the original starting point.

It seems then that the Pythagorean conventions of ordinal enumeration inhibited the development and communication of the new Dyadic doctrine of arithmetic generation, but this is not to say that the problems they encountered are solved with our modern numerical system. Rather, if

---

* Book II, Ch 6, 3. [26, p. 237]. This analogy of the Monad with the point was common and fits with the '•' or 'α' notation. Theon says the point...holding the same place as the Monad does in arithmetic. [28, p. 74]

it is the Brownian ordinals that they were trying to express then the expression of these numbers take us to the very limits of the possibility of notation. Consider in Brownian arithmetic that the first re-entered mark is in the very image of the First Distinction, and so the origin and the *first-born*—and every subsequent marking—are the same. The Word of the Gospel might be telling us that *God-the-father* is one, as I am one as you all are one through me, but this is difficult to express in our modern notation. This would amount to identifying '0' with '1' and also with any '+1', where these latter 'and ones', if ordinal, could themselves be regarded as *other-*

> **Notating the Ordinal Origin**
>
> In *L'arithmetique* (1585) Simon Stevin of Bruges sorted out this problem of Greek inheritance in the notational system of 10 characters. He puts the zero first, as the beginning of the ordinal numbers—'0 signifiant commencement de nombre'—but it is not itself a number. The claim that it is a number would only come much later when the 0 appears in the number line flanked right and left by the positive and negative numbers. In his argument for beginning with '0' rather than '1', he discusses both cardinal and ordinal numbers. It is in the progression of the ordinals that zero *is to* number what the point *is to* the line. This conforms to his expression of geometric progressions by using what are almost our exponents. Thus, to use our notation, the exponent 0 is the beginning of the exponent series, e.g., $2^0, 2^1, 2^2, 2^3, \ldots$

to-one and so as *not*-one! A similar problem is found with Leonard Cohen's I am the one who loves changing from nothing to one. How would you notate that?

There is also a very ordinary contradiction in the way we moderns say that the zero comes 'first'. Surely the celebration of the arrival of the 0, the zero, as the 'first' counting numeral is to a certain extent a celebration of a confusion. There must be a presence before there is an absence, a thing before a *no-thing*. If there are no green bottles sitting on the wall before there is even one of them, then there are also no pink elephants sitting on the wall. The counting zero is a *relative* absence, relative to the presence of the numbered. And even if the first presence is regarded as an absence, then, is it right to say that this 'zero' is '1st'?* In Brownian notation we have the same problem in reverse: can the 'presence' that is the 'first' Distinction really be called the 'origin'? It is a presence with a potent absence and yet it isn't the true origin, which is the absolute zero,

---

* Compare with Hesiod's cosmogony: in the beginning was the gap [*Theogony*, line 115-7] as discussed in [26], p. 116n2.

the mystical absence, the unmarked space that cleaves itself, the *no*-one-*that-will-become*-one. The high teachings of all the great mysticisms make every effort to point out that the origin of the notable (the nameable) is in the unnotable (the unnameable). Irrespective of whether we find the First Distinction to be equivalent to the common ordinal '0' or to the '1', there remains a question of its notation. I can indicate it by marking it on the page, and yet there is a sense in which it is already marked as the border of the blank page, and it is already named, 'the page'.

As author of this book, I find full sympathy with the Pythagoreans because these confusions are the very fragility of every description of the Form in my account. But after all, this is what should be expected because this fragility only reflects the instability of the Form itself, which is its very tendency to generate. The genius of Spencer Brown's notation is the way it is able to treat all these issues of the arithmetic in a direct manner, with a minimum of confusion consequential of the inadequacy of its notation to its expression.

What I suggest by this interpretation of the ancient Dyadic doctrine is that we might have a case here where the insight into the elementary form of arithmetic was in advance of the ability (the willingness?) to give notational expression to it. Because of this notational handicap, Plato and the first Academics were unable to explicate their insight clearly enough so that it could be conveyed to us unambiguously across two millennia. Thus, the Dyadic arithmetic lay dormant and barely discernible in the tradition for 2,000 years. That is, until G W Leibniz—the last of the great Christian Pythagoreans—finally developed an expression of the Dyadic emanation using the notational zero. And so, however limited we may also find the notation in the light of *Laws of Form*, it is nonetheless Leibniz who presents on the page for the first time a notational expression of the Dyadic emanation.

Chapter 14

THE DYADIC OF LEIBNIZ
An Arithmetic of Creation

> There is an old saying that God created everything according to weight, measure and number. But there are things which cannot be weighed, these namely which have no force or power. There are also things which have no parts and hence admit of no measure. But there is nothing which is not subordinate to number. Number is thus a basic metaphysical figure, as it were, and arithmetic is a kind of statics of the universe by which the powers of things are discovered.
>
> Men have been convinced ever since Pythagoras that the deepest mysteries lie concealed in numbers. It is possible that Pythagoras brought over this position, like many others, from the Orient to Greece. But, because the true key to the mystery was unknown, more inquisitive minds fell into futilities and superstitions, from which there finally arose a kind of popular Cabbala, far removed from the true one, and that multitude of follies which is falsely called a kind of magic and with which books have been filled. Meanwhile there remained deep-rooted in men the propensity to believe that marvels can be discovered by means of numbers, characters, and a certain new language, which some called the Adamic language: Jacob Boehme called it the *Natursprache*.
>
> But perhaps no mortal has yet seen into the true basis upon which everything can be assigned its characteristic number. For the most scholarly men have admitted that they did not understand what I said when I incidentally mentioned something of the sort to them. And, although learned men have long since thought of some kind of language or universal characteristic by which all concepts and things can be put into beautiful order, and with whose help different nations might communicate their thoughts and each read in his own language what another has written in his, yet no one has attempted a language or characteristic which includes at once both the arts of discovery and of judgment, that is, one whose signs or characters serve the same purpose that arithmetical signs serve for numbers, and algebraic signs for quantities taken abstractly. Yet it does seem that, since God has bestowed these two sciences on mankind, he has sought to notify us that a far greater secret lies hidden in our understanding, of which these are but the shadows.
>
> Some unknown fate has brought it about, however, that when I was a mere boy I became involved in these considerations, and, as first inclinations usually do, they have remained strongly fixed in my mind ever since.
>
> Leibniz, *Plus Ultra*, 1679

ENTHUSIASTIC MATHEMATICS

A Universal Notation

The greatness, the true greatness of G W Leibniz (1645-1716) in his contribution to mathematics and mathematical philosophy is as much his penetrating brilliance as it is his unity of purpose. The purpose that is ever apparent throughout his career is to establish all science in its elementary form. He wanted to build from first principles the foundations to all the formal sciences, including linguistics (logic), music, geometry and arithmetic. He recognised from the outset that a big part of this task was to reform the notational systems so that they directly expressed the elementary forms. In order to serve the empirical sciences, he was looking to find notational systems that directly expressed the real form of things, what he sometimes called real characteristics. His ultimate goal was a real characteristics able to express all knowledge, and he sometimes called this a universal characteristics. He never achieved this final unifying goal, but, like the ancient Pythagoreans before him, his obsessive purposefulness brought rewards along the way. The elementary arithmetic that he called 'Dyadic' was one of these, and his enthusiasm for it over many years suggests that he held out hope that this elementary calculus would one day serve his grand design to unify all science upon mathematical principles.

Leibniz first played with binary numbers while in Paris in the early 1670s, returning to them again and again with heightening interest. By 1679 he had come to regard the dyadic progression as the complete and ultimate analytic calculus. [40, p. 218] Then in May 1696 he announced that his Dyadics is the very form of the arithmetic emanation from the original One. In that year he wrote a paper entitled:

> The wonderful expression of numbers of everything through 1 and 0 representing the origin of things from God and nothing.
> [40, p. 225]

And if the significance of this discovery for Leibniz were in doubt, I should add his alternative title *The Mystery of Creation*. In this essay Leibniz says of this binary notation that since the most powerful use of the human sciences is...

> ...that they lead us to God, as if by his hand, and they show the wonderful vestiges of the divine author in things; I dare to say that scarcely anything is revealed in the mathematical sciences which better raises the soul to God. For since the mystery of creation is among the most powerful

wonders of God it is unknown to heathens... and since the essences of things are as of numbers, as has been wisely said by philosophers, and therefore nature itself shows wonders in numbers by way of likeness to essences, it has been said that everything does not come from God and matter but from God and nothing.*

The doctrine of *Creation-from-nothing* distinguished a strict monotheism from the doctrine of Creation involving primary matter. In the Western tradition it was overwhelmingly through the Aristotelian influences that a primary matter is introduced to the Creation story, and Aristotelian-style cosmogony is found in 'heathen' Hellenistic doctrines. Matter and its generation also come into an aligned with 'evil' in 'Gnostic' Christian texts and the cosmogony of the Jewish Cabala. The problem for monotheism is thus: if the Creator is given to so much as act upon a primary matter, then there is something *other than*, and *coeval with*, the one Creator-God. As Leibniz said of this cosmogony: it gives the Creator as a principle that produces nothing, but only informs [matter]. [44, p. 97]

It is Saint Augustine who is credited with defining Christian theology away from the confusion introduced with any doctrine of a *substantial-other-to-God*; and it is the Augustinian tradition within Christianity that holds most strongly to this point. After Augustine there were developments in the other direction, including advances in the theology of an evil power and persona associated with ungodly matter through the sins of corporal desire. Nevertheless, by the time the three great monotheistic establishments, Judaism, Christianity and Islam, had overwhelmed continuing Hellenistic theosophy, *Creation-from-nothing* had become the explicitly stated orthodox in each of them.

The doctrine of *Creation-from-nothing* is often described as a 'mystery' because, just like the Christian 'mystery' of the Trinity, it is regarded as unexplained, unexplainable, and yet a necessary truth revealed by God. What Leibniz is claiming is that his notation of the Dyadic progression actually gives expression to this truth: *it dispels this mystery in a scientific account*. His analogy between the generation of numbers and the generation of things is a new confirmation of the Christian religion in regard to a sublime

---

* [40, p. 228] Leibniz's analogy of God's *creation-of-all-things-from-nothing* with the generation of numbers does have a private history prior to extravagant declarations of 1696. In 1679 he suggested that there may be only one thing that is conceived through itself, namely God himself; and besides this there is nothing, or privation, and that this is made clear by an admirable simile which is the way all numbers are expressed by unity and nothing. [41, pp. 2–3] The analogy is mentioned in an essay of about 1690 called 'On the True Mystical Theology' [42, p. 368] and in the 1695 dialogue on the origins of evil [43, p. 113–4]. An extract from this dialogue is below, in the box on p. 284.

article of the faith. [40, p. 247] For Leibniz this analogy is a magnificent example of the advantages that science can give to religion, and of why science should be supported and continued: science saves religion by explaining the mysteries and replacing dogma with understanding. Faith without knowledge says Leibniz comes not of the spirit of God but of the dead letter or the empty echo.

> Faith without light awakens no love but only fear or hope, and is not living.
> [42, p. 369]

Such an argument for science had all but collapsed at the end of the 17th century often with grave consequences for those still advancing it, and also for the science advocated in this way. In hindsight we can see that Leibniz was playing a losing game. The boldness of his specific claim in the climate of the late 17th century may already be palpable to the reader. Suffice is to say for now Leibniz is expressing his Renaissance enthusiasm for science in a monumental claim that is at the same time a monumental transgression of science to the very heart of Christian theology. His arithmetic of Creation is a far greater transgression of Church doctrine than anything Copernicus had ever said about planetary motion, or that Darwin ever would say about the differentiation of the species.

Creation from Nothing in Augustine

...we correctly believe that God made all things from nothing. For, though all formed thing were made from this matter, this matter itself was still made from absolutely nothing. For we should not be like those who do not believe that Almighty God could have made something from nothing, when they observe that carpenters or any workmen cannot produce anything unless they have something out of which to make it...Almighty God did not have to be helped by anything that he had not made so that he could make what he wanted. For if something that he had not made helped him to make those things he wanted to make, he was not almighty...

Augustine
On Genesis

The Dyadic Creation Analogy

Leibniz's arithmetic analogy to the Creation story brings together three doctrines of his tradition, the Christian doctrine of *Creation-from-nothing* and two further doctrines of the Christian Pythagoreans. The first of these is the doctrine of continuous Creation, or emanation. The second is the analogy between things and numbers expressed in the motto: the essence of things is as of the essence of numbers.* Together they give the generation of things as of the form of the generation of numbers. Leibniz had already pushed to the limit the analysis of number and so reducing it to its elementary form in the Dyadic progression. With this progress he believed he had arrived at an arithmetic that is non-arbitrary, that is no human invention, but that which nature itself has prescribed.# The *necessary* consequence of this line of thought is that Dyadic generation must conform to the generation of all things by God. So, a natural step for Leibniz would be to find whether it conformed to the cosmogony revealed directly to Moses by God. And to his delight it did.

> Φ
>
> ...to simply say that all the numbers are formed by the combinations of unity with nothing, and that the nothing suffices for diversifying them. It seems also believable to say that God has made everything from nothing without attending to any primary matter; and that there are only two primary principles, God and nothing: God of perfection, and nothing of imperfection or void of essence.
>
> Φ

In the analogy of Creation, the cosmogony in *Genesis* is read such that God is the one origin of things, and that he created all things in a void. This Biblical void, in which all things are generated, is itself generated by God, and it is (or subsequently becomes) 'Earth' in the opposition Heaven/Earth: God created Heaven and the void, and in the void he creates Earth. The first act of Creation in the void is a negation of this negative, just as light negates darkness: *Let there be light!* and it became light. Leibniz thought this could be illustrated to please the human eye with an image of the Mosaic 'spirit of God' shining over the darkness over the waters. After *Let there be light!* Leibniz leaves it to Moses: the light was good, it was divided from darkness, and the first evening and morning commence the day/night alternations of Earthly time, by which all else is created.+ Leibniz roughly aligns the Mosaic negatives of the 'void,' the 'waters' and the 'darkness', but he does not push the formal alignment too far—and nor

---

* Other expressions and translations include: the essences are numbers, or that they are like the numbers. For Leibniz using the Latin essentiae rerum sunt ut numeri and the French les essence sont comme les nombres, see for example [45], p. 38 & p. 136.
# For 'pushing the limit', see Zacher [40] p. 251, and Widmaier [45] p. 136–7. For nature's prescription, see Zacher [40] p. 218.
+ See for example the full letter to Rudolf in the collected writings [46], p. 119, Reihe I, Band XIII, N. 75. Consider that 'light' as a metaphor works well with the analogy because light is both the power of (biological) generation and the predominant means of perception (the foundation of knowledge).

ENTHUSIASTIC MATHEMATICS

could he because the story presents as an overlapping amalgamation of two previous accounts. The all-important alignment for Leibniz is in regards to the *from-nothing* doctrine of the Creation, and so the void in which things are generated corresponds with the first '0' with which he always begins the Dyadic progression.

Further straining the Mosaic imagery, Leibniz makes it clear that he wants his first 0 to be regarded as the absolute **zero** prior to all Creation by the original **One**. Later, while discussing the precedent to his Dyadics in ancient China, he points out that this first 0 could signify the void which precedes the creation of Heaven and Earth. The first void is not a void relative to Heaven, but prior to it, a void prior even to the first line of Genesis.* If we now try an alignment of the Leibnizian arithmetic Creation story with our story of Formal Re-Entry, then the first '0' of the Dyadic series would be the unmarked space of the First Distinction, while the First Distinction itself corresponds to the Creator itself as the Form of Creation: This Form constitutes implicitly its negation, the void, in which, by entering it (*The God of light says: Let there be light!*), all form of things are created.

Leibniz makes some effort to give expression to his new vision of the form of the Creator prior to Creation. In his first notes on the Creation analogy, the table giving the Dyadic series from 0, has written above it UNUM NECESSARIUM.# This *necessary*-one-*alone* hovering above the void is called 'one', but Leibniz never notates it as '1'. It could not be any ordinary unit because, by Leibniz's account, it is nothing, in that it is nothing in particular (it is no creature of the Creation). A few months later Leibniz, the enthusiast for notation that he was, offers a symbol to express the character of this mystical origin. As a 1697 New Year greeting gift for a benefactor, Rudolf August, Leibniz gives specifications for the design of a medallion to commemorate his discovery of the arithmetic of Creation.+ This medallion would include a sample of the

UNUM
NECESSARIUM

0	0
1	1
10	2
11	3
100	4
101	5
110	6
111	7
1000	8
1001	9
1010	10
1011	11
1100	12
1101	13
1110	14
1111	15
10000	16
10001	17
10010	18
10011	19
10100	20
10101	21
10110	22
10111	23
11000	24
11001	25
11010	26
11011	27
11100	28
11101	29
11110	30
11111	31
100000	32

---

* [40, p. 285]. See also the extended quote below in the box, p. 316.
\# The table and the original German text is found in Zacher [40] p. 231. These notes from May 1696 are under the heading Wunderbarer ursprung aller zahlen aus 1 und 0... The text can also be found in [46] Reihe 1, Band 12, N.67 p66-68. Compare unum necessarium with the Vulgate Bible, Luke 10:41-2, where Jesus advises: Martha, Martha! sollicita es et turbaris erga plurima porro unum est necessarium.
+ [46] p. 119, Reihe 1, Band 13, N. 75. Rudolf August (1627-1704) was head of a branch of the House

arithmetic and an image of the Creation according to the Mosaic description. Its overarching motto would be: For all things to be derived from nothing THE ONE SUFFICES. Leibniz stipulated that the SUFFICIT UNUM of this Latin motto should be emphasised (hence his use of capitals) because in itself it has the sense and depth of meaning of the whole verse. And finally he offered a mystical symbol of the creation of all things from nothing. This symbol consists of '1' superimposed over '0,' similarly to the Greek Φ.* He calls this UNUM AUTEM NECESSIUM. I read this UNUM, sufficient and necessary, as referring not so much to the Creation, but rather to the Creator—one, absolute, timeless, and yet in itself potent with all Creation. Could there be a better symbol expressing the origin as the Platonic *coincidence-of-opposites* than the superimposition of the two characters that mark those opposites?

Leibniz was very excited about this one/zero Creation symbol. He would present it as the epitome of his arithmetic discovery over and over again and to the very end of his Earthly life. Even beyond: he made sure the Φ symbol would be etched on his coffin under a declaration of *all-for-one*, OMNIA AD UNUM.#

Rudolf seemed to share some of Leibniz's enthusiasm. While we don't know whether the medallion depicting the Creation was ever forged, we do know that Rudolf worked on some designs incorporating the symbol, and that at least in letters addressed to Leibniz, Rudolf used a seal with this symbol encircled by the motto: UNUS EX NIHILO OMNIA BENE FECIT.+

Leibniz and Rudolf had good reason to be excited. Leibniz had achieved a breakthrough in the elementary Pythagorean science of arithmetic emanation. Leibniz's alternating 0↔1 progression presents for the first time a notation for the elementary values of Pythagorean arithmetic, the *just* and the *excessive*. This alternating double presents the generation of numbers as a perpetual '*othering*' of the original One, and the degrees

---

of Brunswick–Wolfenbuttel. Leibniz was in the employ of the House of Brunswick–Luneburg (Hanover) from 1676 until his death. In this time he made friends with Rudolf, who had more of an interest in philosophy and religion than government. In 1691 Leibniz was appointed director of the Wolfenbuttel Library.

* This 'Φ' is not to be confused with the 'Φ' representing the Golden Mean, which was first used long after Kepler and Leibniz, when Leibniz's symbol for the rational Creator was long forgotten. To avoid confusion here, I use serif font for Leibniz's 1-0 origin (Φ) while the Golden Mean is represented in san serif font (Φ).

\# The coffin was decorated with etchings according to instructions Leibniz left with his secretary Echhart. See Antognazza [47], p. 545.

+ The motto can be translated as 'the One has made everything from nothing'. See Zacher [40] p. 236, and [46], Reihe 1, Band 13 p. 121-128.

of the arithmetic build in the *justly-just* hierarchy of the elementary geometric progression of **double**. But more than this, by introducing the Φ *just-excessive* symbol, Leibniz has found a way to use the notational **zero** (that the Greeks did not have) with the notational **one** to show that the original **One** is a union of opposites and in doing so also final escape centuries of confusion with the *first-born*-**One** and its progeny.

In Pythagorean terms Leibniz's achievement was magnificent. At long last someone had solved the mystery of the Platonic Monad-Dyad doctrine, breathing life back into the dogma with a unencumbered notation expressing its raw beauty. But you would barely know the traditional significance of the arithmetic from reading Leibniz. He keeps the Pythagorean terminology to a bare minimum. To this day the link to ancient mathematical philosophy remains obscure in its reception. Before and after the revival of interest in binary numbers at the advent of the cybernetic age, Leibniz's Dyadics is generally regarded as novel, not traditional; and the Creation analogy presents as but a courtly flourish—it has never been assessed as a serious attempt to express a formal generation.*

Modern readers can be forgiven for missing the Platonic connection. Consider again this coincidence of the elementary mathematical opposites expressed in the symbol Φ. In his defining, denoting and celebrating the origin of Creation, he never uses the most obvious Platonic term for it, the 'Monad'. That he avoids calling the Creator, the 'Monad' is striking because, after all, the 2nd and 3rd century Church fathers did so, and not just the excessively Hellenistic Alexandrians, Clement and Oregon, but also Dionysius, the very Patriarch of Rome. And Leibniz himself used it elsewhere to express the elementary identity of *being*. It is also striking that Leibniz does not so much as mention Plato, nor the Pythagoreans, in the discussions—the best we get is 'the philosophers' or 'the arithmeticians'—because it is as a Platonist that Leibniz saw his genius. If someone should reduce Plato to a system, wrote Leibniz in a reflective moment at the end of his life, he would render a great service to the human race. He then predicts: it will be seen that I have made some approximation to this.

Systematizing Plato? The Dyadic emanation had come down to the Renaissance as the great summit of Plato's teaching, but it was a doctrine without an expression, without a notation, without a system...which is to

---

* The mathematical historian Florian Cajori in 1916 was unusual in addressing directly the 'image of creation', but only to dismiss it as but an interesting chapter in modern religious mysticism. [48, p. 565]. It is as religious symbolism (and after the cybernetic revival of binary counting) that it receives a more sympathetic treatment by Michael Kerze under the heading of 'Binary Symbolism' in *The Encyclopaedia of Religion* [49].

say, *without a characteristics*. Solving that problem would surely have been irresistible to Leibniz. Yet, if his Dyadics of Creation has anything to do with the Platonic Dyadic emanation, he was not letting on. All we have is the name, and even that he avoids in his later public writings, Latinising it instead to the now more familiar 'binary'.*

What then could explain the absence of the obvious links to Platonism that is otherwise the heart and soul of his work? It could be that Leibniz saw no connection with the Platonic Dyad. But this is unlikely. So it seems that Leibniz is purposefully avoiding an explicit alignment of his Creation analogy with the Platonic emanation. And there is one very good reason for him doing this. The clue comes when we consider that Leibniz avoids altogether the other Creation story in the Bible, namely, the quasi-Platonic cosmogony found in the prologue to the Gospel of John. This account of Creation is emphatically sympathetic with the Leibniz's Dyadics. Yet, if Leibniz were to invoke the Monad and the Dyad to 'solve' the mystery of *Creation-from-nothing* in terms of this Logos that was God, then he would only herald the very first, the most famous, and the most divisive of all Christian heresies, namely, the Arian heresy of the Holy Trinity.

Arius and the New Testament Creation Controversy

As we have already seen above (page 216), the prologue to John says that the Logos was in the *principle-origin* with God and that the Logos *was God*. John then goes on to say that all things come into being through this Logos which is as of an only-begotten [*monogenous*] of a Father. [1:3,14] Here, John presents Creation in a paradox. On the one hand, the Logos was/is with God in the timeless and absolute presence that is the *arche*, the *principle-origin*. There he is identical with God. Yet, on the other hand, he is born of God, as Son of the Father. Now, for us this paradox has been

---

* For use of 'Monad' as a name for the Godhead by the ante-Nicene fathers, see Stead 'The Platonism of Arius'. [50, p. 18] For Leibniz aiming to systematize Plato, see [51], Bk III, p. 637. Regarding the avoidance of the term by Leibniz in his Dyadic writings, see where Cook and Rosemont note the absence of the terminology of the monads in Leibniz's 'Discourse on the Natural Theology of the Chinese', which includes an explication of his Dyadics (see below, p. 329-31). They point out that this absence is especially odd since a more famous text now known as 'The Monadology' was addressed a year earlier to the same correspondent. [44, p. 7] This might also strike some of my readers as especially odd if they were introduced to Leibniz in university philosophy courses where 'The Monadology' is often given great prominence and seen as encapsulating Leibniz's philosophical view. It is not that 'The Monadology' is found in conflict with the Dyadic writings, but only that its sympathy is obscured by a separation of terminology and by the avoidance of any mathematical elaboration. For a typical modern philosophical introduction to Leibniz, see this [52] influential English language selection, first published in 1902. The term 'Dyadics' is also avoided in Leibniz's published essay and in his more public writings. Evidently, after 1705 Leibniz entirely abandoned use of the Greek term.

resolved. In the light of *Laws of Form,* John's *arche* is viewed as a Pythagorean arithmetic origin (namely the Monad as the First Distinction or the Form), and the Logos is the *ratio-of-the-opposites* potent in it—but also, the Logos issues from it as its first manifestation, the *first-born*-one. No one has ever seen God, but the only begotten Son who is in the bosom of the Father declares him. In this view the manifest Logos-Son is both born of God and also identical with God in the unity of his original uncreated and obscure form. While that might have resolved the paradox for us, and while it might have resolved it in sympathy the Platonism of the author, it does seem that some of the influential bishops of the early Church could not, in any terms, find the simple beauty behind this contradictory account of the Logos. As a consequence they struggled with it in a bitter, divisive and lengthy controversy began at the very event organised to bring together all the once subversive Christian communions and unite them under a general creed for the new state-sanctioned Church.

At the foundation council of a united Roman Christian Church in Nicea (325 AD), the interest in the Trinity was all about the Father and the Son. It is true that the 'Nicene Creed' (recited in the modern churches to this day) integrates the Holy Spirit into the Father-Son story. However, in the creed of final assent at the Council of Nicea, ...and the Holy Spirit is tacked on to the end of the affirmation of the faithful as though an afterthought.* So, at this council convened by the lately converted Emperor Constantine, the 'Trinitarian' debate reduced to—or at least, it *began as*—a debate over the nature of the priority of the Father over the Son.

Let's consider this paternal priority. In the doctrine of the Logos-Son we cannot get away from the fact that he is generated by *God-the-Father.* If he is generated, then can we talk of God prior to his fathering? This priority would be in the *principle-origin*; the timeless, absolute presence that is beyond the temporal genesis beginning with the generator-Logos. This gives the Logos—the *first-born,* the generator and the medium of all things—as the secondary and the temporal principle derived from the

---

* Throughout the entire subsequent history of the Church, an effervescence of popular heresies would flip this ecclesiastic formula upon its head by declaring the *Spirit-of-God* first, as the inspiration of all truth including where it is found in canonic scriptures. The rejection of the 'external' church and its dogma for the primacy of the internal god as *in-spir*-ation unifies diverse heresies down through the ages. See the collection of sources presented in *The Birth of Popular Heresy,* which includes an account of a proud 11th century Manichean willing to die a painful death rejecting the fabrications which men have written on the skins of animals for the law written within us by the Holy Spirit. [53, p. 14] It should also be noted that the Nicean creed also integrates Jesus as identical with the *Son-God.* The founder of their church had already been canonically identified with the messiah promised to the Jew. Now, following this declaration of his divinity in Nicea, there would ensue great controversy, including in the difficulty of relating his divinity to the divinity of his Earthly Mother—indeed, it in turn contributed to her assent in status as the Mother of God.

timeless, unseen *principle-origin*. In this way, the Logos can be seen as Godly, yet a product of God—he is not identical with himself as the *principle-origin*. To follow this way of thinking you must next deal with the problem of how the Logos-Son is generated in a fathering of the origin, and from what. If the Logos is from the one God, but yet he is not God, then his difference is in the negation of God. The distinction of Logos must be in, *it must come out of*, what was not. A true monotheism can only allow that he be created by the original *being* from *non-being*, which is to say formally, by the original One from the *not*-One. And all else must be created by this means. This is precisely the position Arius of Alexandria (?–336) took to his peril. Before he was generated, Arius says of the Logos, he did not exist.

> We say that the Son has an origin, but God is without origin. For that reason we are persecuted, and because we say that he is from what is not. And this we say because he is neither part of God nor derived from any matter.

For Arius, there is a timeless condition of the Godhead when the son was not. And he makes this claim specifically in rejection of *Creation-from-matter* (as proposed by the Gnostics). If we are true to our monotheism and deny anything coeval with God then it follows of necessity that he had his being from the non-being.*

What is often obscured later in the continuing Church controversy over the unity of God is that it all began very much as the problem of how to understand the new Christian doctrine of the means of Creation as given in the Gospel of John. It began as the problem of how to explain the emanation of all things without falling into the trap of introducing a material principle. This problem was soon lost to the dispute, and the ecclesiastical condemnation of Arius, lead famously by his Bishop in Alexandria, Athanasius. Their objection came down to a rejection of the logical necessity that the Logos-Son must be generated by God from nothing; this was precisely because it contradicted John's testimonial that the Logos was God.

The Trinitarian controversy at Nicea resulted in the defeat of Arius and his Eastern Church supporters to the dissatisfaction of many others. The Council resolving to allow that the statements, *The Father is God* and *The Son is God*, are equally true, and the priority of Father over Son is both denied and affirmed. The politics of the jargon precipitated the mess

---

* See the letter of Arius to Eusebius, Bishop of Nicomedia and the account of Socrates of Constantinople translated in Bettenson [54] p. 56 & 57.

that became the Church doctrine of the Son inscrutable to most Christians. The reader herself may have one day paused after reciting the line *begotten not made, of one being with the Father* and wonder what *that* was all about. Of course, what these words hover about is the very 'mystery' of the Trinity. And as we have seen, the anti-Arian doctrine effectively supported the obscuring of another doctrine, because, whatever the bishops might say, they could never explicitly deny creation by the **One** from his *not*; all they could do was muddle and obscure the account in terms of the Logos.* There was always the account in *Genesis* to fall back on, which, however muddled, was at least beyond the terms of the Hellenistic controversy, just as it would be for Leibniz.

The danger for Leibniz in meddling with the doctrine of the Logos-Son is all the more apparent when we consider that Arius was quoted as calling this medium 'the Dyad'. Due to the successful suppression of his work it is difficult for us to establish just how important the name 'Dyad' was for Arius and his early followers. What is clear is that naming the ratio of the generation the 'Dyad' is but to announce its secondary nature. And if there were any doubt in post-Renaissance Europe that this were a Platonic heresy, then the widely circulated translations of Plotinus would have removed it: the Dyad is a secondary, announces Plotinus, derived from the Monad.[#] After Arius, 'Dyad' as a name for the medium of Creation falls out of the Christian controversy; and, likewise, the name 'Monad' for John's *arche*, so popular among the ante-Nicene Fathers, also disappears. Moreover, with the eventual defeat of Arianism, the two aspects of the Christian emanation, *by* Logos and *from not*-**One**, are placed beyond controversy in an abuse of the pagan notion of 'mystery'.

The mystery status of the Trinitarian was an attempt to absorb into state dogma the confusing and confounding doctrine of duplicity in the godhead, but if this was supposed to lock it out of the way of controversy, then the only mystery might have been its Platonic inspiration. Its origins in that Christian tradition would be ever open to anyone who could read the canonical Greek texts of Christianity prior to its elevation as the state religion. And so the controversy over the Trinity would go on to become the most factious and enduring controversy of the next two millennia.

---

* As the Council of Nicea agreed, the Logos was not 'made' but he was the medium of all making: through him all things were made, things in Heaven and things on Earth.
# *The Enneads*, Ennead V, Tract 1, 5.

Immediately after Nicea, widespread dissatisfaction with the outcome meant that the issue could not be ignored, but progressive attempts at grammatical compromises soon descended into absurdity, with obscure heretical positions remaining strong. For a time Arianism was even triumphant, and it was during this time that the Goths were converted. This meant that in the polarisation around the Gothic wars, Arianism became the principal doctrinal distinction on which the battles were staged. The name we still use to distinguish the Eastern Church originates from the forgotten distinction of this conflict: **Orthodox (not-Arian)**. If Islam is viewed as a Christian heresy, then at its theological core is a return to strict monotheism. In the West, the absence of any suggestion of the Trinity in the Bible was corrected by an interpolation in John's Gospel for the standard Latin translation.* But, beyond the political manoeuvring and the slogans, there was no decree of the bishops that could prevent private reflection on these awkward teachings about the very nature of the Creator, the very Christian *theo*-logy. Brutal suppression only ever delayed the re-emergence of 'anti-Trinitarians' down through the history of the Western churches.

One such revival emerged out of obscurity across Western Europe during the 16th century. The 3-in-1 nature of the Godhead was one of the key doctrines brought into question in the reform movement that brought the Reformation. Yet this is one teaching that the successful reformed churches were astute to leave alone, and in fact it was not long before they undertook a vigorous campaign to persecute the rampant outbreaks of anti-Trinitarianism in their own protestant territories. Symbolic for our story is the famous case of Michael Servetus, the very model of a Renaissance scientist, remembered in medicine for his publication of a description of pulmonary circulation. After studying the Christian texts in their original languages, he challenged various dogmas of both the reformed and continuing churches, most prominently the unreformed dogma of the Trinity, only to find both sides colluding to hunt him down so that he was eventually burned alive in Calvin's Geneva. In those bloody Reformation years there was no where safe in all of Christendom for a declared anti-Trinitarian to flee, and this predicament continued through to the end of the century when another great Renaissance scientist, Giordano Bruno, would also burn as a proclaimed anti-Trinitarian. In fact, for those who questioned the Trinitarian orthodoxy a brutal untimely death was the real

---

* This interpolation (at 1 John 5.7) seem to have passed unnoticed until the original Greek manuscripts were re-examined in the Renaissance.

prospect almost until the New World opened up as something of a refuge, but even there persecution continued. By the late 17th century the risk was more to livelihood than life, but we should not forget that even the British Act of Toleration of 1689—that celebrated beachhead of liberalism—makes a point of excluded Arianism as an intolerable non-conformity. It was only in the 18th century that some heretics were finally able to affirm themselves as 'Unitarians'.

Many of those who have been lampooned as Arians may not have held to a unitarian doctrine of the Creation. As their teaching are lost to history, we will never know for sure. However, for some there can be no doubt, and perhaps the most well documented of any anti-Trinitarians were among Leibniz's correspondents at Cambridge. Extensive studies of the teaching of the ante-Nicene Church Fathers redeemed Arius in the eyes of some Cambridge Platonists and resident mathematicians. William Whiston (1667-1752), Newton's chosen successor to the Lucasian Chair of Mathematics, was remarkably open about his findings in a Cambridge of Puritans ascendency. In 1710 he lost the chair after a well publicised hearing, and then published his views in his *Primitive Christianity Revived*. While well regarded for his natural science, it was on account of his Arianism that he was excluded from the Royal Society. Other professors, from William Chillingworth (1602-43) to Samuel Clarke (1675-1729), were more discrete. [55] But we know of none so secretive as the most celebrated president of the Royal Society. Sir Isaac Newton's Arianism was widely rumoured after his death. But like so much else about this hero of the Enlightenment, it was obscured to later generations; that is, until 1942, when J M Keynes finally forced us to face the fact that Newton was among those who came to see the Church that defeated Arius as diabolical—and the seriousness in which he held this belief gives a credible explanation for why he avoided ordination, and for his refusal of the sacrament upon his deathbed.*

With the Arian controversy re-awakening in England and continuing to smoulder on the continent, Leibniz would have been faced with the problem that his Dyadics was addressing the very same issue that the Nicean proclamations upon the Logos-Son never resolved. And of course his Dyadics could easily support an Arian interpretation. Leibniz had God creating everything from nothing by means of the Dyad. There is no second 'person' in his origin, only God…and nothing. Yet there is the

---

* For Newton's Arianism see Keynes [11], Vol X, Ch 35, and Wiles [55] p. 77–93. For its possible connection to rejection of the sacrament, see the discussion of belief about the Church in apostasy in the note below on p. 334-5.

Dyadic generator, born of the one-God entering his *not*. This *becoming-other-to*-God is the means of the generation of all things, so it must be understood as the *ratio*-nal means of Creation, the Logos. Now, while *we* can see how this generative ratio is already potent in the original One, this may not be so evident to an inquisitor. What would be evident to an inquisitor, and to all who read Leibniz's accounts of the Creation, is that the 1↔0 Dyad is *created*, and that it is created (by God) *from nothing*. In short, if Leibniz had used the term 'Monad' and related his Dyadics to the Platonic 'Dyad', he might just as well have gone straight out and quoted Arius, as officially preserved heretical in his condemnation by the Church:

The Monad was, but the Dyad was not before it came to be.*

In the promotion of his new arithmetic, the Holy Trinity is one mystery that Leibniz was wise to avoid.

In fact Leibniz did expend a great deal of energy on the problem of the Trinity. But this was as part of an entirely different scholarly enterprise given the working title: *The Catholic Demonstration*. This apologetic project reads alien to his work towards a unification of the science. And it is alien. For, what we may see as a conflict between the defence of received dogma and proper scientific demonstration, Leibniz saw (more in the model of Augustine than Thomas Aquinas) as the divide between revealed and natural theology. For him, reveal theology is about defending the essential Judeo-Christian teachings *revealed* by God that are not *discoverable* by ordinary scientific investigations. The Reformation brought most of these doctrines into heated and bloody conflict that was continuing unabated. Leibniz, who was deeply involved in the German reunification movement, showed little interest in entering controversy over any of these dogmas, except the one that the state-Protestant churches did not dispute with Rome, namely the Trinity.

When the English anti-Trinitarian controversy exploded into print during the 1690s, Leibniz took a keen interest, managing to acquire the key heretical pamphlets that were often circulated secretly and always anonymously. His Trinitarian apologetic is mostly in response to these.

For Leibniz, a proper defence of the Trinity consist not in demonstrating the truth of the teaching *per se*, but in demonstrating it as according to the words of Scriptures and as interpreted by the true Catholic Church.# But

---

* [56, p. 82] This is Athanasius quoting Arius's *Thalia*.
\# Translated, quoted and interpreted by Antognazza [57] p. 116.

while it is not *discoverable* by reason it must be found reasonable nonetheless. In this he finds agreement with Locke's *Reasonableness of Christianity*, where Locke defended himself against accusations that his empirical epistemology promoted a form of 'natural religion' that no longer required revelation. Such a mid-road defence was required because some of Locke's radical followers where using his epistemology in a renewed 'Deism'. All of Christianity, including the Trinity, could be established by reason and the senses, so claimed John Toland and the post-Lockean 'Deists'. Leibniz would never make such a claim, and his objection to using mathematical method to demonstrate the truth of orthodox Trinitarianism does suggests that he found it indefensible by any scientific methodology. [57, Ch 8] And at the same time his arithmetic analogy of the Creator—where THE ONE SUFFICES—draws him into closer and closer conflict with this teaching. Perhaps the same could be said for his mature theory of living beings, which he describes as 'Monads'.

Leibniz's theory of Monads proposes that all (organic) life is aggregates of the indissoluble unites of active/passive power. He often presents this theory of living unity as a modification of the prevailing Aristotelian ontology that gives primary matter as a separate source of being. [52, pp. 251–272] For Leibniz, matter reduces to privation, and so to the passive power—just as in his Dyadics where passive matter is identified with nothing and 0. Why there is no (known) attempt by Leibniz to integrate this ontology with his Dyadics creationism is a mystery. Reticence due to the dangers of presenting a Monad/Dyad theology may not be the full story, but nonetheless there are further sympathies in his fragmentary legacy with our self-referencing systems view.

While a consistent system in Leibniz's Monadic ontology is difficult to find, it is at least clear that he is attempting to avoid external ontology, and we can see this especially when the *being* of material objects is placed in perception, and then the Monad is identified with the perceiver, or as we would say 'the observer'. In this way he found sympathy with George Berkeley's 'immaterialism' when it arrived late in his life, only objecting to Berkeley's ontology (in a rather confused way) by affirming his own 'monadology' where true beings are Monads or perceivers.* Here Leibniz seems very close to our *self-observing-I*, but it is where he explains his Dyadic emanationism as an ontology of *'non plus ultra'* that he helps to bring unity to our entire historical narrative.

---

* Leibniz's marginalia on Berkeley's *Treatise* is translated and quoted by Antognazza [47] p. 539. See above Chapter 1 (expecially p. 14 & p. 26) for discussions of Berkeley on perception.

The Dyad and the Limited Nature of Things

In order for Leibniz to be able to communicate without censure his magnificent vision of self-generation, it was necessary to cut the patristic bridges to Platonism that are the various Platonic terms. But he left one bridge—the name 'Dyadics'—which, once crossed, enables us to rebuild all the other bridges to the grand and ancient tradition of the *mathematici*. In doing so we can see how the Dyadics was something of a culmination of Leibniz's neo-Pythagorean theological investigations.

Consider first his *positive* theology of a perfect and all-powerful Creator. If God is the only power, then the Creation is a self-generation *of* God *in* God; that is, God involves perpetual action in himself. Self-generation is a rule of nature that Leibniz finds through natural reason: If nothing is active by its own nature, there will be nothing active at all. And as all action involves change then there must be in the nature of things a tendency towards internal change associated with temporal succession. Time is a measure of God's continuous Creation. Leibniz always emphasised that this Creation is ongoing, that it is life itself. God created all from nothing, and *makes it still*, says Leibniz, and so the conservation of the *being* of things is just one continuous creation. While the Creator himself is timeless in his absoluteness, all creation is in a state of constant change and motion. Apparent stillness in things is only when the motion is relatively infinitesimal.* In sum, Leibniz's theology determined his elementary vision of the physical world as the living expression of a formal emanation from the original **one**.

This positive reasoning upon the *necessary-and-sufficient-*one*-generator-of-all* informs his negative theology of the infinite origin of the generation. That the all-powerful Creator is infinite, or unlimited, we know by his Creation, which is the limited expression of his power. This limitedness of manifest creatures has two seemingly paradoxical attributes. On the one hand it corresponds to their negation—their *non plus ultra*, their *not-being-more-or-otherwise*. On the other hand it is their very definition. This theology is explained in a dialogue on the origins of evil that Leibniz wrote in 1695—the year before the appearance of the Dyadic Creation analogy (see an extract on page 284). Leibniz uses the circle, as limited by its circumference, to show how all things are bounded or imperfect by virtue of the principle of negation or of nothingness they contain. The limitedness that they contain is their lack of infiniteness, their lack of the perfection of their origin, the Creator.

---

* See for example in the collection [42], p. 352, 398 & 544.

A -   ...To account for sin there must be another infinite cause capable of counterbalancing the influence of divine goodness.
B -   I can name you such a thing.
A -   You would therefore be a Manichean, since you admit two principles, one of good and the other of evil.
B -   You yourself will acquit me of this charge of Manicheanism when I name this other principle.
A -   Then please name it now, sir.
B -   It is nothingness
A -   Nothingness? But is nothingness infinite?
B -   No doubt it is; it is infinite, it is eternal, and it has many attributes in common with God...The Platonists and Saint Augustine himself have already shown us that the cause of good is positive, but that evil is a defect, that is, a privation or negation, and consequently, it arises from nothingness or non-being.
A -   I do not see how nothingness, which is nothing, can enter into the composition of things.
B -   Yet you know that, in arithmetic, **zero** joined to **ones** make up different numbers, such as **10, 100, 1 000**; a witty fellow, having written several **zeros** in a row, wrote above them: on the other hand, a **'one'** is needed too. But, without going so far, you would admit that all created things are limited, and that their limits, or their *non plus ultra* if you wish, constitute something negative. For example, a circle is limited on account of the fact that the separation of the compass used to inscribe that circle was not larger. Thus the boundaries or the *non plus ultra* of this separation determine the circle. It is the same for all other things, for they are bounded or imperfect by virtue of the lack of an infinity of perfections in them, and which are only a nothingness with respect to them.

Leibniz, 1695
[43] p. 113–4

Chapter 14: The Dyadics of Leibniz

For Leibniz, limitedness is the very determination and condition of things. The sum of all the lacks of the infinite perfections of the Creator determines the creature, and this is but a nothingness relative to it, and, paradoxically, *contained within* it.

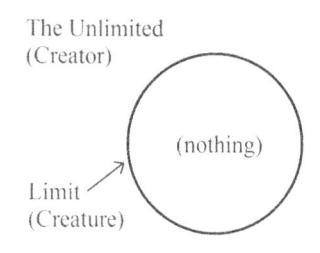

The Unlimited (Creator)

(nothing)

Limit (Creature)

The containment of nothingness in all definite things is an elementary affirmation of the contradiction of the *other-in-the-same* in an apparent defiance of the law of contradiction, which, we should point out, Leibniz never rejects. On the contrary: The great foundation of mathematics, he wrote in 1715,...

> ...is the principle of contradiction or identity, that is, that a proposition cannot be true and false at the same time, and that therefore **A** is **A** and cannot be **not-A**. This second part is sufficient to demonstrate every part of arithmetic and geometry, that is, the principles of mathematics.
> [58, p. 15]

What it is important for us to recognise here is that the *not-cum-nothing* was a breakthrough in Leibniz's thinking at a very elementary level. As he so candidly celebrates in the dialogue extract on the opposite page, this *nothingness* is an *other* that may be generative of difference and yet non-contradictory. Nothing *is other to* something, as 0 *is to* 1. But in its opposition there is no (positive) contradiction. With it he can still allow that **A is A and not not-A**, but yet if **not-A** is nothing to **A** then it can be contained within the identity **A** as its limit—in fact it is its *de-finit*-ion, its very *de-limit*-ing. This is only true of the **one**-*and-its-other* when the *other* is this *not-cum-nothing*, and so the binary is a unity and montheism is saved.

Leibniz's excitement at his discovery of the true power of *nothing* is palpable in this 1695 dialogue and it persisted. He would go on to use its specific limit-circle analogy, and more generally the notion of limitation, when describe the products of Dyadic generation. The Dyadic calculus is, he says,...

> ...an admirable symbol of creation, which is to say of the origin of all things from God alone, and from nothing without any pre-existing matter; and that the nothing is not absolute, but relative, which is to say the limitation which essentially finds itself in creatures, a measure of their imperfection, this limitation being none other than a negation of the further progress of pure

reality, or of the pure act, like when a circle is marked out by its circumference which sets its *non-plus-ultra*.*

The other side to this limit-circle of Creation is the *unlimited* circle of the absolute (i.e., *lack-less*) Creator, and although it is not mentioned in the accounts of the Dyadic Creation, this can only be the great Hermetic paradoxical sources; that is, the pseudo-Egyptian Hellenistic image of God revived in the Renaissance and invoked by Leibniz elsewhere: *a circle whose centre is everywhere and whose circumference is nowhere*. The Creator that has no limit is absolute *being*, while the limits of the creatures defines their *being/non-being* as they are, and as they are all distinguished from God. In the dialogue again: In the same way that an infinite circle is impossible, since any circle is bounded by its circumference, an absolutely perfect created thing is also impossible. And in an essay 'On the True Mystical Theology': No creature can be without non-being; otherwise it would be God.# In the controversy over the status of the infinitesimals in the calculus, Leibniz says that, while mathematics expresses potential infinities in infinite series, and the infinitesimal calculus expresses imaginary infinities fit for determining real finite values, the only real infinity is perhaps the absolute as an attribute of God, the origin and Creator who is anterior to all composition (i.e., it does not have parts) and yet contains all finitude as an active power having parts eminently.+

Defining *creature* by the double negation of limitedness—as a lack of the unlimitedness of the original *being*—gives an elegant *via negativa:* just as finite creatures can be defined negatively in terms of the infinite source, so too in reverse, this real infinity can be defined as *not* a definite or definable thing.

It is when this lack of an infinity of perfections in all things, their relative nothingness, is mistaken for a positive nature that we find the error of primary matter, and also the error of 'evil'. The origin of evil was a perennial problem for Leibniz, as for the entire Christian tradition, but as the 1695 dialogue explains, it is only to follow the Platonists and Augustine to recognise evil as a defect, a privation or negation, and this can now be understood as arising from the nothingness contained in all things and original with the *non-being* of God.++

---
* Translation of the French original in Zacher [40], p. 279–80. Also in Widmaier [45] p. 183.
\# Leibniz says: All creatures derive from God and from nothingness. Their self-being from God, their non-being is of nothing. (Numbers too show this in a wonderful way, and the essence of things are like the essence of numbers.) No creature can be without non-being otherwise it would be God...Sin is not from God but original sin has arisen in some creatures from their non-being and hence out of nothingness. [42, p. 368]
\+ Paraphrased from a 1698 letter to Joh. Bernoulli in [18] Vol III, p. 499–500. See also Ch 17 of Leibniz's 'New Essay on Human Understanding', quoted in [20] p. 423.
++ For the doctrine of limits supplanting a doctrine of evil, see in his pre-Dyadic writings, in 1686, the

When in the following years the Dyadic generation is aligned with the Creation, it is this notion of *generation-as-limitation* that would explain not only how God made everything from nothing, but that everything that He made was Good. That which is not-Good is a limitation, or lack. Thus, by way of this language of limits, the Dyadics is able to expose the error of a positive primary evil, and so affirm the Platonic (Augustinian) position on a third mystery of Christian monotheism, usually described as a problem, 'the problem of evil'. The solution can be given by our typographical convention: It's all Good(not not-Good). Leibniz explained this in his proposed design of the celebratory medallion depicting the creation describe in *Genesis* where the binary table in the centre to show how this orderly creation by the one God is all God/Good.*

When using this language of limitation, Leibniz presents us with one unlimited, original power that generates limited creatures through a process of limitation effected by self-negation. And it should not be forgotten that he saw the living nature of this *power-to-limit* as perpetually active in our created world. When discussing another contemporary theory of limitation with Joh Christian Schulenburg in 1698, Leibniz begins by agreeing that truly, boundaries or limits are of the essence of creatures, they are indeed something private to them and consist in the negation of further advance. But the creature is not a passive recipient of limitation in this sense; rather, it obtains a power from God that is positive and beyond its boundaries, a power that remains a living force in all Creation.# That is, *created life has an autonomous power of self-limitation*. In his Dyadic Creation analogy, which he then proceeds to invoke, this is the power of God within things, as a power to exceed their limitation and so generate further limitation from their negation. There is no end to this process of continuous Creation and so it is always incomplete and indeterminate: incomplete in that the limitation does not stop at some terminus (e.g., a bounded universe, a

---

'Discourse on Metaphysics': ...there was an original limitation or imperfection connatural to all creatures....And to this I believe the opinion of St Augustine and other authors should be reduced who hold that the root of evil lies in nothingness, that is in the privation or limitation of creatures.... [42, p. 322] The dialogue quoted above on page 284 goes on to explain that there was no positive evil in created things at the beginning, but they always lacked many perfections. [43, p. 114] Later, when introducing his Dyadics, he says that imperfections of things only consist in negations; from this comes what St Augustine has said very well, that the bad comes from nothing. [40, p. 243]

* See translation of Leibniz's letter to Rudolph in Glaser [59] p. 31. In Western Christian theology this doctrine, often called *summum bonum*, has its origins in Christian Platonism. The Platonic sources include the discussion of the education of the philosopher-rulers in *Republic*, see especially p. 509e and 517b. In Plato, the doctrine is associated with mathematics and the One as the origin of arithmetic emanation, including in accounts of his notorious lecture on 'The Good'. According to Aristotle (via Aristoxenus), this was not as expected a lecture on ethics but on mathematical demonstrations that finished on the declaration that good is one. See Aristoxenus, *Elementa harmonica* II, p. 30-31.

[18, Vol VII, p. 239] For a discussion of Leibniz's references to this Hermetic notion of the infinite mystical source, see Rosemont and Cook [44], p. 82n.

physical atom, an infinitesimal value); indeterminate in that it does not itself ever constitute a containment beyond which it cannot be more. This is what Leibniz meant by his famous and seemingly contradictory claim that Nature knows no limits.*

The account of Creation in the language of limitation was useful for Leibniz to bring the Platonic solution to the problem of evil into alignment with the Dyadics, but also, implicitly, it brings the early Pythagorean doctrine of limitation (see above on page 174-5) into harmony with the innovation to their doctrine that Aristotle famously attributes to Plato. That is, if in the Creation analogy Leibniz is offering an interpretation of the Platonic Monad and indeterminate Dyad, then in presenting this Creation *as limitation*, he could also be giving us his interpretation of the first lines of the first Pythagorean *Peri Physios*, where the whole world and everything in it is said to be connected from the unlimited and limiting. And this language of limitation has a further advantage for us in that it helps to find the alignment of the identity in Leibniz's image of arithmetic creation with the 'limit' identity in *Laws of Form*—that is, an alignment of Leibniz's *necessary-and-sufficient*-One with Spencer Brown's 'Distinction'. However, here we arrive at a confusion perpetuated, so it seems, by Leibniz's notation.

Where Spencer Brown's genius is in reducing the notation to one mark, Leibniz's Dyadics has two, '1' and '0', which yet defy his vision of the sufficiency of the One. In that the 0 marks *none*, it tends to suggest that this negativity is, itself, a positive identity distinct from one. This suggestion is reinforced when Leibniz aligns the 1 and 0 with God and nothing as the two primary principles, and then with various pairs of binary opposites:

> And this is the origin of things from God and nothing, positivo and privativo, perfection and imperfection, power and limitedness, active and passive...

His list of the binary attributes of Creation sometimes include 'form and matter', but only to meet the prevailing Aristotelian dogma, and to reduce their matter to a formless stuff inactive through itself, except that it opposes. [18, Vol VII, p. 239] Against doctrines of an original matter, or an origin of evil, Leibniz will insist that everything comes from the One, and that the *nothing* of everything is only relative to it. As we saw above, the *nothing-of-things* is

---

* [42, p. 512] This is according to the principle of continuity much referred to by Leibniz. See [42] p. 30–1. Lovejoy traces the history of the use of this principle/law in his famous lectures on the *Great Chain of Being* [60]. Leibniz rejects atoms of matter as contrary to reason. [43, p. 142].

no more than the limitation essential to their being, their *non plus ultra*: they are bounded or imperfect by virtue of the principle of negation or of the nothingness they contain. In principle, in things, the **one** contains its *not*. Yet sometimes when giving the notation of this arithmetic of Creation, there is still a sense that the original *nothing* is something separate from the original **One**, and this likewise, for the relative naughts of the created **units**. The problem seems to be that Leibniz's *binary* notation does not support his *unary* vision of arithmetic generation. He announces that only one is necessary, that the *other* is only its self-contained negation, but then in marking this *nothing* he indicates it as *something else*. Notwithstanding this confusion, it is when Leibniz uses the language of limitation that the affinity of his vision with the vision of *Laws of Form* is most evident, and in finding this affinity he provides us with a bridge from the most ancient Pythagoreans to the present.

Commensurating the Incommensurables

Long before the Creation analogy, Leibniz already announced that in the Dyadics he had uncovered the elementary arithmetic. That was in the year of 1679, and it should not go without mention that this was a remarkable year for his investigations into the foundations of the formal sciences. For it was in this same year that he planted the seeds for the revival of what he saw as a pure geometry—an analysis of figure prior to mensuration—by sending an outline of his '*analysis situs*' to Hugyens for safe keeping, for posterity. For us. [42, p. 250] Although he doubted that his contemporaries would be able to recognise their significance, by 1679 he believed that he now had in hand an elementary geometry (i.e., a topology) and an elementary arithmetic. These did not come out of the blue, and nor did he claim them entirely novel. Rather, they emerged out of the context of his re-examination of Euclid's *Elements*, where the 2000 year old stone-set dogma of its definition melted before his eyes, and where he began to see all sorts of alternatives, including the new definition of the straight line mentioned earlier: a curve each part of which is similar to the whole. Not surprisingly these breakthroughs instilled great confidence, and in this year he also re-invented his youthful vision of an *Ars combinatoria* as his project for a universal characteristics. This would be a calculus of universal applicability; well that at least is the way he put it in an enthusiastic introduction of his projected 'universal encyclopaedia', revived in 1679 under the new title, '*Plus Ultra*'. (See the extract at the head of this chapter.)

Leibniz's initial pragmatic aim in finding the foundations of arithmetic was to investigate a problem in the relationship between number and figure that emerged long before Euclid, and that had never since been entirely resolved. This is the problem of the incommensurable ratios of geometric analysis. Remember that these *asymmetricals* were permissible only after Eudoxus was able to realign the analysis of figures away from *arithmos* and towards the neutral ground of Logos. (See above, page 224.) Yet, the need to commensurate the various sets of incommensurable ratios remained. And the more advanced and complex the geometry (and algebra) became, the more the imperfections of irrational arithmetic expressions tended to become enfolded within it. He needed to find the true relationship of the various types of incommensurable magnitudes with the underlying ratio (the Logos) from which they were geometrically derived.* Success here would reveal the true and natural alignment of arithmetic with shape. In this Leibniz had already made some progress before he applied the Dyadics progression to the problem in 1679.

During his youthful mathematical indulgence in Paris, Leibniz had discovered an expression for π that is an alternate adding and subtracting of the inverse odd series. In this expression, the area of the circle drawn within a unit square is given as:

$$1/1 - 1/3 + 1/5 - 1/7 + 1/9 - 1/11 + \ldots$$

As the series progresses it osculates closer and close to the true but inexpressible value for the area (i.e., $\pi/4$) in a similar way that the ratio's in Theon's series osculate closer and closer to $\sqrt{2}$, and likewise with that other ratio that later came to be known also by the Greek letter 'Φ'.# Leibniz saw his infinite series for π as giving rational expression to the true value, and so it contains at once all the approximations to it. In the recognition of this discovery Leibniz believed that the useless effort to find the true ratio in a single (rational) number would cease. [42, p. 274] He formed the general view that while the incommensurables are indeterminate as a single ratio, their true expression can be found as *infinite* rational series.+

---

* Leibniz used the Latinised 'incommensurable'.
\# On these two usages of 'phi', see the note above on page 273.
+ Long after he came to this view, he would recount it (in a 1705 letter to Cesar Caze) when introducing the principle use of his Dyadics to be to perfect geometry in relation to the determined expression of infinite series (*l'expression des series infinies determinées*). Starting with infinite expressions in decimal numeration, where rational fractions like 1/7 have recurring patterns, he says that, for irrationals, the law of progression to infinity is always determined, although often difficult to know. See Zacher [40] p. 349.

Chapter 14: The Dyadics of Leibniz

In is important to pause here and consider how Leibniz's view of his infinite expression for π agreed with Kepler on his infinite arithmetic expression of Φ but differed from Leibniz's view of the infinite series in the infinitesimal calculus. The infinitesimal calculus is a technique only—a means to an ends. The infinitesimals of the calculus are not real, but they are fit for determining real values, just as the 'imaginary roots' have been found fit for solving algebraic equations of higher degrees.* In explaining this role of the calculus, Leibniz would often start with the familiar progression by ratio, the geometric progression. Such a progression can be used in infinite equations like the successive division expressed in Zeno's paradoxes (see above on page 238), or in a variation often used by Leibniz, which is:

$$1/_1 + 1/_2 + 1/_4 + 1/_8 + 1/_{16} \ldots = 2.\ ^\#$$

This series is an 'image', or an arithmetic representation, of the equivalent finite value, but it is not, itself, that value. Nor does it have an actual smallest term, an infinitesimal. The infinitesimal is just an idea that delivers the calculation to exactly the place were we want it to take us.

Leibniz's account of the infinitesimals withstands surprisingly well the attacks on their status in the ensuring controversy of the early 18th century; in fact in him we find agreement without contradiction with much of what Berkeley later had to say against computing with these ghosts of departed quantities.[+] And much of the ensuing scepticism about the calculus would touch lightly upon Leibniz's account of it—and lightly upon his account of infinity generally. What is important for us to understand here is that while the equations of the infinitesimal calculus are not real identities, the expression of *asymmetrical* ratios as infinite rational series are their *true rational expression*. It is in the very indeterminacy of these expressions that they can be regarded as numerical expressions of the original ratio.[++] In this understanding of *asymmetrical* ratios Leibniz is

---

* [18, Vol III, p.499–500] Leibniz often discussed the imaginary root √-2. Square roots of negative numbers first appeared in Gerolamo Cardano's *Ars Magna* (1545), where they were revealed necessary to the solutions of algebraic equations of the 4th degree. Leibniz wished to determine their true status in arithmetic. It should be noted here that George Spencer Brown presents an analogy between √-1 and the re-entering Form in his preface to the first American Edition [61, p. xv] to show how our arithmetic of geometry already involves contradiction. Kauffman explore this analogy further. [36]

\# [18, Vol IV, p. 92–3] translated by Loemker [42] p. 543. Leibniz frequently outlined his view of the different types of infinities, see for example, in a letter to Joh. Bernoulli in [18], Vol III, p. 499–500.

\+ Following the widespread use of the infinitesimal calculus, there was much consternation over the mathematical status of the infinitesimals. The most systematic critiques of the calculus behind Newton's mechanics of 'fluxion' came when Bishop Berkeley published *The Analyst* in 1734, which was long after both inventors of the calculus were dead.

\++ Compare this idea of an irrational number to the conventional notion that it is a point on a continuum called the 'real number line'. This unattainable point is real while the process used to approximate it is only a representation. The similarity of this representation of the real number to the representation in representationalist epistemology is not coincidental. See the box on p. 292.

ENTHUSIASTIC MATHEMATICS

advancing in accord with the Pythagorean tradition: his understanding of his rational expression for π is similar to Kepler's understanding of his expression for the Golden Ratio, and with Theon's understanding of the ancient √2 series. Indeed, Leibniz's view is entirely in accord with what we propose to have been the solution to the crisis of the *logos a-logos* taken up by Plato and Eudoxus all those centuries ago.

We now have an important context for Leibniz's discovery in 1679 of the Dyadic progression as the elementary arithmetic. In this notation of arithmetic removed of all arbitrary contrivance, he hoped to find the infinite series expressing all variety of incommensurables, and including transcendental and imaginary numbers. In this way he could commensurate the incommensurables and thereby bring geometry into a new alignment with arithmetic. This is what he meant when he later explained that the principle usage of the Binary Arithmetic would be to perfect Geometry.

Graphic Expression for Leibniz's Exemplar Infinite Equation

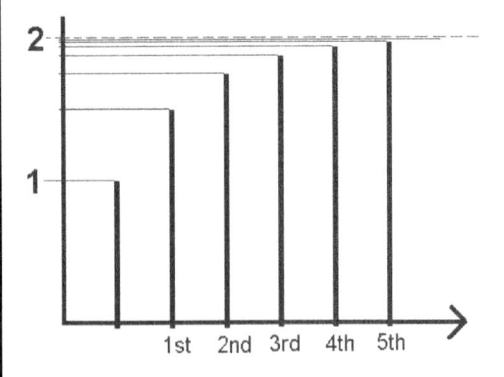

$$2 = 1 + \frac{1}{2} + \frac{1}{4} + \frac{1}{8} + \frac{1}{16} + \frac{1}{32} \ldots$$

It may be helpful to compare the work of the infinitesimal calculus to photographs of a painting using successively decreasing pixel sizes. As the pixels get smaller the image of the painting gets finer and so 'truer' to it. However, the pixels never reach **zero** size and never become continuous with each other. They never become the painting itself but always constitute a representation. This is one way to imagine the essence of the problem of representing real systems in discrete mathematical models called the 'Butterfly Effect'. Similarly, the nature number 2 is *not* equal to Leibniz's infinite series, and nor is 2 a place on the 'Real Number Line'. The equating of this line with a real spatial continuum is like Leibniz's equation above and like a photo with pixel size smaller than perceptible—they are useful illusions. The analogy in elementary Brownian terms is to equating the Distinction with the result of its Re-entry. This is not a real equation, as the latter is a derivation of the former. The real and indistinct is not found at the end of distinguishing, but prior to it—which returns us again to the elementary error endemic in modern epistemology and to the epitome of its condition:

292

One approach was to find the laws of the infinite arithmetic expression for each irrational. He was hoping that, just as $^1/_3$ has a regular decimal expression as 0.33333..., and $^1/_7$ as 0.142857 (where the six digits repeat), incommensurable values displaying no order in their infinite *decimal* expression might display their true symmetry when expressed in the elementary Dyadics. [40, p. 349] It did not take long to find the binary periodicity of some unit fractions, and also a general rule for the length of their period. [59, p. 48] But these investigations never advanced beyond the trivial. Jacques Bernoulli offered Leibniz a binary expression of π to 118 places, but alas, no period for this (or any other) irrational was ever found in the strings of 1s and 0s. [18, Vol III, p. 97]

Another approach to this investigation of Dyadic infinities was to begin by writing out various infinite series, and then examining the periods found in each place-value column. The thinking was as follows. Conventional denary place-value counting moves through nine values in each place before recording this cycle in a higher place and returning to a mark of absences (the '0'), whereas in the Dyadic there is only one value alternating with its absence. In Dyadic counting the first and elementary progression, the arithmetic series, proceeds to generate all numbers by a simple rule. This is the rule of alternation: the rule of alteration provides for continuation. [59, p. 31] This rule applies up the order of place by progression of the geometric double. Thus, the period in the 1st column is 01, then in the 2nd it has doubled to 0011, then doubled again to 00001111, and so forth (see the table on page 272). Thus so, the arithmetic progression can be generated merely *by the law of periodicity* in the columns of powers, that is, *without any calculation*. For Leibniz, it was easy to show how various arithmetic series—e.g., counting by 2s or by 3s—also have their own law of periods in these columns, but what of other progressions? Could this elementary calculus reveal their own true law of alternation?

With this hypothesis, Leibniz proceeded to examine the columnar periods in other number series so that he might find the law of their periodicity. The first he tried in 1679 was the odd series because it was the arithmetic series involved in his expression for π. Later, (in his début paper at the French academy—more about that below) he gives tables demonstrating the columnar periods for the progression by threes, fives and sevens, the series of square numbers and the series of cubic numbers. But these were only the beginning: in his notes and letters he shows how the triangular numbers, pyramid numbers, other figured numbers and several geometric series are found to follow this law of periods so that their progression can be determined without calculation.*

Leibniz envisaged that once he found the law of periods in the binary place-value columns for geometric series, for figured numbers, and even for the series of primes, then these could be progressed indefinitely, not through calculation, but by the law of their columnar periodicity. And all these laws of progression could be shown as derivative of, and reducible to, the law of the Dyadic progression, which in an elementary way contains them all. This would give a general law of arithmetic generation that could then progress forward towards an involvement of the infinite *rational* series that express the incommensurable ratios of geometry.

That was the vision. Yet, despite his initial and continuing enthusiasm, the investigation of columnar periods did not progress beyond the first stage. And, in contrast to his infinitesimal calculus, that was eventually picked up, applied and extended by some of the greatest mathematicians of his day, these same men were unable to help him progress the new arithmetic toward a unified theory of number. All too conscious of his lack of progress, still he never lost faith, and he continued unashamed, promoting his arithmetic to philosophers and mathematicians, to princes and princesses, to electors and kings, until the very end of his life.#

In hindsight we might say that Leibniz's vision of reducing all mathematics and geometry to the form of *one-and-nothing* was bound never to be realised because of an insufficiency deeply embedded in the Logos-emanation tradition. In this tradition, if degrees of the Dyad were given then they were given as the powers of the 'geometric double'. After reducing place-value counting to its extreme, Leibniz failed to recognise that he still remained stuck in an order of degrees that does not arise autonomously out of the original **One**. He did not realise that instead of trying to make the figured number series fit his place-value binaries, he would have been better to start with the arithmetic that they so naturally express. In fact, if we take up his project using instead our Brownian hierarchy of arithmetic (see above page 204-5), then some progress can be

---

* These results found in Leibniz's notes were reported in his published *Explication*: It happens again that square numbers, cubes, and other powers, also triangular numbers, pyramid, and other figure numbers, have similar periods, of a sort that one can write the table without calculation. Translated by Glaser [59], p. 41.

For example, Leibniz promoted his new arithmetic though his friend Sophie Electrice of Hanover (in line to the British Crown when she died in 1714) and in a letter to the Russian Czar, Peter the Great. Accounts of Leibniz's arithmetic of creation did get published again, by Wideburg in 1718 and by Nolte in 1734. Both included illumination of the image of creation, while Nolte included the Letter to Rudolf and *Explication*. See Zacher [40] and Glaser [59] p. 32–35. However, Dyadics was never progressed as a science.

Chapter 14: The Dyadics of Leibniz

made in the expression of key irrationals by his law of alternation. Before ending this chapter let me briefly show how.

Mensuration

So far in our notation we have used the geometric space of the page to express time. With the procession of dots across and down the page, and with the marks within marks, the 'arrow of time' in the emanation proceeds through the space of the page. This is comfortable for us as it conforms to conventions deeply embedded in our tradition, if only in the conventional graphic use of Cartesian space, where the x-axis often expresses time's arrow from left to right. But now consider what happens when we first apply our pure Formal arithmetic to measure geometric space. This time it is the other way around. Space is expressed by time.

To see what I mean, first consider the application of the arithmetic to *logistical* counting. When counting cattle, pure *ordinal* counting is used to mark each cow as a separate Distinction at the same 'depth'. *Logistical* counting is the translation of Brownian order into Brownian number. It is to 'call' each 'cross'. And we make such a translation even when we undertake our *analysis* of the expansion of Formal expressions in the arithmetic. For example, when we count all the marks in the *Tetraktys*, we count them in timely order, from 1 to 10.

Counting Number by Order
One way to imagine the application of arithmetic to *logistical* counting is with the expansion of this expression:

By generating a single mark at each successive depth, it calls by order, as if to say '...and 1':

Now consider metering linear space in the same way. The lengths are measured logistically in Brownian number:

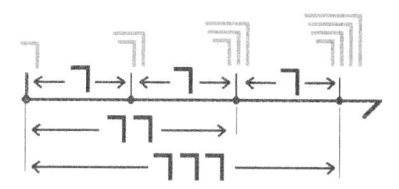

Let's take this as the way to apply Brownian arithmetic to linear geometry for the treatment of its ratios.

295

ENTHUSIASTIC MATHEMATICS

Now, in two dimensional space, consider 2^{D-2}, the square number series.

If, as with the linear series, distance is metered precisely by time then the emanation would not expand in squares but radiate outwards on the arch of a circle. Consider the difference between the distance along the diagonal to this arch and then out to the corner of the square. This difference is the length indicated by '?'. It is the side-to-diagonal difference of the unit square, which is $\sqrt{2} - 1$. This 'fractional component' of $\sqrt{2}$ is its irrational component. This can be found by an interpretation of 2^{D-2} that we will call 'fractional analysis'.

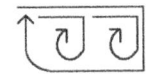

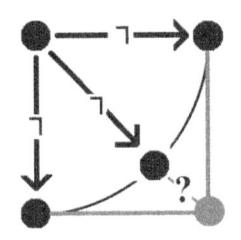

Fractional Analysis

In Pythagorean dot notation it is easy to see how 2^{D-2} expresses the square number series with it first generation from 1 to 3. Previously, we interpreted this as unity generating three offspring, or a branching by trifurcation. However, we could also interpret it as division by 3 where the ratio 1:3 is interpreted as the fraction ⅓. Now, if we continued with this fractional analysis, then we can interpret this infinite number as an infinitely continued fraction.

In doing so, notice the denominator is made up of three branches, two of which continue in the ratio of 1:1. These side branches can both be interpreted as the continued fraction 1/1/1/..., an infinite expression equivalent to 1. The other branch along the diagonal is like a stem repeating this division into two of these unit branch and one continuing the stem. The stem divides again into 1 + 1 = 2 branches and 1 stem, then again 2 branches plus 1 stem, and so on.

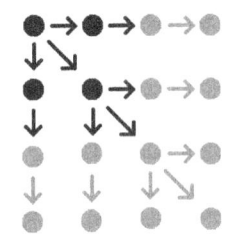

Chapter 14: The Dyadics of Leibniz

This recursive division can be represented as the infinite continued fraction that is recognisable as the fractional component of the infinite continued fraction that has long been used to give the value for the diagonal of the unit square. Thus, with this 'fractional analysis', we can see that the Brownian number 2^{D-2} has inherent in it not only all square numbers, but also the infinite ratio by which the diagonal of any square exceeds the length of its sides. And this series closely related to the geometric expansion given by Theon to express the same infinite value.

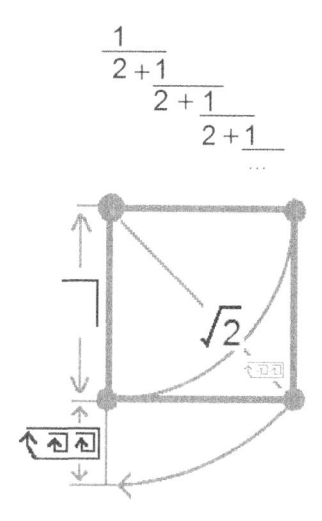

$$\cfrac{1}{2+\cfrac{1}{2+\cfrac{1}{2+\cfrac{1}{\ldots}}}}$$

Infinite continued fractions have been found to express many geometric ratios, including all the diagonals of rectangles with sides in whole number ratio. These 'square roots' are all constructed of unit fractions only with differing denominators. Consider as another example, the ratio for the diagonal of the 1:2 rectangle, or $\sqrt{5}$. Here is the continued fraction:

$$2 + \cfrac{1}{4 + \cfrac{1}{4 + \cfrac{1}{4 + \cfrac{1}{\ldots}}}}$$

This can be expressed by a Brownian expression interpreted as a fraction:

Here the two components of the number are easily identified. The initial two marks express the linear measurement in the 1st degree. This 2 is the finite component of the ratio equivalent to the length of the long side. The second component is infinite. It is a 2nd degree expression that we saw earlier generating the plane 'hexagonal' numbers (see in Table 10.2, page 198). However, by fractional analysis it can also be used in the 1:2 rectangle to mediate between its sides and the plane across which the diagonal traverses.

ENTHUSIASTIC MATHEMATICS

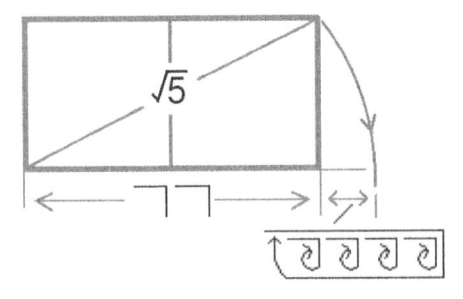

Such compound Brownian numbers can also mediate between the linear and higher dimensions. Consider for example a simple medium between the 1st and the 3rd dimension, which is the diagonal of the cube, √3. This time two unit fractions alternating down the continuing division:

$$1 + \cfrac{1}{1 + \cfrac{1}{2 + \cfrac{1}{1 + \cfrac{1}{2 + \cfrac{1}{\cdots}}}}}$$

This 1↔2 alternation of the denominator is expressed in Brownian notation by punctuating the divisions with an inserted mark. This introduces a repeating two step process:

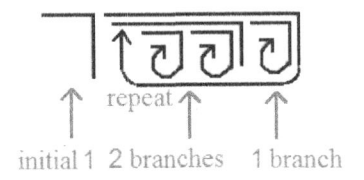

↑ initial 1   ↑ repeat ↑ 2 branches   ↑ 1 branch

In this interpretation, the elementary Re-Entry has the same value as the elementary mark, and so, for example, √3 can also be obtained from a compound Brownian number where the second term is a 1st degree number:

Chapter 14: The Dyadics of Leibniz

Other diagonals have more complicated periods requiring multiple punctuations. For example, √7 has 1,1,1 and then 4 branches before repeating. This can be found by fractional analysis in this expression:

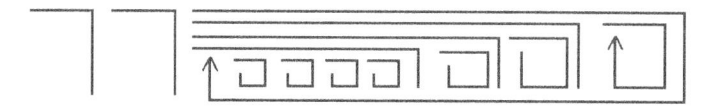

The multiple punctuations in this number provides a window into more complex expressions where a program of repeating procedures can be sequentially staged thus:

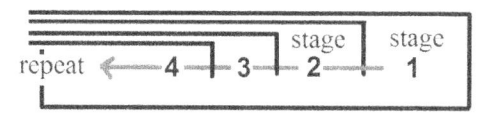

If we return to the analysis of diagonals in the plane, we note that the even Brownian numbers in the 2nd degree have a special relationship with the diagonals in rectangles with length-to-width ratios of 1:1, 1:2, 1:3, 1:4, 1:5, and so forth. This relationship is shown in Table 14.1. At the head of this table are the 2nd degree **zero** and **one**. This **one** is of special note. We will recall that it generates the triangular numbers, the first three iterations of which generates the *Tetraktys* sacred to the Pythagoreans. In fractional analysis it also delivers the Golden Ratio, Φ.

All those years ago Plato had set the mission of finding the generative nature of the symmetrical and the asymmetrical in relation to one another. Late in the Platonic revival, Leibniz took up the challenge of finding the formal ratio of common measure, the ratio of *one-becoming-two*. To this purpose, he reduced arithmetic to the Dyadic form. But he failed to proceed much further with Plato's mission. And now we know why.

    Leibniz failed not, as so many others had before, by failing to understand the generative role of the *nothing-qua-negation*. Rather, he failed because he was unable to maintain the passive hiddenness of this **not-one** in his binary notation. Our success in progressing investigations into the Dyadic emanation is due to the Brownian unary notation. Its elementary versatility we have demonstrated through several powerful interpretations of the Dyadic form. Firstly we interpreted it for logic, giving analogues for Boolean operations. Next we interpreted it for ordinal counting, with

ENTHUSIASTIC MATHEMATICS

Table 14.1: 2nd degree numbers and diagonal values related through 'fractional analysis'

2-D Numerical Value	Brownian Notation	Figured N° Name	Fractional Analysis giving the infinite rational value	Geometric Analogue
0		Linear 1 stem 0 branches	$\dfrac{1}{\tfrac{1}{1}} = 1$	
1		Triangular 1 stem 1 branch	$1 + \cfrac{1}{1 + \cfrac{1}{1 + \cfrac{1}{1 + \cfrac{1}{1+1}}}} = \Phi$ An alternative expression for Φ is as $1 + 1/\Phi = \Phi$	
2		Square 1 stem 2 branches	$1 + \cfrac{1}{2 + \cfrac{1}{2 + \cfrac{1}{2+1}}} = \sqrt{2}$	$\sqrt{2}$
4		Hexagonal 1 stem 4 branches	$= \sqrt{5}$	$\sqrt{5}$
6		Octagonal 1 stem 6 branches	$= \sqrt{10}$	$\sqrt{10}$
8		Decagonal 1 stem 8 branches	$= \sqrt{17}$	$\sqrt{17}$
10		Dodecagonal 1 stem 10 branches	$-10- = \sqrt{26}$	$\sqrt{26}$

higher degree infinite numbers developing in accord with the Pythagorean hierarchy of plane and solid figured numbers. Lastly, just now we have shown how this way of developing the higher degrees of arithmetic presents another way of aligning arithmetic with geometry so that the asymmetrical ratios of plane geometry are found to be symmetries within the arithmetic itself.

With these brief elaborations, the hope is that others will take up where Leibniz left off and other symmetries will be brought into alignment with this *ratio-of-the-one-to-its-other*. Those interested in this project

Chapter 14: The Dyadics of Leibniz

should not confine their investigations to the interpretations already offered here and elsewhere, for there is no limit to the ways of interpreting this dynamics of Form.

For example, instead of counting every iteration in an expansion, count only the odd iterations (or the even ones). This would be as though counting waves arriving at a pier, where iterations in the **unmarked** state are troughs between **marked** peaks. Consider also that odd iterations could be counted as positive numbers while even iterations are counted as negative numbers. If we do this, and then invert the values, there is an interesting result in the case of the square numbers.

For this interpretation of $2^{2\text{-D}}$, first count the odd *gnomons* as positive and the even *gnomons* as negative to gives the series: [1], -3, +5, -7 +9, -11 +.... Then interpret this sequence in ratio with the original **one** to give the sum:

1/1 - 1/3 + 1/5 - 1/7 + 1/9 - 1/11 +...

This adding and subtracting of the smaller and smaller inverted ratios of the square *gnomons* delivers Leibniz's infinite expression for the area of the circle inside the unit square (i.e., $\pi/4$, see above, page 290). This diagram shows how it can be related to $2^{2\text{-D}}$ interpreted as an emanating arch of square numbers.

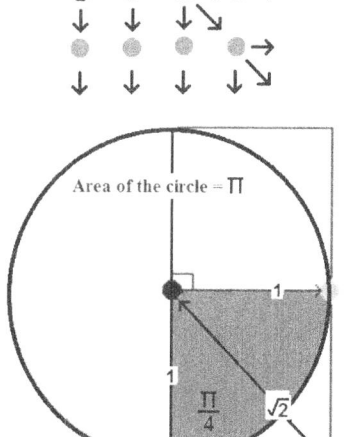

In hindsight we can see that Leibniz's vision for a new unified geometric arithmetic might be achievable, but only after abandoning his binary notation for a unitary notation that more properly express the Dyadic emanation. In hindsight we can also see just how suited Leibniz's calculus would be to notate processes in electronic computing, where the binary **zero** is at base merely an absence (of current). But there was no sign of this utility in Leibniz's life time. In fact, with the failure of his attempts to commensurate the incommensurables, he struggled to find any application at all. Nonetheless his persistent promotion was rewarded in a most surprising way.

When Leibniz was elected to the French Royal Academy he was invited by its secretary Bernard le Bovier de Fontenelle (1657-1757) to submit a paper for its new annual journal. Leibniz saw this as an opportunity to promote his Dyadics and duly wrote an essay. Leaving aside his analogy of Creation, it is in this essay that he pushes most strongly the columnar analysis of periods in the hope that members would assist with these investigations, but he asked Fontenelle to hold off publication in the hope of further progress. The essay was read to the Academy in 1701 but it solicited no interest. This was not encouraging for Fontenelle who failed to appreciate the elementary significance of the binary system. In the end they agreed that a paper would not be published in the Academy's journal unless an utilite palpable were given. Try as he may, Leibniz could not find any useful application for his Dyadics.

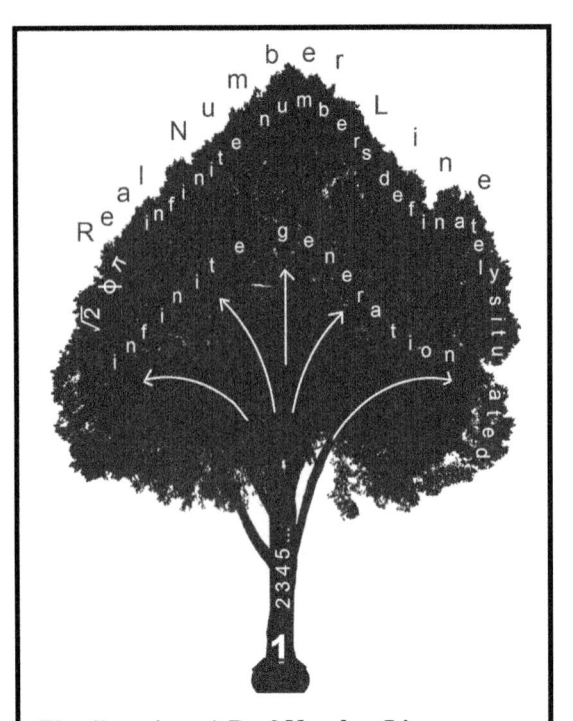

The (Imaginary) Real Number Line

Our approach to arithmetic and its application to geometry presents a non-conventional view of the hierarchy of numbers. Irrational values are seen as infinite rational emanations according to particular interpretations used for geometrical mensuration. Conventionally, the Real Number Line is a continuum of difference with places for the irrationals and rational numbers. However, in our view this line is not real but only a useful imagination for analytic geometry. The hierarchy of numbers in themselves is better understood in an analogy of a tree with branches diminishing in size until they form the limit silhouette. The silhouette boundary is where the irrationals are distributed and definitely situated. And yet, like the shoreline of the Koch Island, no place on this line can be absolutely located. Thus, while, conventionally, imaginary numbers start one step beyond real numbers (i.e., on the complex plane) what we have found is that the Real Number Line is already entirely imaginary.

Chapter 14: The Dyadics of Leibniz

But then in April 1703, when hopes for publication must have been fading, just such a utility arrived in the mail. It was contained in a letter from China sent on its long journey 17 months before. Leibniz immediately incorporated this discovery into his paper and sent it off to Fontenelle. Thus so, a short article appeared in the 1703 issue of the Academy's journal, bound, nonetheless with a scathing review by Fontenelle.*

---

* For an account of the road to publication see Zacher [40] Ch 3, or for a briefer account in English see Antognazza [47] p. 432–3. In his review, Fontenelle gave scientific priority for the discovery of binary numeration to unpublished work by Thomas De Lagny. For a discussion of Fontenelle's review, for a partial translation and a full facsimile of the original, see Glaser [59] p. 43–6 & p. 186–192. The publication of this 1703 memoire was delayed until 1705 [62, p. 251].

Chapter 15

DYADICS DISCOVERED in ANCIENT CHINA

In ancient times when the sages made the Yi [Jing],
They took the principle of flowing with the current
to nature and to heaven's mandates.
They used this to determine the Dao of Heaven
and called it Yin and Yang;
to determine the Dao of the Earth
and called it weak and hard;
to determine the Dao of men
and called it benevolence and righteousness.
They combined to 3 powers and doubled them.
Thus in the Yi, 6 lines completes a hexagram.
A division of Yin, a division of Yang,
which by turns used weak or strong.
Thus in the Yi are the 6 positions
which complete the essay.

Heaven [111] *and Earth* [000] *determine their positions.*
Mountain [001] *and lake* [110] *interchange their Qi energy.*
Thunder [100] *and wind* [011] *excite each other.*
Water [010] *and fire* [101] *do not fight each other.*
The eight trigrams grind together.
The numbering of the past is flowing with the current.
The knowledge of the future is counter-current.
This causes the Yi to count backwards.

Shuo Gua, Yi Jing

Chapter 15: Dyadics Discovered in Ancient China

When Leibniz's 'Explication de l'arithmetique binaire' appeared in the *Memoires de l'Academie Royale des Sciences*, after an outline of the method of columnar analysis, the brief essay continued:

> What is astounding in this calculus is that this arithmetic by 0 and 1 happens to contain the mystery of the lines of an ancient King and Philosopher named Fu Xi, who is believed to have lived more than 4,000 years ago and who the Chinese regard as the founder of their Empire and of their science. There are several linear figures that are attributed to him which all come back to this arithmetic. But it suffices to show here the figure of eight *gua*, as they are called, which pass as fundamental, and to join to them the explication, which can be seen [in the table below] provided that one notices firstly that a whole line ——— signifies unity, or 1, and secondly that a broken line — — signifies zero or 0.

000	001	010	011	100	101	110	111
0	1	10	11	100	101	110	111
0	1	2	3	4	5	6	7

> The Chinese have lost the significance of these *gua* or lineation of Fu Xi, perhaps more than one thousand years ago, and they made commentaries beneath them where they have gathered I know not what far removed meanings, of the sort that it is necessary that their true explication now come from Europeans. Here is how: It is hardly more than two years ago that I sent to R P Bouvet, the celebrated French Jesuit, who resides in Beijing, my method of counting by 0 and 1, and he needed no further assistance to make the observation that this is the key to the figures of Fu Xi. When thus he wrote me on November 14, 1701, he sent me this princely philosopher's grand figure which goes to 64, and leaves no room to doubt the truth of our interpretation, such that one could say that this priest has deciphered the enigma of Fu Xi, with the aid of that which I had communicated to him. Since these figures are perhaps the most ancient monument of science which exists on this Earth, this restitution of their meaning after so long an interval of time would seem all the more curious.

[18, Vol VII, p. 226–7]

The Lines of FuXi

The *Yi Jing* (I Ching) or 'Book of Change' is an extraordinary document that plays a key role throughout the entire recorded history of Chinese philosophy. Consisting of multiple layers of commentary built up over many centuries, it has always been used as a divination tool much like tarot cards. At its core is the 64 arrangements of six lines of two types, broken and unbroken. The 64 '*gua*' have been known in the West since the 17th century as 'hexagrams'. These hexagrams are themselves made up of all the combinations of the eight *gua*, or 'trigrams', and it is these components that Leibniz gives above in his 'Explication'. The basic elements of these trigrams, the broken and unbroken lines, are a notation of Yin and Yang. Yin and Yang are the elementary dynamic concept in the philosophy of '*Yi*' or 'Change', for which this collection is the canon. In fact, they are really but one concept, one dynamic binary unity, as expressed in the symbol now ubiquitous in the West. With Yin the female and receptive side and Yang male and active, they are most susceptible to an interpretation as the 0 and 1 of the Leibnizian Dyad.

The order of the 64 *gua* in the *Yi Jing* is not the order one would expect if they were conceived as a place-value binary arithmetic. However, legend has it that this order is not the original order, but rather this is a rearrangement made by King Wen, at the time of the Zhou ascendency over the Shang around 1100 BC. Legends suggest that in ancient times other *Yi* books were circulating; for example, there was a 'Change' book of the Shang people giving a different order of the 64 *gua*. And prior to arrangements of the 64 *gua* was the eight *gua*, and at the very beginning was the eight *gua* arrange in the order called *xiantian* or '*before-Heaven*'. It is the circular *before-Heaven* arrangement of the lines that has been secretly transmitted down the millennia from the founder of the first Chinese Dynasty, FuXi ['Fu Xi' or 'Fu Hsi']. Sometimes it is even said that Emperor FuXi did not himself invent this notation, but rather it was revealed to him on the back of a turtle emerging from the river. This remarkable

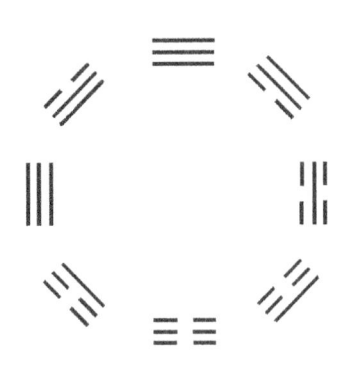

The '*before-Heaven*' arrangement of the 8 trigrams or 'change' characters (*Xiantian gua*) attributed to Fu Xi

Chapter 15: Dyadics Discovered in Ancient China

story of a most ancient, enigmatic and seminal code, revealed openly only relatively recently, attracted great interest among Western scholars in the 17th century. And it turned out that it was this pristine arrangement of the lines that is receptive to the interpretation as binary numbers.*

A foreigner in China, FuXi is credited not only with the foundation of Chinese civilisation but also with the invention of Chinese writing characters and with the foundation of the grand tradition of ancient Chinese science. FuXi's trigrams are themselves often regarded as an essential notation of an essential science: they express the principles of difference and change in the natural world, and so they give the principle of the generation and destruction of all things. It was both the high antiquity and the elementary epistemological significance attributed to FuXi's trigrams that captured the interest of the Jesuit missionary, Joachim Bouvet (1656-1730). His interest in turn caused Leibniz to consider them a candidate for his long sort universal characteristics—if Bouvet could just decipher them. But it was only after Leibniz sent Bouvet his binary numbers—as an evangelical tool to illustrate the Christian Creation doctrine—that Bouvet was able to crack the code, finding them also a binary arithmetic.

History of the Decipherment

The Jesuit mission to China began with Matteo Ricci's extraordinary feat of penetrating to the court in Beijing late in the 16th century. Ricci set the Jesuits working towards the big prize: the conversion of an Emperor with a dominion far more extensive than that of the Roman, Constantine. And they were prepared to take their time about it, as generations of missionaries followed Ricci's lead and put in the long hard work necessary to open up the channels of communication in an alien language, culture and religion. An aspect of the Jesuit missionary strategy was to teach and promote Western ('Christian') science, especially geometry and astronomy. Elevated to mandarins in the imperial court, they achieved some success in this regard, but it was exaggerated claims about the Emperor's interest in these sciences that prompted the idea of sending a mathematical mission to China. Louis XIV was persuaded to support this venture, and so six French Jesuit mathematicians were hastily assembled in Paris for departure to China in 1685.

---

* Invented by FuXi according to the 'Great Commentary' of *Yi Jing*, Sect 2, Ch 2. See [63], p. 328–9.

This mission marked a high period of cultural exchange between the European and Chinese civilisations before disputes over missionary attitudes and methodology, already fouling the air, got out of control and prompted directives from the highest Christian authorities against cultural sympathy. This window of opportunity remained more or less open for the latter half of the 17th century, during which time Chinese culture commanded heightening interest among the European *literati*. And of all the various Christian missions in China at the time, it was the Jesuits who were largely responsible for the appearance in Europe of some remarkably well-informed accounts of Chinese culture and history. Early among these is a history published by the missionary Martin Martini S J in 1658. It includes an account of the *Yi Jing* that taps into the legend of FuXi and presents for the first time in Europe his (*before-Heaven*) order of the 64 hexagrams (in a square) as synoptic of this most ancient text. This arrangement of the lines (that Bouvet would later interpret binary) Martini introduced as a mystic philosophy very similar to that of the Pythagoreans, concerning fate, judiciary astrology and certain principles of nature.*

A decade later, Athanasius Kircher's *China Illustrated* was enormously popular, and although mostly fanciful, it was significant for sparking fascination with Chinese civilisation among many European intellectuals, including Leibniz.# Meanwhile, other Jesuits were preparing a more scholarly publication to feed this new interest. It included a history of China, an analysis of the language, and a collection of translated Confucian classics.

Confucius Sinarum Philosophus, an exposition of Chinese science published in Paris in 1687, was edited by Filippe Couplet, the Belgian Jesuit who had three years earlier persuaded Louis XIV to sponsor the mathematical mission now establishing itself in Beijing. [66] His extensive preface showcases evidence of the true religion in ancient China and includes a table titled 'DUO RERUM PRINCIPIA' that illustrates the generation of the eight trigrams from 'the two principles', Yin and Yang, via the intermediate step of 'the four images', consisting of the four combinations of the two

---

* [64, pp. 1–7] Below the Fu Xi arrangement of the hexagrams Martini writes: The Chinese have a book called the *Yi Jing*, all of which is expressed in these figures; for them the book is of great value in the interpretation of arcane matters which they persuade themselves are hidden there. To me it seems to be a certain mystic philosophy and very similar to the Pythagoreans, although earlier by many centuries; in fact it had its origins in Fu Xi,... [Translation for the author by Ralph Humphries]

[65] From the height of his expertise late in life, Leibniz would come to see the loss of the original arithmetic understanding of FuXi characters and their subsequent symbolic interpretation as comparable to Kircher's fanciful symbolic misinterpretations of Egyptian Hieroglyphs of which he understands nothing. [44, p. 134] This may have been true of the famous Jesuit scholar, but Kircher's role in the revival of ancient wisdom cannot be dismissed. However dubious his speculation, Kircher's *Oedipus Aegyptiacus* of 1652 gave a great boost to Egyptology just as his book on China did for Sinology.

Chapter 15: Dyadics Discovered in Ancient China

lines. This repeats the conventional graphic interpretation of a description of their generation given in 'The Great Commentary' of the *Yi Jing*.* On the same page the eight trigrams are presented again in the *before-Heaven* circle numbered, in a figure-8, from 1 to 8. [67, p. xlii] This is also a standard interpretation (although the Chinese numerals are usually inscribed on the outside). The numbering from 0 to 7 given by Leibniz is in the opposite direction and is found nowhere in the Chinese archive.

Joachim Bouvet arrived in Beijing to work for the mathematical mission in 1688. His correspondence with Leibniz began in 1697 while Bouvet was in Europe canvassing support for the mission. On the eve of his return, Bouvet sent a note commending Leibniz on his introduction to a publication called *The Latest News from China* [*Novissima Sinica*]. Enclosed with the letter was his *Historical Portrait of the Chinese Emperor*.

Leibniz received this letter at the time when his revelation of the secret of Creation as a Dyadic emanation was still fresh, and he had already sent an account of it to the mission, as he explained in the 1697 New Years letter to Rudolf:

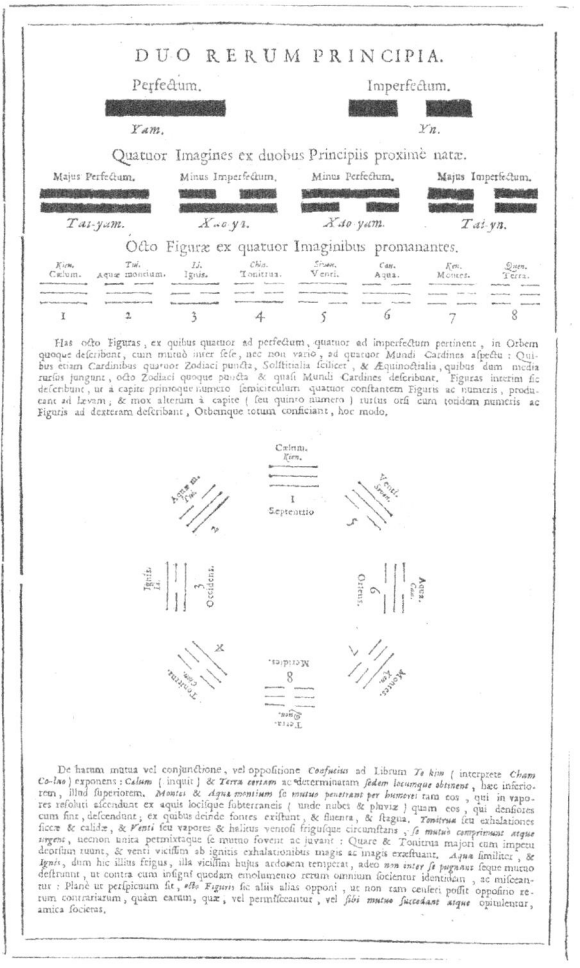

The exposition of Chinese science published by Couplet in 1687 [67] includes an explanation of the elementary principles of generation summarized in this table.

---

* *Yi Jing*, Great Commentary, Section I, Chapter 11, as quoted below, p. 322.

> I am corresponding with Jesuit Father Grimaldi, who is currently in China and also president of the Mathematical Tribunal there, with whom I became acquainted in Rome, and who wrote me during his return trip to China from Goa. I have found it appropriate to communicate to him these number representations in the hope, since he had told me himself that the monarch of this mighty empire was a lover of the art of arithmetic and that he had learned to figure the European way from Father Verbiest, Grimaldi's predecessor, that it might be this image of the secret of creation which might serve to show him more and more the excellence of the Christian faith.
> [59, p. 33]

The letter to Grimaldi to which Leibniz refers gives a two-page explanation of the Dyadic calculus and includes his Φ, his insculpi mysticum symbol of the Creation of all things from nothing by the One. [45, pp. 35–9] Leibniz's meeting with Grimaldi in Rome was back in 1689, and his correspondence from that time with him and other Jesuits expresses a vigorous appetite for Chinese religion and science. This letter also expresses his interest in the Chinese writing characters, which, as a system based around ideograms, could serve as a model for his projected universal characteristics. But there was another reason for promoting to the mission his universal characteristics, and his philosophy generally; namely, to build a fail-safe tool of conversion.

The idea of this practical application of his philosophy was not new. Back in 1679, in his draft introduction to *Plus Ultra* (see above, pages 267 and 290) this initial proposal of the universal characteristics outlines the advantages of its achievement. In the first place it would mark the end of the unrelenting quarrels over theology. In that it would reduce all knowledge to numbers, its results would be as indisputable as the relative weights of an object given by scales. This 'arithmetic' reasoning can apply not only to absolute truths but also to probabilities and so …

> …anyone who is certainly convinced of the truth of religion and its consequences, and so embraces others in love that he desires the conversion of mankind, will surely admit, if he understands these matters, that nothing will be more influential than this discovery for the propagation of the faith, unless it be miracles, the holiness of an apostle, or the victories of a great monarch. Where this language can once be introduced by missionaries, the true religion, which is in complete agreement with reason, will be established, and apostasy will no more be feared in the future than would an apostasy of men from the arithmetic or geometry which they have once learned.
> [42, pp. 224–5]

He was still of this opinion in 1697 when he wrote to Antoine Verjus S J, Louis XIV's confessor and monitor of the French mission, that his characteristics seems to me to have very great consequences for the propagation of religion and for the missions. [45, p. 56] Then, in his response to Bouvet's first letter he goes further and outlines his entire philosophical approach, which is, he emphasises, unlike the too materialistic philosophy of the Cartesian, solidly founded in the philosophy of the ancients. He continues:

> ...the introduction of Philosophy to the Chinese serves a grand effect by preparing their minds more near to receiving the true religion; this is why it seems important to consider how we teach philosophy, for to render it more solid, more convincing and more suitable for this effect.
> [45, p. 64]

In response, Bouvet brings into parallel the 'solid' foundations of Chinese philosophy in *their* ancients, which has also been corrupted in modern times, while the philosophy preserved in their ancient texts has an affinity with the ancient philosophy of Europe. [45, p. 74] In this way, Bouvet will bring Leibniz around to the idea that the Chinese already have the true philosophy, and that it is by reacquainting them with the ancient roots of *their own tradition* that they can be brought into preparation for the revelations of the true (Christian) religion.

In these letters, Bouvet and Leibniz are discussing the history of philosophy in accord with a common Christianity strategy for dealing with the recognition of its own teaching in pre-Christian civilisations—of which there was by then a mass of information in the form of commentaries, speculations and translations that had begun to flowing from the printing presses within decades of the first Guttenberg Bible. According to this approach to non-Christian philosophy, it was by 'natural reasoning' that the Greeks, and others, were able to establish truths in alignment with the true religion, and that this prepared them for the revelations of the mysteries of the true religion—revelations of truths beyond the capacity of human reasoning. In this approach, sound natural reasoning, including that of Christian and pagan science, is not contrary to Christianity, but preparatory to it. It was not that Christianity borrowed from the Greeks, but rather that the sages of Greece, in a different way to the Jewish prophets, were preparing the way for the coming of the Christ.

Whilst using this language of 'natural religion' Bouvet and Leibniz would soon reveal to each other that they were of a more radical and opposing tendency. They soon discovered a mutual inclination towards the

Renaissance belief that the source of this pagan wisdom was not natural but divine, transmitted with varying degrees of clarity from enlightened sages of the earliest times. Such belief in an 'ancient theology' underpinned the theosophy of Renaissance science, which by the end of the 17th century was on the wane after a sustained push from the time of the Reformation for the purification of Christianity from pagan influences. But back at its height in the Florentine Renaissance, the ancient theology/philosophy was proclaimed as a tradition *independent* of the Judeo-Christian tradition. In the face of the persecution begun well before, but yet exemplified by the burning in 1600 of the notorious promoter of pagan philosophy, Giordano Bruno, there was soon a retreated to narratives familiar in the Christian patriarchs of a lineage from all and any pagan sources back to Moses, or even beyond and back to Noah or Adam. The highest antiquity was required for this pan-Christian syncretism due to the belief that certain Hellenistic texts were authored as they proclaim by the most ancient of sages. Especially significant among these texts was the *Corpus Hermetica*, believed to be

The Ancient Theology of Renaissance Christianity: Moses conversing with Hermes in the presence of Isis (above); Greek philosophers mingling with Renaissance masters (below). Both painting may still be viewed in the Vatican.

The pavement of the Siena Cathedral presents Hermes (below) as most prominent among those who foretold the Christian revelation of the One-Creator and his Son; labelled a contemporary of Moses, the Egyptian sage is apparently petitioned by the Jewish lawgiver to 'take up your letters and law'.

Chapter 15: Dyadics Discovered in Ancient China

written by the Egyptian sage Hermes Trismegistus, who was situated historically either (most heretically) as antecedent to Moses, or (most Biblically) as his teacher [as per Acts 7, 22], and then (more tolerably) as his wise contemporary.

Even after the debunking of the high antiquity of these sources (e.g., of the *Hermetica* in 1614) and despite the persecution of this pagan revival, late 17th century investigations of the undeniably ancient philosophical tradition of China were still motivated by this search for traces and echoes of the divine pristine wisdom, and also of the pristine language—perhaps the God-given language Adam used to name the animals, or otherwise that used by Noah and by the builders of Babel even after the flood but before God thwarted their project with the introduction of linguistic diversity. As much as the language is tied to the wisdom it expresses, so too is the script that preserves it—perhaps even preserving it on the Ark or in stone through the great deluge. The hunt was on for the original notation expressing this language, a notation primitive even to the hieroglyphs of Egypt. Leibniz's interest in ancient scripts as a model for his universal characteristics was influenced by this Renaissance belief, and it resonated with Bouvet who confidently predicted that one day we will arrive at an analysis which will reduce [the Chinese Characters] to Egyptian hieroglyphs and demonstrate that they both are writing used among the learned before the flood.* So while the door was closing on this way of involving foreign and ancient cultures, this historiography did survive and continued to motivate and inform the study of Chinese language, script and philosophy.

By the time of the Bouvet-Leibniz correspondence, a potential Chinese source of the ancient theology had already been found in the legendary philosopher-king FuXi and his notation of broken and unbroken line. Bouvet refers Leibniz to these lines as they appear in the preface to *Confucius Sinarum Philosophus* (a book in Leibniz's personal library), and says that if he had the time he would make a great study of them because he believes they contain a real key to the whole tradition.# These characters…

> …were composed with a marvellous artifice and represent in a very simple and natural manner the principles of all sciences, or better said, this is a system completed of a perfect metaphysics, of which the Chinese have lost

---

* [45, p. 73]. Translated by Swiderski [66] p. 138
\# The idea of a '*veritable clef*' or '*clavis sinica*' has a significance not evident here. Leibniz corresponded with Andreas Muller and Christian Mentzel who both claimed to have devised a 'key to Chinese' but neither publicly produced any such key. See Rosemont & Cook [44] p. 11.

> it seems the knowledge long before Confucius. Besides the true intelligence of this system of characters, for which the Chinese have an extraordinary regard, that which they do not understand can well serve not only for re-establishing the principles of the true and legitimate philosophy of the ancient Chinese, and to be able to bring back to all their nation the knowledge of the true God; but also to establish the natural method to be followed in all the sciences, which much earlier we find the ancient following when the light of reason was the more pure. So you see, Sir, that I have the good fortune of entertaining absolutely your sentiments to know that to prepare the mind of the Chinese to receive the true Religion, it is only necessary to teach them the ancient philosophy, and even that same of the ancient Chinese, which I do not believe is any different from that which passes amongst us as the most solid...
> [45 p.74]

Here in a nutshell Bouvet presents the rationale for the French Jesuit mathematical mission to China notoriously advocated by Couplet and Bouvet in a controversy between the Jesuits and their enemies that was already raging in Paris at the very time of this correspondence. While Couplet had claimed that the Chinese got their ancient wisdom prior to Moses—for Shem, the third son of Noah who went to the East—Bouvet would speculate that the 'foreign' FuXi was in fact a Western sage, perhaps Hermes himself, who had brought this system of characters to China as an epitome of the true religion. Leibniz had started out with Bouvet by offering support to the strategy of the Jesuits to promote Christianity through a grounding in Western (Platonic) philosophy, but Bouvet responds by saying that *the Chinese already have it*. What is required for conversion is, paradoxically, to revive their own philosophy lost to them long before Confucius, (i.e., long before even the 5th century BC flowering of Greek philosophy). True to the mission of these mathematical enthusiasts, Bouvet redefines the missionary task in an extreme version of the strategy of cultural 'accommodation' for which the Jesuits had already been severely censured.*

Late in the same year, 1698, in a letter to Verjus, Leibniz shows not only assent to Bouvet's radical approach, but he incorporates it into a narrative of his own vocation:

> It is since my youth that I have thought a new characteristics, which gives one the method not only [to signify in the same way that the Chinese

---

* The 'Noachide' theory for the transmission of divine knowledge was popular among the Jesuits, but not only among them. The Franciscan Antonio Caballero Santa Marie de Prémare [1666-1736], in attacking the prevailing Jesuit view, still presumed that the Chinese are descendants from Noah. See [44], p. 98n & [68], p. 35. See also Bouvet's 'decipherment letter' [40, p. 272] for the suggestion that FuXi might be Zoroaster, Hermes or Enoch.

characters do], but also to calculate exactly those thing that until now one could reason only vaguely. I have succeeded a little in my new infinitesimal calculus, to improving the alliance of geometry with physics, and in another method yet to be published which I call *Calculum Situs* [i.e., topology]. But I claim of still greater advance, if God gives me more life, and also leisure or help for this, and I do not believe that there is nothing which could give more to human reason, than a characteristics could achieve. Bouvet hopes to write to me of the decipherment of certain old characters which are of veneration for the Chinese and that he believes has a relation with philosophy, which could suggest a means to serve our Theology. I thought that one could maybe accommodate one day these characters if one is well informed not only to represent as ordinary characters but even to calculate and to aid imagination and thought in a manner which astonishes the spirit of the people and which gives us a new means of instructing and winning them. Besides, this view of the characteristics which I have had for a long time, and of which I speak in a small book that I made when I was barely 20 years old [i.e., his '*Ars combinatoria*', 1666] is one of the most important which I know. But I am afraid that it will perish.
[45, p. 87]

In a letter of 1701 Leibniz explains directly to Bouvet for the first time his Dyadics, complete with an exalted account of the Creation analogy. He is offering it to the mission once again as an evangelical tool—a new confirmation of the Christian religion—and he suggests that the Emperor might even be interested to learn of it. Then he returns to the topic of his characteristics project:

I remember I spoke to you of an extraordinary design of characters; this would be a means of painting not the words but thoughts, as algebra in mathematics. In putting the discourse in these characters, one would calculate and demonstrate in reasoning. I believe one could find a way of combining this with the old Chinese characters which are already the subject of your thoughts.

To achieve this result, Leibniz proposes, would perhaps be the greatest means one could invent to establish the truth of religion by the voice of reason. [40, p. 248]

This letter took only ten months to reach Bouvet in China late in 1701. Meanwhile, before it was even sent, Bouvet had penned another letter to Charle Le Gobien (a Parisian Jesuit acting as a conduit of information to and from the Chinese mission) specifically asking for a copy to be forward to Leibniz. This letter shows that Bouvet was very close to the binary decipherment already, and if he had not read of the Dyadic in Leibniz's much earlier letter to Grimaldi, then this may have been without the aid of Leibniz's elementary arithmetic. Bouvet writes that he has

ENTHUSIASTIC MATHEMATICS

finally discovered the whole mystery, or at least a road very sure and easy to make pure, and that he can tell from those who know the philosophy of numbers that it is no mere conjecture when he claims that the figures of FuXi express a system that actually contains all other sciences. In that they consist of a double sequence of numbers, plane and solid, they are in effect the same system as that of Plato.*

After Leibniz's letter arrived in Beijing, Bouvet replied with an explicit account of his decipherment, including the 64 hexagrams carefully laid out in binary sequence. When this letter finally came to Leibniz (via Le Gobien) in April 1703, it revealed that what he had envisaged as an ancient characteristics

> Φ
>
> It seems that
> the 8 gua were elementary for the Chinese,
> and it can be understood that Fu Xi even
> presents the creation by One and nothing,
> and that he advances
> the same account as in the story of Genesis.
>
> That is,
> 0 can mean void,
> which precedes the creation of Heaven & Earth,
> and then
> by the commencement of 7th days
> everything exists.
>
> At the beginning of the 1st days 1 exists,
> that is to say God.
> At the beginning of the 2nd, 2,
> Heaven & Earth,
> being created on the 1st.
>
> Finally,
> at the beginning of the 7th, all exist,
> and so the 7th is the most perfect
> and the Sabbath,
> because everything is now filled,
> with 7 written as 111 and so without 0.
> And it is only in this way, by using 0 and 1,
> that the perfection of the 7th appears sacred,
> remarkable that this is,
> his characters give an account of
> the Trinity.
>
> Φ

turned out to be an ancient version of his Dyadic arithmetic. While Bouvet remained confident that these lines might be the historical and formally primitive elements of Chinese writing characters, Leibniz was not convinced; and, now that he knew them to be a version of his Dyadics, he was less persuaded to the possibility that they could form the basis of a universal notation of science. It is curious that despite often promoting his vision of a characteristics as a kind of arithmetic, Leibniz never tried to build his characteristics from his elementary Dyadic arithmetic. Both these

---

* For the full letter see [45], p. 122–128. For a discussion of its significance see Zacher [40], p. 104–6.

elementary notations were introduced first in 1679 (one as already realised, the other only ever projected) but they were always kept separate, even though they were often later juxtaposed in successive paragraphs of the same letter. This separation is all the more curious after the Chinese lines, so keenly sort to realise the dream of the one, turned out to be a version of the other.*

A Sober Review of Bouvet's Interpretation

Bouvet's decipherment of the lines of FuXi has been discredited by modern scholars on many levels. Here is a summary.

- There is no evidence that the *gua* were ever regarded as a binary notation at any time prior to Bouvet, whereas there is plenty of evidence that they were thought of otherwise. Basically, they are the permutations and combination of two possible values in three places, that is, 2 x 2 x 2 = 8 possibilities. Thus we cannot conclude that the correspondence with Leibniz's binaries extends beyond the purely formal.#
- The ancient Chinese were not even equipped to invent such a calculus without first inventing something which they clearly did not have, that is a notational **zero**. We know that this was not introduced until the 8th century, and only then under Indian influence.+
- That the FuXi arrangement of the *gua* is of ancient origins is not at all conclusive. The ancient *Shuo Gua* (quoted above, page 304) is seen to name the trigrams paired across the diameter of this *before-Heaven* circle, but this description does not unambiguously define this arrangement. In fact, this '*before-Heaven*' arrangement makes its first appearance in the archive during the Sung Dynasty (960–1279 AD) where it is associated with the original FuXi invention that is only vaguely described in the ancient *Yi Jing* passages. This arrangement could well have been invented at that time as a late interpretation of these passages.++

---

* For an example of where Leibniz juxtaposes his discovery of the elementary arithmetic beside his search for a universal 'characteristics', see the final paragraph of his 'Explication' [59, p. 43]. The separation of the two projects has few exceptions. For where the Dyadics is more in line with the characteristics project see 'Discourse on the Natural Theology of the Chinese' [44, p. 133], where, very late in life he relates his Dyadics to the proto-characteristics subject of his youthful, *Ars combinatoria*.
\# See Aiton [62] p. 247–8.
+ See for example Cammann [69], p. 245.
++The rejection of the binary interpretation of the FuXi *gua* is a modern response to what was seen as previous uncritical acceptance among the zealous few Westerners who took an interest. Early

ENTHUSIASTIC MATHEMATICS

In responding to this resounding criticism I should first say that the hypothesis of the *before-Heaven* arrangement as an ancient binary system continues to suffer from a lack of evidence. However, the case against it is not so strong as to warrant the dismissal it has received at the hands of modern scholars. In fact, most of the arguments for rejecting Bouvet's interpretation display a lack of sympathy with arithmetic emanationism, whereas if such a sympathy is indulged, then a predisposition to just such an invention among the ancient Chinese becomes apparent. It is only this predisposition that I defend here in order to keep the case open until it is decided by a more thorough investigation of the surviving evidence.

Firstly, let's deal with the origins of the notation. Two ancient practices of divination historically associated with the *Yi Jing* give some suggestions as to the origin of these Yin and Yang lines. In the first, a hot poker is inserted into a drill-hole made in a piece of tortoise shell, or flat bone. This causes radiating cracks which are then interpreted. The *gua* may have been drawn to resemble these heat-induced fissures. The second practice is still used in conjunction with the *Yi Jing*. It is where the numerical results of chance (achieved by throwing and collecting yarrow sticks rather than coins or die) are written under each other. Because the importance in these results is whether the number is odd (auspicious) or even (inauspicious), it might have been that a short hand developed (i.e., the *gua*) that indicates only this in each place, and so we get the *gua* core of the *Yi Jing* as a listing of the possible combination notated in this way. [72, p. 84]

If this speculation about the origins of the notation is on the right track, then it goes against Bouvet's assent to the neat story of the *before-Heaven* arrangement as a pristine philosophy introduced by the legendary founder of Chinese civilisation, FuXi. However, this does not foreclose on the possibility that at some time after they came into use (let's say conservatively, after 1000 BC) and before the revelations and interpretations of the Sung Dynasty (around 1000 AD), a Chinese mathematical cult arranged the lines in this way and interpreted the 'Change' they described as arithmetically binary.

---

promotion of Bouvet's interpretation came in 1705 when Wilhelm Tentzel published an account expanded by private correspondence with Leibniz [40, p. 154–64] [59, p. 49]. The modern rejection began in 1863 when the historian of mathematics Moritz Cantor came to the view that Leibniz was mistaken because the *gua* were symbols of nature and not of numbers. His reasoning was challenged by Paul Carus through an account of Chinese philosophy uncommonly informed for the late 19th century. [70, p. 229] [59, p. 51]. Later, the historian of mathematics Florian Cajori was almost mocking, calling Bouvet's interpretation a curious blunder [48, pp. 564–5]. Cajori thought that Leibniz's minor invention... afforded him a satisfaction out of proportion to its importance. This came before the power of binaries was rediscovered with electronic computing. In the light of this rediscovery, an *Encyclopaedia of Religion* article on 'Binary Symbolism' revives the old spirit [49]. But scholarly scepticism remains, including that of the sinologist Schuyler Cammann who dismisses Bouvet's interpretation of the FuXi *gua* if only for the lack of an ancient Chinese notational of zero. However, in this very dismissal, Cammann

Chapter 15: Dyadics Discovered in Ancient China

There does not seem to have been any ancient Chinese cults as mathematically sophisticated as the Pythagoreans, but there are nonetheless some hints of mathematical mysticism found in writings as early as the Han Dynasty (206 BC – 220 AD). [69] [71] Retrospective support to this evidence comes from two further diagrams revealed in the Sung renaissance along with the *before-Heaven* arrangement of the trigrams. These diagrams were claimed to be the ancient and secret 'Lo-Shu' (or Lo River Writing) and 'He Tu' (Yellow River Map) referenced obscurely in ancient writings.* Apart from the conventional alignment of Yin and Yang with even and odd, they display various arithmetic patterns, the most obvious being those of Western 'magic squares'. But even if mathematical cults are considered to have existed, still Western scholarship tends to dismiss the binary numbers hypothesis with the problem of **zero**. It is fortunate that our preceding discussion of the notation for **zero** (see above, pages 181 and 264) allows us to appreciate that the ancient Chinese lacked nothing in this regard.

Firstly, they had the concept of the place-value **zero** in the empty place on their counting boards. [75, pp. 269–283] The Chinese numerals that eventually came into use are still evidently representations of arrangements of the unit rods on these boards, and it is just as evident that the notational **zero** was introduced to represent the empty place so as to overcome a problem not

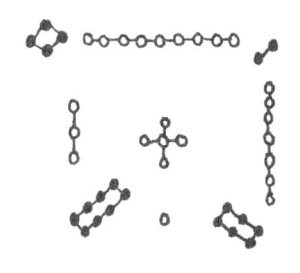

Luo Shu

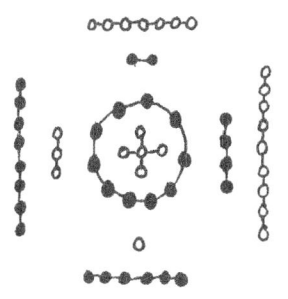

He Tu

Notice that these figures integrate arithmetic with topology, and that the expression of the numbers is similar to the topological notation use by the Pythagoreans. The difference here is that the even (Yin) and odd (Yang) values are distinguished by the dark shading of former.

---

supports their invention as well prior to their first publication during the Sung Dynasty [71, p. 585–88].
* Textual reference to such diagrams date back to the time of Confucius. See *Yi Jing*, Great Commentary, Part I, Chapter 11.8 [63, p. 320]. Reference to the 'River Chart' is made in the Confucian *Analects*, VIII, 9. See the discussion in Feng Yu-lan's history [73] Vol II, p. 8, as well as Cammann [74], p. 188, and Carus [70], p. 204–6. Both diagrams were first revealed in their present form in the 12th century by Ts'ai Yuang-ting. Evidence that these diagrams existed before the 12th century, or that they have any relationship to the diagrams referred to in the ancient texts, consists only of stories of their secret transmission down a line of masters.

319

previously encountered when using these physical calculators. Secondly, they had in the concept of Yin, the very model of the **zero** of Leibniz's binaries. We should remember that this **zero** is no ordinary cipher. It is both nought and not. It is a passive and receptive absence, implicit in the one as its negation. This is precisely how Yin is described in relation to Yang, and the underlying principle of Yin-Yang philosophy is their constant alternation. This alternation has always been seen as expressed in the odd-even alternation of the counting numbers, and also in the elementary temporal progression of day and night—light and dark being an ancient symbolisation of Yang and Yin perhaps as old as the *gua*. Here already, in an elementary way, we have Bouvet's interpretation well supported.

The final obstacle to the plausibility of an ancient binary invention is the probability that the ancients would apply place-value to express the powers of the double. Place-value was already in use to express the powers of ten in the columns of the counting board, but this does not explain why it was found necessary to build powers in the Yin-Yang alternation. Reason for this is found when we consider that trigrams were regarded as expressions of elementary natural change; they are an elementary physics, a physics of waxing and waning, coming and going, of growth and decay. Such physical change constitutes both space and time.

Consider space first. Space is easily found to have powers in its dimensional magnitudes, and if the Yang-Yin double is elementary to the arithmetic progression as successive 'odd-even' pairs, then this **double** would also constitute the elementary magnitude. So the elementary length in a binary geometry would be this **double**. If the elementary line is double, then the elementary plane is **double-double** and the elementary solid is **double** to the 3rd power. The formal similarity with mystical Platonic geometry is not superficial or arbitrary (see the interpretation of the passage in the *Epinomis* above on page 260). Thus, if the FuXi arrangement of the trigrams is interpreted binary then they can be seen as expressions of the progressive generation (and the progressive decay) of the three dimensions of physical things in the wax (and wane) of the Yang value in its three degrees. And while the three-tiered eight trigrams are associated with solid physical things, in support of this interpretation there is even a suggestion that two-tiered 'bi-grams' were associated with the plane figures.

In the 'Change' writings there is reference to an intermediate set of four stacks of two lines known by the wonderfully evocative name '*xiang*'. (See the 'quattuor imagines' given by Couplet above on page 309 and the Change commentary quoted below on page 322). Among other things, '*xiang*' means 'images,' or 'symbols'; and thus, in fact, all Change line arrangements are '*xiang*' in that they are given to notate the Change, which otherwise goes on un-notated. Images, symbols and characters marked on surfaces are, of course, ready examples of 2-dimensional figures in the plane, and so it makes sense that these 'bigrams', as the calculus in the 2nd degree, are specifically called *xiang*.

If we next consider the progression of time, we find that while it is not evidently symmetrical like the degrees of cubic geometry, there are nonetheless natural orders of astronomical time. If the primary alternation of Yin and Yang is expressed in the continuous alternation of night and day, and one day is counted as *one-day-and-night*, then higher orders of time can be measured by the cycles of the planets, especially the 28-day phases of the moon (and menstrual) cycle and the 12 lunar cycles in every solar (and agricultural) cycle. In ancient times the wax and wane of the moon was often associated with the wax and wane of Ying, and moon phase charts are sometimes found superimposed over the trigrams.*

The non-Arbitary Topology of the Yin Yang lines
The notation of Yin and Yang can itself be derived in an analogy with the 3-D geometry of things. Imagine the primary solid as a sphere (e.g., the Earth or Moon). Its cross-section gives the 2-D circle. Sectioned again gives the 1-D Yang line as its diameter. Next, imagine the primary void as a hollowed sphere (e.g., a stone-fruit with its stone removed). Its cross-section is a disc containing a void. Its section again gives a broken diameter, the Yin line. A cube, or any other (genius 0) solid, and that solid hollowed, with give the same two results in the first dimension. Thus, by regressive analysis, the —— and — — can be seen as non-arbitrary topological symbols of presence and absence in the first dimension. We should also note that the divination technique of entering a hot poker into the hole in the bone could be imagined here as the entry of —— into the void of — —. The sexual connotation is entirely in sympathy with the Yin-Yang philosophy, as it is with the rod-in-circle of the Hindu Lingam-Yoni, and as it is with Shakespeare's joke in Hamlet about laying the I in the O between a lady's legs.

---

* See Louis [76, p. 164–5] for an incomplete before-Heaven (*xiantian*) arrangement with moon phases that may date from before the Sung Dynasty. The moon phases alignment is associated with Buddhist influences,

ENTHUSIASTIC MATHEMATICS

Again, there is no positive case here, only a defence against those arguments used to dismiss Bouvet binary interpretation. And we can't escape the fact that there is no direct evidence of base-2 place-values ever being assigned to the Change lines. Instead, the reading of arithmetic place-value into the lines is contradicted by two conventional classifications of the trigrams and hexagrams. The first of these is the classification according to the tally of Yang lines irrespective of place. Thus, for example, 100 and 010 and 001 would be in the same class because they each contain one Yang. The logic of the ordering of the 64 hexagrams in the *Yi Jing* conforms to this classification. The second classification, more sympathetic to a binary interpretation, is derived from this famous passage in the Great Commentary:

> Therefore in the *Yi* there is the Great Axis [*Tai ji*]
> which produced the 2 elemental forms.
> These 2 produce the 4 images [*xiang*].
> The 4 images produce the 8 trigrams.*

After the Sung renaissance, this passage is commonly interpreted as giving the generation of the trigrams, and thereby the hexagrams, as by way of successive dichotomous division. Various tables and diagrams were used to express this interpretation that gives the *geometric double* as the primary generator, which only indirectly generates the binary alternation across each level of the hierarchy. Of course, this ancient passage need not be interpreted as primarily in the geometric progression. Instead, it could be interpreted as expressing the hierarchy of powers as they are seen to develop on the

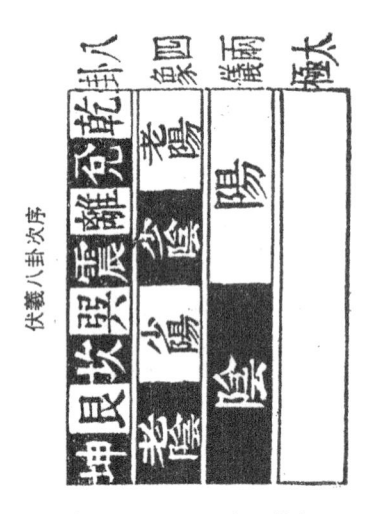

This table expresses the dichotomous generation of the trigrams reading from right to left published in a survey by Hu Wei, 1706.#

---

see Robinet [77], especially Figure A1. Also see *Yi Jing*, Great Commentary, Section II, Ch 5 [63, p. 338–9] for discussion of solar and lunar alternations.
* *Yi Jing*, Great Commentary, Section I, Ch 11.5 [63, p. 318]
\# Diagram from Hu Wei *I-t'u ming-pien* ('Illuminating and differentiating the *Yi Jing* Diagram') published in 1706. For discussion of Hu Wei's historical investigations in parallel with the Jesuits, see Mungello [68], p. 62–4.

322

Chapter 15: Dyadics Discovered in Ancient China

counting board in the elementary arithmetic series, cycling through the units, and then the 10s, to the 100s and so forth, except here the primary arithmetic is a binary alternation with orders of doubling. The question is then: *Is the elementary order of the Change* 1, 2, 3...or 1, 2, 4...? For evidence of the interpretation as a Yin-Yang alternation in the arithmetic series, we must pick up on a tradition that made much of what is historically the most important word in this passage from the Great Commentary on the Change, that is, 'the Great Axis' or 'Great Ridgepole,' the *Tai ji* ['T'ai Chi'].

Consider first that in ancient times the *Tai ji* is closely related to the *Tai yi*, or 'Supreme One', a god popularly believed to reside at the pole star at the centre of the sky and around which all the heavens revolve. Of this legend the Sinologist Schuyler Cammann recently wrote:

> The idea of a cosmic journey on an S-shaped celestial course, and the emphasis on centrality in these diagrams [i.e., the Luo Shu He Tu], also found expression in Chinese mythology. The fact that the sky at night appears to be revolving on an invisible pivot marked by the North Star (Stella Polaris) led the early Chinese to think that that point must mark the center of the sky, the place of the 'Sky Door' which led to the World Beyond the Sky; and sometime toward the end of the Chou [1046–256 BC] they conceived the idea that the chief god—who in Ch'in [Qin, 221–206 BC] and Han times, if not earlier, was called *T'ai-yi*, the 'Supreme One'—lived at that place and travelled in the Nine Halls...T'ai-yi's travels were later explained by saying that he left his palace at the center to visit each of the first four directions in the sky, marked by individual trigrams; then he came home to rest at the center, before resuming his S-shaped tour; finally he visited the last four directions indicated by the remaining trigrams.*

The ancient say goes: 'Tai yi gathers the numbers by travelling the nine halls'. His journey is usually associated with the more common King Wen arrangement of the trigrams, but could this once have been the *before-Heaven* arrangement enumerated? One hint to this is that the *before-Heaven* arrangement was always associated with the eight (compass) directions—to which the legend refers. [74] If we imagine that this Supreme One resides in the centre of the *before-Heaven* circle, then his journey could correspond to the figure-8 counting required for the binary interpretation as shown in the sketch below:

---

* [69, p. 240] Cammann was using this legend for a different purpose: to help align the King Wen arrangements of the trigrams to the 'Lo Shu' diagram (see above p. 319).

323

ENTHUSIASTIC MATHEMATICS

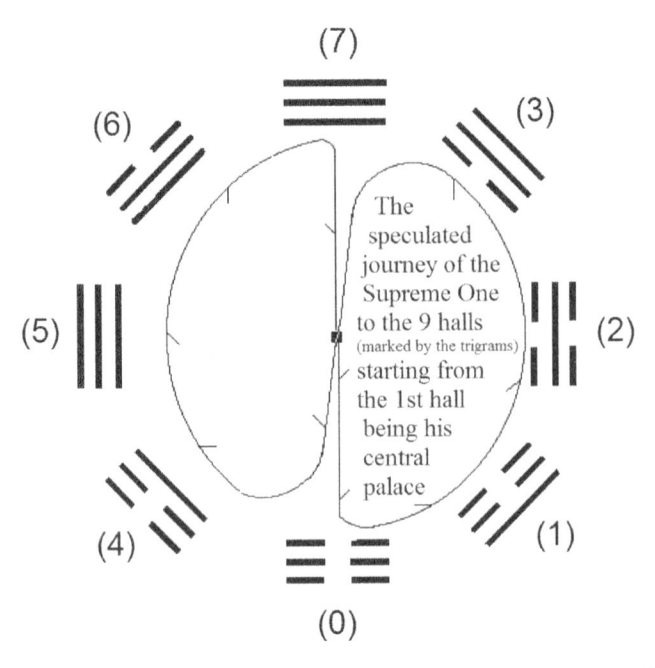

(7)
(6)
(3)
(5)
(2)
(4)
(1)
(0)

The speculated journey of the Supreme One to the 9 halls (marked by the trigrams) starting from the 1st hall being his central palace

In this tradition we also find the notion of an ordinal zero, the '*Wu ji*', the 'no-ridgepole', given as the unchanging nothing that corresponds to the place of rest at the centre of things. In that *Wu ji* corresponds to the Platonic *principle-origin*, we do well to observe that in this tradition it is more properly defined as the ordinal **zero**—there is no confusion of it with the *first-born*-**one** or the cardinal **unit**.

Wu ji: unchanging stillness, the unlimited primary nothingness

As we have already seen, when the *before-Heaven* arrangement emerged in the Sung renaissance, it was often enumerated in the figure-8 of my speculated *Tai yi* journey, but in reverse order to the binary 'rising Yang'; and counting not from 0 to 7, but instead from 1 to 8. We could count in reverse a binary 'rising-Yin' as the symmetrically opposite destruction, or waning, of Ying by giving that — — is 1 and ——— is 0. However, this is not it, because the synchronicity is thrown by starting the numbering with 1 and not 0. *But what is the appearance of this 1 to 8 enumeration telling us?* It could be speculated on the binary hypothesis that when these numbers from 1 to 8 were assigned to the trigrams, the binary understanding of the notation had been lost, but that nonetheless, the scribes were cognisant that tradition gave the trigrams as expressing the arithmetic series operating in the figure-8. Now, everybody knows that Yin is even and Yang is odd, but the only way to match the outer Yin and Yang lines with the even and odd numerals written around them is by *counting in reverse*. Thus so, the Sung enumeration of the trigrams could be a corruption of the original binary interpretation.

In the Ming Dynasty (1368-1643) the '*Tai ji* diagram'—the black and white swirls familiar to us all—is found drawn inside the *before-Heaven* arrangement as an expression of the Change given in the outer lines. Many versions of this diagram appeared during the Ming, but the line of distinction between the Yin and Yang is always a reverse-S. If the *Tai ji* were drawn to an S-shape then it could be seen to express the proportion of Yang and Yin as proportions of light and dark across the rotating diameters of the circle. Unlike the more common modern *Tai ji* drawn upon semi-circles, the earliest *Tai ji* often approximate these proportions but in mirror image. Thus, if these *Tai ji* diagrams were reversed then they would present a dynamic phase-chart expressing at once all the phases of the counting in the outer *before-Heaven* circle, where the ridgepole is a diameter rotating around half the circle before flipping to make the figure-8, and so allowing the Supreme One 'to gathering the numbers'.

The above arrangement of the *Tai ji* diagram within the *before-Heaven* (*xantian*) trigrams was published in an historical survey by Hu Wei in 1706.* Yang (———) rising is unshading. Yin (— —) rising is shading. The *Tai ji* gives the proportions of the diameter at each trigram (0:7, 1:6, 2:5...) that support the binary interpretation except in mirror image. The proposal original design is below.

---

* From Hu Wei *I-t'u ming-pien*, 1706.

There are some early S-shaped expressions of the Change suggesting this as an earlier form of the *Tai ji*, but here we are only speculating, and until further evidence is found that is all that we can do.*

The doctrine of *Tai ji* has a strong historical affinity with Daoism (in it, the *Wu ji* ordinal origin is often identified with 'the unnameable Dao') and if there were ever a binary interpretation of the *before-heaven* arrangement then it is likely to have come from this tradition. The Daoist scholar, Isabella Robinet finds a distinctiveness in the Daoist readings of the Change in contrast to the dichotomous generation of the Great Commentary (quoted above, page 322) that is in sympathy with the generation describe in Chapter 42 of *Dao De Jing*:

> The Dao begot 1
> 1 begot 2
> 2 begot 3
> And 3 begot the myriad of things
> The myriad of things carry Yin and embrace Yang.
> They achieve harmony by combining these forces.

Here the primary generation is the 1, 2, 3,..., the basic odd-even series. *Dao De Jing* also offers an understanding of the name '*before-Heaven*' [*xiantian*]. This is in the first section of Chapter 25:

> Something mysteriously formed,
> Born before Heaven and Earth.
> In the silence and the void,
> Standing alone and unchanging,
> Ever present and in motion.
> Perhaps it is the mother of the myriad things.
> I do not know its name.
> Call it Dao.
> For lack of a better word, I call it great.

And then the final lines:

> Man follows the Earth.
> Earth follows Heaven.
> Heaven follows the Dao.
> The Dao following what is natural.#

---

* There is some evidence for an S-shaped diagram, including one drawn inside a *before-Heaven* arrangement from the 14th century that is reproduced by Louis [76] as his Fig. 10. Louis also reproduces other old decorative figures (Fig. 15, 16 & 17) with the *Tai ji* in the S-shaped. I presented this proposal for the origin of the *Tai ji* in an unpublished paper to the University of Melbourne HPS Post-Graduate conference, Mt Evelyn, Victoria, Australia, 15 March, 1996.
\# This is the Gia-Fu Feng translation of 'Tao Te Ching' [Dao De Jing] by 'Lao Tzu' [Laozi] only with

Heaven and Earth are the primary manifestations of Yang and Yin in 'Change' cosmogony. The motion 'before Heaven' would then be a motion of the Dao prior to Creation. As the Great Commentary says: that which is antecedent to physical form is called the Dao.*   So this is a motion not actual or particular, silent and void, ever-present, yet still in motion. If we were to interpret Platonically a Daoist motion *before-Heaven-and-Earth*, then we could say, without force, that this motion prior to Creation is of *numbers-in-themselves* (i.e., *arithmetic*, not *logisitic*, formal not actual) generating themselves around the **zero**-point in a potent, endless cycle corresponding, for non-arbitrary reasons, with what has become in the West the symbol for infinity.

'10,000' replaced by 'myriad'. [78] See also *Yi Jing*, Great Commentary, Section I, Ch 9 [63, p. 308]: Heaven is 1, Earth is 2, Heaven is 3, Earth is 4 Heaven is 5....
* See *Yi Jing*, Great Commentary, Section I, Ch 12, translated by Wu Jing-Nuan [79].

Chapter 16

THE END OF THE ROAD

Leibniz's reply to Bouvet's decipherment letter was not answered. Nor by any of his subsequent letters was Leibniz able to solicit a response, and his contact with the mathematical missionaries in Beijing was lost forever. Research by Bouvet and the other Jesuit mathematicians in China was being censured and suppressed by their superiors. In 1712 we still find Bouvet advocating the wisdom of the *Yi jing*, but also complaining bitterly of not being able to complete his grand project which was to do with the wisdom of the ancient Far East what others had already done with the ancient West, namely, to establish the credibility of all the mysteries of the Gospels...by arguments drawn from the pagans themselves.* And there is little wonder this project was being suppressed in view of the fact that such an approach to scholarship was placing in jeopardy not only the Jesuit mission in China, but the Jesuit order itself.

In 1700 a set of propositions derived from Couplet's preface to *Confucius Sinarum Philosophus* and from later Jesuit publications—which presented Christianity flourishing in China during the two millennia before the birth of Christ—went on trial in the Sorbonne. This trial sparked a notorious controversy that ended in devastating defeat. And this was on top of everything else. For their critics, the methodological error of the Jesuit mission began with Ricci's use of a traditional Chinese name for God, 'shan-ti', to translate the names of the one true God. Against the prevailing Jesuit view, some argued that an entirely new Chinese word is required—perhaps even a transliteration of the Latin, *Deus*.# Thus was the 'term controversy', but then there was also the 'Confucian rites controversy'. The rites and practices of ancestor worship were tolerated

---

* Letter to the Abbe Bignon, 15 September 1704 concerning general ideas of the *Yi jing*, translated in Walker [80], p. 227.
\# For the Sorbonne controversy see Walker [80] Ch 6. Walker supports the Jesuit argument that such pan-Christian claims were not exclusive to the Jesuits. See also Mungello [68] p. 19. Perhaps more extreme than Bouvet was Joseph Henri Marie de Prémare who would identified *Wu ji* with the Christian God. See Mungello [68] p. 22 & Walker [80] p. 199.

among the Chinese Christian converts by the Jesuits. They regarded them as merely 'civil' practices and not pagan religious practices incompatible with Christianity.* Many a missionary, including Dominicans, Franciscans and some Jesuits, strongly opposed this toleration, as did many a vocal churchman back in Europe. And eventually so did the Pope: in 1715, after a century of debate, he made a final ruling against the accommodation of the Confucian rites. It is important to place in this context Bouvet's long letter to Leibniz that containing the decipherment. This was published within a year of its receipt so as to exemplify everything wrong with the Jesuit approach. It and subsequent correspondence within the Jesuit fraternity continued to embroil Bouvet in a growing controversy over the Society's missionary methods as one of its more unrelenting exponents.#

Although Leibniz lost direct contact with the mathematical mission, he still had his indirect sources, and he continued to research and discuss Chinese theosophy to the very end of his life. Indeed, there was no moderation of his Jesuit-inspired approval in the face of the increasing hostility. In fact, in the very year of the Papal Bull against toleration of Confucian rites he set about writing his most extended and sympathetic study of the topic. Apparently this was prompted by him finally receiving copies of two notorious texts hostile to Chinese theosophy, sent by the French Platonist, Nicholas Remond, in September 1715 with a request for comment.+

Leibniz answered in what he refers to as his 'Discourse on the Natural Theology of the Chinese' by first pleading that European interpreters show due respect to such a grand tradition. It is not only for its greatness in size and history that Chinese civilisation commands this respect, but more because of the political, social and religious harmony it has achievement upon this scale. It has orderly government and a public morality admirable in certain regards, conjoined to a...natural theology, venerable by its antiquity, established and authorised for about 3,000 years. For this reason...

> It would be highly foolish and presumptuous on our part, having newly arrived compared with them, and scarcely out of barbarism, to want to condemn such an ancient doctrine simply because it does not appear to agree at first glance with our ordinary scholastic notions.
> [44, p. 78]

---

* Swiderski notes that Bouvet was among a group of Jesuits who presented a memorial to the emperor in 1700 asking his support against those who called Chinese rites heathen and forbade Chinese converts from continuing their practice. Leibniz had sided with these Jesuits already in his 'Latest News from China'. [66, p. 139]
\# For full publication details of Bouvet's decipherment letter, see Zacher [40] p. 262. Bouvet sent one more letter to Leibniz, but this was in 1702, before he had received a response to the decipherment.
+ Only a year earlier Leibniz had sent the now more famous essay called 'The Monadology'.

One of these ordinary scholastic notions was Aristotelian primary matter. And a major concern of this Discourse is to counter an interpretation of Chinese theosophy as materialism. Just such an interpretation is made in one of the books under review, written by a Jesuit, Nichola Longobardi (1565-1655) more than 100 years earlier.

Longobardi was a maverick among the Jesuits in his unreserved hostility to Chinese theosophy and in his penchant for street preaching over scholarship. Yet he was Ricci's chosen successor and the head of the Jesuit mission from 1610 to 1622. [68, p. 26] In this text, suppressed by the Jesuits for many years, Longobardi interprets the Chinese '*Li*' as equivalent to Aristotelian primary matter. Leibniz sees it as nothing of the sort, and finds Longobardi imposing the scholastic Aristotelian framework on a system that it clearly does not fit. The Chinese quite evidently do not make the error of a substrate independent of the supreme *creator-of-all*. And even if they did, then it cannot be the *Li*, because primary matter is only receptive and passive, whereas this is clearly an active power. Using Longobardi's own citations against him, Leibniz finds that on the contrary, this *Li* corresponds to our divinity. The Chinese recognise that…

> …all things are active only by participation of the *Li*, i.e., the same original Spirit (God), which gives them all their perfection. And matter itself is only a production of this same primary cause…Thus everything emanates from [Li] as from a central point…. The saying [of the Chinese] that *all is one*… means that God is everything by eminence, as the perfection of effects are in their cause, and not formally as if God is the aggregate of all things…
> [44, p. 95]

In finding 'matter' as but a product of this *principle-origin*, the *Li*, Leibniz finds Chinese philosophy to be more Christian than Christian Aristotelianism:

> In consequence of this production of prime matter by the primary principle, or primitive Form, by pure activity, by the operation of God, Chinese philosophy more closely approaches Christian theology than the philosophy of the ancient Greeks who considered matter as coeval with God, a principle which produces nothing but only informs it.
> [44, p. 97]

The entire Discourse is an enthusiastic advocacy of ancient Chinese theosophy, and at one point Leibniz gushes that what he finds in the Chinese is quite excellent and quite in accord with natural theology. He goes as far as to claim

Chapter 16: The End of the Road

that it is pure Christianity and only qualifies this with an obeisance to revealed religion:

> It is pure Christianity in so far as it renews the natural law inscribed in our hearts—except for what revelation and grace add to it to improve our nature.*

In the final section of the Discourse he recounts the decipherment of the FuXi lines before grabbing the opportunity for another explication of his binary numbers. But then the text breaks off incomplete. 'The Discourse on the Natural Theology of the Chinese', written over the last year of his life, was left unfinished among his papers when he died in November 1716.

****

Leibniz's last years were not spent basking in his fame as one of the great mathematicians of his day. Instead he found himself increasingly isolated and the subject of increasing hostility within the two small communities in which he had long subsisted, namely, the Hanoverian court and the European scientific community. The bitter controversy over the invention of the infinitesimal calculus, into which he was drawn, would serve to alienate him from both these circles. Newton had invented his calculus long before Leibniz, and he used it magnificently to develop his theory of planetary orbits, but he also kept it secret for many years. While Newton was lying low in his Cambridge digs, Leibniz published his own invention, using a notation that gained acceptance across continental Europe during the first years of the 18th century. This new technique that was revolutionising the mathematical analysis of motion (and of change generally) carried in almost every instant the unmistakable mark of Leibniz; and if this was offensive to its first and true inventor, then it did not help that the pretender to the invention was openly critical of the underlying principles of his (Newton's) physics.

The controversy was already simmering along in learned discussion and correspondence when in 1697 a member of the Royal Society published an article attributing the discovery to Newton alone and attacking

---

* Translation from Rosemont and Cook [44] p. 105. This reiterates what he said to De Bosses in 1708: And thus, as far as I understand, I think the substance of the ancient theology of the Chinese is intact and, purged of additional errors, can be harnessed to the great truths of the Christian religions. [44, p. 73]

Leibniz. Leibniz was himself a long-standing member of the Society, elected in 1673 when he impressed the London assembly with a demonstration of his mechanical computer; but when Leibniz eventually complained about the article, the English scientists closed ranks around their most famous fellow who by 1703 had become their exulted president. Without giving Leibniz a hearing, and after much delay, the Society published its finding that there had been no slander against Leibniz. There could not be, because the complainant had in fact derived his calculus entirely from Newton.

This finding was published in 1712 and within a few years Leibniz's dispute with the Royal Society became something of an international embarrassment for his employer at the court in Hanover due to the extraordinary turn of events that saw Georg Ludwig of Hanover, the Elector of Brunswick, become King George I of England. Newton, the most celebrated living scientist, was not only president of the scientific society of London, to which the former Georg Ludwig of Hanover was now the royal patron, but he was also the new King George's Master of the Mint. As for Leibniz, when the Court moved to London in 1714, he was left behind in Hanover, which had become a province of the Britain Crown.

Georg Ludwig was never fond of the frail fogy, a courtier since his childhood, whom he had left behind ostensibly to finish his history of the House of Brunswick (of which the Hanoverians were a branch). It was his father and not him who had promoted Leibniz to Privy Counsellor. In these dark times Leibniz's few friends at court seemed to be mostly women, one of whom was his student, defender and confidant, the young Caroline, now Princess of Wales. But things got decidedly worse for Leibniz when comments he sent her about the decay of natural religion (this term began to supplant 'natural theology' during the 18th century) in her new homeland were passed on to members of the Royal Society.

Leibniz's criticisms of both John Locke and Isaac Newton prompted a reply from Samuel Clarke in defence of Newton. The exchange of letters that ensued were widely circulated and then published by Clarke shortly after Leibniz's death. In these letters Leibniz addresses a number of recurring themes now familiar to the reader, not the least important of which emerges in his criticism of Newtonian absolute space, where Leibniz finds once again the spectre of Arisototelian primary matter.

For Leibniz, space, and empty space, is only *relative-to-things*. This is consistent with the dialogue extract above on page 284, where *nothing* is relative to *things*, and consistent with the Dyadics where *not*-one is relative to one. In the discussion with Clarke, Leibniz proclaims space as something purely relative just like time; it is an order of coexistence, as time is an order of successions. This was against the idol of some modern Englishmen which is a real absolute space. [58, pp. 25–6] Leibniz considered absolute space to be a version of Aristotelian primary matter, whether as a being independent of the Creator or as a medium of material objects independent from him. Either way, Leibniz saw an error of principle and (what amounted to the same thing) a defiance of natural religion.

Newton's absolute space was influenced by a similar doctrine of his Cambridge senior Henry More. More's version was found objectionable to the prevailing relativism of 17th century science, and Descartes opposed it accordingly in an earlier exchange of letters.* Leibniz takes up the case again, arguing against the priority of space and so the possibility of absolute void, and also against what he saw as consequential, including the notion of the material atom, the simultaneity of things in space, and, accordingly, the simultaneity of events across space in time.# Leibniz's arguments are (even by the standards of the time) strikingly *a priori* and rarely empirical: these ideas of nature and the universe are wrong *in principle*. Not surprisingly he argued in vain, and the debate barely progressed, with Clarke blindly repeating unreasonable presuppositions.

Perhaps Leibniz could not see as we can see now: that by this time it was all over. The Aristotelianism paragon was on the rise again and all the empirical data was set to conform to it. In this case, primary matter had arisen in the guise of a presupposed place and context of things, coming in on the coattails of the success and fame of Newton's theory of planetary orbits, and defended with the political clout of the Royal Society. Indeed, we can now see in hindsight how truly resilient was this absolute space, which Descartes and Leibniz found indefensible, but which would yet keep relativism heretical in physics and cosmology, and right up until Einstein two centuries later.+

It was also all over in the debate over the epistemology of that other esteemed theorist of the Society, John Locke. Locke unequivocally turned all the epistemological attention away from the formal source of ideas and

---

* See Koyré [13] Ch 5.
# According to Leibniz's rule of the identity of discernible, two things in two different places could not be regarded as the same unless they were in fact one, and likewise two events at two different times could not be regarded as the same as each other except if they were one and the same event. In Leibnizian space-time every spatial-temporal place in the emanation is unique. This was not so in Newtonian space, and one of the great breakthroughs of Einstein on the way to Relativity was his critique of simultaneity.
+ See Einstein's historical discussion of theories of space, where he says the general theory of relativity confirms Descartes' conception in a roundabout way. [81, p. 136]

towards the presupposed material object; an object of knowledge represented in our senses but yet existing beyond any sense of it. Although Clarke's letters to Leibniz presented such a representationalist epistemology as a matter of course, this was not an object of their debate.* But Leibniz had already faced up to Locke's empiricism directly, including in a book-length dialogue addressing point-by-point Locke's *Essay on Human Understanding*. In his *New Essay*, Leibniz argues that contrary to Locke, we do have 'innate ideas,' and then he goes as far as to propose that all the thought and actions of our soul come from its own depths and could not be given to it by the senses.# But there was no longer much tolerance for such a position in learned discourse, and as we have already seen in Chapter 1, such a position was soon regarded as entirely fantastic—as an epistemology bereft of any ontology. Science had now shifted from its murky old metaphysical ways. In fact, the society of scientists sanctioned by the British Crown had already begun to rewrite the history of science in the image of this new way of explaining itself; and there was no room in this story for mystics, no room for Platonists, nor for mathematical reductionists of any kind. There was certainly no room for Leibniz.

Natural *theology* was banished as atheistic in order to introduce a science that was itself void of theology, and thereby unthreatening to the spiritual authority of the Church. For Locke and the Royal Society under Newton, science as 'Natural Religion' became the study of things, not in their generation by God, but as already generated in an external insensible spatio-temporal context from where they transmit sensible data in their image. For Leibniz, this represented a corruption of the long tradition of Western science to the point where it had turned its back on God for the worship of such idols. And he didn't mind saying so. And for this he paid a price. Leibniz's end was indeed symbolic of the changing times. It may be true that his intellectual isolation in later years was exacerbated by his reputation for avoiding Christian practice. What we know is that his secretary would later publish that he was never known to take communion; and he did defer, and so avoid, Holy Rite upon his deathbed.+ But it was

---

* By way of explaining what Newton meant by space as God's sensorium, Clarke presented a similitude with the mind of man which, by its immediate presence to the pictures or images of things formed in the brain by the means of the organs of sensation, sees those pictures as if they were the things themselves.... [58, p. 13]
# [82, p. 74 (standard pagination)] Leibniz's criticism of Locke was well known to his correspondence but it should be remembered that very little of Leibniz's voluminous writing was published in his lifetime. His *New Essay* was finished around the time of Locke's death in 1705, but it was not published until 1765.
+ This is according to the biography written by his secretary Eckhart (1779) and an account of Leibniz's death in two letters by Johann Vogler. See Aiton [62] p. 348–9. It would be an anachronistic mistake to view the rejection of the sacraments at the time by Leibniz, Newton and others, as a sign of obstinate atheism. Rather, it was more likely (and more likely viewed as) a sign of a belief in the

Chapter 16: The End of the Road

more on account of his bold attempts to solve the great conundrums of Christian theology that his name became (much like that of the Jewish heretic Baruch Spinoza) a byword for heresy among the devout churchmen, and at the same time an object of mockery among the Enlightened materialists of the 18th century salons.*

When the Privy Councillor finally died, having served the House of Hanover for 40 years, King George and much of his court were in Germany, nearby Hanover, yet no members of the court attended the funeral, and Leibniz was buried in an unmarked grave. Thus so, a late great wave of enthusiastic science flared and crashed to nothing, as spectacular and futile as an ocean swell arriving at the coast. Leibniz died during the 16th year of the 18th century, and by this time there was no doubt that the revival of mathematical mysticism was defeated by a counter-Renaissance backlash. After two centuries of epistemology wars, Logical Empiricism had achieved its incredible triumph.

---

apostasy of the state church, whether Catholic or Protestant. Since the late Middle Ages, various heresies had emerged among the *literati* that included the belief that the Church had fallen into apostasy at some stage after the apostolic period, including at the Council of Nicaea (325 AD) on the doctrine of the Trinity. Sometimes this apostasy was even viewed in terms of the apocalyptic tradition as the rise of the anti-Christ, and so acceptance of a sacrament from the state church would be to act against the true Christ.

* [47, p. 546] In a 1737 critique of Alexander Pope's 'Essay on Man', the Swizz Huguenot logician Jean-Pierre de Crousaz accuses Pope of promoting the deterministic philosophy of Leibniz, which was seen as dangerous in that it promoted a fatalism that serves (religious) scepticism. On the other hand, in *Candide* (1759), Voltaire mock's Leibniz's version of Augustinian *Summum Bonum* as naïve (religious) optimism.

ACKNOWLEDGEMENTS

It was after a seminar in the austral spring of 1991 that I went up to Niklas Luhmann and said 'I think I finally get it'. A short discussion ensued before I asked him 'If I were to go down this path then where should I start?' There was no ambiguity in his response. 'You should read *Laws of Form*.' It was the worst career advice I ever had. But it has been a wonderful intellectual adventure and it has resulted in this book.

In one form or another this work has been with me most of my adult life. I can scarcely remember all those who have contributed to its evolution. I do hope that my mentioning some of them does not suggest that I am ungrateful to the others.

In the preparation for publication (2016-8) I thank Randy Dible for getting me moving again. My new readers included Eddie Shubert, Martin Cohen, Jim Bowery and Charlie Ambrose. I thank them for their comments, as also Rebecca Dempsey for her careful proof-reading. In 2017 Ben Hughson designed our little 'Dynamic of Form' computer program to facilitate the explorations of the 2nd and 3rd degree arithmetic that had always been difficult with pencil and paper. This program was used to clarify and consolidate the new work presented at the end of Chapters 10 and 14.

The development of this book into its current form during 2007-9 would not have been possible without the help and support of my wife Kelsey Hegarty. She encouraged re-engagement with the project (mostly for therapeutic reasons!) and then afforded generous time and space for its undertaking. Kelsey corrected every draft of every chapter of the 2009 version, which her friend Chris Dowrick then read through and became its first fan.

The original book under the title 'Remedy for Enthusiasm' was drafted during 2002-4 with the support and encouragement of Arimbi Winoto, and corrected by Peter Nihill. (Historical chapters removed from later versions may one day yet appear.)

Back in the early 1990s it was when David Roberts said 'the unity of the form is in the distinction' that everything started to tumble into place. After Luhmann sent me on my way, the *Laws of Form* community was most welcoming. I fondly recall discussions with Dick Shoup, James Flagg, Jack Engstrom and Jim Bowery. Special thanks goes to Lou Kauffman for the patient induction of a non-mathematician into Form Dynamics. Thea Winoto, Ralph Humphries and Steven Kilsby opened up the parallel world of Leibniz through their translations. For her support during this period (and especially during the difficult times when my doctoral candidature was becoming untenable) I am ever indebted to Arimbi Winoto.

Before *Laws of Forms*, Eric Timewell opened my eyes to the world of ideas. A chance discussion of the 'problem of reference' left me transfixed and determined to find the solution. In those days I rode tandem on an intellectual adventure with Ralf Humphries. Thanks go to him and the many others who joined our long conversations, whether across the kitchen table at Blyth St or for hours after lectures in the Agora of La Trobe University.

NOTES

NOTES PART I LOGICAL EMPIRICISM

[1] A. Arnauld & P. Nicole, *Logic or the Art of thinking* ('The Port Royal Logic'). Cambridge University Press, 1996.
[2] M. de Montaigne, *Michel de Montaigne - The Complete Essays*. Penguin Classics, 1993.
[3] J. Locke, *An Essay Concerning Human Understanding*. Penguin Classics, 1998.
[4] J. S. Mill, *A System of Logic*. CreateSpace, 2016.
[5] R. Porter, *Enlightenment: Britain and the Creation of the Modern World*. Penguin, 2001.
[6] B. Russell, *Philosophical Essays*. London: Longmans, 1910.
[7] R. Rorty, *Objectivity, Relativism, and Truth*. Cambridge University Press, 1991.
[8] R. Rorty, *Philosophy and the Mirror of Nature*. Princeton University Press, 1979.
[9] R. Monk, *Ludwig Wittgenstein: the Duty of Genius*. London: Cape, 1990.
[10] L. Wittgenstein, *Philosophical Investigations*. Oxford: Basil Blackwell, 1953.
[11] W. V. Quine, 'Main Trends in Recent Philosophy: Two Dogmas of Empiricism', *The Philosophical Review*, vol. 60, no. 1, pp. 20–43, 1951.
[12] H. R. Maturana & F. J. Varela, *Autopoiesis and Cognition*, Translation of 'De Maquinas y Seres Vivos', Chile, 1972. Boston: D. Reidel, 1980.
[13] H. R. Maturana and F. J. Varela, *The Tree of Knowledge*, Rev ed Boston: Shambhala, 1992.
[14] J. Locke, *The Works of John Locke*, 3d. ed. London: A. Bettesworth, 1727.
[15] M. W. Cranston, *John Locke: A Biography*. Oxford University Press, 1985.
[16] G. Berkeley, *A Treatise Concerning the Principles of Human Knowledge*. Indianapolis: Hackett, 1982.
[17] G. Berkeley, *Berkeley's Principles and Dialogues: Background Source Materials*. Cambridge University Press, 2000.
[18] G. Berkeley, *Three Dialogues Between Hylas and Philonous*. Indianapolis: Hackett, 1979.
[19] Voltaire, *Philosophical Dictionary*, Rev. ed. edition. Penguin Classics, 1984.
[20] G. Buchdahl, *The image of Newton and Locke in the Age of Reason*. London: Sheed & Ward, 1961.
[21] J. Boswell, *The Life of Samuel Johnson*, Abridged ed. New York: Penguin Classics, 1979.
[22] R. Descartes, *Discourse on Method and The Meditations*. Penguin Classics, 1968.
[23] R. Descartes, *Descartes: Selected Philosophical Writings*. Cambridge University Press, 1988.
[24] R. Skidelsky, *John Maynard Keynes Volume One: Hopes Betrayed 1883-1920*. London, Macmillan, 1983.
[25] P. Levy, *Moore: G. E. Moore and the Cambridge Apostles*. London: Weidenfeld & Nicolson, 1979.
[26] V. Descombes, *Modern French Philosophy*. Cambridge University Press, 1980.
[27] R. Monk, *Bertrand Russell : The Spirit of Solitude 1872-1921*. New York: Free Press, 1996.
[28] F. P. Ramsey, *The Foundations of Mathematics and Other Logical Essays*. Psychology Press, 2001.
[29] B. Russell, *The Last Philosophical Testament: 1943-68*. London: Routledge, 1997.

[30] D. Davidson, 'Reality Without Reference', *Dialectica*, vol. 31, no. 3–4, p. 247–258, 1977.
[31] B. Russell, *The Problems of Philosophy*. Oxford University Press, 1959.
[32] R. Crawshay-Williams, *Russell Remembered*. Oxford University Press, 1970.
[33] B. Russell, *Mysticism and Logic and Other Essays*. London: Penguin Books, 1953.
[34] E. Mach & C. M. Williams, *The Analysis of Sensations, and the Relation of the Physical to the Psychical*. Chicago: Open Court, 1984.
[35] C. C. Gillispie, *Dictionary of Scientific Biography*. New York: Scribners, 1970.
[36] A. Einstein, *Autobiographical Notes*, Centennial ed. Chicago: Open Court, 1979.
[37] B. Russell, *Principles of Mathematics*. London: Routledge, 2009.
[38] B. Russell, *My Philosophical Development*, Rev ed. London: Routledge, 1995.
[39] H. Poincaré, *Science and Method*. London: Thomas Nelson, 1914.
[40] B. Russell, History of western philosophy. London: Routledge, 1996.
[41] Diogenes Laertius, *Lives of Eminent Philosophers*, 2 vols. Harvard University Press (Loeb #184 & #185), 1925.
[42] Aristotle, *On Sophistical Refutations. On Coming-to-be and Passing Away. On the Cosmos*. (Loeb #400) Harvard University Press, 1955.
[43] I. M. Copi, 'The Burali-Forti Paradox', *Philosophy of Science*, vol. 25, no. 4, p. 281–286, 1958.
[44] A. N. Whitehead & B. Russell, *Principia Mathematica to *56*. Cambridge University Press, 1997.
[45] P. Edwards, Ed., *The Encyclopedia of Philosophy*. Macmillan, 1972.
[46] L. Wittgenstein, *Tractatus Logico-Philosophicus*, Corrected Edition. London: K. Paul, Trench, Trubner, 1933.
[47] G. Spencer-Brown, *Laws of Form*. New York: Dutton, 1979.
[48] R. Marcus & M. McEvoy, *An Historical Introduction to the Philosophy of Mathematics: A Reader*. London: Bloomsbury, 2016.
[49] M. Dummett, *Truth and Other Enigmas*. London: Duckworth, 1978.
[50] Aristotle, *The Metaphysics*, 2 vols. Harvard University Press (Loeb #271 & 287), 1933 & 1935.
[51] Aristotle, *On the Soul. Parva Naturalia. On Breath.*, Rev ed. Cambridge, Mass.: Harvard University Press (Loeb #288), 1957.
[52] T. M. Robinson, (Editor), *Heraclitus: Fragments*. University of Toronto Press, 1987.
[53] Aristotle, *The Basic Works of Aristotle*. New York: Random House, 1941.
[54] A. N. Whitehead, *Symbolism: Its Meaning and Effect,* Rev ed. New York: Fordham University Press, 1985.
[55] Augustine, *On Christian Doctrine*. Liberal Arts Press, 1958.
[56] Augustine, *Confessions*. London: Penguin Classics, 1961.
[57] J. Derrida, *Margins of Philosophy*. Brighton: Harvester, 1982.
[58] E. Durkheim, *Emile Durkheim: Selected Writings*. Cambridge University Press, 1972.
[59] P. L. Berger & T. Luckmann, *The Social Construction of Reality*. London: Penguin, 1984.
[60] K. Marx & F. Engels, *The German Ideology, including Theses on Feuerbach*. Amherst, N.Y: Prometheus Books, 1998.
[61] T. S. Kuhn, *The Structure of Scientific Revolutions*, 2nd ed. University of Chicago Press, 1970.
[62] M. Foucault, *The Order of Things*. New York: Vintage, 1994.
[63] J. Derrida, *Dissemination*. University of Chicago Press, 1983.
[64] J. Derrida, *Of Grammatology*. Johns Hopkins University Press, 1977.
[65] B. Russell, *A Critical Exposition of the Philosophy of Leibniz*, 2nd ed. London: Routledge, 1992.

NOTES PART II MATHEMATICAL EPISTEMOLOGY

[1] L. Wittgenstein, *Tractatus Logico-Philosophicus*, Corr Ed. London: K. Paul, Trench, Trubner, 1933.
[2] L. Wittgenstein, *Philosophical Investigations*. Oxford: Basil Blackwell, 1953.
[3] L. Wittgenstein, *Remarks on the Foundations of Mathematics*, Rev ed. MIT Press, 1978.
[4] G. Spencer-Brown, *Laws of Form*. New York: Dutton, 1979.
[5] Nicomachus of Gerasa, *Introduction to Arithmetic*. New York: Macmillan, 1926.
[6] R. Crawshay-Williams, *Russell Remembered*. Oxford University Press, 1970.
[7] Proclus, *Stoicheīosis Theologikē* = *The Elements of Theology*, 2nd ed. Edited by E. R. Dodds, Oxford: Clarendon Press, 1963.
[8] B. B. Mandelbrot, *The Fractal Geometry of Nature*, Updated and augmented. New York: W. H. Freeman, 1983.
[9] G. W. Leibniz, *Selections*. Translated by Philip Wiener, New York: Scribner, 1951.
[10] G. Galilei, *Discoveries and Opinions of Galileo*. New York: Doubleday Anchor, 1957.
[11] I. E. Gordon, *Theories of Visual Perception*, 3rd Ed. Hove, East Sussex, England: Psychology Press, 2004.
[12] H. Bergson, *Creative Evolution*. London: Macmillan, 1911.
[13] F. J. Varela & H. R. Maturana, 'De Máquinas y Seres Vivos: Una teoría sobre la organización biológica', Santiago de Chile: Editorial Universitaria, 1973.
[14] H. R. Maturana & F. J. Varela, *Autopoiesis and Cognition : the Realization of the Living*, Translation of 'De Maquinas y Seres Vivos', Chile, 1972. Boston: D. Reidel Pub. Co, 1980.
[15] F. Varela, H. Maturana, & R. Uribe, 'Autopoiesis: the organization of living systems, its characterization and a model.', *Currents in Modern Biology*, vol. 5, no. 4, p. 187, 1974.
[16] L. von Bertalanffy, 'Der Organismus als physikalisches System betrachtet', *Naturwissenschaften*, vol. 28, no. 33, pp. 521–531, 1940.
[17] L. Von Bertalanffy, *General Systems Theory*. New York: Braziller, 1968.
[18] G. W. Leibniz *Die Philosophischen Schriften von Gottfried Wilhelm Leibniz*, 7 vols. Edited by C I Gerhardt, Berlin: Weidmannsche, 1875.
[19] M. R. Antognazza, *Leibniz: An Intellectual Biography*, Cambridge University Press, 2011.
[20] R. Penrose, *The Emperor's New Mind*. Oxford University Press, 1989.
[21] T. L. Heath, *A History of Greek Mathematics*, 2 vols. Oxford: Clarendon Press, 1921.
[22] Lucretius, *On the Nature of Things*, 2nd Rev Ed. Harvard University Press (Loeb #181), 1924.
[23] Nicholas of Cusa, *On Learned Ignorance : a translation and an appraisal of De docta ignorantia*. Jasper Hopkins (trans), Minneapolis: A.J. Benning Press, 1981.
[24] A. Koyré, *From the Closed World to the Infinite Universe*. Baltimore: Johns Hopkins Press, 1957.
[25] G. Endress, *The Works of Yaḥyā Ibn 'Adī : an analytical inventory*. Wiesbaden: Reichert, 1977.
[26] D. Janos, *Ideas in Motion in Baghdad and Beyond*. Leiden: Brill, 2015.
[27] Muḥammad Ḥusayn Ṭabāṭabā'ī, Ed., *A Shi'ite Anthology*. London: Muhammadi Trust of Great Britain & Northern Ireland, 1981.
[28] E. Hoffmann & R. Klibansky, *Nicolai de Cusa Opera Omnia: De Coniecturis*, vol. 3, 22 vols. Hamburg: In aedibus Felicis Meiner, 1972.
[29] Nicholas of Cusa, *On God as not-other : a translation and an appraisal of De li non aliud*. Jasper Hopkins (trans), University of Minnesota Press, 1979.

[30] Plato, *Euthyphro. Apology. Crito. Phaedo. Phaedrus*. Harvard University Press (Loeb #36), 1904.
[31] L. Kauffman, *Laws of Form: An Exploration in Mathematics and Foundations*. Book in progress. http://homepages.math.uic.edu/~kauffman/Laws.pdf
[32] J. Francisco & G. Varela, 'A Calculus for Self-Reference', *International Journal of General Systems,* vol. 2, no. 1, pp. 5–24, Jan. 1975.
[33] L. H. Kauffman & F. J. Varela, 'Form dynamics', *Journal of Social and Biological Structures*, vol. 3, no. 2, p. 171–206, Apr. 1980.
[34] R. Descartes, *Descartes: Selected Philosophical Writings*. Cambridge University Press, 1988.
[35] J. A. Egan, *The Works of John Dee: Modernizations of his Main Mathematical Masterpieces*. CreateSpace, 2012.
[36] Plutarch, *Moralia, Volume V.* (Loeb #306) Harvard University Press, 1936.
[37] J. B. Pritchard, *Ancient Near Eastern Texts Relating to the Old Testament with Supplement*. Princeton University Press, 2016.
[38] L. Lamy, *Egyptian Mysteries: new Light on Ancient Knowledge*. London: Thames and Hudson, 1981.
[39] J. de Voragine, *The Golden Legend of Jacobus de Voragine*. Granger Ryan & Helmut Ripperger (trans), New York: Arno Press, 1969.
[40] M. Warner, *Alone of All Her Sex: the myth and the cult of the Virgin Mary*. New York: Vintage, 1983.
[41] Lao Tsu, *Tao Te Ching*. Gia-fu Feng (trans), London: Wildwood House, 1972.
[42] R. Llull, *Romancing God: contemplating the Beloved*. Brewster, Mass.: Paraclete Press, 1999.
[43] R. Llull, *The Book of the Lover and the Beloved*. Warminster, England: The Centre for Mediterranean Studies, University of Bristol, 1995.
[44] M. Porete, *The Mirror of Simple Souls*. E. L. Babinsky (trans), New York: Paulist Press, 1993.
[45] N. Luhmann, 'European rationality', *Observations on Modernity*, pp. 22–43, 1998.
[46] S. Freud, *On Metapsychology: the theory of psychoanalysis*. Penguin, 1984.
[47] S. Freud, *An Outline of Psycho-Analysis*, The Standard Edition edition. New York: W. W. Norton & Company, 1989.
[48] S. Freud, *New Introductory Lectures on Psychoanalysis*. Penguin, 1973.
[49] S. Freud, *The Freud Reader*. London: Vintage, 1995.

NOTES PART III ENTHUSIASTIC MATHEMATICS

[1] H. Diels, *Die Fragmente der Vorsokratiker, griechisch und deutsch*, 5. Aufl. Edited by Walther Kranz, Berlin: Weidmann, 1934.
[2] H. Diels, *Ancilla to the Pre-Socratic Philosophers : a complete translation of the Fragmentis in Diels, Fragmente der Vorsokratiker* by Kathleen Feeman. Oxford: Blackwell, 1948.
[3] T. L. Heath, *The Thirteen Books of Euclid's Elements*, 2nd ed., 3 vols. New York: Dover Publications, 1956.
[4] T. L. Heath, *A History of Greek Mathematics*, 2 vols. Oxford: Clarendon Press, 1921.
[5] R. Lawlor, *Sacred Geometry : philosophy and practice*. London: Thames & Hudson, 1982.
[6] S. Weil, *Intimations of Christianity among the Ancient Greeks*. London: Routledge, 1957.
[7] T. Taylor, *Theoretic Arithmetic*. London: Valpy, 1816.
[8] J. Burnet, *Greek Philosophy. Part I, Thales to Plato*. London: Macmillan, 1914.
[9] J. M. Dillon, *The Middle Platonists : a Study of Platonism, 80 B.C. to A.D. 220*. London: Duckworth, 1977.
[10] H. Tarrant, *Scepticism or Platonism? : the Philosophy of the Fourth Academy*: Cambridge University Press, 1985.
[11] J. M. Keynes, *The Collected Writings of John Maynard Keynes*. London: Macmillan, 1971.
[12] F. A. Yates, *Giordano Bruno and the Hermetic Tradition*. London: Routledge and Kegan Paul, 1964.
[13] A. Koyré, *From the Closed World to the Infinite Universe*. Baltimore: Johns Hopkins Press, 1957.
[14] J. Kepler, *The Harmony of the World*. Philadelphia: American Philosophical Society, 1997.
[15] Proclus, *A Commentary on the First Book of Euclid's Elements*. Translated by Glenn R. Morrow: Princeton University Press, 1970.
[16] J. A. Egan, *The Works of John Dee: Modernizations of his Main Mathematical Masterpieces*. CreateSpace, 2012.
[17] I. Bulmer-Thomas, (Tranlator), *Greek Mathematical Works*, 2 vols. (Loeb #335 & #362): Harvard University Press, 1939.
[18] G. W. Leibniz, *Mathematische Schriften*, 7 vols. Edited by C. I. Gerhardt, Halle: Schmidt, 1858.
[19] B. B. Mandelbrot, *The Fractal Geometry of Nature*, Updated and augmented. New York: W. H. Freeman, 1983.
[20] G. W. Leibniz, *Selections*. Translated by Philip Wiener, New York: Scribner, 1951.
[21] L. F. Richardson, 'The problem of contiguity: an appendix to statistics of deadly quarrels', *General Systems Yearbook*, vol. 6, p. 139–187, 1961.
[22] B. B. Mandelbrot, 'How long is the coast of Britain', *Science*, vol. 156, no. 3775, p. 636–638, 1967.
[23] Diogenes Laertius, *Lives of Eminent Philosophers*, 2 vols. (Loeb #184, #185): Harvard University Press, 1925.
[24] J. Barnes, *Early Greek Philosophy*. London: Penguin, 1987.
[25] T. M. Robinson, Ed., *Heraclitus: Fragments*: University of Toronto Press, 1987.
[26] Nicomachus of Gerasa, *Introduction to Arithmetic*. Translated by M. L. D'Ooge with essays by F. E. Robbins & L. C. Karpinski, New York: Macmillan, 1926.
[27] Theon Smyrnaeus, *Expositio rerum mathematicarum ad legendum Platonem utilium*. Translated by Eduard Hiller, Leipzig: Teubneri, 1878.
[28] Theon of Smyrna, *Mathematics Useful for Understanding Plato*. Translated by R. Lawlor & D. Lawlor, San Diego: Wizards Bookshelf, 1979.

NOTES PART III ENTHUSIASTIC MATHEMATICS

[29] A. E. Taylor, 'Forms and numbers: a study in Platonic metaphysics (I)', *Mind*, vol. 35, no. 140, p. 419–440, 1926.
[30] J. Mcleish, *Number*. London: Bloomsbury, 1991.
[31] Iamblichus, *On the Pythagorean Way of Life*. Translated by J. M. Dillon & J. P. Hershbell, Atlanta, Georgia: Scholars Press, 1991.
[32] W. K. C. Guthrie, *A History of Greek Philosophy: Volume I, The Earlier Presocratics and the Pythagoreans*, Rev ed. Cambridge University Press, 1979.
[33] C. B. Boyer & U. C. Merzbach, *A History of Mathematics*, 2nd ed. New York: Wiley, 1991.
[34] M. Livio, *The Golden Ratio: The Story of Phi, the World's Most Astonishing Number*. New York: Broadway Books, 2003.
[35] D. W. Thompson, *On Growth and Form*, 2nd ed. Cambridge University Press, 1942.
[36] L. Kauffman, *Laws of Form: An Exploration in Mathematics and Foundations*. Book in progress. http://www.math.uic.edu/~kauffman/Laws.pdf.
[37] M. E. Baron, *The Origins of the Infinitesimal Calculus*. New York: Dover, 1987.
[38] F. Nesselmann, *Versuch einer kritischen Geschichte der Algebra*. Minerva-Verlag, 1842.
[39] A. E. Taylor, *Plato: the Man and his Work*, 4th ed. London: Methuen, 1937.
[40] H. J. Zacher, *Die Hauptschriften zur Dyadik von G.W. Leibniz*. Frankfurt: Klostermann, 1973.
[41] G. W. Leibniz, *Philosophical Writings*. Translated by Mary Morris, New rev. ed. London: Dent, 1973.
[42] G. W. Leibniz, *Philosophical Papers and Letters*. Translated by L. E. Loemker, 2nd ed. Dordrecht: Reidel, 1976.
[43] G. W. Leibniz, *Philosophical Essays*. translated by R. Ariew & D. Garber, Indianapolis: Hackett, 1989.
[44] G. W. Leibniz, *Writings on China*. Edited by H. Rosemont & D. Cook, Chicago: Open Court, 1994.
[45] G. W. Leibniz, *Leibniz korrespondiert mit China : der Briefwechsel mit den Jesuitenmissionaren (1689-1714)*. Edited by Rita Widmaier, Frankfurt: Klostermann, 1990.
[46] G. W. Leibniz, *Samtliche Schriften und Briefe*. Darmstadt: O. Reichl, 1923.
[47] M. R. Antognazza, *Leibniz: An Intellectual Biography*. Cambridge University Press, 2011.
[48] F. Cajori, 'Leibniz's "Image of Creation"', *The Monist*, vol. 26, no. 4, p. 557–565, 1916.
[49] M. A. Kerze, 'Numbers: Binary Symbolism', in *Encyclopedia of Religion*, vol. 10, L. Jones, Ed. Detroit: Macmillan, 1987, p. 19–21.
[50] G. C. Stead, 'The Platonism of Arius', *The Journal of Theological Studies*, p. 16–31, 1964.
[51] G. W. Leibniz, *Die philosophischen Schriften*, 7 vols. Edited by C. I. Gerhardt, Berlin: Weidmannsche, 1875.
[52] G. W. Leibniz, *Discourse on metaphysics: Correspondence with Arnauld; Monadology*. Translated by G. R. Montgomery, La Salle, Ill.: Open Court, 1979.
[53] R. I. Moore, *The Birth of Popular Heresy*. London: Edward Arnold, 1975.
[54] H. Bettenson, *Documents of the Christian Church*, 2nd ed., Oxford University Press, 1963.
[55] M. F. Wiles, *Archetypal Heresy: Arianism through the centuries*. Oxford: Clarendon Press, 1996.
[56] R. C. Gregg & D. E. Groh, *Early Arianism – a view of salvation*. London: SCM Press, 1981.
[57] M. R. Antognazza, *Leibniz on the Trinity and the Incarnation: reason and revelation in the seventeenth century*. Translated by G. Parks, New Haven : Yale University Press, 2007.

[58] G. W. Leibniz & S. Clarke, *The Leibniz-Clarke Correspondence: Together with extracts from Newton's Principia and Opticks*. Edited by H.G. Alexander, Manchester University Press, 1956.
[59] A. Glaser, *History of Binary and other Nondecimal Numeration*. Southampton, Pa: Tomash, 1971.
[60] A. O. Lovejoy, *The Great Chain of Being: a study of the history of an idea*. Harvard University Press, 1936.
[61] G. Spencer-Brown, *Laws of Form*. New York: Dutton, 1979.
[62] E. J. Aiton, *Leibniz : a Biography*. Bristol: A. Hilger, 1985.
[63] R. Wilhelm (translator from Chinese), *The I Ching, or, Book of Changes,* 3rd ed. rendered into English by C. F. Baynes, London: Routledge & Kegan Paul, 1968.
[64] M. Martini, *Sinicae historiae decas prima*. Amsterdam, Joannem Blaev, 1659.
[65] A. Kircher, *China monumentis, qua sacris quà profanis, nec non variis naturae & artis spectaculis, aliarumque rerum memorabilium argumentis illustrata, auspiciis Leopoldi primi*. Amsterdam: Jacobum à Meurs, 1667.
[66] R. M. Swiderski, 'Bouvet and Leibniz: A Scholarly Correspondence', *Eighteenth-Century Studies,* vol. 14, no. 2, p. 135–150, 1980.
[67] P. Couplet, *Confucius Sinarum philosophus: sive, Scientia sinensis*. Paris: Danielem Horthemels, 1687.
[68] D. E. Mungello, *Leibniz and Confucianism, the Search for Accord*. University Press of Hawaii, 1977.
[69] S. Cammann, 'Some Early Chinese Symbols of Duality', *History of Religions,* vol. 24, no. 3, p. 215–254, 1985.
[70] P. Carus, 'Chinese Philosphy', *The Monist*, vol. 6, no. 2, p. 188–249, 1896.
[71] S. Cammann, 'Chinese Hexagrams, Trigrams, and the Binary System', *Proceedings of the American Philosophical Society*, vol. 135, no. 4, p. 576–589, 1991.
[72] Chang Cheng-Lang, *et al*, 'An interpretation of the divinatory inscriptions on early Chou Bronzes', *Early China*, vol. 6, p. 80–96, 1980.
[73] Feng Yu-lan, *A History of Chinese Philosophy*, 2nd ed. Princeton University Press, 1952.
[74] S. Cammann, 'The Origins of Circular Trigrams in Ancient China', *Bulletin of the Museum of Far Eastern Antiquities*, vol. 62, p. 185–212, 1990.
[75] G. Ifrah, *The Universal History of Numbers: From Prehistory to the Invention of the Computer*. New York: Wiley, 2000.
[76] F. Louis, 'The Genesis of an Icon: The "Taiji" Diagram's Early History', *Harvard Journal of Asiatic Studies*, vol. 63, no. 1, p. 145–196, 2003.
[77] I. Robinet, 'The Place and Meaning of the Notion of Taiji in Taoist Sources Prior to the Ming Dynasty', *History of Religions*, vol. 29, no. 4, p. 373–411, May 1990.
[78] Lao Tsu, *Tao Te Ching*. Translated by Gia-Fu Feng, London: Wildwood House, 1972.
[79] Wu Jing-Nuan (Tranlator), *Yi Jing*. Washington, D.C: The Taoist Centre, 1991.
[80] D. P. Walker, *Ancient Theology: Studies in Christian Platonism from the 15th to the 17th Century*. London: Gerald Duckworth, 1972.
[81] A. Einstein, *Relativity: The Special and the General Theory*. Translated by R. Lawson, New York: Crown, 1961.
[82] G. W. Leibniz, *New Essays on Human Understanding*. Cambridge University Press, 1996.

GREEK GLOSSARY

Transliteration	Greek	Meaning: Pythagorean (general & other*) *See: Liddell and Scott's Greek-English Lexicon
alogia	αλογια	Irrational
analogia	αναλογια	Proportion, geometric series (analogy; correspondence) [inTheon] αναλογια εναλλαξ is a converging series
anamnesis	αναμνησις	[In Plato] knowing as remembering (recollection)
aoristos	αοριστης	Indeterminate [Dyad]
apeiron	απειρον	Unbounded; limitless
aphaireseôs	αφαιρεσεος	[In Aristotle] abstract entities; that which is taken away from things
apodeixis	αποδειξις	[In Aristotle] logical demonstration or proof (setting forth)
arche	αρχη	First principle; origin; beginning
arithmos	αριθμος	Number (number; quantity; rank)
asymmetros	ασυμμετρος	Incommensurable; irrational
autokineton	αθτο-κινετον	[In Proclus] the self-moved; [Also in Proclus is αυταρκες, autonomous generator]
chaos	ψαος	Void; gap; chasm
character	χαρακτερ	Notation (mark or token impressed or stamped on a coin or seal)
diairesis	διαιρεσις	A dividing or division
dyas / dyada	δυας / δυαδα	[In Platonism] the Dyad (two / duality)
dynamis	δυναμις	Value as power; potential (power)
eidos	ειδος	Form; idea; species
empeiria	εμπειρια	Experience
entheos	εν-θεος	Full of god; inspired. Hence: enthusiastic
episteme	επιστημη	Knowledge
epistreptikos	επιστρεπτικος	[In Proclus] self-observation
genus	γενος	Type by birth or generation (by descent)
gignomai	γιγνομαι	Generate or produce [Various similar word derived from the root γενω.]
gnomon	γνωμων	The successive additions in a figured number series; the sundial rod; the carpenter's square (that by which a thing is known; marker)
harreton	αρ-ρητος	[Arithmetically] inexpressible (unsaid)
hartios	αρτιος	Even number; just
hule	υλη	Subject matter (wood; material)
hupo-keimenon	υπο-κειμενον	Primary matter (underlying matter)
logos	λογοσ	Ratio (reasonable account; reason; word)
Mathematici	μαθηματικι	Mathematicians
megethos	μεγεθος	Magnitude
mesotes	μεσοτης	Mean (middle)
meteche	μετεχω	To partake. [in Plato] things partakes of their ideal form [also used are μετοχη and μετα-λαμβανω.]
metreo	μετρεω	To measure
monas / monada	μονας /μοναδα	[In Platonism] the Monad or original one and its clones (solitary / singularity)
mysteria	μυστερια	Mysteries, secret rites
oud-hen	ουδ-εν / ουδ-εις	Not-one; none
peri / peras	περι / περας	About; around / limit
perissos	περισσος	Odd number; excessive [Athenian variant: περριτος]
physios	φυσος	Nature [Also φυσικιος as 'natural', e.g., the natural number series]
protogenes	πρωτογενης	First-born
psyche	ψυχη	Breath, life-spirit
pythmen	πυθμην	Stock; the elementary form
retos / ar-retos	ρητος / αρ-ρητος	Expressed / unexpressed (unsaid)
riza	ριζα	Root
semeion	σημειον	Point [of emanation]
spermatikos	σπερματικως	Like a seed, seminal, potent origin [Hence the Stoic 'seminal logos']
symmetresis	συμμετρησις	Measuring by a standard measure
tauton	ταυτον	Same
theos	θεος	God [Also θεοτοκος, god-bearer or mother of god]

INDEX

abacus and counting board: 74, 161
  & zero, 181
  in China, 319-20
Academy, Plato's: 35, 50n, 154
  & *logos*, 156
  & unwritten teachings, 157
  scepticism period of, 158
  & Proclus, 132;
  demise and diaspora, 154, 159
algebra: 57
    Babylonian, 183
    Boolean logical, 116-7
    Boolean arithmetic, 117-19
    & Pythagoreans, 183, 238
analogia (proportion): 209-15
  & Aristotle, 216
  & *logos*, 216
  & Golden Section, 216
  & irrationals, 222
  & the natural number series, 242
  & 'turn about the double', 259-60
  & fractals, 212-3
  alternating *analogia*, 234-38, 245-6
analysis:
    Aristotle's tool, x, 35, 36n
    logical, 35-36
    semantic, 55-7
    arithmetic, 114-16, 295-6
    fractional, 296-300
analytic geometry: 198-9
Analytic Philosophy: 21
  & Frege, 41-2
anamnesis, *see* recollection
Anaximander: 174-5, 177
Ancient Theology: 312-3
antinomy, *see* paradox
anti-Trinitarianism, *see* Arianism
apeiron (limitless): 174-5

arche (principle-origin): 174
  & arithmetic emanationism, 177, 182
  & generation of dimensions, 194
  & the seminal *logos*, 235
  in Gospel of John, 216, 275-7
Archytas: 98-9, 244, 263
  & unbounded universe, 98-9
  & geometric mean, 211
  & arithmetic *analogia*, 242
Arianism: 275-81
Aristotelianism: ix-xii: 32-3
  Medieval, 11, 39, 161, 166
Aristotle: ix-xi;
  Lyceum of, 31;
  logic of, x-xi, 31, 35, 57
  form/matter ontology, ix, 11, 51-2
  & Liar Paradox, 39;
  & other-reference, 42-48
  against self-reference, 49-51
  & closed universe, 99
  account of the Pythagoreans, 157-8, 174, 239-41, 248-9
arithmetic:
    Pythagorean, 170-180
    & logistic, 180-1
    Brownian, 107-116
    Brownian higher degrees, 201-6
    as mystical, 74-5
    & identity, 54
    & Analytic Philosophy, 41-2
Arius of Alexandria: 277, 281
Arnauld, Antoine: 58-9, 128, 128-9
Atheism: 3, 5, 24
Augustine of Hippo: 101, 160, 269-70
  his *On Genesis*, 98
  on creation from nothing, 270
Autopoiesis: 85-88
Bacon, Francis: 3, 165
Barnsley fern: 206

INDEX

Bergson, Henri: 23, 62-3, 85-6
Berkeley, Bishop George: 13-26, 66, 92-3
  & Leibniz, 282, 291
binary numbers, *see* Dyadic numeration
blind spot: 83
Boethius: 161, 167
Boltzmann, Ludwig: 28
Boole, George: 117
Boolean algebra, *see* algebra
Boswell, James: 17
Bouvet, Joachim (SJ): 307-17, 328-9
Brahe, Tycho: 1
Brouwer, Luitzen: 20n, 32n
Bruno, Giordano: 279, 312
Buddhism: 142, 321n
Cantor, Georg: 33-4, 40
  Cantor dust, 199, 212, 216
Clarke, Samuel: 280, 332-4
Condillac, Étienne de: 16n
Constantinople, fall of: 32, 161-2
continued fractions: 296-300
contradiction (logical): 36-8, 241
  & *reducto ad absurdum*, 239-40
Couplet, Filippe (SJ): 308-9, 314, 328
Creation:
  from nothing (*ex nihilo*), 101n, 269
  in Genesis, 270-2
  in Gospel of John, 216
  in Augustine, 270
  in Proclus 132
  in Arius, 275-7, 281
  Dyadic 268-73
  & feminine void, 133-7
Daoism: 137, 326-7
Dee, John: 3, 132n, 153, 164-5, 214n
Deism: 281-2
Derrida, Jacques: 61-2, 65-6
Descartes, René: ix, 18
  mathesis universalis, 65-6;
  cogito ego sum, 128-9
  mind/body, 146
  & scepticism, 61, 65;
  & relativity, 99, 333,
differential calculus, *see* infinitesimal calculus
Distinction:
  in pre-communicative knowing, 70-1
  in *Laws of Form*, 95-105
  & *apeiron*, 182
  & Leibniz's *non plus ultra*, 283-8
division:
  Platonic *diairesis*, 253-5
  Egyptian method of, 254
Durkheim: 63n

Dyad (*duas*): 249;
  in Plotinus 278
  in Arius 281&
  Christian Logos, 275-9
Dyadic emanation: 156-7
  original doctrine of, 248-51
  modern reception, 168-9
  of Leibniz, 268-75
  & degrees of double, 256-61
  & problem of zero, 261-66
  & creation from nothing, 268-72
  & *non plus ultra*, 283-9
  & infinite expressions for irrationals, 289-94
  & *Yi Jing*, 305-7, 315-27
  & *Tai ji*, 323-26
dynamis (power):
  as ontological potential in Aristotle, 43, 215-6
  & degrees of arithmetic, 194
  of the Monad, 235
Einstein, Albert:
  & Mach's Phenomenology, 28n
  & unbounded universe 99, 105n
  & absolute space, 333
Eleatic school: 37-8
  & modern scepticism, 61
emanationism: xi, 5
  Pythagorean arithmetic, 35, 177-80
  geometric, 233-4
  Dyadic, 157-8, 250-1
  Gnostic, 158
  of the dimensions with figured numbers, 193-201
  of irrationals, 234-5, 296-301
  by means of Logos, 156
  in Proclus, 132, 159
  in Kepler, 164;
  in Dee, 164-5
  & self-reference, 46
  & the foundations of science, 152
  & Re-Entry of Form, 182, 193
  compared to Logical Empiricism, 53
Enlightenment (18th Century): xii-xiii, 3
  against Renaissance epistemology, 163-5
  against mysticism, 142
  & Representationalism, 15, 20, 65, 129
  & anti-Trinitarians, 280
enthusiasm: xiii-xiv, 5, 18
  & madness, xv, 18
Epicurus/Epicureanism: 2, 158
Epinomis (text): 179-80, 184, 150, 170
  & problem of irrationals, 225
  turn about the double, 258-60

INDEX

Eubulides: 38
Euclid of Alexandria: 154, 159, 161
   Proclus on, 163
   Dee's preface to, 164-5
   Christian reception of, 161, 166, 168
   on Golden Section, 216-19
   & new definition of *logos*, 224
   & arithmetic *analogia*, 242
   Leibniz revising, 289-90
Eudoxus: 156
   new definition of *logos*, 156, 224
   method of exhaustion, 239
evolution theory: 23, 85, 91-2
   & Aristotelian taxonomy, 53n
Fibonacci sequence: 125, 226-29, 299-300
Fibonacci: 226
Ficino, Marsilio: 162
Figure/Ground ambiguity: 96-7
Figured/figurate numbers: 187-201
   & Fractional Analysis, 296-301
Fontenelle, Bernard le Bovier de: 302-3
Forms: 44
   as translation of *eidos*, 43, 76
   of Plato, ix, 26, 11n, 44
   participation in, 76
   of Aristotle, ix, 43-5, 51
   in Thomas Aquinas, 11, 44
   see also Laws of Form
Fractional Analysis: 296-301
Frege, Friedrich: 30, 41-2
Freud, Sigmund: 146-7
FuXi ['Fu hsi']:
   trigrams, 305-8
   legend of, 313-16
Galileo Galilei: 1, 77
Gassendi, Pierre: 9n
Genesis (Book of the Bible): 98
   Augustine on, 270
   & Dyadics, 271-2, 278, 287, 316
Geometric expansion: 208-11
   of Golden Section, 217-20
   of the square, 233-4,
Geometry:
   analytic, 198-9
   non-Euclidian, 105n
   fractal: 171, 206, 212
   as arithmetic applied to shape, 183-4
   Egyptian origins of, 155n
   Frege on the primacy of, 42
   Creator as geometer, 166-7
   & the crisis of irrationals, 221-5
   inscription at the entrance to the Academy, 168
   see also Topology

gnomon:
   in figured numbers, 187, 190
   as the first derivative, 196
   in ancient Greek science, 190n
Gnostic Christianity: 101, 158, 269, 277
Golden Section/Mean: 215-21
   & Fibonacci sequence, 225-9
   in Fractional Analysis, 299-300
Gospel of John, *see* John's Gospel
Hegel, Georg: 21, 26
Hellenistic: 32n
Heraclitus: 43, 94, 175-7, 211, 234
   logos of, 207, 215
   & *diairesis*, 253
Hermes Trimegistus: 162n, 312-3
   statue of: 43-44
   & *FuXi*, 314
Hesiod: 126, 265n
Hexagrams (*Yi Jing*): 306, 308, 316, 322
Hierarchy of Types: 39-41
   & Wittgenstein, 73
Hobbes, Thomas: 63n
Husserl, Edmund: 26
Hypatia: 154
I Ching, see Yi Jing
Iamblichus: 155, 191
imaginary numbers: 291-2, 302
incommensurables, *see* irrationals
infinite:
   Cantor on, 33
   Russell on, 33-4, 40
   universe as, 99
   Degrees of arithmetic as hierarchy of, 193, 198-201, 203-5
   Leibniz's types of, 283, 285-6, 291
   Pi as, 290-1
   equation, 292
   irrational numbers as, 228, 238, 290-3, 296-301.
infinitesimal calculus:
   historical development of, 239
   reception of, 294
   infinitesimals controversy, 286, 291
   invention controversy, 331-2
Intuitionism: 20, 23-4, 62, 128
   Russell against, 20, 23,75
   Ramsey against, 20
irrational numbers/values: 156, 221-4
   $\sqrt{2}$, 230-41
   see also Golden Mean
   see also and Pi
Jesuits in China: 307-8
   & missionary controversies, 328-31

INDEX

John's Gospel:
  logos in, 214-6
  & Arian controversy, 275-6
Kant, Immanuel: vii-viii, 10, 13, 19-20, 25
  influence on phenomenology, 25-7
Kauffman, Louis: 123n, 124, 291n
Kepler, Johannes: 1, 163-5
  & Copernican revolution, 163
  & Proclus, 163-4
  & Newton, 163
  & Fibonacci sequence, 225-9
Keynes, John Maynard: 165, 280
Kircher, Athanasius: 308
Koch Island/Snowflake: 212-3, 216
Laozi (Lao Tzu, Dao De Jing): 94, 120, 137, 326
Laws of Form (book): 95, 151-2, 182-3
  & injunction, 73n
  notation of, 112
  laws of number and order, 113
Leibniz, G W: 268ff
  universal characteristics of, 66, 106
  juris non facti, 77
  self-referencing, 80
  against Primary Matter, 89-90, 269, 271
  Dyadic arithmetic, 268ff
  on infinity 290-1
  his Monadology essay, 275n, 282
  reduction of ontology to perception, 282
  & the Enlightenment, 165, 169
  & limitation, 283ff
Leonard of Pisa, *see* Fibonacci
Leonardo da Vinci: 1, 154
  & Golden Mean, 219
Liar Paradox: 37-9
Lingam-Yoni (Hindu): 321
Llull, Ramon: 160
Locke John: viii, xv, 9-10, 13, 15, 18
  on semiotics, 64-5
  on self-observation, 130-1
  & Deism, 282
logistic: 180-2
logos: 156, 209ff
  of Heraclitus, 207
  Christian, 134, 214-6
  & the crisis of irrationals, 224
Longobardi, Nichola (SJ): 330
Mach, Ernst: 27-9
Machiavelli, Niccolò: 63n
magnitude: 183-5
Mandelbrot, Benoit: 76n, 171, 213n, 216
Manicheanism: 101
  Leibniz on, 284
Martini, Martin (SJ): 308

Mary, Mother of God: 134-7
Matter, Primary: ix, 43-6
  as logical, 51
  of Thomas Aquinas, 11
  Leibniz's rejection of, 268-9
  Arius' rejection of, 277
  & sculpture analogy. 43-4
  & gnostic creation, 101, 158, 269, 277
  & Berkeley, 15-19
  & Russell, 22
  & modern physics, 11, 27
Maturana, Humberto: 86-7
mean proportional: 208
Monad (*monas, monada*): 249-51
  & Eudoxan Revolution, 156
  self-moving, 50
  as *psyche*, 50
  & zero, 261-64
  & *Wu ji*, 324
monotheism:
  & self-creation, xi
  & creation from nothing, 132, 158, 269, 277
  mathematical, 167
  of Islam, 99, 269, 279
  & otherness, 99-100, 109
  & evil, 101, 287
Moore, G E: 19-20,
More, Henry: 333
Moses: 145, 271-3
  & Ancient Theology, 312-3
multiplication, Egyptian method of: 254
mysticism:
  Aristotle against, ix, 42-3
  & enthusiasm, xiv, xv
  & madness, xv, xv
  & state theology, xv-xvi, 5
  Russell against, 23, 73
  of Wittgenstein, 72-3
  of mathematics, 31, 75-6
  of Platonic forms, 76
  & *via negativa*, 100, 142
  of the unmarked space, 102, 137
  of the First Distinction, 128
  in Daoism, 134
  as ontological foundation, 141, 14
  & scepticism, 158;
Naturalism: 2-3
Newton, Isaac: 1-2, 10, 15
  promoting empiricism, 15n
  anti-Trinitarian, 280
  infinitesimal calculus, 331-2
  absolute space, 332-3
  & Kepler, 163, 165

INDEX

Nicea, Council of, 160, 276
   creed of, 280-1, 278
Nicholas of Cusa:
   on unbounded finite universe, 99
   & *via negativa*, 100, 142
Nicomachus of Gerasa: 74
   translated by Boethius, 167
   on figured number hierarchy, 195-8, 201
   on arithmetic *analogia*, 242
   on Monad & Dyad, 250-1, 262-3
   & problem of zero, 263-4
Noah, Noa(c)hide theory: 312, 313-4
Origen of Alexandria: 160
Orphism: 154, 157
Paradox, Russell's logical: 33-35, 37-8, 48
   & Frege, 41-2
   & Poincaré, 57
   See also Zeno's paradox
Parmenides of Elea: 37
   Plato's esteem for, 156
Pascal's triangle: 199-200
Paul of Venice: 39
Penrose, Roger: 90
Phenomenology: 26-29
Philo of Alexandria: 160
Philolaus: 156, 175, 177-8, 240-1
Pi (the ratio): 290, 293, 301
Plato:
   monotheist, xi
   Pythagorean, xii, 31
   on enthusiasm, xiv-xv
   his Theory of Forms, 26, 76
   on recollection (*anamnesis*), 76, 150, 233
   his method of division (*diairesis*) 253-5
   & opposites, 104
   on mind's eye, 126
   unwritten teachings of, 157;
Platonism: 31-2, 132, 154, 156
   Old Academy, 35, 179-80
   Academic scepticism, 158
   is Hellenistic Pythagoreanism, 156-7, 162
   diaspora of, 159
   Alexandrean syncretism, 159-60
   Christian, 161-2, 275-81,163-9
   Timaean, 43n, 158
   neo-Platonism (Plotinus), 159,168, 278
   & *Anima Mundi*, 50n;
Plotinus: 101, 157, 159
   on Dyad, 278
Poincaré, Henri: 37, 41, 57
Porete, Marguerite: 138
Port Royal Logic: 58-60, 64, 139

Primary Matter, *see* Matter
Proclus: 120, 132, 157, 159, 167
   & Mystical Theology, 168
   Kepler on, 163-4;
proportion, *see analogia*
psyche: 49-50
   as self-moving monad, 50
Psychoanalysis: 146-7
Pythagoras: 31, 154-5, 175
Pythagoras' Theorem: 231, 233
Pythagoreanism: 153-69
Ramsey, Frank: 20
ratio, *see logos*
Real Number Line: 199, 291n, 292, 302
recollection (*anamnesis*), Plato's doctrine of: 76, 150, 233
Re-Entry of the Form: 123-5
Representationalism: 10-13
Restoration of the British Monarch: xiv-xv, 3, 5
Ricci, Matteo: 307, 328, 330
Rorty, Richard: 12, 62
Royal Society of London: xiv-xv, 1, 10, 28, 165
   Newton president of, 280
   Leibniz member of, 331
   & infinitesimal calculus controversy, 332
Rudolf August: 272, 273
Russell, Bertrand: 12, 20-1
   his *Problems of Philosophy*, 21-5
   his Hierarchy of Types, 39-41
   against mysticism, 23
   on instincts, 22-3
   against self-reference, 38-9, 47-8
   & solipsism, 22
   & Frege, 41
   & Poincare, 57
Ryle, Gilbert: 146
scepticism:
   & logical paradox, 33-4
self-reference: xii
   Aristotelian opposition to, 38-39, 48-51
   in biological systems theory, 80-2
   as Autopoiesis, 85-89
Seminal (*spermatikos*) Logos: 235
Servetus, Michael: 279
set theory: 33
Society of Jesus, *see* Jesuits
solipsism: 22, 29, 82, 84
Spencer Brown, George: 41n, 95, 151-2, 182-3
   see also, Laws of Form
Stevin, Simon: 265

INDEX

Stoicism: 158, 214-5, 243
    & the term 'logic', 36n
    & *spermatikos logos*, 235n
    & Christian *logos*, 210, 214-5
Sufism: 137, 138n, 145
surds, *see* irrationals
syllogism: 36
    in Brownian algebra, 119
systems theory: 86-88
Tai ji (Tai Chi): 323, 325-6
Tai yi: 323-4
Tetraktys: 191-2, 200, 206, 299
Thales of Miletus: 155, 174,
Theaetetus: 156
Theon of Smyrna: 159, 167
    on *logos*, 210
    on ratio of identity, 212
    on alternating *analogia*, 236
    on arithmetic *analogia*, 242
    on Monad, 251, 263, 264n
    & infinite expression for $\sqrt{2}$, 234-8, 244, 297
Theotokos, *see* Mary
Thomas Aquinas (Saint): 10-11, 161, 166,
topology: 74-5, 289
    & Distinction, 105
Trigrams (ancient Chinese): 304, 306-9
    & *Tai ji*, 323-7
Types, Theory of, *see* Hierarchy of Types
Universals, Medieval philosophy of: 161
Varela, Francisco: 86-7, 123n
Voltaire: 15-16

Weil, Simone: 30, 150
    on Eudoxan Revolution, 224
Whiston, William: 280
Whitehead, Alfred North: 34
    his shift away from logical reductionism, 38n, 57
Wittgenstein: 72
    on contradiction, 30
    on the sign, 69
    on showing and saying, 72-3, 74
    & Russell's introduction to *Tractatus*, 73
Wu ji: 324
Xenocrates: 35, 157
    on *psyche*, 50,
Yi Jing (I Ching): 304, 306ff
Yin/Yang: 103, 137
    in *Yi Jing*, 304
    notation of, 305-6, 308-9
    emanation by, 308-9, 230, 322-3
    & zero, 320
    & Lingam/Yoni, 321
Zeno of Elea: 37
    his paradoxes, 238, 245, 291
Zero:
    unmarked on the counting board, 181
    unmarked in Brownian notation, 113-4, 181
    Pythagorean problem with, 261-4
    of Stevin, 265
    its Formal relationship with one and infinity, 203, 205

Printed in Great Britain
by Amazon